T0332533

Real-Time Systems

Real-time systems need to react to certain input stimuli within given time bounds. For example, an airbag in a car has to unfold within 300 milliseconds in a crash. There are many embedded safety-critical applications and each requires real-time specification techniques. This textbook introduces three of these techniques, based on logic and automata: Duration Calculus, Timed Automata, and PLC-Automata.

The techniques are brought together to form a seamless design flow, from real-time requirements specified in the Duration Calculus, via designs specified by PLC-Automata, and into source code for hardware platforms of embedded systems. The syntax, semantics, and proof methods of the specification techniques are introduced; their most important properties are established; and real-life examples illustrate their use. Detailed case studies and exercises conclude each chapter.

Ideal for students of real-time systems or embedded systems, this text will also be of great interest to researchers and professionals in transportation and automation.

E.-R. OLDEROG is Professor of Computer Science at the University of Oldenburg, Germany. In 1994 he was awarded the Leibniz Prize of the German Research Council (DFG).

H. DIERKS is a researcher currently working with OFFIS, a technology transfer institute for computer science in Oldenburg, Germany.

REAL-TIME SYSTEMS

Formal Specification and Automatic Verification

ERNST-RÜDIGER OLDEROG[1] AND HENNING DIERKS[2]

[1] Department of Computing Science, University of Oldenburg, Germany
[2] OFFIS, Oldenburg, Germany

CAMBRIDGE
UNIVERSITY PRESS

CAMBRIDGE
UNIVERSITY PRESS

Shaftesbury Road, Cambridge CB2 8EA, United Kingdom

One Liberty Plaza, 20th Floor, New York, NY 10006, USA

477 Williamstown Road, Port Melbourne, VIC 3207, Australia

314–321, 3rd Floor, Plot 3, Splendor Forum, Jasola District Centre, New Delhi – 110025, India

103 Penang Road, #05–06/07, Visioncrest Commercial, Singapore 238467

Cambridge University Press is part of Cambridge University Press & Assessment, a department of the University of Cambridge.

We share the University's mission to contribute to society through the pursuit of education, learning and research at the highest international levels of excellence.

www.cambridge.org
Information on this title: www.cambridge.org/9780521883337

First published 2008

A catalogue record for this publication is available from the British Library

ISBN   978-0-521-88333-7   Hardback

Contents

Preface

Computers are used more and more to provide high-quality and reliable products and services, and to control and optimise production processes. Such computers are often embedded into the products and thus hidden to the human user. Examples are computer-controlled washing machines or gas burners, electronic control units in cars needed for operating airbags and braking systems, signalling systems for high-speed trains, or robots and automatic transport vehicles in industrial production lines.

In these systems the computer continuously interacts with a physical environment or plant. Such systems are thus called reactive systems. Moreover, common to all these applications is that the computer reactions should obey certain timing constraints. For example, an airbag has to unfold within milliseconds, not too early and not too late. Reactive systems with such constraints are called real-time systems. They often appear in safety-critical applications where a malfunction of the controller will cause damage and risk the lives of people. This is immediately clear for all applications in the transport sector where computers control cars, trains and planes.

Therefore the design of real-time systems requires a high degree of precision. Here formal methods based on mathematical models of the system under design are helpful. They allow the designer to specify the system at different levels of abstraction and to formally verify the consistency of these specifications before implementing them. In recent years significant advances have been made in the maturity of formal methods that can be applied to real-time systems.

Structure of this book

In this advanced textbook we shall present three such formal approaches:

- Duration Calculus (DC for short), a logic and calculus for specifying high-level requirements of real-time systems;
- timed automata (TA for short), a state-transition model of real-time systems with the advantage of elaborate tool support for the automatic verification of real-time properties;
- PLC-Automata, a state-transition model of real-time systems with the advantage of being implementable, for example in the programming language C or on Programmable Logic Controllers (PLCs for short), a hardware platform that is widespread in the automation industry.

This book is the first one that presents the above three approaches to the specification of real-time systems in a coherent way. This is achieved by combining the approaches into a design method for real-time systems, reaching from requirements down to executable code as illustrated in Figure 0.1. Here:

- Real-time requirements are specified in the Duration Calculus or subsets thereof.
- Designs are specified by PLC-Automata.
- Implementations are written as C programs with timers or as programs that are executable on PLCs.
- Automatic verification of requirements is performed using the model-checking tool UPPAAL for timed automata.
- A tool MOBY/RT, built for PLC-Automata, allows the user to invoke algorithms for generating C or PLC code from such automata, and to automatically verify properties specified in a subset of Duration Calculus by using UPPAAL as a back-end verification engine.

The connection is that PLC-Automata have both a semantics in terms of the Duration Calculus and an equivalent one in terms of timed automata. To verify that a PLC-Automaton satisfies a given real-time requirement expressed in the Duration Calculus, there are two possibilities: either a proof can be conducted in the Duration Calculus exploiting the corresponding semantics of the PLC-Automaton, or, for certain types of requirement, an automatic verification is possible using the tool UPPAAL and the timed automata semantics of the PLC-Automaton.

How to read this book

The titles and dependencies of the chapters are shown in Figure 0.2. First, the introduction in Chapter 1 should be read. Here two case studies (railroad

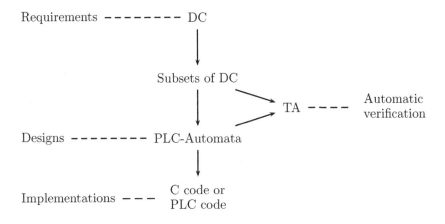

Fig. 0.1. Overview of design method

crossing and gas burner) provide a feeling for the delicacies of real-time systems. Then one can continue with Chapter 2 (Duration Calculus) or Chapter 4 (Timed automata).

Chapter 2 presents the basic knowledge of the Duration Calculus. First, the syntax and semantics of the logic are defined. Then the proof rules of the calculus are introduced, including a simple induction rule. These rules are applied to the case study of the gas burner.

Chapter 3 presents advanced topics on the Duration Calculus. First, decidability results are discussed for the cases of discrete and continuous time domains. Then a subset of the Duration Calculus that is closer to the implementation level is presented, the so-called DC implementables. Finally, Constraint Diagrams are introduced as a graphic representation for requirements with a semantics in the Duration Calculus.

Chapter 4 presents the basic facts of timed automata. In particular, the most prominent result of timed automata is shown: the decidability of the reachability problem. It is then explained which variant of timed automata and properties the model checker UPPAAL can decide.

Chapter 5 introduces PLC-Automata as a class of implementable real-time automata. First, these automata are motivated using an example of a real-time filter. Then it is described how PLC-Automata can be compiled into code that is executable on Programmable Logic Controllers (PLCs). To link the PLC-Automata with the Duration Calculus, their semantics are defined in terms of this logic. As a consequence, a general result estimating the reaction times of PLC-Automata to input stimuli can be proved. Also, an algorithm is discussed that synthesises a PLC-Automaton from a given set of DC implementables provided this set is consistent. Finally, hierarchical PLC-Automata are defined.

Chapter 6 ties together the results of Chapters 4 and 5 for the purposes of automatic verification. It turns out that certain real-time properties of PLC-Automata can be proven automatically using the model checker UPPAAL for timed automata. To this end, an alternative and equivalent semantics of PLC-Automata in terms of timed automata is defined. Then it is shown that real-time requirements expressed in a subset of Constraint Diagrams can be verified against PLC-Automata by checking the reachability of certain states with UPPAAL. This is all supported by the tool MOBY/RT, which is described briefly as well. Also, MOBY/RT enables the user to compile PLC-Automata into PLC code or C code.

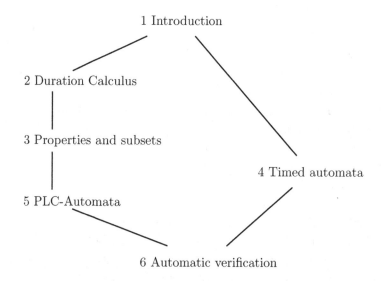

Fig. 0.2. Dependency of chapters

Actually, only Section 5.5 (Synthesis) of Chapter 5 depends on Section 3.2 (DC implementables) of Chapter 3. The remainder of Chapter 5 can thus also be read immediately after Chapter 2.

Intended audience

This textbook is appropriate for either a course on formal methods for real-time systems in the upper division of undergraduate studies or for graduate studies in computer science and engineering. It can also be used for self study, and will be of interest for engineers of embedded real-time systems. Readers are expected to have a basic understanding of mathematical and logical notations.

Courses based on this book

Our own course on real-time systems at the University of Oldenburg is for M.Sc. and advanced B.Sc. students in computer science with an interest in embedded systems; it proceeds as follows:

Course at Oldenburg	
Introduction	1
Duration Calculus	2
Properties and subsets	3.1–3.2
Timed automata	4
PLC-Automata	5.1–5.5
Automatic verification	6 (only short indication)

The course takes one semester with three hours of lectures and one hour of exercises per week.

At Oldenburg an in-depth study of Chapter 6 (Automatic verification) with the use of the tools UPPAAL and MOBY/RT is delegated to practical work of the students in separate labs on real-time systems. There LEGO Mindstorm robots are used for implementing the systems. Once desirable real-time properties have been verified, the compiler from PLC-Automata to C is applied to generate code for the LEGO Mindstorms.

An alternative usage of the material of this book could be in (part of) a course on timed automata as follows:

Course based on timed automata	
Introduction	1
Timed automata	4
PLC-Automata	5.1–5.3 and 5.6
Automatic verification	6

Further information and additional material can be found on the webpage
http://csd.informatik.uni-oldenburg.de/rt-book.

Acknowledgements

Our first inspiring contacts with real-time systems were in the context of the basic research project ProCoS (Provably Correct Systems) funded by the European Commission from 1989 to 1995. This project was planned by Dines Bjørner (Technical University of Denmark), Tony Hoare (Oxford University), and Hans Langmaack (University of Kiel). Its goal was to develop a mathematical basis for the development of embedded, real-time, computer systems.

Returning from a sabbatical at the University of Austin at Texas, Tony Hoare was impressed by the work of Robert S. Boyer and J Strother Moore on mechanical verification exemplified in a case study known as the "CLInc Stack". Talking to Dines Bjørner and Hans Langmaack, a project on the foundation of verification of many-layered systems was conceived: ProCoS. The different levels of abstraction studied in this project became known as the "ProCoS Tower". They comprise (informal) expectations, (formal) requirements, (formal) system specifications, programs (occam), machine code (for transputers), and circuit diagrams (netlists). During the project the case study of a gas burner was defined in collaboration with a Danish gas burner manufacturer.

At the project start in 1989 the first author of this book moved from Kiel to Oldenburg to take up a professorship in computing science at the University of Oldenburg and became one of the site leaders of ProCoS. He is very grateful for six rewarding years of research contacts with the members of the ProCoS project group, in particular Hans Langmaack, Tony Hoare, Dines Bjørner, Zhou Chaochen, He Jifeng, Jonathan Bowen, Michael R. Hansen, Anders P. Ravn, Hans Rischel, Kirsten M. Hansen, Martin Fränzle, Markus Müller-Olm, Stephan Rössig, and Michael Schenke. Two highlights evolved during the ProCoS project: the case study of the gas burner and the Duration Calculus, both featuring prominently in this book.

In the first years of ProCoS the second author of this book was a student of computing science and mathematics at Oldenburg. His first contact with the real-time systems of ProCoS was during his master thesis on "The production cell as a verified real-time system" – formalised using the Duration Calculus.

The next decisive step was the collaborative project UniForM (Universal Workbench for Formal Methods) together with Bernd Krieg-Brückner and Jan Peleska (University of Bremen) as well as Alexander Baer and Wolfgang Nowak (company Elpro AG in Berlin). One of the challenges of this project was to develop a formal method to support the real-time programming of tram control systems targeted at Programmable Logic Controllers. Motivated by this challenge the second author developed the concept of a PLC-Automaton, which serves for design specifications in this book.

Inspired by ProCoS and UniForM the research on specification and verification of real-time systems gained momentum at our group on "Correct System Design" at Oldenburg. In particular, we wish to thank Cheryl Kleuker, who contributed Constraint Diagrams, Jochen Hoenicke, who can spot even subtle errors in a minute, and Andreas Schäfer, who saw how to extend the Duration Calculus to cope with space and time. Under the guidance of Josef Tapken the tool MOBY/RT was developed to provide support for the theory presented in this book. We are particularly grateful to the following people who helped create this tool: Hans Fleischhack, Marc Lettrari, Michael Möller, Marco Oetken, Josef Tapken, and Tobe Toben.

The second author spent an extended research visit at the Aalborg University to work with the UPPAAL group on automatic verification and planning of timed automata. He would like to thank Kim Larsen, Gerd Behrmann, Alexandre David, Anders P. Ravn, Wang Yi, and Paul Petterson for inspiring cooperation.

Both authors are pleased to acknowledge the research momentum gained by the Collaborative Research Center AVACS (Automatic Verification and Analysis of Complex Systems) which has been funded by the German Research Council (DFG) since 2004. AVACS groups at the universities of Oldenburg, Freiburg and Saarbrücken, as well as the Max-Planck Institute for Informatics in Saarbrücken, address automatic verification and analysis of real-time systems, hybrid systems, and systems of systems. In the research area of real-time systems we would like to thank our close colleagues Werner Damm, Bernd Becker, Reinhard Wilhelm, Johannes Faber, Roland Meyer, Ingo Brückner, Heike Wehrheim, Bernd Finkbeiner, Andreas Podelski, Andrey Rybalchenko, Viorica Sofroni-Stokkermans, Bernhard Nebel, Jörg Hoffmann, and Sebastian Kupferschmid. We also thank Willem-Paul de Roever for his support of this large-scale project and for many refreshing remarks and suggestions over the years.

Everyone who has written a book knows how difficult it is to find the time to work intensively on the manuscript. Very helpful in this respect was a sabbatical of the first author in the winter semester 2004/05 at ETH Zürich. Many thanks to my perfect hosts David Basin and Barbara Geiser. The first author would also like to thank Krzysztof R. Apt, with whom he wrote his first book, for setting a lucid example of how a book should look and for many pieces of invaluable advice during the past years.

We are very grateful to Michael Möller for creating a draft on which the cover design of this book is based. Last but not least we wish to thank David Tranah and his team from Cambridge University Press who have been very supportive throughout this book project.

List of symbols

1

Introduction

1.1 What is a real-time system?

This book is about the design of certain kinds of reactive systems. A *reactive system* interacts with its environment by reacting to inputs from the environment with certain outputs. Usually, a reactive system is not supposed to stop but should be continuously ready for such interactions. In the real world there are plenty of reactive systems around. A vending machine for drinks should be continuously ready for interacting with its customers. When a customer inputs suitable coins and selects "coffee" the vending machine should output a cup of hot coffee. A traffic light should continuously be ready to react when a pedestrian pushes the button indicating the wish to cross the street. A cash machine of a bank should continuously be ready to react to customers' desire for extracting money from their bank account.

Reactive systems are seen in contrast to *transformational systems*, which are supposed to compute a single input–output transformation that satisfies a certain relation and then terminate. For example, such a system could input two matrices and compute its product.

We wish to design reactive systems that interact in a well-defined relation to the real, physical time. A *real-time system* is a reactive system which, for certain inputs, has to compute the corresponding outputs within given time bounds. An example of a real-time system is an *airbag*. When a car is forced into an emergency braking its airbag has to unfold within 300 milliseconds to protect the passenger's head. Thus there is a tight upper time bound for the reaction. However, there is also a lower time bound of 100 milliseconds. If the airbag unfolds too early, it will deflate and thus lose its protective impact before the passenger's head sinks into it. This shows that both *lower* and *upper* time bounds are important. The outputs of a real-time system may depend on the *behaviour* of its inputs over time. For instance, a *watchdog* has to raise an alarm (output) if an input signal is absent for a period of t seconds.

Real-time constraints often arise indirectly out of safety requirements. For example, a gas burner should avoid a critical concentration of unburned gas in the air because this could lead to an explosion. This is an untimed safety requirement. To achieve it, a controller for a gas burner could react to a flame failure by shutting down the gas valve for a *sufficiently large period of time* so that the gas can evaporate during that period. This way the safety requirement is reduced to a real-time constraint.

The gas burner is an example of a *safety critical* system: a malfunction of such a system can cause loss of goods, money, or even life. Other examples are the airbag in a car, traffic controllers, auto pilots, and patient monitors.

Real-time constraints are sometimes classified into *hard* and *soft*. Hard constraints must be fulfilled without exception, whereas soft ones should not be violated. For example, a car control system *should* meet the real-time requirements for the air condition, but *must* meet the real-time constraints for the airbag.

In constructing a real-time system the aim is to control a physically existing environment, the *plant*, in such a way that the controlled plant satisfies all desired timing requirements: see Figure 1.1.

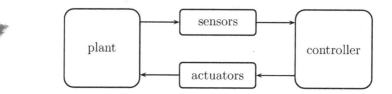

Fig. 1.1. Real-time system

The *controller* is a digital computer that interacts with the plant through *sensors* and *actuators*. By reading the sensor values the controller inputs information about the current state of the plant. Based on this input the controller can manipulate the state of the plant via the actuators. A precise model of controller, sensors, and actuators has to take *reaction times* of these components into account because they cannot work arbitrarily fast.

In many cases the plant is distributed over different physical locations. Also the controller might be implemented on more than one machine. Then one talks of *distributed systems*. For instance, a railway station consists of many points and signals in the field together with several track sensors and actuators. Often the controller is hidden to human beings. Such real-time systems are called *embedded systems*. Examples of embedded systems range from controllers in washing machines to airbags in cars.

When we model the plant in Figure 1.1 in more detail we arrive at *hybrid systems*. These are defined as reactive systems consisting of continuous and discrete components. The continuous components are time-dependent physical variables of the plant ranging over a continuous value set, like temperature, pressure, position, or speed. The discrete component is the digital controller that should influence the physical variables in a desired way. For example, a heating system should keep the room temperature within certain bounds. Real-time systems are systems with at least one continuous variable, that is time. Often real-time systems are obtained as abstractions from the more detailed hybrid systems. For example, the exact position of a train relative to a railroad crossing may be abstracted into the values *far_away*, *near_by*, and *crossing*.

Figure 1.2 summarises the main classes of systems discussed above and shows their containment relations: hybrid systems are a special class of real-time systems, which in turn are a special class of reactive systems.

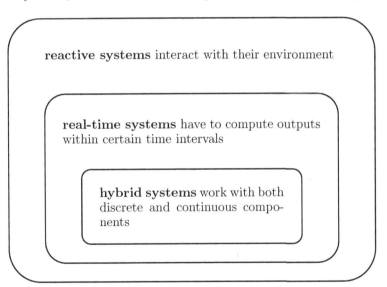

Fig. 1.2. Classes of systems

Since real-time systems often appear in safety-critical applications, their design requires a high degree of precision. Here, formal methods based on mathematical models of the system under design are helpful. They allow the designer to specify the system at different levels of abstraction and to formally verify the consistency of these specifications before implementing them. In recent years significant advances have been made in the maturity of formal methods that can be applied to real-time systems.

When considering formal methods for specifying and verifying systems we have the reverse set of inclusions of Figure 1.2, as shown in Figure 1.3: formal methods for hybrid systems can also be used to analyse real-time systems, and formal methods for real-time systems can also be used to analyse reactive systems.

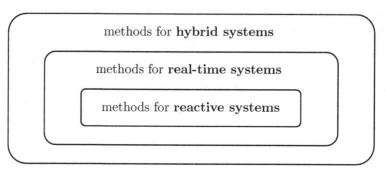

Fig. 1.3. Formal methods for systems classes

1.2 System properties

To describe real-time systems formally, we start by representing them by a collection of time-dependent *state variables* or *observables* obs, which are functions

$$\mathsf{obs} : \mathsf{Time} \longrightarrow \mathcal{D}$$

where Time denotes the time domain and $\mathcal{D}$ is the data type of obs. Such observables describe an infinite system behaviour, where the current data values are recorded at each moment of time.

For example, a gas valve might be described using a Boolean, i.e. $\{0,1\}$-valued observable

$$G : \mathsf{Time} \longrightarrow \{0, 1\}$$

indicating whether gas is present or not, a railway track by an observable

$$\mathsf{Track} : \mathsf{Time} \longrightarrow \{empty, appr, cross\}$$

where *appr* means a train is approaching and *cross* means that it is crossing the gate, and the current communication trace of a reactive system by an observable

$$\mathsf{trace} : \mathsf{Time} \longrightarrow Comm^*$$

where $Comm^*$ denotes the set of all finite sequences over a set $Comm$ of possible communications. Thus depending on the choice of observables we can describe a real-time system at various levels of detail.

There are two main choices for time domain Time:

- **discrete time:** Time $= \mathbb{N}$, the set of natural numbers, and
- **continuous time:** Time $= \mathbb{R}_{\geq 0}$, the set of non-negative real numbers.

A discrete-time model is appropriate for specifications which are close to the level of implementation, where the time rate is already fixed. For higher levels of specifications continuous time is well suited since the plant models usually use continuous-state variables. Moreover, continuous-time models avoid a too-early introduction of hardware considerations. Throughout this book we shall use the continuous-time model and consider discrete time as a special case.

To describe desirable properties of a real-time system, we constrain the values of their observables over time, using formulas of a suitable logic. In this introduction we simply take *predicate logic* involving the usual logical connectives $\neg$ (negation), $\wedge$ (conjunction), $\vee$ (disjunction), $\implies$ (implication), and $\iff$ (equivalence) as well as the quantifiers $\forall$ (for all) and $\exists$ (there exists). When expressing properties of real-time systems quantification will typically range over time points, i.e. elements of the time domain Time. Later in this book we introduce dedicated notations for specifying real-time systems.

In the following we discuss some typical types of properties. For reactive systems properties are often classified into safety and liveness properties. For real-time systems these concepts can be refined.

Safety properties. Following L. Lamport, a safety property states that *something bad must never happen*. The "bad thing" represents a critical system state that should never occur, for instance a train being inside a crossing with the gates open. Taking a Boolean observable $C :$ Time $\longrightarrow \{0,1\}$, where $C(t) = 1$ expresses that at time t the system is in the critical state, this safety property can be expressed by the formula

$$\forall t \in \text{Time} \bullet \neg C(t). \tag{1.1}$$

Here $C(t)$ abbreviates $C(t) = 1$ and thus $\neg C(t)$ denotes that at time t the system is not in the critical state. Thus for all time points it is not the case that the system is in the critical state.

In general, a safety property is characterised as a property that can be *falsified* in bounded time. In case of (1.1) exhibiting a single time point t_0 with $C(t_0)$ suffices to show that (1.1) does not hold.

In the example, a crossing with permanently closed gates is safe, but it is unacceptable for the waiting cars and pedestrians. Therefore we need other types of properties.

Liveness properties. Safety properties state what may or may not occur, but do not require that anything ever does happen. Liveness properties state what must occur. The simplest form of a liveness property guarantees that *something good eventually does happen*. The "good thing" represents a desirable system state, for instance the gates being open for the road traffic. Taking a Boolean observable $G : \text{Time} \longrightarrow \{0, 1\}$, where $G(t) = 1$ expresses that at time t the system is in the good state, this liveness property can be expressed by the formula

$$\exists t \in \text{Time} \bullet G(t). \tag{1.2}$$

In other words, there exists a time point in which the system is in the good state. Note that this property cannot be falsified in bounded time. If for any time point t_0 only $\neg G(t)$ has been observed for $t \le t_0$, we cannot complain that (1.2) is violated because *eventually* does not say how long it will take for the good state to occur.

Such liveness property is not strong enough in the context of real-time systems. Here one would like to see a time bound when the good state occurs. This brings us to the next kind of property.

Bounded response properties. A bounded response property states that a desired system reaction to an input occurs *within a time interval* $[b, e]$ with lower bound $b \in \text{Time}$ and upper bound $e \in \text{Time}$ where $b \le e$. For example, whenever a pedestrian at a traffic light pushes the button to cross the road, the light for pedestrians should turn *green* within a time interval of, say, $[10, 15]$. The need for an upper bound is clear: the pedestrian wants to cross the road within a short time (and not *eventually*). However, also a lower bound is needed because the traffic light must not change from *green* to *red* instantaneously, but only after a *yellow* phase of, say, 10 seconds to allow cars to slow down gently.

With $P(t)$ representing the pushing of the button at time t and $G(t)$ representing a green traffic light for the pedestrians at time t, we can express the desired property by the formula

$$\forall t_1 \in \text{Time} \bullet (P(t_1) \implies \exists t_2 \in [t_1 + 10, t_1 + 15] \bullet G(t_2)). \tag{1.3}$$

Note that this property can be falsified in bounded time. When for some time point t_1 with $P(t_1)$ we find out that during the time interval $[t_1 + 10, t_1 + 15]$ no green light for the pedestrians appeared, property (1.3) is violated.

Duration properties. A duration property is more subtle. It requires that for observation intervals $[b, e]$ satisfying a certain condition $A(b, e)$ the *accumulated time* in which the system is in a certain critical state has an upper bound $u(b, e)$. For example, the leak state of a gas burner, where gas escapes without a flame burning, should occur at most 5% of the time of a whole day.

To measure the accumulated time t of a critical state $C(t)$ in a given interval $[b, e]$ we use the integral notion of mathematical calculus:

$$\int_b^e C(t)dt.$$

Then the duration property can be expressed by a formula

$$\forall b, e \in \mathsf{Time} \bullet \left(A(b, e) \Longrightarrow \int_b^e C(t)dt \leq u(b, e) \right). \qquad (1.4)$$

Again this property can be falsified in finite time. If we can point out an interval $[b, e]$ satisfying the condition $A(b, e)$ where the value of the integral is too high, property (1.4) is violated.

1.3 Generalised railroad crossing

This case study is due to C. Heitmeyer and N. Lynch [HL94]. It concerns a railroad crossing with a physical layout as shown in Figure 1.4, for the case of two tracks. In the safety-critical area "Cross" the road and the tracks intersect. The gates (indicated by "Gate") can move from fully "closed" (where the angle is 0°) to fully "open" (where the angle is 90°). Moving the gates up and down takes time. Sensors at the tracks will detect whether a train is approaching the crossing, i.e. entering the area marked by "Approach".

1.3.1 The problem

Given are two time parameters $\xi_1, \xi_2 > 0$ describing the reaction times needed to open and close the gates, respectively. In the following problem description time intervals are used that collect all time points in which at least one train is in the area "Cross". These are called *occupancy intervals* and denoted by $[\tau_i, \nu_i]$ where the subscripts $i \in \mathbb{N}$ enumerate their successive

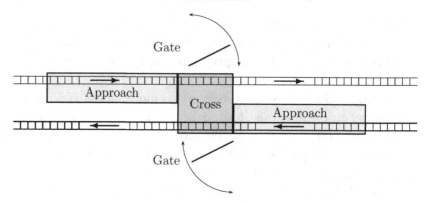

Fig. 1.4. Generalised railroad crossing

occurrences. As usual, a closed interval $[\tau_i, \nu_i]$ is the set of all time points t with $\tau_i \leq t \leq \nu_i$. Moreover, for a time point t let $g(t)$ denote the angle of the gates, ranging from 0 (closed) to 90 (open).

The task is to construct a controller that operates the gates of the railroad crossing such that the following two properties hold for all time points t:

- **Safety:** $t \in \bigcup_{i \in \mathbb{N}} [\tau_i, \nu_i] \implies g(t) = 0$, i.e. the gates are closed inside all occupancy intervals.
- **Utility:** $t \notin \bigcup_{i \in \mathbb{N}} [\tau_i - \xi_1, \nu_i + \xi_2] \implies g(t) = 90$, i.e. outside the occupancy intervals extended by the reaction times ξ_1 and ξ_2 the gates are open.

This problem statement is taken from the article of Heitmeyer and Lynch [HL94]. Note that the safety and utility properties are consistent, i.e. the gate is never required to be simultaneously open and closed. To see this, take a time point t satisfying the precondition (the left-hand side of the implication) of the utility property. Then in particular,

$$t \notin \bigcup_{i \in \mathbb{N}} [\tau_i, \nu_i],$$

which implies that t does not satisfy the precondition of the safety property. Thus never both $g(t) = 0$ and $g(t) = 90$ are required.

Note, however, that depending on the choice of the time parameters ξ_1, ξ_2 and the timing of the trains it may well be that in between two successive trains there is not enough time to open the gate, i.e. two successive time intervals

$$[\tau_i - \xi_1, \nu_i + \xi_2] \quad \text{and} \quad [\tau_{i+1} - \xi_1, \nu_{i+1} + \xi_2]$$

may overlap (see also Figure 1.5).

In the following we formalise and analyse this case study in terms of predicate logic over suitable observables.

1.3.2 Formalisation

The railroad crossing can be described by two observables:

$$\begin{aligned}
\text{Track} : \text{Time} &\longrightarrow \{\text{empty, appr, cross}\} &&\text{(state of the track)} \\
g : \text{Time} &\longrightarrow [0, 90] &&\text{(angle of the gate).}
\end{aligned}$$

Note that via the three values of the observable Track we have abstracted from further details of the plant like the exact position of the train on the track. The value empty expresses that no train is in the areas "Approach" or "Cross", the value appr expresses that a train is in the area "Approach" and none is in "Cross", and the value cross expresses that a train is in the area "Cross". The observable g ranges over all values of the gate angle in the interval $[0, 90]$. We will use the following abbreviations:

$$\begin{aligned}
E(t) &\quad\text{stands for}\quad \text{Track}(t) = \text{empty} \\
A(t) &\quad\text{stands for}\quad \text{Track}(t) = \text{appr} \\
Cr(t) &\quad\text{stands for}\quad \text{Track}(t) = \text{cross} \\
O(t) &\quad\text{stands for}\quad g(t) = 90 \\
Cl(t) &\quad\text{stands for}\quad g(t) = 0.
\end{aligned}$$

Requirements. With these observables and abbreviations we can specify the requirements of the generalised railroad crossing in predicate logic. The safety requirement is easy to specify:

$$\text{Safety} \overset{\text{def}}{\Longleftrightarrow} \forall t \in \text{Time} \bullet Cr(t) \Longrightarrow Cl(t) \tag{1.5}$$

where $\overset{\text{def}}{\Longleftrightarrow}$ means *equivalence by definition*. Thus whenever a train is in the crossing the gates are closed. Note that this formula is logically equivalent to the property **Safety** above because by the definition of $Cr(t)$ we have

$$\forall t \in \text{Time} \bullet Cr(t) \Longleftrightarrow t \in \bigcup_{i \in \mathbb{N}} [\tau_i, \nu_i],$$

i.e. $Cr(t)$ holds if and only if t is in one of the occupancy intervals.

Without the reaction times ξ_1 and ξ_2 of the gate the utility requirement could simply be specified as

$$\forall t \in \text{Time} \bullet \neg Cr(t) \Longrightarrow O(t).$$

However, the property **Utility** refers to (the complements of) the intervals $[\tau_i - \xi_1, \nu_i + \xi_2]$, which are not directly expressible by a certain value of the observable Track. In Figure 1.5 the occupancy intervals $[\tau_i, \nu_i]$ and their extensions to $[\tau_i - \xi_1, \nu_i + \xi_2]$ are shown for $i = 0, 1, 2$. Only outside of the latter intervals, in the areas exhibited by the thick line segments, are the gates required to be open.

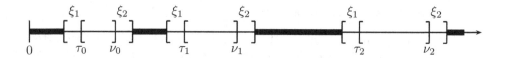

Fig. 1.5. Utility requirement

We specify this as follows. Consider a time point t. If in a suitable time interval containing t there is no train in the crossing then $O(t)$ should hold. Calculations show that this interval is given by $[t - \xi_2, t + \xi_1]$. Thus $\neg Cr(\tilde{t})$ should hold for all time points $\tilde{t}$ with $t - \xi_2 \le \tilde{t} \le t + \xi_1$. This is expressed by the following formula:

$$\text{Utility} \overset{\text{def}}{\iff} \forall t \in \text{Time} \bullet \tag{1.6}$$
$$(\forall \tilde{t} \in \text{Time} \bullet t - \xi_2 \le \tilde{t} \le t + \xi_1 \implies \neg Cr(\tilde{t}))$$
$$\implies O(t).$$

Note the subtlety that $t - \xi_2$ may be negative whereas $\tilde{t} \in \text{Time}$ is by definition non-negative. It can be shown that this formula **Utility** is equivalent to the property **Utility** above (see Exercise 1.2).

For the generalised railroad crossing all functions Track and g are admissible that satisfy the two requirements above. These functions can be seen as *interpretations* of the observables Track and g. They are presented as *timing diagrams*. Figure 1.6 shows an admissible interpretation of Track and g.

Assumptions. In this case study Track is an *input observable* which can be read but not influenced by the controller. By contrast, g is an *output observable* since it can be influenced by the controller via actuators. The correct behaviour of the controller often depends on some assumptions about the input observables. Here we make the following assumptions about Track:

- Initially the track is empty: Init $\overset{\text{def}}{\iff}$ $E(0)$.

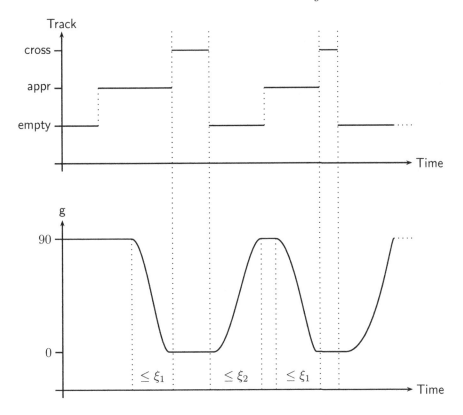

Fig. 1.6. An admissible interpretation of the observables Track and g

- Trains cannot enter the crossing without approaching it:

$$\text{E-to-Cr} \quad \overset{\text{def}}{\Longleftrightarrow} \quad \forall b, e \in \text{Time} \bullet (b \le e \wedge E(b) \wedge Cr(e))$$
$$\Longrightarrow \exists t \in \text{Time} \bullet b < t < e \wedge A(t).$$

- Approaching trains eventually cross:

$$\text{A-to-E} \quad \overset{\text{def}}{\Longleftrightarrow} \quad \forall b, e \in \text{Time} \bullet (b \le e \wedge A(b) \wedge E(e))$$
$$\Longrightarrow \exists t \in \text{Time} \bullet b < t < e \wedge Cr(t).$$

Some assumptions about the speed of the approaching trains are also needed. If a train could approach the crossing arbitrarily fast, a typical reaction time of half a minute for the gates to close would not suffice. We assume that the fastest train will take a time of ρ to reach the crossing after being detected in the approaching area. Here $\rho > 0$ is another time parameter. On the other hand, trains which are arbitrarily slow in the approaching area are not acceptable in the presence of the utility requirement. Therefore we assume that trains need not more than ρ' to pass through the approaching area.

- Fastest train:

$$\text{T-Fast} \overset{\text{def}}{\iff} \forall c, d \in \text{Time} \bullet (c < d \wedge E(c) \wedge Cr(d)) \implies d - c \geq \rho.$$

- Slowest train:

$$\text{T-Slow} \overset{\text{def}}{\iff} \forall c \in \text{Time} \bullet A(c) \implies (\exists d \in \text{Time} \bullet c < d < c + \rho' \wedge \neg A(d)).$$

1.3.3 Design

For the design of the controller we stipulate that the gate is closed at most ξ_1 seconds after detection of an approaching train:

$$\text{Des-G} \overset{\text{def}}{\iff} \forall c, d \in \text{Time} \bullet d - c \geq \xi_1 \wedge$$
$$(\forall t \in \text{Time} \bullet c < t < d \implies \neg E(t)) \implies Cl(d).$$

Under the assumptions

$$\text{Asm} \overset{\text{def}}{\iff} \text{Init} \wedge \text{T-Fast} \wedge \rho \geq \xi_1$$

we can then prove that the following implication holds:

$$(\text{Asm} \wedge \text{Des-G}) \implies \text{Safety}.$$

Thus for all interpretations of Track and g satisfying Asm and Des-G, the safety requirement Safety holds.

Proof:
See Exercise 1.3. □

1.4 Gas burner

This case study was introduced in [RRH93, HHF+94] during the EU project ProCoS (Provably Correct Systems, 1989–95, [BHL+96]). The physical components of the plant are shown in Figure 1.7.

1.4.1 The problem

The desired functionality of the gas burner is as follows:

- If the thermostat signals to switch on the heating the gas valve opens and the burner tries to ignite it for a short period of time.

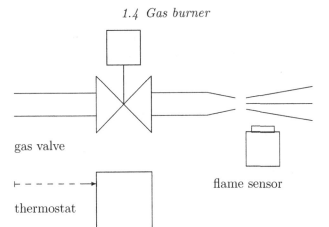

Fig. 1.7. Gas burner

- If the thermostat signals to switch off the heating the gas valve closes.

Important is the following *safety-critical* aspect of the gas burner. If gas effuses without a burning flame in front of the gas valve the concentration of unburned gas can reach critical limits and thus cause an explosion. This has to be avoided. To this end, the following real-time constraint on the system is introduced:

- For each time interval with a duration of at least 60 seconds the (accumulated) duration of gas leaks is at most 5% of the overall duration.

Note that this requirement does not exclude short gas leaks because they are unavoidable before ignition. If the system satisfies this requirement the gas burner is safe.

1.4.2 Formalisation

We concentrate on the safety aspect of the gas burner and introduce two Boolean observables: G describes whether the gas valve is open, and F whether the flame is burning as detected by the flame sensor.

$$G : \text{Time} \longrightarrow \{0, 1\}$$
$$F : \text{Time} \longrightarrow \{0, 1\}.$$

The safety-critical state L describes when gas *leaks*, i.e. when G holds but F does not. It is formalised by the Boolean expression $L \stackrel{\text{def}}{\Longleftrightarrow} G \wedge \neg F$, which is time dependent just as G and F are:

$$L : \text{Time} \longrightarrow \{0, 1\}.$$

Figure 1.8 exhibits an example of interpretations for F and G and the resulting value for L.

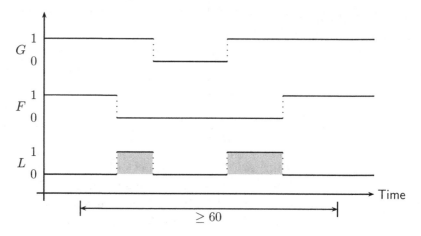

Fig. 1.8. Interpretations for F, G, and L

The real-time requirement is that for each time interval of at least 60 seconds duration the shaded periods do not exceed 5%, i.e. one-twentieth of that duration. To measure in a given interval $[b, e]$ the sum of the durations of all subintervals in which $L(t) = 1$ holds, we use the *integral notation*

$$\int_b^e L(t)dt.$$

Here L is considered as a function from real numbers to real numbers, which is integrable under suitable assumptions. The requirement can now be formalised as follows:

$$\text{Req} \stackrel{\text{def}}{\Longleftrightarrow} \forall b, e \in \text{Time} \bullet \left(e - b \geq 60 \Longrightarrow \int_b^e L(t)dt \leq \frac{e-b}{20} \right). \quad (1.7)$$

Looking at this high-level requirement it is difficult to see how to construct a controller that guarantees it.

1.4.3 Design

As a step towards a controller we make the design decision to introduce two real-time constraints that seem easier to implement and that together imply the requirement Req.

(i) The controller can stop each leak *within a second*:

$$\text{Des-1} \overset{\text{def}}{\Longleftrightarrow} \forall b, e \in \text{Time} \bullet (\forall t \in \text{Time} \bullet b \leq t \leq e \Longrightarrow L(t))$$
$$\Longrightarrow e - b \leq 1.$$

   This constraint restricts the duration of each leak state to at most one second.

(ii) After each leak the controller *waits for 30 seconds* before opening the gas valve again:

$$\text{Des-2} \overset{\text{def}}{\Longleftrightarrow} \forall b, e \in \text{Time} \bullet (L(b) \wedge L(e) \wedge$$
$$\exists t \in \text{Time} \bullet (b < t < e \wedge \neg L(t)))$$
$$\Longrightarrow e - b \geq 30.$$

   This constraint requests a *distance* of at least 30 seconds between any two subsequent leak states. This is illustrated in Figure 1.9.

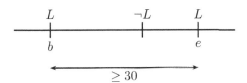

Fig. 1.9. Real-time constraint Des-2

From these design constraints it is possible to prove the desired requirement because the following implication holds:

$$(\text{Des-1} \wedge \text{Des-2}) \Longrightarrow \text{Req},$$

i.e. for all interpretations of G and F satisfying Des-1 and Des-2, the safety requirement Req holds.

1.5 Aims of this book

Using predicate logic as a specification language for real-time systems has several disadvantages. First, as we have seen in the examples above, we have to spell out explicitly all quantifications over time. Second, there is no support for an automatic verification of properties that one might want to prove about such specifications. Third, there is no obvious way to implement a real-time system once it is specified in predicate logic.

To overcome these disadvantages we shall consider three dedicated formal specification languages for real-time systems: Duration Calculus, timed automata, and PLC-Automata.

1.5.1 Duration Calculus

The *Duration Calculus* (abbreviated DC) was introduced by Zhou Chaochen in collaboration with M.R. Hansen, C.A.R. Hoare, A.P. Ravn, and H. Rischel. The DC is a temporal logic and calculus for describing and reasoning about properties that time-dependent observables satisfy over time intervals. In particular, safety properties, bounded response, and duration properties (hence the name of the calculus) can be expressed in DC.

Example 1.1

The safety requirement Req for the gas burner that we formalised in Section 1.4.2 using predicate logic can be expressed in DC more concisely by the duration formula

$$\Box \left(\ell \geq 60 \implies \int L \leq \frac{\ell}{20} \right).$$

It states that for all observation intervals ($\Box$) of length at least 60 seconds ($\ell \geq 60$) the accumulated duration of a gas leak ($\int L$) is at most 5%, i.e. one-twentieth of the length of the interval ($\leq \frac{\ell}{20}$). Note that in contrast to the formula in predicate logic this DC formula avoids any explicit quantification over time points. ∎

An advantage of DC is that it enables us to express a high-level declarative view of real-time systems without implementation bias. We shall therefore use DC as a specification language for system requirements. The price to pay is that for the continuous-time domain the satisfiability problem of the DC is in general undecidable. Thus we cannot hope for automatic verification procedures for the full DC. Also direct tool support for the DC is at present rather limited.

1.5.2 Timed automata

Timed automata (abbreviated TA) were introduced by R. Alur and D. Dill as operational models of real-time systems that extend finite-state automata by explicit, real-valued clock variables.

Example 1.2
The timed automaton in Figure 1.10 is due to K.G. Larsen and models a *light controller*. It has three states called *off, light, bright* and four transitions labelled with the input action **press?** modelling the effects of pressing the light switch. Additionally, this timed automaton uses a clock variable x. The value of this clock can be tested and reset with the transitions.

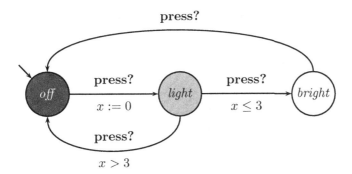

Fig. 1.10. Timed automaton

The timed behaviour specified by this automaton is as follows. Initially, the automaton is in state *off*. When the switch is pressed once, the light goes on. If the switch is pressed twice quickly (within 3 seconds) the light gets bright. Otherwise the light will be switched off with the second pressing. ∎

A strong advantage of TA is that they come with automatic verification procedures for certain properties like reachability of states. The model checker UPPAAL developed at the universities of Uppsala and Aalborg is the leading tool for carrying out such verifications. We shall therefore use TA and UPPAAL when we want to verify properties of real-time systems automatically. In particular, a subset of DC can be translated into semantically equivalent TA and thus used as a specification language for properties in such an automatic verification.

However, since the complexity of automatic verification grows exponentially with the number of clocks, the current verification technology based on TA quickly reaches its limits when the real-time systems get larger. Another limitation of TA is that they are not always implementable because they allow for nondeterministic backtracking, perfect timing, and time-locks.

1.5.3 PLC-Automata

PLC-Automata were introduced by H. Dierks as a special class of real-time automata that model a cyclic behaviour consisting of sensor reading, state transformation, and actuator writing.

Example 1.3

Figure 1.11 shows a PLC-Automaton specifying a watchdog. The automaton

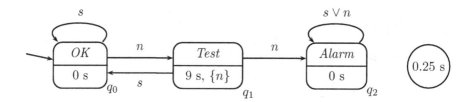

Fig. 1.11. PLC-Automaton

has three states q_0, q_1, q_2 and polls with a cycle time of 0.25 seconds the current sensor value. If in its initial state q_0 the sensor value s (*signal present*) is read, the automaton outputs *OK*. If n (*no signal*) is read the automaton switches to the state q_1 and outputs *Test*. The inscription in the lower part of this state indicates that here further readings of the sensor value n will be ignored for 9 seconds. However, reactions to the sensor value s are still possible and will cause a switch to the initial state q_0 with output *OK*. If after having been 9 seconds in state q_1 still the sensor value n is read, the automaton switches into the state q_2 and outputs *Alarm*. The automaton will then stay in this state. ∎

A strong advantage of PLC-Automata is that they can be implemented on a standard hardware platform known as *Programmable Logic Controllers* (abbreviated PLCs). This explains the name of the automata model. We shall therefore use PLC-Automata as a stepping stone towards an implementation of real-time systems. Once such a system is represented as a network of cooperating PLC-Automata it can be compiled automatically into PLC code. Moreover, it is also possible to compile it into code for other hardware platforms as long as they satisfy certain minimal requirements.

1.5.4 Tying it all together

Figure 1.12 gives an overview of a design process for real-time systems that forms the backbone of our exposition on formal specification and automatic verification in this book.

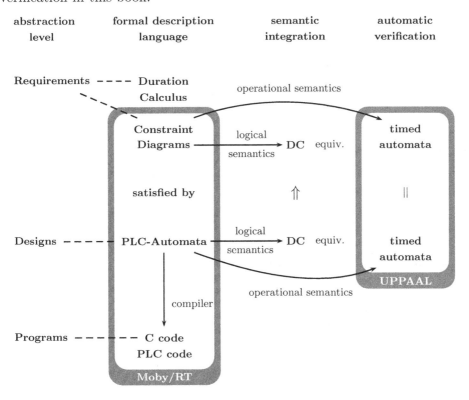

Fig. 1.12. Overview

We consider three levels of abstraction:

- requirements will be specified in Duration Calculus,
- designs will be specified as PLC-Automata,
- programs will be written as C code or PLC code.

Further on,

- automatic verification will be performed using timed automata and the model checker UPPAAL.

PLC-Automata are connected to the two other specification languages, DC and timed automata, in that they have a logical semantics in terms of DC formulas and an equivalent operational semantics in terms of timed automata. This enables us to automatically verify properties specified in subsets of DC via translation into timed automata. The verification can be performed using any model checker for timed automata. In this book we shall use the tool UPPAAL for this purpose.

1.6 Exercises

Exercise 1.1 (System properties)
State for each of the following classes of system properties one requirement for an elevator:

- safety properties,
- liveness properties,
- bounded response properties,
- duration properties.

Exercise 1.2 (Utility)
Prove that the formula Utility in (1.6) is equivalent to the original property **Utility** required for the generalised railroad crossing.

Exercise 1.3 (Safety property)
Prove that in the generalised railroad crossing case study the following implication holds:

$$(\mathsf{Asm} \wedge \mathsf{Des\text{-}G}) \implies \mathsf{Safety}$$

where Asm, Des-G, and Safety are defined as in Section 1.3.

Exercise 1.4 (Single-track line segment)
Consider the railroad system in Figure 1.13. The two circular tracks share a safety-critical section: a line segment with a single track only. Suppose that there are exactly two trains driving in opposite directions along this segment. We assume that the trains cannot change their direction. Each entry of the critical section is guarded by a block signal. The points can be assumed to be switched into the right direction when a train is approaching the critical section.

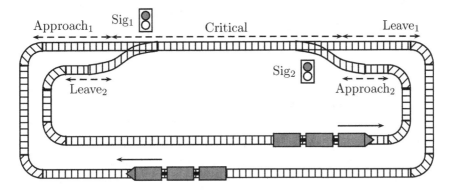

Fig. 1.13. Single-track line segment

(a) How can the positions of the trains and the states of the block signals be described by observables? Give suitable data types for these observables and argue whether a discrete- or continuous-time domain is a more suitable choice.

(b) Use formulas of predicate logic as in the case study of the generalised railroad crossing to describe the following requirements:

– Safety: "There are never two trains at the same time in the critical section."
– Bounded response: "If a train approaches a block signal, it will show a green light within ξ_{wait} time."

(c) Formalise the following design specifications in predicate logic:

– A train needs at most ξ_{cross} time units to pass the critical section.
– A train enters the critical section only if the block signal shows green.
– If one of the block signals shows green, the other one shows red.

(d) Explain in which case a railroad system that satisfies all design specifications of (c) can nevertheless fail to satisfy the safety requirement.

1.7 Bibliographic remarks

Real-time (and hybrid) systems is a very active field of research. The current research on real-time systems is presented in journals, at various specialised conferences such as RTSS (IEEE Real-Time Systems Symposium), EuroMicro, FTRTFT (Formal Techniques in Real-Time and Fault-Tolerant Systems), FORMATS (Formal Modelling and Analysis of Timed Systems), Hybrid Systems and HSCC (Hybrid Systems: Computation and Control), and as part of more general conferences. The IEEE Computer Society has a special Technical Committee on Real-Time Systems.

Only a few books summarising aspects of this large area exist today. The book by H. Kopetz [Kop97] discusses a wide range of concepts needed for the design of distributed embedded real-time systems, including the notion of time, fault-tolerance, real-time communications, time-triggered protocols and architectures. It contains a wealth of examples drawn from industrial, in particular automotive applications. The presentation is mostly informal, it does not introduce formal methods to reason about properties of real-time systems. A. Burns and A. Wellings introduce in their book [BW01] many concepts of real-time systems including scheduling, and present in depth important concepts and languages for programming concurrent and real-time systems. They do not discuss formal methods for specifying and verifying real-time systems. The book by J.W.S. Liu [Liu00] is devoted to scheduling algorithms for real-time systems, but also discusses real-time communication protocols and real-time operating systems. A very good overview on different methods in scheduling theory, and the specification and verification of real-time systems, is provided in a book edited by M. Joseph [Jos96]. Another collective work is the book edited by C. Heitmeyer and D. Mandrioli where the generalised railroad crossing (see Section 1.3) case study is used to illustrate and compare various formal specification methods for real-time systems [HM96]. A monograph devoted to the Duration Calculus and its extensions is authored by Zhou Chaochen and M.R. Hansen [ZH04]. The book by J.C.M. Baeten and C.A. Middelburg presents a process-algebraic approach to real-time systems [BM02]. A specific process algebra, i.e. Real-Time CSP, is presented in [Dav93]. Reactive systems, specified by Milner's Calculus of Communicating Systems (CCS) and timed automata, are presented in the book [AILS07].

In the following we give some pointers to the literature on topics touched upon in this introduction. Subsequent chapters of this book give more detailed bibliographic remarks on the topics discussed there.

Case studies. The case study of the *Generalised Railroad Crossing* was introduced by C. Heitmeyer and N. Lynch [HL94]. Since then it has been used as a benchmark to compare different approaches to the specification and verification of real-time systems (see e.g. [HM96]).

The case study of the *Gas Burner* was introduced in the collaborative European research project ProCoS (Provably Correct Systems) [HHF+94, BHL+96]. The safety requirement Req (see Subsection 1.4.2) was defined in cooperation with engineers of a company producing gas burners. The first formal specification and correctness proof of the gas burner appeared in [RRH93].

Another prominent case study is the *Steam Boiler* by J.R. Abrial, E. Börger and H. Langmaack, to which various approaches to the specification and verification of real-time systems have been applied and compared [ABL96].

Temporal logics. For reasoning about the infinite computations of reactive systems *temporal logic* has been introduced by A. Pnueli [Pnu77]. In this logic safety and liveness properties of reactive systems [OL82] can be specified and proven [MP91, MP95]. Whereas safety properties represent requirements that should be continuously maintained by the system, liveness properties represent requirements whose eventual realisation must be guaranteed, for instance that every query is eventually answered or that a process has infinitely often access to a critical resource. Safety properties can be checked by looking at the finite prefixes of a computation, but liveness properties can be checked only by looking at the whole infinite computation, and are thus more difficult to prove. B. Alpern and F.B. Schneider [AS85, AS87] and Z. Manna and A. Pnueli [MP90] presented different characterisations of safety and liveness properties, as a partition or as a hierarchy of properties, respectively.

Logics for reasoning about properties of real-time systems are mostly extensions of temporal logics for reactive systems. Only if the time domain is discrete can one use the same temporal logic as for reactive systems, for example CTL (Computation Tree Logic) [CES86]. For the continuous-time domain MTL (Metric Temporal Logic) [Koy90] and TCTL (Timed Computational Tree Logic) [ACD93] have been proposed. Lamport advocates an "old-fashioned recipe" for real time which rejects using any special notation but takes a normal temporal logic augmented with explicit clock variables [AL92]. In our opinion this leads to complicated reasoning similar to that in Sections 1.3 and 1.4 based on predicate logic. These are all point-based temporal logics. By contrast, the *Duration Calculus*, which is used in this book, is an interval-based temporal logic for real time extending previous work on Interval Temporal Logic [Mos85].

Logic is often claimed to be an obstacle for direct use by engineers. Therefore formal *graphic notations* have been proposed for the specification of behavioural properties. Well known are MSCs (Message Sequence Charts) developed for applications in telecommunication systems [ITU94, MR94]. In their original form MSCs describe only typical communication traces of a reactive system. To overcome this shortcoming, MSCs have been extended to LSCs (Live Sequence Charts), a graphic notation for a fragment of temporal logic [DH01]. To specify real-time properties graphically, *Constraint Diagrams* have been proposed [Die96]. Their semantics is defined in terms of the Duration Calculus. We shall introduce Constraint Diagrams in Chapter 3 of this book.

State-transition models. The most popular description technique for reactive systems is state-transition models. *Finite automata* are well understood since the early days of computing and come with a graphic representation that appeals to engineers. This basic model has been extended in many ways: *Büchi automata* accept infinite sequences [Tho90], *Petri nets* have an explicit representation of concurrency [Rei85], *statecharts* have this as well but also a concept of hierarchy [Har87], *action systems* add infinite data domains to the finite control state space [Bac90]. All these state-transition models have been extended to deal with time. In this book we shall deal with two such models for continuous real time.

Timed automata were introduced by R. Alur and D. Dill as an extension of Büchi automata by real-valued clocks [AD94]. The most interesting result on timed automata is that certain important properties like the emptiness problem for timed languages and the reachability problem for states are decidable [ACD93, AD94]. This is remarkable because timed automata, although they have only finitely many control points, describe systems with infinitely many (in fact, uncountably many) states due to their use of clocks ranging over the real numbers. This result has triggered the development of tools for the automatic verification of properties of timed automata, in particular UPPAAL [LPW97], KRONOS [Yov97], and HyTech [HHW97].

Although timed automata are an operational model of real-time systems, they cannot always be implemented. This is because a timed automaton is just an acceptor of the desired infinite runs of a real-time system. If after finitely many steps the timed automaton cannot extend its computation to an infinite run meeting the required timing conditions, these steps are just not accepted. Operationally speaking, the timed automaton has then to *backtrack*, which is impossible for an implementation representing a controller of a real-time system.

PLC-Automata were developed by H. Dierks as a state-transition model of real-time systems that can be implemented on a simple hardware platform, i.e. PLCs (Programmable Logic Controllers) [Die00a]. PLCs are widespread in industrial control and automation applications [Lew95]. PLC-Automata are not only useful when PLCs serve as an implementation platform. They can be implemented on any hardware platform that performs a non-terminating loop consisting of inputting sensor values, updating the state in accordance with timer values, and outputting actuator values.

PLC-Automata are well connected to both the Duration Calculus and timed automata in that they have (equivalent) semantics in each of these other specification languages [DFMV98]. This enables us to use PLC-Automata as design specifications for real-time systems and verify their properties, specified in subsets of the Duration Calculus, using the model-checking techniques that are available for timed automata.

Process algebras. The essence of process algebras is to use *composition operators* like parallel composition to structure state-transition models and to study algebraic laws of these operators under certain notions of behavioural equivalence of state-transition models like *bisimulation* [Mil89]. The most prominent process algebras are CCS (*Calculus of Communicating Systems*) [Mil89], CSP (*Communicating Sequential Processes*) [Hoa85, Ros98], and ACP (*Algebra of Communicating Systems*) [BW90].

All these process algebras have been extended by timing operators, for instance CCS to Timed CCS [Yi91], CSP to Timed CSP [Dav93, DS95, Sch95], ACP to a Real-Time Process Algebra [BB91]. A difficulty with these algebras is that their semantics is based on certain scheduling assumptions on the actions like urgency, which are difficult to calculate with. We do not pursue the process algebraic approach here, but apply some of their composition operators such as parallel composition and restriction to timed automata.

Synchronous languages. The so-called *synchronous languages* like ESTEREL [BdS91], LUSTRE [CPHP87], and SIGNAL [BlGJ91] are specification languages for real-time systems that are based on the discrete-time model and the *synchrony hypothesis* that there is no reaction time between input and output. This idealised model is justified when the computation time is negligibly small, for example when the system is implemented on a single computer but does not suffice for reasoning about distributed systems. By contrast, PLC-Automata, our model reflecting the implementation level, are based on the continuous-time model and the assumption that computation and reaction do take time. The latter is essential for their implementability on hardware platforms like distributed networks of PLCs.

Programming languages. To program real-time systems several well-known programming languages offer (extensions with) real-time constructs like timers and scheduling facilities, in particular Ada, Real-Time Java, C/POSIX, and occam2. For details we refer to the book by A. Burns and A. Wellings [BW01]. Additionally, some languages dedicated to particular hardware platforms have been developed, for instance ST (*Structured Text*) for programming PLCs. ST is a standard in the automation industry; it comprises control structures of an imperative programming language and timers [IEC93]. This language will be discussed briefly in Chapter 5 of this book.

Scheduling theory. Scheduling theory can be viewed as a verification technique for real-time systems that are specified as sets of *tasks* [LL73]. In its simplest setting, only certain time parameters of each task are known, for instance the period (when the task has to be executed), the worst-case execution time (an upper bound of how long the execution may take), and the deadline (an upper time bound before which the execution needs to be completed). A scheduling algorithm will then order the execution of the tasks in an attempt to meet all deadlines, and it will compute the worst-case behaviour. Thus it constructively solves the problem of whether certain bounded response properties are satisfied. For more details see for example the books [Jos96, Liu00, BW01].

A task system abstracts from the input and output data and their functional dependency, which is specified along with the real-time constraints in a high-level specification of a real-time system as shown in this introduction. Task systems appear when a real-time system is to be implemented using a *real-time operating system* [But02]. The topics of real-time operating systems, scheduling theory, and the analysis of worst-case execution times (WCET) of programs is not part of this book. Our considerations on implementation of real-time systems end at the level of distributed programs with certain *assumptions* on the upper bounds of their execution cycles. These assumptions have to be discharged separately.

Verification tools. For the verification of properties of specifications at the requirements or design level we discuss automatic and deductive approaches. Since the pioneering work by Clarke and Emerson [CE81] and by Queille and Sifakis [QS82] *model checking*, i.e. the automatic verification of (mostly temporal) properties of (mostly finite state) systems, has been developed and applied to an impressive range of cases [CGP00]. As mentioned earlier, Alur, Courcoubetis and Dill have shown that model checking can also be applied to verify properties of real-time systems modelled as timed automata [ACD93, AD94]. This is remarkable because timed automata have an infinite state space due to their real-valued clocks. This has led to the development of tools like UPPAAL [LPW97], KRONOS [Yov97], and HyTech [HHW97]. However, the complexity of this automatic verification grows exponentially with the number of clocks.

Despite the successes in model checking, tackling the huge state spaces that easily arise when considering systems consisting of a parallel composition of many components or of many real-time clocks remains a problem of current research. To apply model-checking techniques, some preparatory abstraction from the details of the system is therefore necessary. To reason about such abstractions *interactive theorem provers* can be used.

In the area of real-time PVS (*Prototype Verification System*) [ORS92] is often used because it combines the expressive power of higher-order logic with some efficient decision algorithms, in particular for real-number arithmetic. Mostly, PVS is used to build a direct model of the application problem in higher-order logic and to reason about this model (see e.g. [FW96]). Other approaches proceed by first embedding a more specific real-time logic into PVS and then using the embedded logic for dealing with applications [Ska94].

For the Duration Calculus some tools supporting verification have been developed. For the case of discrete time the validity problem of the Duration Calculus is decidable [ZHS93]. P.K. Pandya has exploited this result for the construction of the tool DCVALID [Pan01]. For the case of continuous-time Duration Calculus, J.U. Skakkebæk provided proof support via an embedding of the calculus into the logic of PVS [Ska94]. Similar work was done by S. Heilmann on the basis of the interactive theorem prover Isabelle [Hei99]. The Moby/DC tool provides a semi-decision procedure for a subset of (continuous-time) Duration Calculus [DT03], and the Moby/RT tool offers model checking of PLC-Automata against specifications written in this subset [OD03].

2

Duration Calculus

The Duration Calculus (*DC* for short) was introduced by Zhou Chaochen, C.A.R. Hoare, and A.P. Ravn. It is an interval temporal logic for continuous time that enables the user to specify desirable properties of a real-time system without bothering about their implementation. A DC formula describes how time-dependent state variables or observables of the real-time system should behave in certain time intervals. In particular, this interval-based view can measure the accumulated *duration* of states. Depending on the choice of observables both abstract, high-level and concrete, low-level specifications can be formulated in the Duration Calculus.

This chapter is organised as follows. After an informal preview of the Duration Calculus, we introduce its syntax, semantics, and proof rules. Among the proof rules we present an induction rule that is simpler to apply than the classic induction rule of the Duration Calculus. We explain how to use the Duration Calculus as a specification language for real-time systems and illustrate this with the gas burner example introduced in the introductory chapter. Properties and subsets of the Duration Calculus will be discussed in the subsequent chapter.

2.1 Preview

In Chapter 1 we modelled (examples of) real-time systems by collections of time-dependent state variables or observables obs, i.e. functions of the form

$$\mathsf{obs} : \mathsf{Time} \longrightarrow \mathcal{D}$$

where Time denotes the time domain, usually the non-negative real numbers, and $\mathcal{D}$ is the data type of obs. Duration Calculus is a logic (and calculus) that is tailored to expressing properties of such observables in a concise way.

As a first contact with Duration Calculus, let us look once more at the examples of Chapter 1.

Examples 2.1

For the railroad crossing of Section 1.3 let us take E, A, Cr, O, and Cl, introduced as abbreviations in Subsection 1.3.2, as independent Boolean observables

$$E, A, Cr, O, Cl : \mathsf{Time} \longrightarrow \{0, 1\}$$

denoting an empty track, an approaching train, a train crossing the gate area, an open gate, and a closed gate, respectively.

Often one wishes to specify that a certain property holds throughout an observation interval. To this end, the Duration Calculus offers the *every-where* operator written by embracing the property with ceiling brackets $\lceil \ \rceil$. For example, an arbitrary time interval where the track is empty is expressed by the formula $\lceil E \rceil$. Similarly, $\lceil A \rceil$ and $\lceil Cr \rceil$ denote intervals where a train is approaching and where a train is crossing the gate area, respectively.

To specify behaviour patterns consisting of several intervals, the Duration Calculus offers the *chop operator* ; of interval logic. It "chops" larger intervals into smaller subintervals. For example, a behaviour where first the track is empty, then a train is approaching, and finally it is crossing the gate area is expressed by the formula

$$\lceil E \rceil \; ; \; \lceil A \rceil \; ; \; \lceil Cr \rceil .$$

To measure the *length* of an interval the operator ℓ is used. For example,

$$\lceil A \rceil \wedge \ell = 10$$

expresses an interval of length 10 (seconds) where a train is approaching. To specify that *any* approaching phase cannot last longer than 15 (seconds), we use implication and write

$$\lceil A \rceil \implies \ell \le 15.$$

Informally, this formula states that approaching trains are not driving too slow. To specify that every E–A–Cr behaviour pattern has a duration of at least 10 (seconds) we write

$$(\lceil E \rceil \; ; \; \lceil A \rceil \; ; \; \lceil Cr \rceil) \implies \ell \ge 10. \qquad (2.1)$$

There is one subtlety with this formula. Since the implication should hold for *every* E–A–Cr pattern, the boundary intervals $\lceil E \rceil$ and $\lceil Cr \rceil$ may be arbitrarily small. Thus in (2.1), ℓ actually measures the length of the approaching phase $\lceil A \rceil$. Informally, it states that approaching trains are not driving too fast.

To specify the safety property that the gate is closed whenever a train is in the crossing, we simply state the implication

$$\lceil Cr \rceil \Longrightarrow \lceil Cl \rceil \, ,$$

i.e. for every interval where a train is in the crossing the gate is closed. In contrast to the predicate calculus formula (1.5) in Section 1.3, no explicit quantification over time is needed in this Duration Calculus formula.

The Utility property requires that the gate must open when there is no train in the crossing for a sufficiently long time. In Duration Calculus, this can be expressed as follows:

$$(\lceil \neg Cr \rceil \wedge \ell > \xi_1 + \xi_2) \implies \Diamond \lceil O \rceil . \tag{2.2}$$

This formula states that in every observation interval where there is no train in the crossing and which has a sufficient length (here greater than $\xi_1 + \xi_2$, the time needed to open and close the gate), a subinterval can be found where the gate is open. The existence of this subinterval is formalised by the *diamond* operator $\Diamond$, which in Duration Calculus is an abbreviation:

$$\Diamond \lceil O \rceil \iff (\text{true}; \lceil O \rceil \, ; \text{true}).$$

Thus the subinterval where O holds throughout is surrounded by two arbitrary intervals specified by true. Note that (2.2) is much shorter than the corresponding predicate calculus formula (1.6) in Section 1.3.

For the gas burner of Section 1.4 let us take L as an independent Boolean observable

$$L : \text{Time} \longrightarrow \{0, 1\}$$

standing for a gas leak. In Duration Calculus, the safety requirement (1.7) of Section 1.4 that gas must not leak too long can be expressed using the integral operator $\int$:

$$\ell \geq 60 \implies \int L \leq \frac{\ell}{20}.$$

This formula states that in each observation interval of length at least 60 (seconds) the duration of L, i.e. the accumulated time where the gas burner leaks, is one-twentieth of that length. In contrast to the predicate calculus formula (1.7), no explicit quantification over the integral time bounds is needed in this Duration Calculus formula. The name Duration Calculus

stems from the ability to (conveniently) specify accumulated durations of
states with the integral operator. ∎

The examples show two characteristics of the Duration Calculus:

- Whereas the predicate calculus formulas of Chapter 1 used time points to
  express properties of observables, the Duration Calculus uses time intervals. This allows for a convenient way of specifying patterns of behaviour
  sequences.
- Unlike the predicate calculus formulas of Chapter 1, the Duration Calculus avoids references to time at the explicit syntactic level and pushes
  quantification over time interval to the implicit semantics level. This results often in very concise specifications.

2.2 Syntax and semantics

We now turn to the formal definition of the Duration Calculus. In this
section we introduce its syntactic constituents *together* with their meaning
or *semantics*. The calculus consists of *state assertions*, *terms*, and *formulas*,
constructed from certain symbols which we introduce first.

2.2.1 Symbols

We start from the following sets of symbols:

- A set of *function symbols* with typical elements f, g, each one with a
  certain *arity* $n \in \mathbb{N}$. Function symbols of arity 0 are called *constants*. We
  assume the presence of the constants 0, 1 and in fact m for all $m \in \mathbb{N}$,
  and of the binary function symbols $+$ and $\cdot$.
- A set of *predicate symbols* with typical elements p, q, each one with a
  certain *arity* $n \in \mathbb{N}$. We assume the presence of two predicate symbols
  of arity 0, namely true and false, and of the binary predicate symbols
  $=, <, >, \leq$, and $\geq$.
- A set GVar of *global variables* with typical elements x, y, z, to be used as
  parameters of a real-time system that do not change over time.
- A set Obs of time-dependent *state variables* or *observables* with typical elements X, Y, Z, each one of a certain (mostly finite) data type $\mathcal{D}$. *Boolean*
  observables are those of data type $\{0, 1\}$.
- A set of further symbols comprising the logical connectives $\neg, \wedge, \vee, \Longrightarrow$,
  and $\Longleftrightarrow$, the quantifiers $\forall$ and $\exists$, and the symbols $\ell, \int, ;, \bullet$, and
  elements d taken from the data types $\mathcal{D}$ of observables.

Semantics. The meaning of the symbols involves the sets $\{\mathsf{tt}, \mathsf{ff}\}$ of the truth values "true" and "false", $\mathbb{R}$ of the real numbers, and Time of time, with typical element t. Mostly we consider $\mathsf{Time} = \mathbb{R}_{\geq 0}$ (continuous time) and only in Subsection 3.1.1 alternatively $\mathsf{Time} = \mathbb{N}$ (discrete time).

The semantics of an n-ary function symbol f is a function, denoted by $\hat{f}$, with

$$\hat{f} : \mathbb{R}^n \longrightarrow \mathbb{R},$$

and the semantics of an n-ary predicate symbol p is a function, denoted by $\hat{p}$, with

$$\hat{p} : \mathbb{R}^n \longrightarrow \{\mathsf{tt}, \mathsf{ff}\}.$$

In particular, for $n = 0$ we have $\hat{f} \in \mathbb{R}$ and $\hat{p} \in \{\mathsf{tt}, \mathsf{ff}\}$.

Examples 2.2

The semantics of the function and predicate symbols mentioned above is fixed throughout this book. The most important cases are as follows:

- $\widehat{\mathsf{true}} = \mathsf{tt}$ and $\widehat{\mathsf{false}} = \mathsf{ff}$,
- $\hat{0} \in \mathbb{R}$ is the number *zero*,
- $\hat{1} \in \mathbb{R}$ is the number *one*,
- $\hat{+} : \mathbb{R}^2 \longrightarrow \mathbb{R}$ is the *addition* of real numbers,
- $\hat{\cdot} : \mathbb{R}^2 \longrightarrow \mathbb{R}$ is the *multiplication* of real numbers,
- $\hat{=} : \mathbb{R}^2 \longrightarrow \{\mathsf{tt}, \mathsf{ff}\}$ is the *equality* relation on real numbers,
- $\hat{<} : \mathbb{R}^2 \longrightarrow \{\mathsf{tt}, \mathsf{ff}\}$ is the *less than* relation on real numbers.

The remaining cases can be defined as abbreviations in the usual way. Since this semantics is the expected one, we shall often simply use the symbols $0, 1, +, \cdot, =, <$ when we mean their semantics $\hat{0}, \hat{1}, \hat{+}, \hat{\cdot}, \hat{=}, \hat{<}$. ∎

The semantics of a global variable is not fixed, but given by a *valuation*. This is a mapping $\mathcal{V}$ that assigns to each global variable x a real number

$$\mathcal{V}(x) \in \mathbb{R}.$$

We use Val to denote the set of all valuations, i.e. $\mathsf{Val} = \mathsf{GVar} \longrightarrow \mathbb{R}$. The adjective *global* indicates that the value of a global variable is *independent* of the time.

By contrast, the semantics of a state variable is *time-dependent*. It is given by an *interpretation* $\mathcal{I}$, which is a mapping that assigns to each state variable X of type $\mathcal{D}$ a function

$$\mathcal{I}(X) : \mathsf{Time} \longrightarrow \mathcal{D}$$

such that $\mathcal{I}(X)(t)$ denotes the value in $\mathcal{D}$ that X has at $t \in$ Time. For the interpretation of X we shall also write $X_\mathcal{I}$ instead of $\mathcal{I}(X)$. Such an interpretation can be displayed by a *timing diagram*.

Example 2.3
Consider an observable X of data type $\{\text{up}, \text{down}\}$. The following timing diagram shows (an initial part) of an interpretation $\mathcal{I}$ of X, i.e. a function $X_\mathcal{I} : \text{Time} \longrightarrow \{\text{up}, \text{down}\}$:

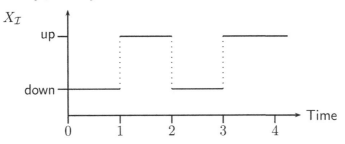

Thus in the formal account on Duration Calculus we carefully distinguish between syntax and semantics of observables. An observable like X is just a syntactic name which can be interpreted semantically by any function $X_\mathcal{I}$ from Time to the data type of X, here $\{\text{up}, \text{down}\}$. Later in Subsection 2.2.3 we restrict the set of admissible functions $X_\mathcal{I}$ somewhat. ∎

The meaning of the logical connectives and the quantifiers is standard: $\neg$ denotes *negation*, $\wedge$ denotes *conjunction*, $\vee$ denotes *disjunction*, $\Longrightarrow$ denotes *logical implication*, $\Longleftrightarrow$ denotes *logical equivalence*, $\forall$ denotes the universal quantifier *for all*, and $\exists$ denotes the existential quantifier *there exists*. The meaning of the symbols ℓ, $\int$, $;$, $\bullet$, and $d \in \mathcal{D}$ will be explained in the following subsections when they are needed.

2.2.2 *State assertions*

State assertions are Boolean combinations of basic properties of state variables. The set of *state assertions*, with typical elements P, Q, R, is defined by the following abstract syntax:

$$P ::= 0 \mid 1 \mid X = d \mid \neg P \mid P_1 \wedge P_2$$

where d belongs to the data type $\mathcal{D}$ of the observable X. For a Boolean observable X (with $\mathcal{D} = \{0, 1\}$) we abbreviate the basic property $X = 1$ to X. In the case $P_1 \wedge P_2$ the subscripts 1 and 2 serve to distinguish the first and second subassertion. This notation is helpful when structural induction on state assertions is used as in the definition of semantics below.

For conciseness we show here only the logical connectives $\neg$ and $\wedge$. The other connectives $\vee$, $\Longrightarrow$, and $\Longleftrightarrow$ are considered as abbreviations in the usual way. It is well known that the presence of several binary infix operators may lead to syntactic *ambiguities* when assertions are written as strings. Consider for instance

$$P \wedge Q \Longleftrightarrow R.$$

Does this mean $P \wedge (Q \Longleftrightarrow R)$ or $(P \wedge Q) \Longleftrightarrow R$? There are two standard solutions to this problem: either use brackets (as above) or define *priorities* for the connectives such that a connective of higher priority binds stronger than one of lower priority. We define the following priority groups from highest to lowest priority:

- negation $\neg$,
- the binary connectives $\wedge$ and $\vee$,
- the binary connectives $\Longrightarrow$ and $\Longleftrightarrow$.

For example, $\neg P \wedge Q$ stands for $(\neg P) \wedge Q$. Note that brackets may always be used to clarify the intended structure of an assertion.

Semantics. Obviously, the semantics of a state assertion depends on the interpretation of the state variables occurring in it and is thus *time dependent*. Given an interpretation $\mathcal{I}$, assigning to each state variable X a function $X_\mathcal{I} : \mathsf{Time} \longrightarrow \mathcal{D}$, the semantics of a state assertion P is a function

$$\mathcal{I}[\![P]\!] : \mathsf{Time} \longrightarrow \{0, 1\}$$

such that $\mathcal{I}(P)(t)$ denotes the value of P at $t \in \mathsf{Time}$. This value is defined inductively on the structure of P:

$$\mathcal{I}[\![0]\!](t) = 0,$$
$$\mathcal{I}[\![1]\!](t) = 1,$$
$$\mathcal{I}[\![X = d]\!](t) = \begin{cases} 1, & \text{if } X_\mathcal{I}(t) = d \\ 0, & \text{otherwise,} \end{cases}$$
$$\mathcal{I}[\![\neg P]\!](t) = 1 - \mathcal{I}[\![P]\!](t),$$
$$\mathcal{I}[\![P_1 \wedge P_2]\!](t) = \begin{cases} 1, & \text{if } \mathcal{I}[\![P_1]\!](t) = 1 \text{ and } \mathcal{I}[\![P_2]\!](t) = 1 \\ 0, & \text{otherwise.} \end{cases}$$

For a Boolean observable X we have the following special case of the third clause of this definition:

$$\mathcal{I}[\![X]\!](t) = \mathcal{I}[\![X = 1]\!](t) = X_{\mathcal{I}}(t).$$

The function $\mathcal{I}[\![P]\!]$ is also called an *interpretation of* P and often written as $P_{\mathcal{I}}$ instead of $\mathcal{I}[\![P]\!]$. Using numbers 0 and 1 as values of this interpretation instead of truth values tt and ff is convenient in the next subsection when defining the semantics of terms which are constructed from state assertions. Again, the interpretation $P_{\mathcal{I}}$ can be displayed by a timing diagram.

Example 2.4

For Boolean observables G and F let L be the state assertion $G \wedge \neg F$. Recall our convention for Boolean observables: G abbreviates $G = 1$ and F abbreviates $F = 1$. Thus L actually stands for $G = 1 \wedge \neg (F = 1)$. Consider the following interpretations $F_{\mathcal{I}} : \text{Time} \longrightarrow \{0, 1\}$ and $G_{\mathcal{I}} : \text{Time} \longrightarrow \{0, 1\}$ and the induced semantics $L_{\mathcal{I}} : \text{Time} \longrightarrow \{0, 1\}$ of the state assertion L:

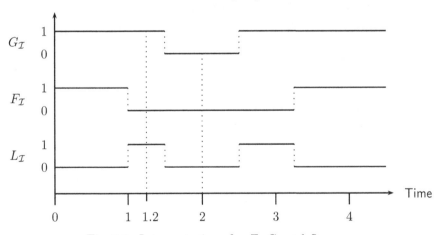

Fig. 2.1. Interpretations for F, G, and L

From the interpretations of Figure 2.1 we see that $L_{\mathcal{I}}(1.2) = 1$ and $L_{\mathcal{I}}(2) = 0$. Formally, this is calculated as follows. At time 1.2 we have

$$
\begin{aligned}
L_{\mathcal{I}}(1.2) &= \mathcal{I}[\![L]\!](1.2) \\
&= \mathcal{I}[\![G \wedge \neg F]\!](1.2) \\
&= 1
\end{aligned}
$$

because $\mathcal{I}[\![G]\!](1.2) = G_{\mathcal{I}}(1.2) = 1$ and

$$\begin{aligned} \mathcal{I}[\![\neg F]\!](1.2) &= 1 - \mathcal{I}[\![F]\!](1.2) \\ &= 1 - F_{\mathcal{I}}(1.2) \\ &= 1 - 0 \\ &= 1. \end{aligned}$$

At time 2 we calculate

$$\begin{aligned} L_{\mathcal{I}}(2) &= \mathcal{I}[\![L]\!](2) \\ &= \mathcal{I}[\![G \wedge \neg F]\!](2) \\ &= 0 \end{aligned}$$

because $\mathcal{I}[\![G]\!](2) = G_{\mathcal{I}}(2) = 0$. ∎

2.2.3 Terms

Duration terms, abbreviated DC terms or just terms, are expressions that denote real numbers that depend on time intervals. The set of *terms*, with the typical element θ, is defined by the following abstract syntax:

$$\theta ::= x \mid \ell \mid \int P \mid f(\theta_1, \ldots, \theta_n)$$

where according to our conventions x is a global variable, P is a state assertion, and f is an n-ary function symbol. The symbol ℓ stands for the *length* operator and the symbol $\int$ for the *integral* operator. A term without the symbols ℓ and $\int$ is called *rigid*.

Note that in this abstract syntax we write function symbols f in prefix notation. However, concrete binary function symbols like $+$ and $\cdot$ we shall write in infix notation as usual. For example, we write $\theta_1 + \theta_2$ rather than $+(\theta_1, \theta_2)$. As for assertions, this may lead to syntactic ambiguities when terms are written as strings, which have to be removed by using brackets or priorities.

Semantics. The semantics of a term depends not only on a given interpretation of the state variables occurring in its state assertions and a given valuation of its global variables, but also on a given time interval. To this end, we introduce the set Intv of all *closed intervals* in the time domain:

$$\text{Intv} \stackrel{\text{def}}{=} \{ [b, e] \mid b, e \in \text{Time and } b \leq e \}$$

where $\stackrel{\text{def}}{=}$ means *equal by definition*. Intervals of the form $[b, b]$ are called *point intervals*. The semantics of a term θ is a function

$$\mathcal{I}[\![\theta]\!] : \mathsf{Val} \times \mathsf{Intv} \longrightarrow \mathbb{R}$$

such that $\mathcal{I}[\![\theta]\!](\mathcal{V}, [b, e])$ is the real number that θ denotes under the interpretation $\mathcal{I}$, the valuation $\mathcal{V}$, and the interval $[b, e]$. This value is defined inductively on the structure of θ:

$$\mathcal{I}[\![x]\!](\mathcal{V}, [b, e]) = \mathcal{V}(x),$$
$$\mathcal{I}[\![\ell]\!](\mathcal{V}, [b, e]) = e - b,$$
$$\mathcal{I}[\![\textstyle\int P]\!](\mathcal{V}, [b, e]) = \int_b^e P_{\mathcal{I}}(t)dt,$$
$$\mathcal{I}[\![f(\theta_1, \ldots, \theta_n)]\!](\mathcal{V}, [b, e]) = \hat{f}(\mathcal{I}[\![\theta_1]\!](\mathcal{V}, [b, e]), \ldots, \mathcal{I}[\![\theta_n]\!](\mathcal{V}, [b, e])).$$

Thus the value of a global variable x depends only on the valuation $\mathcal{V}$, the value of the symbol ℓ is the length of the given interval $[b, e]$, the value of the term $\int P$ is calculated by the integral of the function $P_{\mathcal{I}}$ from b to e, and the value of a composed term $f(\theta_1, \ldots, \theta_n)$ is determined by applying the function $\hat{f}$ inductively to the arguments $\mathcal{I}[\![\theta_1]\!](\mathcal{V}, [b, e]), \ldots, \mathcal{I}[\![\theta_n]\!](\mathcal{V}, [b, e])$.

The integral $\int_b^e P_{\mathcal{I}}(t)dt$ measures the accumulated *duration* that the state assertion P holds (has the value 1) in the time interval $[b, e]$, but we have to ensure that it exists. Since $P_{\mathcal{I}} : \mathsf{Time} \longrightarrow \{0, 1\}$, this function correctly maps (in the case of continuous time) real numbers to real numbers, but it might not be (Riemann-)integrable. For instance, the so-called *Dirichlet function*

$$P_{\mathcal{I}}(t) = \begin{cases} 1, & \text{if } t \in \mathbb{Q} \\ 0, & \text{if } t \notin \mathbb{Q} \end{cases}$$

yielding 1 for rational t and 0 for irrational t is discontinuous everywhere and thus not integrable.

Convention. To exclude such functions, the Duration Calculus considers only interpretations $\mathcal{I}$ satisfying the following condition of *finite variability*:

> For each state variable X and each interval $[b, e]$ there is a finite partition of $[b, e]$ such that the interpretation $X_{\mathcal{I}}$ is constant on each part. Thus on each interval $[b, e]$ the function $X_{\mathcal{I}}$ has only finitely many points of discontinuity.

This is sufficient to guarantee integrability of the functions $P_{\mathcal{I}}$. The following annotated timing diagram illustrates this condition:

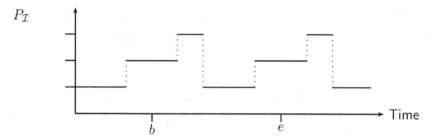

$P_\mathcal{I}$

Time

b e

Remark 2.5

The semantics $\mathcal{I}[\![\theta]\!](\mathcal{V}, [b, e])$ of a term θ is insensitive against changes of the interpretation $\mathcal{I}$ at individual time points. This is a simple consequence of the fact that the integral $\int_b^e P_\mathcal{I}(t)dt$ is insensitive against such changes.

Remark 2.6

The semantics $\mathcal{I}[\![\theta]\!](\mathcal{V}, [b, e])$ of a *rigid* term θ does not depend on the interval $[b, e]$. Thus semantically, rigid terms behave like global variables in that they denote a value that depends only on the valuation $\mathcal{V}$.

Example 2.7

Consider $\theta = x \cdot \int L$. Assume that $\mathcal{V}(x) = 20$ and that $L_\mathcal{I}$ is given by the following timing diagram:

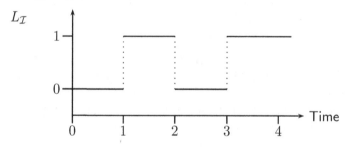

$L_\mathcal{I}$

1

0

Time

0   1   2   3   4

Then the semantics $\mathcal{I}[\![\theta]\!](\mathcal{V}, [1, 4])$ can be calculated as follows:

$$\mathcal{I}[\![\theta]\!](\mathcal{V}, [1, 4]) = \mathcal{I}[\![x]\!](\mathcal{V}, [1, 4]) \; \hat{\cdot} \; \mathcal{I}[\![\int L]\!](\mathcal{V}, [1, 4])$$

$$= \mathcal{V}(x) \; \hat{\cdot} \; \int_1^4 L_\mathcal{I}(t)dt$$

$$= 20 \; \hat{\cdot} \; 2$$

$$= 40.$$

Note that in this calculation we used the ˆ notation for the meaning of the symbol $\cdot$, i.e. multiplication of real numbers, but we omitted it for the meaning of the constants 1, 4, 20, 2, and 40. ∎

2.2.4 Formulas

Duration formulas, abbreviated DC formulas or just formulas, are the core of the Duration Calculus. They describe properties of observables depending on time intervals. The set of *formulas*, with typical elements F, G, H, is defined by the following abstract syntax:

$$F ::= p(\theta_1, \ldots, \theta_n) \mid \neg F_1 \mid F_1 \wedge F_2 \mid \forall x \bullet F_1 \mid F_1 \,;\, F_2$$

where p is an n-ary predicate symbol, $\theta_1, \ldots, \theta_n$ are terms, the symbol $\bullet$ is used for separation in quantified formulas, and the symbol $;$ denotes the so-called *chop operator*.

Formulas of the form $p(\theta_1, \ldots, \theta_n)$ are called *atomic formulas*. Note that true and false are special cases of atomic formulas where the predicate symbol p has arity $n = 0$. A formula is called *rigid* if it contains only rigid terms, i.e. if it does not contain symbols ℓ or $\int$. A formula is called *chop-free* if it does not contain the $;$ operator. Note that quantification is only possible over (first-order) global variables x (representing real numbers), not over (second-order) state variables (representing functions from real numbers to data values).

For conciseness we show here only the logical connectives $\neg$ and $\wedge$, and the universal quantifier $\forall$. The connectives $\vee$, $\implies$, and $\iff$, and the existential quantifier $\exists$ are considered as abbreviations in the usual way. Also we write predicate symbols p here in prefix notation. However, concrete binary predicate symbols like $=$ and $<$ we shall write in infix notation as usual. For example, we write $\theta_1 < \theta_2$ rather than $< (\theta_1, \theta_2)$. As for state assertions, this may lead to syntactic ambiguities when formulas are written as strings, which have to be removed by using brackets or priorities. We define the following five priority groups from highest to lowest priority:

- negation $\neg$,
- the chop operator $;$,
- the binary connectives $\wedge$ and $\vee$,
- the binary connectives $\implies$ and $\iff$,
- the quantifiers $\forall$ and $\exists$.

For example, $\neg F ; G \vee H$ stands for $((\neg F) ; G) \vee H$, and $\forall x \bullet F \wedge G$ stands for $\forall x \bullet (F \wedge G)$.

As usual, quantification leads to the notion of free and bound variables. A global variable x is called a *free* variable of a formula F if it occurs in F outside all subformulas of the form $\forall x \bullet Q$ or $\exists x \bullet Q$, and x is called a *bound* variable of F if it occurs in F inside some subformula of the form $\forall x \bullet Q$ or $\exists x \bullet Q$. By $free(F)$ we denote the set of all free global variables in F. For example, $x \in free(\ell \leq x \wedge \forall x \bullet x + 0 = 0)$. In fact, x occurs also bound in this formula.

An important syntactic operation on formulas F is the *substitution* of a term θ for a variable x in F. We write

$$F[x := \theta]$$

to denote the formula that results from F by performing the following two steps:

(i) F is transformed into $\tilde{F}$ by a renaming of bound variables in F such that no free occurrence of x in $\tilde{F}$ appears within a quantified subformula of the form $\exists z \bullet G$ or $\forall z \bullet G$ for some z occurring in θ.

(ii) $F[x := \theta]$ results from $\tilde{F}$ by textually replacing all free occurrences of x in $\tilde{F}$ by θ.

The first step ensures that there is no clash of a variable z in θ with a bound variable in F. If such a clash cannot occur this step can be omitted. Note that $free(F) = free(\tilde{F})$ and that the formula $F[x := \theta]$ is unique up to a renaming of bound variables only.

Example 2.8

Consider $F \stackrel{\text{def}}{\Longleftrightarrow} (x \geq y \Longrightarrow \exists z \bullet z \geq 0 \wedge x = y + z)$ and $\theta_1 \stackrel{\text{def}}{=} \ell$. Then

$$F[x := \theta_1] \stackrel{\text{def}}{\Longleftrightarrow} (\ell \geq y \Longrightarrow \exists z \bullet z \geq 0 \wedge \ell = y + z).$$

In this substitution no bound renaming of z is needed. This is different if we consider $\theta_2 \stackrel{\text{def}}{=} \ell + z$. Now z needs to be renamed in F, say into $\tilde{z}$, yielding $\tilde{F} \stackrel{\text{def}}{\Longleftrightarrow} (x \geq y \Longrightarrow \exists \tilde{z} \bullet \tilde{z} \geq 0 \wedge x = y + \tilde{z})$, before the replacement of x by θ_2 can take place, yielding

$$F[x := \theta_2] \stackrel{\text{def}}{\Longleftrightarrow} (\ell + z \geq y \Longrightarrow \exists \tilde{z} \bullet \tilde{z} \geq 0 \wedge \ell + z = y + \tilde{z})$$

as the result of the substitution.   ∎

Semantics. The semantics of a formula depends on a given interpretation of the state variables occurring in its terms, a given valuation of the global variables occurring in its terms, and a given time interval. The semantics of a formula F is a function

$$\mathcal{I}[\![F]\!] : \mathsf{Val} \times \mathsf{Intv} \longrightarrow \{\mathsf{tt}, \mathsf{ff}\}$$

such that $\mathcal{I}[\![F]\!](\mathcal{V}, [b, e])$ is the truth value of F under the interpretation $\mathcal{I}$, the valuation $\mathcal{V}$, and the interval $[b, e]$. This value is defined inductively on the structure of F:

$$\mathcal{I}[\![p(\theta_1, \ldots, \theta_n)]\!](\mathcal{V}, [b, e]) = \hat{p}(\mathcal{I}[\![\theta_1]\!](\mathcal{V}, [b, e]), \ldots, \mathcal{I}[\![\theta_n]\!](\mathcal{V}, [b, e])),$$
$$\mathcal{I}[\![\neg F_1]\!](\mathcal{V}, [b, e]) = \mathsf{tt} \text{ iff } \mathcal{I}[\![F_1]\!](\mathcal{V}, [b, e]) = \mathsf{ff},$$
$$\mathcal{I}[\![F_1 \wedge F_2]\!](\mathcal{V}, [b, e]) = \mathsf{tt} \text{ iff } \mathcal{I}[\![F_1]\!](\mathcal{V}, [b, e]) = \mathsf{tt} \text{ and }$$
$$\mathcal{I}[\![F_2]\!](\mathcal{V}, [b, e]) = \mathsf{tt},$$
$$\mathcal{I}[\![\forall x \bullet F_1]\!](\mathcal{V}, [b, e]) = \mathsf{tt} \text{ iff } \text{ for all } d \in \mathbb{R} \text{ the following holds:}$$
$$\mathcal{I}[\![F_1]\!](\mathcal{V}[x := d], [b, e]) = \mathsf{tt},$$
$$\mathcal{I}[\![F_1 \,;\, F_2]\!](\mathcal{V}, [b, e]) = \mathsf{tt} \text{ iff } \text{ there is an } m \in [b, e] \text{ such that}$$
$$\mathcal{I}[\![F_1]\!](\mathcal{V}, [b, m]) = \mathsf{tt} \text{ and }$$
$$\mathcal{I}[\![F_2]\!](\mathcal{V}, [m, e]) = \mathsf{tt}.$$

The first four cases are standard. In case of an atomic formula $p(\theta_1, \ldots, \theta_n)$ the truth value is determined by applying the function $\hat{p}$ to the values $\mathcal{I}[\![\theta_1]\!](\mathcal{V}, [b, e]), \ldots, \mathcal{I}[\![\theta_n]\!](\mathcal{V}, [b, e])$ of the terms $\theta_1, \ldots, \theta_n$. In the cases of negation and conjunction the truth values are defined as expected. In case of the universal quantifier we refer to the *modified valuation* $\mathcal{V}[x := d]$ which agrees with $\mathcal{V}$ on all global variables except for x, where the value is modified to d:

$$\mathcal{V}[x := d](y) = \begin{cases} \mathcal{V}(y), & \text{if } x \neq y \\ d, & \text{otherwise.} \end{cases}$$

The chop operator deserves attention. Intuitively, a formula $F_1 \,;\, F_2$ holds on an interval $[b, e]$ if this interval can be "chopped" into an initial subinterval $[b, m]$ and a final subinterval $[m, e]$ such that F_1 holds on $[b, m]$ and F_2 holds on $[m, e]$.

Example 2.9
With the same $L_{\mathcal{I}}$ as in Example 2.7 we obtain

$$\mathcal{I}[\![\textstyle\int L = 0 \,;\, \int L = 1]\!](\mathcal{V}, [0, 2]) = \mathsf{tt}$$

because

$$\mathcal{I}[\![\int L = 0]\!](\mathcal{V}, [0, 1]) = \left(\int_0^1 L_{\mathcal{I}}(t)dt \,\hat{=}\, 0\right) = \text{tt}$$

$$\text{and} \quad \mathcal{I}[\![\int L = 1]\!](\mathcal{V}, [1, 2]) = \left(\int_1^2 L_{\mathcal{I}}(t)dt \,\hat{=}\, 1\right) = \text{tt}$$

holds.   ∎

Remark 2.10 (Rigid and chop-free)

Let F be a duration formula, $\mathcal{I}$ be an interpretation, $\mathcal{V}$ be a valuation, and $[b, e] \in \mathsf{Intv}$.

- If F is *rigid* then its semantics $\mathcal{I}[\![F]\!](\mathcal{V}, [b, e])$ does not depend on the interval $[b, e]$, i.e.

$$\mathcal{I}[\![F]\!](\mathcal{V}, [b, e]) = \mathcal{I}[\![F]\!](\mathcal{V}, [b', e'])$$

  holds for all $[b, e], [b', e'] \in \mathsf{Intv}$.
- Consider a term θ occurring in F. If F is *chop-free* or θ is *rigid* then in the calculation of the semantics $\mathcal{I}[\![F]\!](\mathcal{V}, [b, e])$ of F, every occurrence of θ in F denotes the same value.

By contrast, in Example 2.9 above, the formula $\int L = 0 \,;\, \int L = 1$ is not chop-free, and in the calculation of its semantics $\mathcal{I}[\![\int L = 0 \,;\, \int L = 1]\!](\mathcal{V}, [0, 2])$ the two occurrences of the term $\theta = \int L$ denote different values, i.e. 1 and 2.

The following Substitution Lemma states that the syntactic operation of substitution corresponds on the semantic side to a suitable modification of the valuation.

Lemma 2.11 (Substitution)

Consider a formula F, a global variable x, and a term θ such that F is chop-free or θ is rigid. Then the following holds for all interpretations $\mathcal{I}$, valuations $\mathcal{V}$, and intervals $[b, e]$:

$$\mathcal{I}[\![F[x := \theta]]\!](\mathcal{V}, [b, e]) = \mathcal{I}[\![F]\!](\mathcal{V}[x := d], [b, e])$$

where $d = \mathcal{I}[\![\theta]\!](\mathcal{V}, [b, e])$.

Proof idea:

Use induction on the structure of F and exploit Remark 2.10.   □

Note that without the restrictions on F and θ the lemma does not hold. For instance, consider

$$F \stackrel{\text{def}}{\Longleftrightarrow} \ell = x \,;\, \ell = x \Longrightarrow \ell = 2 \cdot x$$

and $\theta = \ell$. Then $\mathcal{I}[\![F]\!](\mathcal{V}, [b, e]) = \mathsf{tt}$ for every interpretation $\mathcal{I}$, every valuation $\mathcal{V}$, and every interval $[b, e]$. Thus in particular,

$$\mathcal{I}[\![F]\!](\mathcal{V}[x := d], [b, e]) = \mathsf{tt}$$

for $d = \mathcal{I}[\![\theta]\!](\mathcal{V}, [b, e])$. However, for $b < e$

$$\mathcal{I}[\![F[x := \theta]]\!](\mathcal{V}, [b, e]) = \mathcal{I}[\![\ell = \ell \,;\, \ell = \ell \Longrightarrow \ell = 2 \cdot \ell]\!](\mathcal{V}, [b, e]) = \mathsf{ff}$$

because $\ell = \ell$ is trivially true whereas $\ell = 2 \cdot \ell$ is false.

Abbreviations. The following abbreviations of formulas are often used:

- *point interval*

$$\lceil\rceil \stackrel{\text{def}}{\Longleftrightarrow} \ell = 0.$$

The formula $\lceil\rceil$ holds in an interval $[b, e]$ if this is a point interval, i.e. if $b = e$ holds.

- *almost everywhere P*

$$\lceil P \rceil \stackrel{\text{def}}{\Longleftrightarrow} \int P = \ell \wedge \ell > 0.$$

The formula $\lceil P \rceil$ holds in an interval $[b, e]$ if $b < e$ and P is 1 almost everywhere in $[b, e]$ so that the integral $\int P$ yields $e - b$, the length of the interval. "Almost" reflects the fact that P can be 0 at finitely many time points in the interval $[b, e]$ without affecting the value of the integral. The following two variants of this notation constrain the length of the interval by a time bound $t \in \mathsf{Time}$:

- *P holds for time t*

$$\lceil P \rceil^t \stackrel{\text{def}}{\Longleftrightarrow} \lceil P \rceil \wedge \ell = t.$$

- *P holds up to time t*

$$\lceil P \rceil^{\leq t} \stackrel{\text{def}}{\Longleftrightarrow} \lceil P \rceil \wedge \ell \leq t.$$

- *For some subinterval F holds*

$$\Diamond F \stackrel{\text{def}}{\Longleftrightarrow} \mathsf{true}\,;\, F \,;\, \mathsf{true}.$$

The $\Diamond$ operator is a *modal operator* of interval logic, read as *diamond*. The formula $\Diamond F$ holds in an interval $[b, e]$ if F holds in some subinterval of $[b, e]$, i.e. if $[b, e]$ can be chopped into an arbitrary initial subinterval, a subinterval where F holds, and an arbitrary final subinterval. This is illustrated by the following figure:

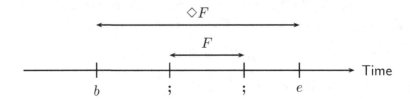

- For *all subintervals* F holds

$$\Box F \stackrel{\text{def}}{\Longleftrightarrow} \neg\Diamond\neg F.$$

The $\Box$ operator is the dual modal operator of interval logic, read as *box*. Its definition by double negation means that there should be no subinterval where F is false. In other words, the formula $\Box F$ holds in an interval $[b, e]$ if F holds in every subinterval of $[b, e]$. This is illustrated by the following diagram:

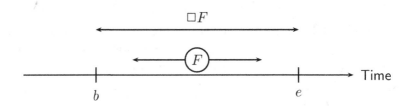

Example 2.12
Assume the following interpretation $\mathcal{I}$ of the observable L:

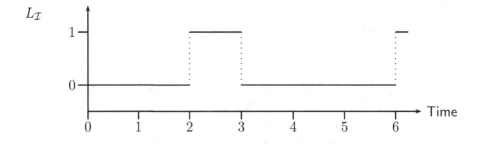

Let $\mathcal{V}$ be an arbitrary valuation. Then the following statements hold:

$$\mathcal{I}[\![\quad \int L = 0 \qquad\qquad\qquad]\!](\mathcal{V}, [0, 2]) = 1,$$
$$\mathcal{I}[\![\quad \int L = 1 \qquad\qquad\qquad]\!](\mathcal{V}, [2, 6]) = 1,$$
$$\mathcal{I}[\![\quad \int L = 0 ; \int L = 1 \qquad\quad]\!](\mathcal{V}, [0, 6]) = 1,$$
$$\mathcal{I}[\![\quad \lceil \neg L \rceil \qquad\qquad\qquad]\!](\mathcal{V}, [0, 2]) = 1,$$
$$\mathcal{I}[\![\quad \lceil L \rceil \qquad\qquad\qquad]\!](\mathcal{V}, [2, 3]) = 1,$$
$$\mathcal{I}[\![\quad \lceil \neg L \rceil \; ; \; \lceil L \rceil \qquad\qquad]\!](\mathcal{V}, [0, 3]) = 1,$$
$$\mathcal{I}[\![\quad \lceil \neg L \rceil \; ; \; \lceil L \rceil \; ; \; \lceil \neg L \rceil \quad]\!](\mathcal{V}, [0, 6]) = 1,$$
$$\mathcal{I}[\![\quad \Diamond \lceil L \rceil \qquad\qquad\qquad]\!](\mathcal{V}, [0, 6]) = 1,$$
$$\mathcal{I}[\![\quad \Diamond \lceil \neg L \rceil \qquad\qquad\quad]\!](\mathcal{V}, [0, 6]) = 1,$$
$$\mathcal{I}[\![\quad \Diamond \lceil \neg L \rceil^2 \qquad\qquad\quad]\!](\mathcal{V}, [0, 6]) = 1,$$
$$\mathcal{I}[\![\quad \lceil \neg L \rceil^2 \; ; \; \lceil L \rceil^1 \; ; \; \lceil \neg L \rceil^3 \;\;]\!](\mathcal{V}, [0, 6]) = 1.$$

Note how the chop operator is used to describe sequential behaviour. For example, the formula $\lceil \neg L \rceil \; ; \; \lceil L \rceil \; ; \; \lceil \neg L \rceil$ expresses that a phase where $\neg L$ holds is followed by a phase where L holds, which is followed by a phase where again $\neg L$ holds. ∎

2.2.5 Validity, satisfiability, and realisability

In the following let $\mathcal{I}$ be an interpretation, $\mathcal{V}$ be a valuation, $[b, e]$ be an interval, and F be a DC formula. Then F *holds* in $\mathcal{I}$, $\mathcal{V}$, $[b, e]$, in symbols

$$\mathcal{I}, \mathcal{V}, [b, e] \models F,$$

iff $\mathcal{I}[\![F]\!](\mathcal{V}, [b, c]) = \mathsf{tt}$. The formula F is *satisfiable* iff F holds in some interpretation $\mathcal{I}$, some valuation $\mathcal{V}$, and some interval $[b, e]$.

We say that $\mathcal{I}$ and $\mathcal{V}$ *realise* (or are *a model of*) F, in symbols

$$\mathcal{I}, \mathcal{V} \models F,$$

iff $\mathcal{I}, \mathcal{V}, [b, e] \models F$ holds for all intervals $[b, e]$. We call F *realisable* iff some interpretation $\mathcal{I}$ and some valuation $\mathcal{V}$ realise F. We say that $\mathcal{I}$ *realises* (or is *a model of*) F, in symbols

$$\mathcal{I} \models F,$$

iff $\mathcal{I}, \mathcal{V}, [b, e] \models F$ holds for all valuations $\mathcal{V}$ and all intervals $[b, e]$.

The formula F is *valid*, in symbols

$$\models F,$$

iff all interpretations $\mathcal{I}$ and all valuations $\mathcal{V}$ realise F.

Remark 2.13

For all DC formulas F the following properties hold:

(i) *Duality*: F is satisfiable iff $\neg F$ is not valid.
F is valid iff $\neg F$ is not satisfiable.

(ii) If F is valid then F is realisable, but not vice versa.

(iii) If F is realisable then F is satisfiable, but not vice versa.

Example 2.14

The formulas

$$\ell \geq 0,$$
$$\ell = \int 1,$$
$$\ell = 30 \iff \ell = 10\,;\ell = 20,$$
$$((F\,;G)\,;H) \iff (F\,;(G\,;H)) \quad \text{(associativity of ;)}$$

are all valid. Note that in the third formula the three occurrences of ℓ all refer to different lengths. For a given interval $[b,e]$ the formula $\ell = 30$ refers to the length $e - b = 30$, whereas (due to the chop operator) $\ell = 10$ and $\ell = 20$ refer to two adjacent subintervals $[b,m]$ and $[m,e]$ of length $m-b = 10$ and $e - m = 20$. The formula

$$\int L \leq x$$

is realisable (and hence satisfiable) by an appropriate interpretation $L_{\mathcal{I}}$ and valuation of x, but it is not valid. The formula

$$\ell = 2$$

is satisfiable, but not realisable. ∎

Initial values of state variables are often important for the correctness of real-time systems. Therefore, we introduce a specialised version of the realisation relation that considers only intervals starting at time 0. We say that $\mathcal{I}$ and $\mathcal{V}$ *realise F from 0* (or are *a model of F from 0*), in symbols

$$\mathcal{I}, \mathcal{V} \models_0 F,$$

iff $\mathcal{I}, \mathcal{V}, [0,t] \models F$ holds for all time points t. Intervals of the form $[0,t]$ are called *initial intervals*. We call F *realisable from 0* iff some interpretation $\mathcal{I}$ and some valuation $\mathcal{V}$ realise F from 0. Again, we simplify the notation if F is independent of the valuation $\mathcal{V}$. Then we say that $\mathcal{I}$ *realises F from 0* (or is *a model of F from 0*), in symbols

$$\mathcal{I} \models_0 F,$$

iff $\mathcal{I}, \mathcal{V}, [0, t] \models F$ holds for all valuations $\mathcal{V}$ and all time points t.

The formula F *is valid from 0*, in symbols

$$\models_0 F,$$

iff all interpretations $\mathcal{I}$ and all valuations $\mathcal{V}$ realise F from 0.

Proposition 2.15

For all interpretations $\mathcal{I}$, valuations $\mathcal{V}$, and DC formulas F the following properties hold:

  (i) $\mathcal{I}, \mathcal{V} \models F$ implies $\mathcal{I}, \mathcal{V} \models_0 F$, but not vice versa.
  (ii) If F is realisable then F is realisable from 0, but not vice versa.
  (iii) F is valid iff F is valid from 0.

Proof:

Re (i): By definition, $\mathcal{I}, \mathcal{V} \models F$ implies $\mathcal{I}, \mathcal{V} \models_0 F$. To see that the converse is false, consider $F = \lceil \rceil \vee \lceil X = 1 \rceil \,; \mathsf{true}$. Then $\mathcal{I} \models_0 F$ means that $X_{\mathcal{I}}$ is 1 initially, but $\mathcal{I} \models F$ requires that $X_{\mathcal{I}}$ is 1 (almost) everywhere.

Re (ii): Again by definition, if F is realisable then F is realisable from 0. To see that the converse is false, we refine the argument above and consider $F = (\lceil \rceil \vee \lceil X = 1 \rceil \,; \mathsf{true}) \wedge (\ell \geq 2 \implies \Diamond \lceil X = 0 \rceil)$. Then F is realisable from 0, e.g. by the following interpretation $X_{\mathcal{I}}$:

$$X_{\mathcal{I}}(t) = \begin{cases} 1, & \text{if } t \leq 1 \\ 0, & \text{if } t > 1. \end{cases}$$

However, F is not realisable in the general sense because the first conjunct of F requires that $X_{\mathcal{I}}$ is 1 (almost) everywhere whereas the second conjunct requires that $X_{\mathcal{I}}$ is 0 infinitely often.

Re (iii): See [ZH04], Theorem 3.1 on p. 44.   □

2.3 Specification and correctness proof

In this section we give an overview of how we shall use the Duration Calculus in the specification and correctness proof of real-time systems. To specify a real-time system we first choose a collection of observables that determine in how much detail we wish to model the system. Then we constrain the possible interpretations of these observables by stating DC formulas whose conjunction we take as the specification Spec of the system. Note that the DC formula Spec may contain free global variables. They can be used to represent *time parameters* of the system, for instance an unknown reaction time. Spec represents the set of all interpretations $\mathcal{I}$ and all valuations $\mathcal{V}$ that realise Spec from 0, i.e. with

$$\mathcal{I}, \mathcal{V} \models_0 \text{Spec}.$$

Mostly, we wish to compare this specification against a second description of the real-time system, representing it at a different level of detail, for example as a controller. If this description is again given as a DC formula, say Ctrl, then we can verify its *correctness* w.r.t. the specification Spec by proving that the implication

$$\text{Crtl} \implies \text{Spec} \tag{2.3}$$

is valid. Then every interpretation $\mathcal{I}$ and all valuations $\mathcal{V}$ that realise Ctrl from 0 also realise Spec from 0. This presupposes that Ctrl and Spec use the *same* observables. This is the simplest possible setting of a correctness relation. We discuss now several variants of (2.3).

If Ctrl and Spec use different observables, say Ctrl uses more concrete observables C and Spec uses more abstract observables A, then we need a *linking invariant* that relates the data values of C and A. If this invariant is described by a DC formula, say $\text{Link}_{C,A}$, then correctness of Ctrl w.r.t. Spec can be verified by proving the validity of the implication

$$\text{Crtl} \wedge \text{Link}_{C,A} \implies \text{Spec}.$$

The linking invariant corresponds to a refinement relation as used in the theory of *data refinement*.

Often the controller will operate correctly only under some *assumptions* on the behaviour of the plant. We shall specify such assumptions as a DC formula Asm on the input observables and verify correctness of Ctrl w.r.t. Spec by proving the validity of the implication

$$\text{Asm} \wedge \text{Crtl} \implies \text{Spec}.$$

Neither the specification nor the controller need to be given in terms of DC formulas. For instance, later in this book we present other formal description techniques for real-time systems such as Constraint Diagrams for the specification and PLC-Automata for the controller. However, for these description techniques we shall define a *predicative semantics* in terms of DC formulas. If Ctrl is given as a PLC-Automaton let $[\![\text{Crtl}]\!]$ denote a DC formula defining its semantics. Analogously, if Spec is given as a Constraint Diagram let $[\![\text{Spec}]\!]$ denote a DC formula defining its semantics. Then verifying correctness of Ctrl w.r.t. Spec is done by proving the validity of the implication

$$[\![\mathsf{Crtl}]\!] \implies [\![\mathsf{Spec}]\!].$$

So far we have compared only two different levels of descriptions of a real-time system, controller and specification. In general, the development of a real-time system can involve intermediate levels. For instance, a top-down fashion might involve a specification Spec, a design Des, and a controller Ctrl. The correctness is established by proving the validity of the implications

$$\mathsf{Crtl} \implies \mathsf{Des} \quad \text{and} \quad \mathsf{Des} \implies \mathsf{Spec}$$

and then concluding by the transitivity of implication that indeed

$$\mathsf{Crtl} \implies \mathsf{Spec}$$

is valid. In our examples, these different variants of correctness arguments will often be combined.

How do we actually prove the validity of the implications? In this book, we use several approaches. In simple cases we conduct the correctness proof by hand on the basis of the semantics of DC formulas supported by the proof rules of the DC to be introduced in Section 2.4. We may also be able to apply a general theorem on the real-time behaviour of certain descriptions like PLC-Automata (Subsection 5.4.1). Finally, for certain classes of controllers and specifications we use algorithms to prove their correctness. These algorithms may even synthesise controllers from specifications (Section 5.5). Mostly, we rely on a semantics preserving translation of controllers and specification into timed automata to exploit the UPPAAL tool for the automatic verification of the correctness relation.

2.3.1 Gas burner revisited

Following up the discussion of the gas burner in Section 1.4, we choose two observables G and F of Boolean data type $\{0, 1\}$. The state assertion $G = 1$ (G for short) represents the flow of *gas* and $F = 1$ (F for short) the presence of the *flame*. Then the state assertion $L \stackrel{\text{def}}{\Longleftrightarrow} G \wedge \neg F$ represents the critical *leak* state: gas flows but the flame is off. The safety requirement for the gas burner can now be expressed by the DC formula

$$\mathsf{Req} \stackrel{\text{def}}{\Longleftrightarrow} \Box(\ell \geq 60 \implies 20 \cdot \int L \leq \ell).$$

The two design decisions discussed in Section 1.4 can be expressed by the following two DC formulas:

- The controller can stop each leak *within a second*

$$\text{Des-1} \stackrel{\text{def}}{\Longleftrightarrow} \Box(\lceil L \rceil \Longrightarrow \ell \leq 1).$$

- After each leak the controller *waits for 30 seconds* and thus enforces a non-leak period of that duration

$$\text{Des-2} \stackrel{\text{def}}{\Longleftrightarrow} \Box(\lceil L \rceil ; \lceil \neg L \rceil ; \lceil L \rceil \Longrightarrow \ell > 30).$$

We want to prove the following statement:

Theorem 2.16
$\models (\text{Des-1} \wedge \text{Des-2}) \Longrightarrow \text{Req}.$

To this end, we first consider a simplified requirement that constrains the duration of the leak period only for short observation intervals:

$$\text{Req-1} \stackrel{\text{def}}{\Longleftrightarrow} \Box(\ell \leq 30 \Longrightarrow \smallint L \leq 1).$$

Lemma 2.17
$\models \text{Req-1} \Longrightarrow \text{Req}.$

Proof:
Assume Req-1. Consider an interval $[b, e]$ of length $\ell = e - b \geq 60$ and let

$$n \stackrel{\text{def}}{=} \left\lceil \frac{e - b}{30} \right\rceil$$

so that $n - 1 < \frac{e-b}{30} \leq n$. We split the interval $[b, e]$ into n adjacent subintervals in the following way:

Each of the first $n - 1$ subintervals has a length of 30, the last subinterval has a length of at most 30. With this partition we estimate an upper bound for the duration of leaks as follows:

$$20 \cdot \int_b^e L_{\mathcal{I}}(t)dt$$

$$= 20 \cdot \left(\sum_{i=0}^{n-2} \int_{b+30 \cdot i}^{b+30(i+1)} L_{\mathcal{I}}(t)dt + \int_{b+30 \cdot (n-1)}^{e} L_{\mathcal{I}}(t)dt \right)$$

$$\leq \quad \{\text{by Req-1 and } e - b - 30 \cdot (n-1) \leq 30\}$$

$$20 \cdot \left(\sum_{i=0}^{n-2} 1 \right) + 20 \cdot 1$$

$$= \quad 20 \cdot n$$

$$< \quad \{\text{since } n - 1 < \frac{e-b}{30}\}$$

$$20 \cdot \left(\frac{e - b}{30} + 1 \right)$$

$$= \quad \frac{2}{3} \cdot (e - b) + 20$$

$$\leq \quad \{\text{since } e - b \geq 60 \text{ and thus } 20 \leq \frac{1}{3} \cdot (e - b)\}$$

$$e - b$$

$$= \quad \ell.$$

Thus Req holds on every interval of length $\ell \geq 60$. □

For the next part of the proof we need some laws of the Duration Calculus about the integral operator.

Theorem 2.18
For all state assertions P and all real numbers $r_1, r_2 \in \mathbb{R}$ the following properties hold:

(i) $\models \int P \leq \ell$,

(ii) $\models (\int P = r_1) \,;\, (\int P = r_2) \Longrightarrow \int P = r_1 + r_2$,

(iii) $\models \lceil \neg P \rceil \Longrightarrow \int P = 0$,

(iv) $\models \lceil \rceil \Longrightarrow \int P = 0$.

Proof:
(of (ii))

$$\models (\textstyle\int P = r_1) \,; (\textstyle\int P = r_2) \Longrightarrow \textstyle\int P = r_1 + r_2$$

iff $\forall \mathcal{I}, \mathcal{V}, [b,e] \bullet \mathcal{I}[\![(\textstyle\int P = r_1) \,; (\textstyle\int P = r_2) \Longrightarrow \textstyle\int P = r_1 + r_2]\!](\mathcal{V}, [b,e])$

iff $\forall \mathcal{I}, \mathcal{V}, [b,e] \bullet \mathcal{I}[\![(\textstyle\int P = r_1) \,; (\textstyle\int P = r_2)]\!](\mathcal{V}, [b,e])$
$$\Longrightarrow \mathcal{I}[\![\textstyle\int P = r_1 + r_2]\!](\mathcal{V}, [b,e])$$

iff $\forall \mathcal{I}, \mathcal{V}, [b,e] \bullet \left(\begin{array}{cc} \exists m \in [b,e] \bullet & \mathcal{I}[\![\textstyle\int P = r_1]\!](\mathcal{V}, [b,m]) \\ \wedge & \mathcal{I}[\![\textstyle\int P = r_2]\!](\mathcal{V}, [m,e]) \end{array} \right)$
$$\Longrightarrow \mathcal{I}[\![\textstyle\int P = r_1 + r_2]\!](\mathcal{V}, [b,e])$$

iff $\forall \mathcal{I}, \mathcal{V}, [b,e] \bullet \left(\exists m \in [b,e] \bullet \displaystyle\int_b^m P_{\mathcal{I}}(t)dt = r_1 \wedge \int_m^e P_{\mathcal{I}}(t)dt = r_2 \right)$
$$\Longrightarrow \int_b^e P_{\mathcal{I}}(t)dt = r_1 + r_2.$$

The last formula follows from the mathematical laws about integrals. The proofs for the remaining claims are left to the reader (see Exercise 2.8). □

With these laws we can prove the following implication:

Lemma 2.19
$\models (\mathsf{Des\text{-}1} \wedge \mathsf{Des\text{-}2}) \Longrightarrow \mathsf{Req\text{-}1}.$

Proof:
Assume Des-1 and Des-2. Then

$$\ell \leq 30$$
$$\Longrightarrow \quad \{\text{by finite variability}\}$$

$$\begin{array}{l} \lceil \rceil \\ \vee \quad \lceil L \rceil \,; (\lceil \rceil \vee \lceil \neg L \rceil) \\ \vee \quad \lceil \neg L \rceil \,; (\lceil \rceil \vee \lceil L \rceil) \\ \vee \quad \lceil \neg L \rceil \,; \lceil L \rceil \,; \lceil \neg L \rceil \\ \vee \quad (\ell \leq 30 \wedge \Diamond(\lceil L \rceil \,; \lceil \neg L \rceil \,; \lceil L \rceil)) \end{array}$$

$\implies$ {by Des-2}

$$
\begin{array}{ll}
& \sqcap \\
\vee & \lceil L \rceil \; ; (\sqcap \vee \lceil \neg L \rceil) \\
\vee & \lceil \neg L \rceil \; ; (\sqcap \vee \lceil L \rceil) \\
\vee & \lceil \neg L \rceil \; ; \lceil L \rceil \; ; \lceil \neg L \rceil
\end{array}
$$

$\implies$ {by Des-1}

$$
\begin{array}{ll}
& \sqcap \\
\vee & (\ell \leq 1) \; ; (\sqcap \vee \lceil \neg L \rceil) \\
\vee & \lceil \neg L \rceil \; ; (\sqcap \vee (\ell \leq 1)) \\
\vee & \lceil \neg L \rceil \; ; (\ell \leq 1) \; ; \lceil \neg L \rceil
\end{array}
$$

$\implies$ {by Theorem 2.18 (i)}

$$
\begin{array}{ll}
& \sqcap \\
\vee & (\int L \leq 1) \; ; (\sqcap \vee \lceil \neg L \rceil) \\
\vee & \lceil \neg L \rceil \; ; (\sqcap \vee (\int L \leq 1)) \\
\vee & \lceil \neg L \rceil \; ; (\int L \leq 1) \; ; \lceil \neg L \rceil
\end{array}
$$

$\implies$ {by Theorem 2.18 (iii), (iv)}

$$
\begin{array}{ll}
& (\int L = 0) \\
\vee & (\int L \leq 1) \; ; (\int L = 0) \\
\vee & (\int L = 0) \; ; ((\int L = 0) \vee (\int L \leq 1)) \\
\vee & (\int L = 0) \; ; (\int L \leq 1) \; ; (\int L = 0)
\end{array}
$$

$\implies$ {by Theorem 2.18 (ii)}

$$\int L \leq 1.$$

Thus **Req-1** holds. $\qquad\qquad\qquad\qquad\qquad\qquad\qquad\qquad\qquad\qquad$ □

Lemmas 2.17 and 2.19 together yield Theorem 2.16.

2.4 Proof rules

So far we have presented syntax and semantics of the Duration Calculus. In this section the *calculus* is introduced. In general, a proof system or calculus $\mathcal{C}$ for DC formulas consists of a set of *proof rules* of the form

$$\frac{F_1, \ldots, F_n}{F} \quad \text{where } cond(F_1, \ldots, F_n, F). \qquad (2.4)$$

The formulas $F_1, \ldots, F_n$ are called the *premises* of the proof rule (2.4), and the formula F is called the *conclusion* of (2.4). All formulas $F_1, \ldots, F_n, F$

have to fulfil the *application condition* $cond(F_1, \ldots, F_n, F)$, which has to be *decidable*. Typically, this condition is a simple syntactic constraint like "$F_1, \ldots, F_n$ do not have x as a free variable". In case of $n = 0$ we call the proof rule an *axiom* and simplify the notation a bit:

$$F \quad \text{where} \quad cond(F).$$

If $cond(F)$ is always satisfied we omit it.

The central concepts of a calculus are that of proof and provability. A *proof* of a formula F from a set $\mathcal{H}$ of formulas in $\mathcal{C}$ is a finite sequence

$$G_1$$
$$\vdots$$
$$G_m$$

of formulas with $G_m = F$ such that each formula G_i with $i = 1, \ldots, m$

- is either in the set $\mathcal{H}$ or
- is an axiom of $\mathcal{C}$ or
- is a conclusion of a proof rule of $\mathcal{C}$ applied to some predecessor formulas in the proof, i.e. there exists a proof rule

$$\frac{F_1, \ldots, F_n}{G_i} \quad \text{with} \quad cond(F_1, \ldots, F_n, G_i)$$

such that $\{F_1, \ldots, F_n\} \subseteq \{G_1, \ldots, G_{i-1}\}$ and $cond(F_1, \ldots, F_n, G_i)$ hold.

The formulas in the set $\mathcal{H}$ are called *assumptions* or *hypotheses* of the proof. The natural number m is also called the *length* of the proof. We say that F is *provable* from $\mathcal{H}$ in $\mathcal{C}$, in symbols

$$\mathcal{H} \vdash_{\mathcal{C}} F,$$

if there exists a proof of F from $\mathcal{H}$ in $\mathcal{C}$. We need a few variations of this notation. For a finite set of hypotheses, $\mathcal{H} = \{H_1, \ldots, H_k\}$, we write $H_1, \ldots, H_k \vdash_{\mathcal{C}} F$ instead of $\{H_1, \ldots, H_k\} \vdash_{\mathcal{C}} F$. If $\mathcal{H} = \varnothing$ we write $\vdash_{\mathcal{C}} F$ instead of $\varnothing \vdash_{\mathcal{C}} F$. A formula F with $\vdash_{\mathcal{C}} F$ is also called a *theorem* of $\mathcal{C}$. If the calculus $\mathcal{C}$ is clear from the context, we omit the subscript $\mathcal{C}$.

A proof rule

$$(R) \qquad \frac{F_1, \ldots, F_n}{F} \quad \text{where} \quad cond(F_1, \ldots, F_n, F)$$

is said to be a *derived* proof rule of a calculus $\mathcal{C}$ iff

$$\{F_1, \ldots, F_n\} \vdash_{\mathcal{C}} F$$

holds whenever the application condition $cond(F_1, \ldots, F_n, F)$ is satisfied. Thus assuming all the premises $F_1, \ldots, F_n$ of R, its conclusion F can be proved in $\mathcal{C}$. Hence R does not increase the proving power of the calculus $\mathcal{C}$. This is made precise in the following remark:

Remark 2.20
For a derived rule R of a calculus $\mathcal{C}$ the following holds for every set $\mathcal{H}$ of formulas and every formula F:

$$\mathcal{H} \vdash_{\mathcal{C} \cup \{R\}} F \text{ iff } \mathcal{H} \vdash_{\mathcal{C}} F.$$

Thus every proof with the rule R can also be done without this rule in the calculus $\mathcal{C}$. Nevertheless, it may be convenient to have a derived rule R as a shortcut in a proof. In the coming subsections we shall see a number of derived proof rules for operators of the Duration Calculus that were introduced as abbreviations.

Provability is defined by application of purely syntactic proof rules. The question arises of how this is connected to the semantics of the proven formulas. The answer is given by the concepts of soundness and completeness of a calculus. A calculus $\mathcal{C}$ is *sound* if

$$\mathcal{H} \vdash_{\mathcal{C}} F \text{ implies } \mathcal{H} \models F.$$

Here $\mathcal{H} \models F$ means that for all interpretations $\mathcal{I}$ the following holds:

$$\text{if } \mathcal{I} \models G \text{ for all formulas } G \in \mathcal{H} \text{ then } \mathcal{I} \models F.$$

Recall that $\mathcal{I} \models F$ iff $\mathcal{I}, \mathcal{V}, [b, e] \models F$ holds for all valuations $\mathcal{V}$ and all intervals $[b, e]$. In case of $\mathcal{H} = \varnothing$ soundness thus requires that

$$\vdash_{\mathcal{C}} F \text{ implies } \models F,$$

i.e. every theorem of $\mathcal{C}$ should be valid.

Of course, every calculus $\mathcal{C}$ should be sound. To show this it suffices to check that all proof rules of $\mathcal{C}$ are sound in the following sense. A *proof rule* (2.4) is *sound* if whenever the application condition $cond(F_1, \ldots, F_n)$ holds,

$$\mathcal{I} \models F_1, \ldots, \mathcal{I} \models F_n \text{ implies } \mathcal{I} \models F.$$

By induction on the lengths of proofs in $\mathcal{C}$, one can prove the following result:

Remark 2.21
If all proof rules of a calculus $\mathcal{C}$ are sound, then $\mathcal{C}$ itself is sound.

The reverse direction of soundness is called completeness. A calculus $\mathcal{C}$ is *complete* if

$$\mathcal{H} \models F \text{ implies } \mathcal{H} \vdash_{\mathcal{C}} F.$$

In particular, every valid formula should be provable in $\mathcal{C}$. It is desirable to have a (sound and) complete calculus, but due to reasons of computability this goal is not always achievable.

Let us investigate what is to be expected for the Duration Calculus. We first state two well-known general facts about proof systems (see for example [EFT96]).

Lemma 2.22
For every calculus $\mathcal{C}$, every set $\mathcal{H}$ of formulas, and every formula F the following holds:

(i) *If $\mathcal{H} \vdash_{\mathcal{C}} F$ then there exists a finite subset $\mathcal{H}_{fin} \subseteq \mathcal{H}$ with $\mathcal{H}_{fin} \vdash_{\mathcal{C}} F$.*
(ii) *It is semi-decidable whether F is a theorem of $\mathcal{C}$.*

Proof:
Re (i): The claim follows from the fact that every proof of F in $\mathcal{C}$ is a finite sequence that can use only finitely many of the hypotheses from $\mathcal{H}$.

Re (ii): Since each proof rule (2.4) has a decidable application condition, it is decidable whether a given sequence of formulas constitutes a proof in $\mathcal{C}$. To check whether F is a theorem of $\mathcal{C}$, systematically enumerate all possible sequences of formulas with F as a final formula. For each such sequence decide whether it is a proof in $\mathcal{C}$. If F is indeed a theorem of $\mathcal{C}$, this procedure will find a corresponding proof of F in $\mathcal{C}$. Otherwise the procedure will never terminate. $\quad\square$

We now apply this lemma to the case of DC formulas.

Theorem 2.23
A sound calculus $\mathcal{C}$ for DC formulas cannot be complete.

Proof:
Consider for an arbitrary state assertion P the formula $F \overset{\text{def}}{\Longleftrightarrow} \lceil\rceil \vee \lceil P \rceil$ and the following infinite set:

$$\mathcal{H} = \{\ell = n \Longrightarrow F \mid n \in \mathbb{N}\}$$

of DC formulas. Then $\mathcal{H} \models F$ because every time interval $[b, e] \subseteq \text{Time}$ has a bounded length, but $\mathcal{H}_{fin} \not\models F$ for every finite subset $\mathcal{H}_{fin} \subseteq \mathcal{H}$.

Suppose there exists a sound and complete calculus $\mathcal{C}$ for DC formulas. The completeness of $\mathcal{C}$ yields that $\mathcal{H} \models F$ implies $\mathcal{H} \vdash_{\mathcal{C}} F$. By Lemma 2.22, there exists a finite subset $\mathcal{H}_{fin} \subseteq \mathcal{H}$ with $\mathcal{H}_{fin} \vdash_{\mathcal{C}} F$. The soundness of $\mathcal{C}$ yields $\mathcal{H}_{fin} \models F$. Contradiction. $\quad\square$

What are the reasons for this incompleteness? The problem is that the validity of DC formulas may depend on facts of the real numbers. For example, $\mathcal{H} \models F$ in the above proof depends on the fact that every real number is bounded by some natural number. Unfortunately, it is impossible to give a complete set of proof rules that characterise all valid facts of the real numbers. (For more details see Subsection 2.4.3.) As a consequence it is impossible to find a complete set of proof rules for the Duration Calculus. Nevertheless, there is a set of proof rules for DC formulas that is *relatively complete* in the following sense: given an "oracle" for the valid arithmetic formulas over real numbers we can always find a proof of F from $\mathcal{H}$ provided $\mathcal{H} \models F$ holds.

In the following we shall present such a proof system. It is structured into several layers.

2.4.1 Predicate calculus

It is clear that a proof system for DC formulas requires reasoning on the underlying first-order predicate logic. The *predicate calculus* is a sound and complete proof system for all valid formulas in predicate logic. Here we need these rules for proving true facts about the logical connectives and the quantifiers in DC formulas. We list only the most prominent rules of the predicate calculus, and note one subtle difference concerning substitution of terms for variables.

Modus Ponens:

$$\frac{F,\; F \Longrightarrow G}{G}. \tag{2.5}$$

$\forall$-Introduction:

$$\frac{F}{\forall x \bullet F}. \tag{2.6}$$

$\forall$-Elimination:

$$\frac{\forall x \bullet F}{F[x := \theta]} \quad \text{where } F \text{ is chop-free or } \theta \text{ is a rigid term.} \tag{2.7}$$

Note that the application condition of the rule for $\forall$-Elimination is not present in the usual predicate calculus. Here it is necessary to guarantee its soundness in the presence of DC formulas F and DC terms θ. When substituting a term θ for the free occurrences of the global variable x in F we have to ensure that all occurrences of θ in

$F[x := \theta]$ denote the same value. By Remark 2.10, the application condition ensures this.

Without this condition, we could for instance (erroneously) deduce from

$$\forall x \bullet \ell = x \,;\, \ell = x \Longrightarrow \ell = 2 \cdot x$$

the formula

$$\ell = \ell \,;\, \ell = \ell \Longrightarrow \ell = 2 \cdot \ell.$$

Whereas the first formula is valid, the latter one is not. The dual rule for ∃-Introduction requires the same application condition.

∃-Introduction:

$$\frac{F[x := \theta]}{\exists x \bullet F} \quad \text{where } F \text{ is chop-free or } \theta \text{ is a rigid term.} \qquad (2.8)$$

2.4.2 Equality

Basic predicate logic does not contain the equality symbol $=$, which is needed prominently in our context when evaluating DC terms. However, it is well known that equality can be axiomatised completely by the following axioms:

Reflexivity:

$$x = x. \qquad (2.9)$$

Symmetry:

$$x = y \Longrightarrow y = x. \qquad (2.10)$$

Transitivity:

$$(x = y \wedge y = z) \Longrightarrow x = z. \qquad (2.11)$$

Leibniz Property:

$$(x_1 = y_1 \wedge \ldots \wedge x_n = y_n) \quad \Longrightarrow \quad f(x_1, \ldots, x_n) = f(y_1, \ldots, y_n) \qquad (2.12)$$
$$(x_1 = y_1 \wedge \ldots \wedge x_n = y_n) \quad \Longrightarrow \quad p(x_1, \ldots, x_n) = p(y_1, \ldots, y_n).$$

2.4.3 Real numbers

Since the semantics of Duration Calculus is based on the continuous-time domain Time $= \mathbb{R}_{\geq 0}$, its calculus needs rules for proving properties of the real numbers. It is known from logic and model theory that this is a difficult issue. Here we discuss only some of the highlights of the axiomatisability of the structure

$$\mathcal{R} = (\mathbb{R},\ \hat{+},\ \hat{\cdot},\ \hat{<},\ \hat{0},\ \hat{1})$$

of the real numbers with the standard constituents: the set $\mathbb{R}$ of real numbers with addition $\hat{+}$ and multiplication $\hat{\cdot}$, the strict order $\hat{<}$, and the constants zero $\hat{0}$ and one $\hat{1}$. The structure $\mathcal{R}$ is a completely ordered field. Thus to begin with, we need the axioms of fields and orders expressed in first-order predicate logic.

Fields. A *field* is a structure with constants 0 and 1, and with binary function symbols $+$ and $\cdot$ that satisfy the following axioms:

Associativity:	$(x + y) + z = x + (y + z)$
	$(x \cdot y) \cdot z = x \cdot (y \cdot z).$
Commutativity:	$x + y = y + x$
	$x \cdot y = y \cdot x.$
Neutral Elements:	$x + 0 = x$
	$x \cdot 1 = x.$
Zero and One:	$\neg(0 = 1).$
Inverse Elements:	$\forall x\, \exists y \bullet x + y = 0$
	$\forall x \bullet \neg x = 0 \implies \exists y \bullet x \cdot y = 1.$
Distributivity:	$x \cdot (y + z) = (x \cdot y) + (x \cdot z).$

Orders. An *(irreflexive) order* is a structure with one binary predicate symbol $<$ that satisfies the following axioms:

Irreflexivity: $\neg(x < x).$

Transitivity: $(x < y \wedge y < z) \implies x < z.$

Totality: $(x < y) \vee (x = y) \vee (y < x).$

The reflexive order symbol $\leq$ is introduced as an abbreviation:

$$x \leq y \overset{\text{def}}{\iff} x < y \vee x = y.$$

Ordered fields. An *ordered* field is a structure with constants 0 and 1, binary function symbols $+$ and $\cdot$, and a binary predicate symbol $<$ that in addition to the field and order axioms satisfies the following axioms stating the intended interplay between the order and the constants and function symbols of the field:

Zero Smaller One: $0 < 1$.

Monotonicity: $x < y \Longrightarrow x + z < y + z$

$$(x < y \wedge 0 < z) \Longrightarrow x \cdot z < y \cdot z.$$

Completely ordered fields. For the following definition we briefly recall some concepts of ordered structures $(D, <)$. A subset $S \subseteq D$ is *bounded from above* if there exists an element $d \in D$ such that

$$\forall s \in S \bullet s \leq d.$$

Then d is called an *upper bound* of S. A *supremum* of S is a least upper bound, i.e. an element $d_0 \in D$ such that d_0 is an upper bound of S and $d_0 \leq d$ holds for all upper bounds d of S. Note that the supremum d_0 does not necessarily exist.

Definition 2.24
An ordered field is called *complete* if for every non-empty subset which is bounded from above there exists a supremum.

While there are many structurally different ordered fields, for instance the rational numbers and the real numbers, the following theorem from mathematical analysis states that the structure of a completely ordered field is unique:

Theorem 2.25
The structure $\mathcal{R}$ of the real numbers is up to isomorphism the only completely ordered field.

Recall that an isomorphism may rename the values representing the real numbers by a bijective mapping but must preserve the structure. Thus the structure $\mathcal{R}$ is unique up to such renamings of its elements. Concerning axiomatisability of $\mathcal{R}$ we recall the following facts from model theory:

(1) The structure $\mathcal{R}$ of the real numbers can be completely axiomatised in *second-order* predicate logic, where quantification is possible not only over real-valued global variables but also over set-valued variables. In particular, Definition 2.24 of *completely ordered* is expressible by a second-order formula.

However, for *second-order* predicate logic there does not exist any complete proof system for deducing all valid formulas – in contrast to *first-order* predicate logic for which there is a sound and complete proof system, the *predicate calculus*.

(2) Let T denote the set of all *first-order* predicate logic formulas that are valid in the structure $\mathcal{R}$. By a theorem of Tarski, the set T is decidable (by using a technique of quantifier elimination). The decision procedure can also be seen as a complete proof system for T. However, in contrast to (1), formulas in this set T cannot state facts about suprema of subsets of real numbers.

We summarise:

For the structure $\mathcal{R}$ of real numbers there is no sound and complete proof system in which one can prove exactly all formulas that are valid in the structure $\mathcal{R}$. In the following we assume the existence of an *oracle* for $\mathcal{R}$, i.e. we assume that all valid formulas over real numbers are given as axioms.

2.4.4 Interval logic

The following axioms and proof rules are due to B. Dutertre and represent a complete axiomatisation of first-order interval logic relative to $\mathcal{R}$:

Length-Pos: $\ell \geq 0.$ $\qquad$ (2.13)

Chop-Asm: $((F \,;\, G) \,;\, H) \iff (F \,;\, (G \,;\, H)).$ $\qquad$ (2.14)

Chop-Overlay: $((F \,;\, G_1) \wedge \neg (F \,;\, G_2)) \implies (F \,;\, (G_1 \wedge \neg G_2))$ $\qquad$ (2.15)
$((G_1 \,;\, F) \wedge \neg (G_2 \,;\, F)) \implies ((G_1 \wedge \neg G_2) \,;\, F).$

Chop-Elim: $(F \,;\, G) \implies F$ $\qquad$ (2.16)
$(G \,;\, F) \implies F$
where F is a rigid formula.

Chop-Ex: $((\exists x \bullet F) \,;\, G) \implies \exists x \bullet (F \,;\, G)$ $\qquad$ (2.17)
$(G \,;\, (\exists x \bullet F)) \implies \exists x \bullet (G \,;\, F)$
where $x \notin \textit{free}(G).$

Chop-Length: $(F \,;\, (\ell = x)) \implies \neg ((\neg F) \,;\, (\ell = x))$ $\qquad$ (2.18)
$((\ell = x) \,;\, F) \implies \neg ((\ell = x) \,;\, (\neg F)).$

Add-Length: $(x \geq 0 \wedge y \geq 0) \implies$
$((\ell = x + y) \iff (\ell = x) \,;\, (\ell = y)).$ $\qquad$ (2.19)

$$\text{Chop-Pnt: } F \Longrightarrow (F \,;\, (\ell = 0)) \tag{2.20}$$
$$F \Longrightarrow ((\ell = 0) \,;\, F).$$

$$\text{Necessary: } \frac{F}{\neg((\neg F) \,;\, G)} \tag{2.21}$$

$$\frac{F}{\neg(G \,;\, (\neg F))}.$$

$$\text{Chop-Mon: } \frac{F \Longrightarrow G}{(F \,;\, H) \Longrightarrow (G \,;\, H)} \tag{2.22}$$

$$\frac{F \Longrightarrow G}{(H \,;\, F) \Longrightarrow (H \,;\, G)}.$$

We comment on (the soundness of) some of these rules. For the rule *Chop-Overlay* note that $F \,;\, G$ chops any given interval $[b, e]$ into a first part $[b, m]$ where F holds and a second part $[m, e]$ where G holds. Thus $\neg(F \,;\, G)$ implies that $\neg G$ holds on $[m, e]$ so that indeed $(F \,;\, (G_1 \wedge \neg G_2))$ holds.

The rule *Chop-Elim* exploits the fact that F is rigid and thus its truth value is independent of any given interval. An instance of this rule is

$$x + 1 > x \,;\, \ell \geq 1 \Longrightarrow x + 1 > x.$$

Without F being rigid the rule becomes unsound, as the counterexample

$$\ell = 1 \,;\, \ell \geq 1 \not\Longrightarrow \ell = 1$$

shows. The rule *Chop-Ex* can expand the scope of the existential quantifier from F to $F \,;\, G$ because x does not occur freely in G and thus the truth value of G does not depend on the valuation of x.

The rule *Chop-Length* exploits the fact that $F \,;\, (\ell = x)$ chops any given interval $[b, e]$ into a first part $[b, m]$ where F holds and a second part $[m, e]$ of length $e - m = x$. Therefore it is impossible to chop the same interval $[b, e]$ according to the formula $\neg F \,;\, (\ell = x)$ because this would imply that $\neg F$ holds on the first part $[b, m]$. Note that in the rule *Add-Length* the condition $x \geq 0 \wedge y \geq 0$ is needed because the global variables x and y range over $\mathbb{R}$ whereas the lengths of intervals are non-negative as stated in axiom *Length-Pos*.

According to the premise of the rule *Necessary* the formula F holds on every interval. Therefore it is impossible to chop a given interval $[b, e]$ into a first part $[b, m]$ where $\neg F$ holds (and a second part $[m, e]$ where G holds).

Derived rules for the modal operators

In Subsection 2.2.4 the modal operators $\Diamond$ (for some subinterval) and $\Box$ (for all subintervals) of the Duration Calculus were defined as follows:

$$\Diamond F \stackrel{\text{def}}{\Longleftrightarrow} \text{true}\,;F\,;\text{true} \quad \text{and} \quad \Box F \stackrel{\text{def}}{\Longleftrightarrow} \neg\Diamond\neg F.$$

With these definitions the axioms and proof rules of the classical *modal logic* S4 can be derived [HC68]:

$$\text{Box-Impl:}\ \Box(F \Longrightarrow G) \Longrightarrow (\Box F \Longrightarrow \Box G). \tag{2.23}$$

$$\text{Box-Elim:}\ \Box F \Longrightarrow F. \tag{2.24}$$

$$\text{Box-Trans:}\ \Box F \Longrightarrow \Box\Box F. \tag{2.25}$$

$$\text{Box-Intro:}\ \frac{F}{\Box F}. \tag{2.26}$$

2.4.5 Durations

Zhou Chaochen and M.R. Hansen presented the following axioms and proof rules for durations:

$$\text{Dur-Zero:}\ \textstyle\int 0 = 0. \tag{2.27}$$

$$\text{Dur-One:}\ \textstyle\int 1 = \ell. \tag{2.28}$$

$$\text{Dur-Pos:}\ \textstyle\int P \geq 0. \tag{2.29}$$

$$\text{Dur-Add:}\ \textstyle\int P + \int Q = \int(P \wedge Q) + \int(P \vee Q). \tag{2.30}$$

$$\text{Dur-Chop:}\ (\textstyle\int P = x)\,;(\int P = y) \Longrightarrow \int P = x + y. \tag{2.31}$$

$$\text{Dur-Logic:}\ \textstyle\int P = \int Q \quad \text{where } P \Longleftrightarrow Q \text{ is a tautology.} \tag{2.32}$$

Note that to calculate the sum $\int P + \int Q$ in the axiom *Dur-Add* the duration $\int(P \wedge Q)$ needs to be added to the duration $\int(P \vee Q)$ to cover the case that the durations of P and Q overlap in time.

Derived rules for the everywhere operator

In Subsection 2.2.4 the point interval $\lceil\rceil$ and the (almost) everywhere operator $\lceil P \rceil$ were defined as follows:

$$\lceil\rceil \stackrel{\text{def}}{\Longleftrightarrow} \ell = 0 \quad \text{and} \quad \lceil P \rceil \stackrel{\text{def}}{\Longleftrightarrow} \textstyle\int P = \ell \wedge \ell > 0.$$

With these definitions the following axioms and proof rules can be derived:

$$\text{P-Mon: } \lceil P \rceil \Longrightarrow \lceil Q \rceil \quad \text{where } P \Longrightarrow Q \text{ is a tautology.} \qquad (2.33)$$

$$\text{P-Chop: } \lceil P \rceil \,; \lceil P \rceil \iff \lceil P \rceil. \qquad (2.34)$$

$$\text{P-Box: } \lceil P \rceil \Longrightarrow \Box(\lceil\rceil \vee \lceil P \rceil). \qquad (2.35)$$

$$\text{P-Neg: } \neg \lceil P \rceil \iff (\lceil\rceil \vee \Diamond \lceil \neg P \rceil). \qquad (2.36)$$

$$\text{P-And: } \lceil P \wedge Q \rceil \iff \lceil P \rceil \wedge \lceil Q \rceil. \qquad (2.37)$$

$$\text{P-Chop-Neg: } \neg(\lceil P \rceil \,; \text{true}) \iff \lceil\rceil \vee \lceil \neg P \rceil \,; \text{true} \qquad (2.38)$$
$$\neg(\text{true} \,; \lceil P \rceil) \iff \lceil\rceil \vee \text{true} \,; \lceil \neg P \rceil.$$

$$\text{P-Chop-And: } ((\lceil P \rceil \,; \text{true}) \wedge \lceil Q \rceil \,; \text{true}) \iff \lceil P \wedge Q \rceil \,; \text{true} \qquad (2.39)$$
$$((\text{true} \,; \lceil P \rceil) \wedge (\text{true} \,; \lceil Q \rceil)) \iff \text{true} \,; \lceil P \wedge Q \rceil.$$

$$\text{P-Chop-Or: } ((\lceil P \rceil \,; \text{true}) \vee \lceil Q \rceil \,; \text{true}) \iff \lceil P \vee Q \rceil \,; \text{true} \qquad (2.40)$$
$$((\text{true} \,; \lceil P \rceil) \vee \text{true} \,; \lceil Q \rceil) \iff \text{true} \,; \lceil P \vee Q \rceil.$$

2.4.6 Induction

Since DC is based on the continuous-time domain, it is at first sight surprising that an *induction rule* can be stated for the DC. However, the idea behind this induction is to exploit the fact that the interpretations of its observables and hence all state assertions are finitely varying.

In the following let F be a DC formula and P be a state assertion:

$$\text{Induction-R:} \quad \frac{\begin{array}{l} (1)\ \lceil\rceil \Longrightarrow F \\ (2)\ F \,; \lceil P \rceil \Longrightarrow F \\ (3)\ F \,; \lceil \neg P \rceil \Longrightarrow F \end{array}}{(4)\ F}. \qquad (2.41)$$

The conclusion (4) of this rule is the DC formula F. The three premises (1)–(3) simplify the proof in that F needs to be shown only under certain assumptions. Premise (1) considers as the *induction basis* the point interval $\lceil\rceil$. Premise (2) assumes by *induction hypothesis* that F holds on an initial subinterval; of the remainder of the interval we can assume only that $\lceil P \rceil$ holds. The idea is that from $\lceil P \rceil$ we can deduce that F holds on the whole interval. Premise (3) considers the complementary case that $\lceil \neg P \rceil$ holds on the rest of the interval.

There is also the following variant of the rule in which the subintervals $\lceil P \rceil$

and $\lceil \neg P \rceil$ are chopped off on the left-hand side of the considered interval:

$$\text{Induction-L:} \quad \frac{\begin{array}{c} \lceil \rceil \Longrightarrow F \\ \lceil P \rceil \, ; F \Longrightarrow F \\ \lceil \neg P \rceil \, ; F \Longrightarrow F \end{array}}{F} \, . \tag{2.42}$$

Example 2.26

As a first application we prove for an arbitrary state assertion P:

$$P\text{-Cover:} \quad \lceil \rceil \vee (\lceil P \rceil \, ; \text{true}) \vee (\lceil \neg P \rceil \, ; \text{true}) \tag{2.43}$$
$$\lceil \rceil \vee (\text{true} \, ; \lceil P \rceil) \vee (\text{true} \, ; \lceil \neg P \rceil).$$

Consider the second of these two formulas and put

$$F \;\overset{\text{def}}{\Longleftrightarrow}\; \lceil \rceil \vee \text{true} \, ; \lceil P \rceil \vee \text{true} \, ; \lceil \neg P \rceil \, .$$

We check whether for this particular choice of F the three premises of the rule Induction-R (2.41) hold.

(1) $\lceil \rceil \Longrightarrow F$ is trivially satisfied.
(2) By (Chop-Mon), the following implication chain holds:
   $F \, ; \lceil P \rceil \Longrightarrow \text{true} \, ; \lceil P \rceil \Longrightarrow F$.
(3) Analogously to (2).

The first formula of P-Cover is proven analogously by rule Induction-L. ■

Next we prove the soundness of the induction rule.

Theorem 2.27

The induction rule (2.41) is sound, i.e. for all interpretations $\mathcal{I}$

$$\mathcal{I} \models \lceil \rceil \Longrightarrow F, \quad \mathcal{I} \models F \, ; \lceil P \rceil \Longrightarrow F \quad \text{and} \quad \mathcal{I} \models F \, ; \lceil \neg P \rceil \Longrightarrow F$$

always imply $\mathcal{I} \models F$.

Proof:

Consider an arbitrary interpretation $\mathcal{I}$. Suppose that for a DC formula F and a state assertion P the three premises (1)–(3) of the DC induction rule are realisable. For $k \in \mathbb{N}$ we define inductively the DC formula $FA^k(P)$:

$$FA^0(P) \;\overset{\text{def}}{\Longleftrightarrow}\; \lceil \rceil$$

$$FA^{k+1}(P) \;\overset{\text{def}}{\Longleftrightarrow}\; FA^k(P) \vee FA^k(P) \, ; \lceil P \rceil \vee FA^k(P) \, ; \lceil \neg P \rceil \, .$$

Here FA stands for "Finite Alternation". For example,

$$FA^1(P) \quad \Longleftrightarrow \quad \lceil\rceil \vee \lceil P \rceil \vee \lceil\neg P\rceil \ ,$$

$$FA^2(P) \quad \Longleftrightarrow \quad \lceil\rceil \vee \lceil P \rceil \vee \lceil\neg P\rceil$$
$$\lceil P \rceil \ ; \ \lceil\neg P\rceil \vee \lceil\neg P\rceil \ ; \ \lceil P \rceil \ ,$$

$$FA^3(P) \quad \Longleftrightarrow \quad \lceil\rceil \vee \lceil P \rceil \vee \lceil\neg P\rceil$$
$$\lceil P \rceil \ ; \ \lceil\neg P\rceil \vee \lceil\neg P\rceil \ ; \ \lceil P \rceil$$
$$\lceil P \rceil \ ; \ \lceil\neg P\rceil \ ; \ \lceil P \rceil \vee \lceil\neg P\rceil \ ; \ \lceil P \rceil \ ; \ \lceil\neg P\rceil \ .$$

In general, $FA^k(P)$ describes all combinations of up to $k - 1$ alternations between $\lceil P \rceil$ and $\lceil\neg P\rceil$.

Proposition 2.28

For all P, $\mathcal{I}$, $\mathcal{V}$, $[b, e]$ there exists a $k \in \mathbb{N}$ with $\mathcal{I}, \mathcal{V}, [b, e] \models FA^k(P)$.

This proposition follows immediately from the finite variability of the interpretation $\mathcal{I}$ of the observables and thus of the state assertion P.

Proposition 2.29

Let the premises (1)–(3) of the DC induction rule be given. Then for all $k \in \mathbb{N}$ we have $\mathcal{I} \models FA^k(P) \Longrightarrow F$.

The proof of this proposition is by (normal) induction on $k \in \mathbb{N}$.

- *Induction basis*: $k = 0$.
  By premise (1) of the DC induction rule, we have $\mathcal{I} \models \lceil\rceil \Longrightarrow F$.
- *Induction step*: $k \longrightarrow k + 1$.
  Suppose $\mathcal{I} \models FA^k(P) \Longrightarrow F$ holds. By rule (Chop-Mon), this implies $\mathcal{I} \models FA^k(P) \ ; \ \lceil P \rceil \Longrightarrow F \ ; \ \lceil P \rceil$. Thus by premise (2) of the DC induction rule, we conclude $\mathcal{I} \models FA^k(P) \ ; \ \lceil P \rceil \Longrightarrow F$. Analogously we infer from premise (3) of the DC induction rule that $\mathcal{I} \models FA^k(P) \ ; \ \lceil\neg P\rceil \Longrightarrow F$ holds. Altogether we have $\mathcal{I} \models FA^{k+1}(P) \Longrightarrow F$ as desired.

To prove the realisability of the conclusion (4) of the DC induction rule consider now arbitrary valuation $\mathcal{V}$ and interval $[b, e]$. By Proposition 2.28, there exists a $k \in \mathbb{N}$ with

$$\mathcal{I}, \mathcal{V}, [b, e] \models FA^k(P).$$

By Proposition 2.29, this implies $\mathcal{I}, \mathcal{V}, [b, e] \models F$ as desired.   □

Remark 2.30

Often we wish to prove implications with the DC induction rule. For the case

$$F \stackrel{\text{def}}{\Longleftrightarrow} (\Box F_1 \Longrightarrow F_2)$$

the premises (2) and (3) of the DC induction rule (2.41) can be specialised as follows:

$$(2) \quad \text{reduces to} \quad (\Box F_1 \wedge F_2 \,;\, \lceil P \rceil) \Longrightarrow F_2, \qquad (2.44)$$

$$(3) \quad \text{reduces to} \quad (\Box F_1 \wedge F_2 \,;\, \lceil \neg P \rceil) \Longrightarrow F_2. \qquad (2.45)$$

Proof:

We prove (2.44):

$$
\begin{aligned}
(2) \quad &\Longleftrightarrow \quad (\Box F_1 \Longrightarrow F_2) \,;\, \lceil P \rceil \Longrightarrow (\Box F_1 \Longrightarrow F_2) \\
&\Longleftrightarrow \quad ((\Box F_1 \Longrightarrow F_2) \,;\, \lceil P \rceil \wedge \Box F_1) \Longrightarrow F_2 \\
&\Longleftrightarrow \quad (\Box F_1 \wedge F_2 \,;\, \lceil P \rceil) \Longrightarrow F_2.
\end{aligned}
$$

(2.45) can be shown analogously. □

Remark 2.31

For the case

$$F \stackrel{\text{def}}{\Longleftrightarrow} (\Box F_1 \Longrightarrow \Box F_2)$$

the premises (2) and (3) of the DC induction rule (2.41) can be specialised as follows:

$$(2) \quad \text{reduces to} \quad (\Box F_1 \wedge \Box F_2 \,;\, \lceil P \rceil) \Longrightarrow F_2, \qquad (2.46)$$

$$(3) \quad \text{reduces to} \quad (\Box F_1 \wedge \Box F_2 \,;\, \lceil \neg P \rceil) \Longrightarrow F_2. \qquad (2.47)$$

Proof:

We prove (2.46). By (2.44), premise (2) is equivalent to

$$(\Box F_1 \wedge \Box F_2 \,;\, \lceil P \rceil) \Longrightarrow \Box F_2.$$

To prove $\Box F_2$ on the right-hand side of the implication, we have to show that F_2 holds for all subintervals of a given interval. To this end, we investigate the possible forms of subintervals satisfying the assumption $\Box F_2 \,;\, \lceil P \rceil$. There are three cases:

$$
\begin{aligned}
\text{(i)} \quad & (\Box F_1 \wedge \Box F_2) \Longrightarrow F_2, \\
\text{(ii)} \quad & (\Box F_1 \wedge \lceil P \rceil) \Longrightarrow F_2, \\
\text{(iii)} \quad & (\Box F_1 \wedge \Box F_2 \,;\, \lceil P \rceil) \Longrightarrow F_2.
\end{aligned}
$$

Case (i) is trivial and case (ii) is a special case of (iii). Thus it remains to show (iii), which is just (2.46). (2.47) can be shown analogously.   □

2.4.7 Application to the gas burner

We shall now apply the induction rule (2.41) to prove the implication

$$\models \text{Req-1} \Longrightarrow \text{Req}$$

of the case study of the gas burner. We recall the definitions:

$$\text{Req-1} \overset{\text{def}}{\Longleftrightarrow} \Box(\ell \leq 30 \Longrightarrow \int L \leq 1),$$
$$\text{Req} \overset{\text{def}}{\Longleftrightarrow} \Box(\ell \geq 60 \Longrightarrow 20 \cdot \int L \leq \ell).$$

By Remark 2.31, it suffices to show the two implications

$$(\text{Req-1} \wedge \text{Req} \,; \lceil L \rceil) \Longrightarrow (\ell \geq 60 \Longrightarrow 20 \cdot \int L \leq \ell), \qquad (\text{I2})$$
$$(\text{Req-1} \wedge \text{Req} \,; \lceil \neg L \rceil) \Longrightarrow (\ell \geq 60 \Longrightarrow 20 \cdot \int L \leq \ell) \qquad (\text{I3})$$

as premises of the induction rule. To prove (I2) we need the following upper bound of the duration of $\lceil L \rceil$:

Lemma 2.32
$\models \text{Req-1} \wedge \lceil L \rceil \Longrightarrow \ell \leq 1.$

Proof:
Suppose $\text{Req-1} \wedge \lceil L \rceil \wedge \ell > 1$. Then

$$
\begin{aligned}
&\quad\ \text{Req-1} \wedge \lceil L \rceil \wedge \ell > 1 \\
&\Longrightarrow \quad \text{Req-1} \wedge (\lceil L \rceil \wedge 1 < \ell \leq 30) \,; \text{true} \\
&\Longrightarrow \quad \{\text{by Req-1}\} \\
&\qquad (\ell = \int L \leq 1 \wedge 1 < \ell) \,; \text{true} \\
&\Longrightarrow \quad \text{false} \,; \text{true} \\
&\Longrightarrow \quad \text{false}.
\end{aligned}
$$

Contradiction! This proves the lemma.   □

From Lemma 2.32 we deduce the following interesting remark concerning the design formula $\text{Des-1} \overset{\text{def}}{\Longleftrightarrow} \Box(\lceil L \rceil \Longrightarrow \ell \leq 1)$:

Remark 2.33
$\models \text{Req-1} \Longrightarrow \text{Des-1}.$

Proof:
Consider an interpretation $\mathcal{I}$, a valuation $\mathcal{V}$, and an interval $[b, e]$ with
$\mathcal{I}, \mathcal{V}, [b, e] \models$ Req-1. We have to show $\mathcal{I}, \mathcal{V}, [b, e] \models$ Des-1. To this end,
take a subinterval $[c, d]$ of $[b, e]$ with $\mathcal{I}, \mathcal{V}, [c, d] \models \lceil L \rceil$. We have to show
$d - c \leq 1$. Note that $\mathcal{I}, \mathcal{V}, [c, d] \models$ Req-1 and thus $\mathcal{I}, \mathcal{V}, [c, d] \models$ Req-1 $\wedge \lceil L \rceil$
holds. By Lemma 2.32, we conclude $d - c \leq 1$, as required. $\qquad \square$

Proof of (I2). We are now prepared for the proof of (I2). Nothing is to be
shown if $\ell < 60$ holds. In case of $\ell \geq 60$ we distinguish two cases:

Case 1: $\ell \geq 90$. Here we argue as follows:

$$\text{Req-1} \wedge \text{Req} \, ; \, \lceil L \rceil \wedge \ell \geq 90$$
$$\implies \quad \{\text{by Lemma 2.32}\}$$
$$\text{Req-1} \wedge \text{Req} \, ; \, (\lceil L \rceil \wedge \ell \leq 1) \wedge \ell \geq 90$$
$$\implies \quad \text{Req-1} \wedge (\text{Req} \wedge \ell \geq 60) \, ; \, \ell = 30$$
$$\implies \quad \{\text{by Req}\}$$
$$\text{Req-1} \wedge (20 \cdot \textstyle\int L \leq \ell) \, ; \, \ell = 30$$
$$\implies \quad \{\text{by Req-1}\}$$
$$(20 \cdot \textstyle\int L \leq \ell) \, ; \, (\textstyle\int L \leq 1 \wedge \ell = 30)$$
$$\implies \quad (20 \cdot \textstyle\int L \leq \ell) \, ; \, (20 \cdot \textstyle\int L \leq \ell)$$
$$\implies \quad 20 \cdot \textstyle\int L \leq \ell.$$

Case 2: $60 \leq \ell < 90$. Then we reason as follows:

$$\text{Req-1} \wedge \text{Req} \, ; \, \lceil L \rceil \wedge 60 \leq \ell < 90$$
$$\implies \quad \text{Req-1} \wedge 60 \leq \ell < 3 \cdot 30$$
$$\implies \quad \{\text{by Req-1}\}$$
$$60 \leq \ell \wedge \textstyle\int L \leq 3$$
$$\implies \quad 20 \cdot \textstyle\int L \leq 60 \leq \ell.$$

Proof of (I3). We now distinguish the following two cases:

Case 1: $\text{Req} \land \ell \geq 60$. Then we conclude as follows:

$$\text{Req-1} \land (\text{Req} \land \ell \geq 60) \,;\, \lceil \neg L \rceil$$
$$\implies \quad \{\text{by Req}\}$$
$$20 \cdot \textstyle\int L \leq \ell \,;\, \lceil \neg L \rceil$$
$$\implies \quad 20 \cdot \textstyle\int L \leq \ell \,;\, \int L = 0$$
$$\implies \quad 20 \cdot \textstyle\int L \leq \ell.$$

Case 2: $\text{Req} \land \ell < 60$. Here we argue as follows:

$$\ell \geq 60 \land \text{Req-1} \land (\text{Req} \land \ell < 60) \,;\, \lceil \neg L \rceil$$
$$\implies \quad \{\text{by Req-1}\}$$
$$\ell \geq 60 \land \textstyle\int L \leq 2 \,;\, \lceil \neg L \rceil$$
$$\implies \quad \ell \geq 60 \land \textstyle\int L \leq 2 \,;\, \int L = 0$$
$$\implies \quad 20 \cdot \textstyle\int L \leq 20 \cdot 2 < 60 \leq \ell.$$

This concludes the proof of the implication $\models \text{Req-1} \implies \text{Req}$. $\square$

2.4.8 Further rules*

The following derived axioms and proof rules for the Duration Calculus are due to A.P. Ravn. They provide additional insights into the operators of the logic.

Interval logic

Chop-False: $F \,;\, \text{false} \implies \text{false}$ \hfill (2.48)

$\qquad\qquad \text{false} \,;\, F \implies \text{false}.$

Chop-Or: $F \,;\, (G \lor H) \iff (F \,;\, G \lor F \,;\, H)$ \hfill (2.49)

$\qquad\qquad (G \lor H) \,;\, F \iff (G \,;\, F \lor H \,;\, F).$

Chop-Length: $F \,;\, G \iff \exists x \bullet ((F \land \ell = x) \,;\, \text{true}) \land (\ell = x \,;\, G).$ \hfill (2.50)

Chop-And: $F_1 \,;\, (G_1 \land \ell = x) \land F_2 \,;\, (G_2 \land \ell = x)$ \hfill (2.51)

$\qquad \iff (F_1 \land F_2) \,;\, (G_1 \land G_2 \land \ell = x)$

$\qquad (G_1 \land \ell = x) \,;\, F_1 \land (G_2 \land \ell = x) \,;\, F_2$

$\qquad \iff (G_1 \land G_2 \land \ell = x) \,;\, (F_1 \land F_2).$

Chop-Neg1: $\neg(F\,;G) \iff \forall x \bullet \ell < x \lor ((\neg F)\,;\ell = x)$ (2.52)
$$\lor \mathsf{true}\,;(\ell = x \land \neg G)$$

$\neg(F\,;G) \iff \forall x \bullet \ell < x \lor (\ell = x\,;\neg G)$
$$\lor (\neg F \land \ell = x)\,;\mathsf{true}.$$

Chop-Neg2: $\neg(F\,;\mathsf{true}) \iff \forall x \bullet \ell < x \lor (\neg F)\,;\ell = x$ (2.53)
$\neg(\mathsf{true}\,;F) \iff \forall x \bullet \ell < x \lor \ell = x\,;\neg F.$

Chop-All: $((\forall x \bullet F) \land \ell = y)\,;G \iff \forall x \bullet ((F \land \ell = y)\,;G)$ (2.54)
$G\,;((\forall x \bullet F) \land \ell = y) \iff \forall x \bullet (G\,;(F \land \ell = y))$
where x is not a free variable in G.

Modal operators

Box-Mon: $\dfrac{F \implies G}{\Box F \implies \Box G}$.   (2.55)

Box-Idem: $\Box\Box F \iff \Box F.$ (2.56)

Box-Neg: $\neg\Box F \iff \Diamond\neg F$ (2.57)
$\Box\neg F \iff \neg\Diamond F.$

Box-Or: $(\Box F \lor \Box G) \implies \Box(F \lor G).$ (2.58)

Box-And: $\Box(F \land G) \iff (\Box F \land \Box G).$ (2.59)

Box-Chop: $(\Box F \land \Box G) \implies \Box(F\,;G).$ (2.60)

Dia-Mon: $\dfrac{F \implies G}{\Diamond F \implies \Diamond G}$.   (2.61)

Dia-Idem: $\Diamond\Diamond F \iff \Diamond F.$ (2.62)

Dia-Neg: $\neg\Diamond F \iff \Box\neg F$ (2.63)
$\Diamond\neg F \iff \neg\Box F.$

Dia-Or: $\Diamond(F \lor G) \iff (\Diamond F \lor \Diamond G).$ (2.64)

Dia-And: $\Diamond(F \land G) \implies (\Diamond F \land \Diamond G).$ (2.65)

Dia-Chop: $\Diamond(F\,;G) \implies (\Diamond F \land \Diamond G).$ (2.66)

Duration operator

Dur-Real: $\dfrac{\mathcal{R} \models p(x_1, \ldots, x_n)}{p(\int P_1, \ldots, \int P_n)}$. $\qquad\qquad$ (2.67)

Dur-Dis: $\int P + \int \neg P = \ell$. $\qquad\qquad$ (2.68)

Dur-Bounds: $0 \leq \int P \leq \ell$. $\qquad\qquad$ (2.69)

Dur-Neg: $(\int \neg P = \ell) \iff (\int P = 0)$. $\qquad\qquad$ (2.70)

Dur-Impl: $(\int (P_1 \Longrightarrow P_2) = \ell) \Longrightarrow (\int P_1 \leq \int P_2)$. $\qquad\qquad$ (2.71)

Dur-And: $(\int (P_1 \wedge P_2) = \ell) \iff (\int P_1 = \int P_2 = \ell)$. $\qquad\qquad$ (2.72)

Dur-Or: $(\int (P_1 \vee P_2) = \ell) \Longrightarrow (\int P_1 + \int P_2 \geq \ell)$. $\qquad\qquad$ (2.73)

Dur-Equiv: $(\int (P_1 \iff P_2) = \ell) \Longrightarrow (\int P_1 = \int P_2)$. $\qquad\qquad$ (2.74)

Dur-Exact: $(x \leq \int P) \Longrightarrow (\int P = x)$; true. $\qquad\qquad$ (2.75)

Dur-Chop-Add: $\qquad\qquad$ (2.76)

$$\dfrac{\mathcal{R} \models (p(x_1, \ldots, x_n) \wedge p(y_1, \ldots, y_n)) \Longrightarrow p(x_1 + y_1, \ldots, x_n + y_n)}{(p(\int P_1, \ldots, \int P_n) \, ; p(\int P_1, \ldots, \int P_n)) \Longrightarrow p(\int P_1, \ldots, \int P_n)}.$$

Classic induction rule

In the original Duration Calculus a more general and more complex induction rule appears. It requires DC formulas of an extended syntax, $H(\mathcal{X})$, where $\mathcal{X}$ is a free *formula variable* of type $\mathsf{Intv} \longrightarrow \{\mathsf{tt}, \mathsf{ff}\}$. With this extension the rule can be stated as follows:

ClassicInduction-R: $\dfrac{\begin{array}{c} H(\lceil\rceil) \\ H(\mathcal{X}) \Longrightarrow H(\mathcal{X} \vee \mathcal{X} \, ; \lceil P \rceil \vee \mathcal{X} \, ; \lceil \neg P \rceil) \end{array}}{H(\mathsf{true})}$. $\qquad$ (2.77)

In this rule $H(F)$ denotes the formula obtained from $H(\mathcal{X})$ by replacing every occurrence of $\mathcal{X}$ in H with F. In particular, $H(\lceil\rceil)$ is the *induction basis* and $H(\mathcal{X})$ is the *induction hypothesis* which should imply the *induction step* $H(\mathcal{X} \vee \mathcal{X} \, ; \lceil P \rceil \vee \mathcal{X} \, ; \lceil \neg P \rceil)$.

There is also the following variant of the rule in which the subintervals $\lceil P \rceil$

and $\lceil\neg P\rceil$ are chopped off on the left-hand side of the considered interval:

ClassicInduction-L: $\quad\dfrac{\begin{array}{l} H(\lceil\rceil) \\ H(\mathcal{X}) \Longrightarrow H(\mathcal{X} \vee \lceil P\rceil \,;\, \mathcal{X} \vee \lceil\neg P\rceil \,;\, \mathcal{X}) \end{array}}{H(\text{true})}.$ $\qquad$ (2.78)

By contrast, in our induction rules (2.41) and (2.42) normal DC formulas suffice in their premises and conclusion. This makes the rule easier to comprehend and to apply.

In the following we prove that for the case

$$H(\mathcal{X}) \stackrel{\text{def}}{\Longleftrightarrow} (\mathcal{X} \Longrightarrow F)$$

the new induction rule (2.41) is equivalent to the classical induction rule (2.77). We first show two lemmas.

Lemma 2.34

For $H(\mathcal{X})$ as above the premises $H(\lceil\rceil)$ and $H(\mathcal{X}) \Longrightarrow H(\mathcal{X} \vee \mathcal{X}\,;\, \lceil P\rceil \vee \mathcal{X}\,;\, \lceil\neg P\rceil)$ are equivalent to the conjunction of the following formulas:

$$
\begin{array}{ll}
(i) & H(\lceil\rceil), \\
(ii) & H(\mathcal{X}) \Longrightarrow H(\mathcal{X}\,;\, \lceil P\rceil), \\
(iii) & H(\mathcal{X}) \Longrightarrow H(\mathcal{X}\,;\, \lceil\neg P\rceil).
\end{array}
$$

Proof:

We use the following equivalences:

$$H(\mathcal{X}) \Longrightarrow H(\mathcal{X} \vee \mathcal{X}\,;\, \lceil P\rceil \vee \mathcal{X}\,;\, \lceil\neg P\rceil)$$
$\Longleftrightarrow \quad \{\text{by definition of } H\}$
$$H(\mathcal{X}) \Longrightarrow ((\mathcal{X} \vee \mathcal{X}\,;\, \lceil P\rceil \vee \mathcal{X}\,;\, \lceil\neg P\rceil) \Longrightarrow F)$$
$\Longleftrightarrow \quad \{\text{predicate calculus}\}$
$$H(\mathcal{X}) \Longrightarrow ((\mathcal{X} \Longrightarrow F) \wedge (\mathcal{X}\,;\, \lceil P\rceil \Longrightarrow F) \wedge (\mathcal{X}\,;\, \lceil\neg P\rceil \Longrightarrow F))$$
$\Longleftrightarrow \quad \{\text{by definition of } H\}$
$$H(\mathcal{X}) \Longrightarrow (H(\mathcal{X}) \wedge H(\mathcal{X}\,;\, \lceil P\rceil) \wedge H(\mathcal{X}\,;\, \lceil\neg P\rceil))$$
$\Longleftrightarrow \quad \{\text{predicate calculus}\}$
$$(H(\mathcal{X}) \Longrightarrow H(\mathcal{X}))\wedge$$
$$(H(\mathcal{X}) \Longrightarrow H(\mathcal{X}\,;\, \lceil P\rceil))\wedge$$
$$(H(\mathcal{X}) \Longrightarrow H(\mathcal{X}\,;\, \lceil\neg P\rceil)).$$

This proves the lemma. $\qquad\qquad\square$

Using this lemma the classic induction rule can be simplified as follows:

$$
\text{Induction:} \quad \frac{\begin{array}{ll}(i) & H(\lceil\rceil) \\ (ii) & H(\mathcal{X}) \Longrightarrow H(\mathcal{X}\,;\,\lceil P\rceil) \\ (iii) & H(\mathcal{X}) \Longrightarrow H(\mathcal{X}\,;\,\lceil\neg P\rceil) \end{array}}{(iv) \quad H(\text{true})} \ .
$$

We compare the premises and the conclusion of this rule with those of the new induction rule (2.41).

Lemma 2.35
The following equivalences hold:

$$(1) \Longleftrightarrow (i), \quad (2) \Longleftrightarrow (ii), \quad (3) \Longleftrightarrow (iii) \quad and \quad (4) \Longleftrightarrow (iv).$$

Proof:
Obviously the equivalences

$$(1) \Longleftrightarrow (\lceil\rceil \Longrightarrow F) \Longleftrightarrow H(\lceil\rceil) \Longleftrightarrow (i)$$

and

$$(4) \Longleftrightarrow F \Longleftrightarrow (\text{true} \Longrightarrow F) \Longleftrightarrow H(\text{true}) \Longleftrightarrow (iv)$$

hold. Next, we show the implication $(2) \Longrightarrow (ii)$:

$$
\begin{array}{ll}
& (2) \\
\Longleftrightarrow & (F\,;\,\lceil P\rceil \Longrightarrow F) \\
\Longleftrightarrow & (F\,;\,\lceil P\rceil \Longrightarrow F) \wedge (H(\mathcal{X}) \Longrightarrow H(\mathcal{X})) \\
\Longleftrightarrow & \{\text{by definition of } H\} \\
& (F\,;\,\lceil P\rceil \Longrightarrow F) \wedge (H(\mathcal{X}) \Longrightarrow (\mathcal{X} \Longrightarrow F)) \\
\Longrightarrow & \{\text{by Chop-Mon}\} \\
& (F\,;\,\lceil P\rceil \Longrightarrow F) \wedge (H(\mathcal{X}) \Longrightarrow (\mathcal{X}\,;\,\lceil P\rceil \Longrightarrow F\,;\,\lceil P\rceil)) \\
\Longrightarrow & \{\text{by the transitivity of } \Longrightarrow\} \\
& H(\mathcal{X}) \Longrightarrow (\mathcal{X}\,;\,\lceil P\rceil \Longrightarrow F) \\
\Longleftrightarrow & \{\text{by definition of } H\} \\
& (ii).
\end{array}
$$

Finally, we prove the implication $(ii) \implies (2)$:

$$(ii)$$
$$\iff H(\mathcal{X}) \implies (\mathcal{X} \,;\, \lceil P \rceil \implies F)$$
$$\implies \quad \left\{ \text{instantiate } \mathcal{X} \text{ with } F \text{ using the sound rule } \frac{H(\mathcal{X})}{H(F)} \right\}$$
$$H(F) \implies (F \,;\, \lceil P \rceil \implies F)$$
$$\iff \quad \{ \text{by definition of } H \}$$
$$(F \implies F) \implies (F \,;\, \lceil P \rceil \implies F)$$
$$\iff F \,;\, \lceil P \rceil \implies F$$
$$\iff (2).$$

Together, this establishes the equivalence $(2) \iff (ii)$. The equivalence $(3) \iff (iii)$ is shown analogously. $\qquad \square$

With Lemma 2.34 and Lemma 2.35, we obtain the desired equivalence result for both induction rules:

Theorem 2.36
- *If F is provable with the new induction rule (2.41) then it is also provable with the classic induction rule (2.77).*
- *If $H(\text{true})$ for $H(\mathcal{X}) \stackrel{\text{def}}{\iff} (\mathcal{X} \implies F)$ is provable with the classic induction rule (2.77) then it is also provable with the new induction rule (2.41).*

2.5 Exercises

Exercise 2.1 (Evaluating DC expressions)
A traffic light for pedestrians is modelled by the observables Light of data type $\{\text{red}, \text{yellow}, \text{green}\}$ and Button of data type $\mathcal{D}_{\text{Button}} = \{\text{press}, \text{release}\}$. Consider an interpretation $\mathcal{I}$ of these observables as given by the timing diagrams in Figure 2.2.

(a) Draw the interpretation of the following state assertion:

$$\mathcal{I}[\![\text{Light} = \text{green} \wedge \neg(\text{Button} = \text{release})]\!]$$

on the interval $[0, 7]$.

(b) Let $\mathcal{V}(x) = 5$. Calculate the real value of the following DC term:

$$\mathcal{I}[\![x \cdot \textstyle\int (\text{Light} = \text{green} \wedge \neg(\text{Button} = \text{release}))]\!](\mathcal{V}, [1, 7]).$$

(c) Calculate the truth values of the following DC formulas:

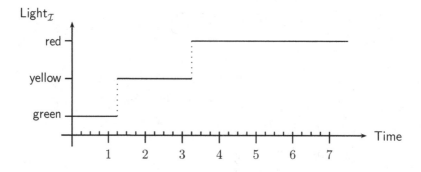

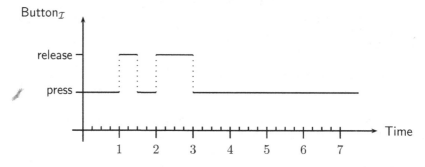

Fig. 2.2. Interpretations $\mathsf{Light}_\mathcal{I}$ and $\mathsf{Button}_\mathcal{I}$

$$\mathcal{I}[\![(\mathsf{true}; (\textstyle\int \mathsf{Light} = \mathsf{green}) = \ell); \mathsf{true}]\!](\mathcal{V}, [1,6])$$

and

$$\mathcal{I}[\![\textstyle\int (\mathsf{Button} = \mathsf{press} \wedge \mathsf{Light} = \mathsf{red}) \le 1]\!](\mathcal{V}, [1,6]).$$

Exercise 2.2
Prove Lemma 2.11.

Exercise 2.3 (Validity and realisability)
(a) State a DC formula F_a containing an integral term that is valid. F_a should be different from the formulas given in Example 2.14.
(b) State a DC formula F_b containing an integral term that is realisable from 0, but not realisable. F_b should be different from the formula used in the proof of Proposition 2.15.

    Prove your claims.

Exercise 2.4 (Interval relations)
In the article "Maintaining knowledge about temporal intervals" published

in *Communications of the ACM*, 26 (1983), J.F. Allen introduced a number of basic relations between intervals. It is proven that from the seven relations between intervals F and G shown in Figure 2.3 together with their inverses, all other possible relations between F and G can be deduced.

State DC formulas specifying these seven relations where F and G are considered as given DC formulas describing the displayed intervals.

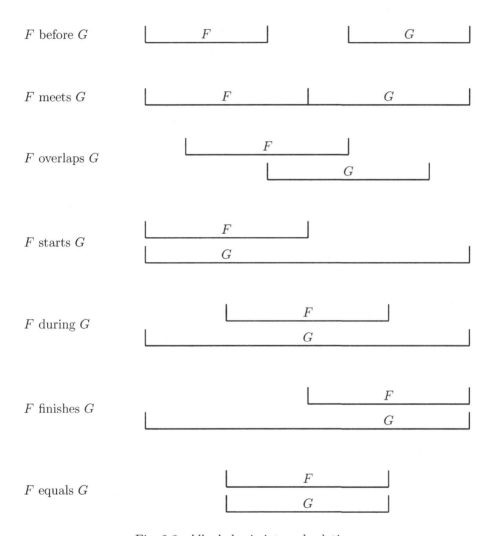

Fig. 2.3. Allen's basic interval relations

Exercise 2.5 (Measuring length)
Let P be a state assertion. Prove the following equivalence with the help of

the DC semantics:

$$\models \left(\forall x \bullet \Box((\lceil \neg P \rceil ; (\lceil P \rceil \wedge \ell = x); \lceil \neg P \rceil) \Longrightarrow x \geq 30) \right)$$
$$\Longleftrightarrow \left(\Box((\lceil \neg P \rceil ; \lceil P \rceil ; \lceil \neg P \rceil) \Rightarrow \ell > 30) \right).$$

Exercise 2.6 (Generalised railroad crossing)
In Section 1.3 we formalised the generalised railroad crossing using predicate
logic. Consider now the following DC specification of some of the properties:

$$\Box(\lceil Cr \rceil \Longrightarrow \lceil Cl \rceil), \qquad\qquad\qquad\qquad (\text{Safety})$$
$$(\lceil E \rceil ; \mathsf{true}) \vee \lceil\rceil, \qquad\qquad\qquad\qquad\qquad (\text{Init})$$
$$\Box((\lceil E \rceil ; \mathsf{true}; \lceil Cr \rceil) \Longrightarrow \ell \geq \varepsilon), \qquad\qquad (\text{T-Fast})$$
$$\Box((\lceil \neg E \rceil \wedge \ell \geq \varepsilon) \Longrightarrow \mathsf{true}; \lceil Cl \rceil). \qquad (\text{G-Close})$$

Explain informally the meaning of each of these formulas. Prove the following implication by using the DC semantics:

$$\mathsf{Init} \wedge \mathsf{T\text{-}Fast} \wedge \mathsf{G\text{-}Close} \Longrightarrow \mathsf{Safety}.$$

Exercise 2.7 (Everywhere operator)
Let P, Q, R be state assertions. Which of the following DC formulas are
valid? Explain your argument or give a counterexample for the claimed
implication or reverse implication.

(a1) $\quad \neg \lceil P \rceil \Longrightarrow \lceil \neg P \rceil$,
(a2) $\quad \neg \lceil P \rceil \Longleftarrow \lceil \neg P \rceil$,
(b1) $\quad (\lceil P \rceil \wedge \lceil Q \rceil) \Longrightarrow \lceil P \wedge Q \rceil$,
(b2) $\quad (\lceil P \rceil \wedge \lceil Q \rceil) \Longleftarrow \lceil P \wedge Q \rceil$,
(c1) $\quad \Diamond(\lceil P \wedge Q \rceil) \Longrightarrow (\Diamond \lceil P \rceil) \wedge (\Diamond \lceil Q \rceil)$,
(c2) $\quad \Diamond(\lceil P \wedge Q \rceil) \Longleftarrow (\Diamond \lceil P \rceil) \wedge (\Diamond \lceil Q \rceil)$.

Exercise 2.8 (Integral)
Prove that for all state assertions P the following properties hold:

(a) $\quad \models \lceil\rceil \Longrightarrow \int P = 0$,
(b) $\quad \models \lceil \neg P \rceil \Longrightarrow \int P = 0$,
(c) $\quad \models \lceil\rceil \Longrightarrow \int P = 0$.

Exercise 2.9 (Proof rules)
Explain the meaning of the following proof rules and argue why they are

sound:

$$(\Box F \wedge \Box G) \Longrightarrow \Box(F;G), \qquad \text{(box-chop)}$$

$$F;(G \vee H) \Longleftrightarrow (F;G) \vee (F;H), \qquad \text{(chop-or)}$$

$$\frac{F}{\Box F}. \qquad \text{(box-intro)}$$

Exercise 2.10 (Proofs with DC rules)
Prove the following implication using the rules *Chop-Mon*, *Chop-Asm*, the definition $\Diamond F = true;(F;true)$, and the proof rules from predicate logic:

$$\Diamond\Diamond F \Longrightarrow \Diamond F.$$

Exercise 2.11 (Induction rule)
Prove the following DC formula with the help of the induction rule:

$$\lceil \rceil \vee \lceil P \rceil \vee \Diamond \lceil \neg P \rceil.$$

2.6 Bibliographic remarks

The Duration Calculus was invented in the context of the European Community Basic Research Action ProCoS (Provably Correct Systems, 1989–1995) [HHF+94, BHL+96] as a new logic and calculus for specifying the behaviour of real-time systems. The first publication on the Duration Calculus is by Zhou Chaochen, C.A.R. Hoare, and A.P. Ravn [ZHR91]. Duration Calculus is an extension of the Interval Temporal Logic of B. Moskowski [Mos85, Mos86] to deal with continuous time. In particular, the ProCoS case study of the gas burner with its safety requirement Req motivated the main new ingredient of the calculus compared with other logics for continuous time: the integral operator enabling the specifier to express duration properties.

Duration Calculus is based on the notion of an observable interpreted as a function from the continuous-time domain to some data domain. A real-time system is described by a set of such observables. This links up well to the mathematical basis found in classical dynamic systems theory [Lue79] and enables extensions to cover hybrid systems [GNRR93]. By choosing the right set of observables, real-time systems can be described at various levels of abstraction in the Duration Calculus (see e.g. [RRH93, ORS96, SO99, Sch99, Die00a, HO02]). The calculus has been investigated carefully and several extensions of the original form have been developed (see e.g. [ZHS93, Rav95, HZ97, Frä04, FH07]). The most comprehensive exposition of its foundation, containing numerous further references, is the monograph [ZH04].

In the proof system for Duration Calculus, the application conditions of the rules for ∀-Elimination and ∃-Introduction in Subsection 2.4.1 are taken from [ZH04]. The completeness of the axioms for equality in Subsection 2.4.2 is often attributed to [Bir35]. For more details on the structure $\mathcal{R}$ of the real numbers, discussed in Subsection 2.4.3, we refer to books on logic like [EFT96, Dal04] or on mathematical analysis like [Rud76]. More specifically, Tarski's quantifier elimination theory for first-order formulas over the real numbers is discussed in [Dri88]. The axiomatisation of interval logic given in Subsection 2.4.4 is due to B. Dutertre [Dut95]. In that paper it is shown that this axiomatisation along with the proof rules of predicate logic is complete relative to the theory of an abstract time domain, which may be chosen as $\mathcal{R}$, the structure of real numbers.

The induction rule introduced in Subsection 2.4.6 appears in the Signed Duration Calculus (SDC) of [Ras02]. It avoids the use of free *formula variables* as in the classic induction rule [ZH04]. In Subsection 2.4.8, we have shown that for proof goals of the form $H(\mathcal{X}) \stackrel{\text{def}}{\Longleftrightarrow} (\mathcal{X} \Longrightarrow F)$ both induction rules are equally powerful. It is interesting to notice that all applications of the classic induction rule in [ZH04] are of this form. The other axioms and proof rules (2.48)–(2.76) stated in Subsection 2.4.8 are taken from [Rav95]. Various examples of formal proofs with the proof rules of the Duration Calculus can be found in [Rav95, ZH04].

A. Schäfer extended the Duration Calculus to a multi-dimensional logic called Shape Calculus [Sch05, Sch06]. It is intended for the specification and verification of mobile real-time systems like robots moving in a physical space over continuous time. As for the Duration Calculus, the logic of the full Shape Calculus has no sound and complete axiomatic proof system. However, a sound proof system that is complete relative to an axiomatisation of a multi-dimensional interval logic has been developed [Sch07].

<h1 style="text-align:center">3</h1>

<h1 style="text-align:center">Properties and subsets of DC</h1>

The Duration Calculus can be used as a high-level specification language for properties of real-time systems. The question arises whether reasoning about such specifications can be automated. To this end, we first discuss the decidability of the *realisability problem* of the Duration Calculus: is there an algorithm that for a given Duration Calculus formula decides whether this formula can be realised. By using proof techniques of Zhou Chaochen, M.R. Hansen, and P. Sestoft, we show that for a subset of the Duration Calculus and the *discrete-time* domain this problem is indeed decidable. However, for the general case of *continuous time* it is not. The proofs of these results shed light on the difference between these two time domains.

Next we introduce the subset of *implementables* due to A.P. Ravn. This subset provides certain patterns of formulas formalising concepts like stability and progress that are convenient for specifying the behaviour of controllers. Finally, we introduce *Constraint Diagrams* due to C. Kleuker as a graphical representation of a subset of Duration Calculus. These diagrams specify timed behaviours in an assumption/commitment style. We show that the implementables all have lucid representations as Constraint Diagrams. In general, Constraint Diagrams are more expressive than implementables.

3.1 Decidability results

Zhou Chaochen, M.R. Hansen, and P. Sestoft showed that the problem whether a given DC formula is satisfiable is decidable for a subset of DC when *discrete* time is assumed [ZHS93]. This result has been exploited by P.K. Pandya in a tool called DCVALID for automatically checking satisfiability and validity of formulas in this subset [Pan01]. The authors of [ZHS93] also proved undecidability of the satisfiability problem for several interesting subsets of DC in the case of *continuous* time. Since the proofs of both results use very interesting constructions, we present them in this section. However, we are not interested in satisfiability but in the question whether a DC formula can be realised by an interpretation. Therefore we consider the decidability of the *realisability* problem. We first present the positive result for discrete time and then explain the negative result for continuous time.

3.1.1 Decidability for discrete time

We consider the subset RDC (Restricted DC) of DC formulas, defined by the following abstract syntax:

$$F ::= \lceil P \rceil \mid \neg F_1 \mid F_1 \vee F_2 \mid F_1 \,;\, F_2$$

where P is a state assertion as defined in Subsection 2.2.2, but with observables of Boolean type $\{0, 1\}$ only. The logical connectives $\wedge, \Longrightarrow$, and $\Longleftrightarrow$ can be considered as abbreviations. Note that global variables are not allowed in this restricted syntax. Thus the truth of an RDC formula F does not depend on any valuation $\mathcal{V}$, so we can omit this parameter here.

Discrete time is modelled by discrete interpretations and discrete intervals. We call $\mathcal{I}$ a *discrete interpretation* if each observable X is interpreted by a function

$$X_{\mathcal{I}} : \mathsf{Time} \longrightarrow \{0, 1\},$$

where $\mathsf{Time} = \mathbb{R}_{\geq 0}$ but all discontinuities are in $\mathbb{N}$. The following timing diagram gives an example of such a function:

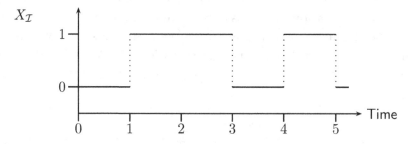

We call an interval $[b, e] \subset \mathsf{Time}$ *discrete* if $b, e \in \mathbb{N}$ holds. We also change the inductive definition of the semantics of the chop operator such that only discrete chopping points are allowed:

$$\mathcal{I}, [b, e] \models F_1 \,;\, F_2$$

iff there exists an $m \in [b, e]$ with $m \in \mathbb{N}$ such that

$$\mathcal{I}, [b, m] \models F_1 \quad \text{and} \quad \mathcal{I}, [m, e] \models F_2.$$

Expressiveness of RDC

At first sight RDC seems to be a very restricted subset of the DC. However, under the assumption of discrete time we can express many interesting properties in RDC. First, we show that we can express $\ell = 1$. Indeed, the formula

$$\ell = 1 \iff (\lceil 1 \rceil \wedge \neg(\lceil 1 \rceil \, ; \, \lceil 1 \rceil)),$$

with its right-hand side expressed in RDC, is equivalent to the DC formula

$$\ell = 1 \iff (\ell > 0 \wedge \neg(\ell > 0 \, ; \, \ell > 0)),$$

which is valid because in discrete time intervals of length 1 are the only non-point intervals that *cannot* be chopped into two non-point subintervals. By contrast, in continuous time the implication

$$\lceil 1 \rceil \Longrightarrow (\lceil 1 \rceil \, ; \, \lceil 1 \rceil)$$

and its equivalent

$$\ell > 0 \Longrightarrow (\ell > 0 \, ; \, \ell > 0)$$

are valid, i.e. every non-point interval can be chopped into two non-point subintervals. In this way we may obtain arbitrarily small non-point intervals. More generally, for every state assertion P the implication

$$\lceil P \rceil \Longrightarrow (\lceil P \rceil \, ; \, \lceil P \rceil)$$

is valid in continuous time, but not in discrete time. Note that the reverse implication

$$(\lceil P \rceil \, ; \, \lceil P \rceil) \Longrightarrow \lceil P \rceil$$

is valid in both time domains (cf. also rule (2.34)).

Using $\ell = 1$, other interesting properties can also be expressed in RDC. The following examples show how some typical DC formulas can be expressed by equivalent RDC formulas:

$$\ell = 0 \qquad\qquad \Longleftrightarrow \quad \neg\lceil 1\rceil,$$
$$\ell = 1 \qquad\qquad \Longleftrightarrow \quad \lceil 1\rceil \wedge \neg(\lceil 1\rceil \;;\; \lceil 1\rceil),$$
$$\text{true} \qquad\qquad \Longleftrightarrow \quad \ell = 0 \vee \neg(\ell = 0),$$
$$\textstyle\int P = 0 \qquad \Longleftrightarrow \quad \lceil \neg P\rceil \vee \ell = 0,$$
$$\textstyle\int P = 1 \qquad \Longleftrightarrow \quad (\textstyle\int P = 0)\,;\,(\lceil P\rceil \wedge \ell = 1)\,;\,(\textstyle\int P = 0),$$
$$\textstyle\int P = k+1 \quad \Longleftrightarrow \quad (\textstyle\int P = k)\,;\,(\textstyle\int P = 1),$$
$$\textstyle\int P \geq k \qquad \Longleftrightarrow \quad (\textstyle\int P = k)\,;\,\text{true},$$
$$\textstyle\int P > k \qquad \Longleftrightarrow \quad \textstyle\int P \geq k+1,$$
$$\textstyle\int P \leq k \qquad \Longleftrightarrow \quad \neg(\textstyle\int P > k),$$
$$\textstyle\int P < k \qquad \Longleftrightarrow \quad \textstyle\int P \leq k-1,$$

where $k \in \mathbb{N}$.

Realisability problem

Let F be an RDC formula. A discrete interpretation $\mathcal{I}$ *realises F from 0 in discrete time*, iff $\mathcal{I}, [0, n] \models F$ holds for all $n \in \mathbb{N}$. We call F *realisable from 0 in discrete time* iff there is a discrete interpretation $\mathcal{I}$ that realises F from 0 in discrete time. The *realisability problem* is described as follows.

Given: An RDC formula F.
Question: Is F realisable from 0 in discrete time?

This problem can be reduced algorithmically to the infinity problem of regular languages: to each RDC formula F we will assign a regular language $\mathcal{L}'(F)$ such that the following holds:

$$F \text{ is realisable from 0 in discrete time}$$
$$\Longleftrightarrow \mathcal{L}'(F) \text{ is infinite.}$$

By the decidability of the latter problem, we shall conclude the decidability of the realisability problem of RDC for discrete time.

Construction of $\mathcal{L}(F)$

Given an RDC formula F we take as the alphabet Σ for the regular language the set of all *basic conjuncts* of the state variables in F.

Example 3.1

Assume that F contains exactly the state variables X, Y, Z. Then

$$\Sigma = \left\{ \begin{array}{llll} X \wedge Y \wedge Z, & X \wedge Y \wedge \neg Z, & X \wedge \neg Y \wedge Z, & X \wedge \neg Y \wedge \neg Z, \\ \neg X \wedge Y \wedge Z, & \neg X \wedge Y \wedge \neg Z, & \neg X \wedge \neg Y \wedge Z, & \neg X \wedge \neg Y \wedge \neg Z \end{array} \right\}$$

is the associated alphabet.   ∎

The idea of this alphabet is that each basic conjunct, i.e. each letter $a \in \Sigma$, describes a discrete interpretation $\mathcal{I}$ on an interval of length 1. Therefore, a word $a_1 \ldots a_n \in \Sigma^*$ describes a discrete interpretation of length n.

Definition 3.2
A word $w = a_1 \ldots a_n \in \Sigma^*$ with $n \geq 0$ and $a_1, \ldots, a_n \in \Sigma$ *describes* a discrete interpretation $\mathcal{I}$ on $[0, n]$ iff for all $j \in \{1, \ldots, n\}$ the property

$$\forall t \in (j-1, j) \bullet \mathcal{I}[\![a_j]\!](t) = 1$$

holds. Here $(j-1, j)$ denotes the open interval $\{t \in \text{Time} \mid j-1 < t < j\}$. For $n = 0$ we put $w = \varepsilon$.

Note that each letter a_j of the word is a basic conjunct and therefore a state assertion. Thus, $\mathcal{I}[\![a_j]\!]$ is defined as a function of type Time $\longrightarrow \{0, 1\}$.

Example 3.3
The word

$$w = (\neg X \wedge \neg Y \wedge \neg Z) \cdot (X \wedge \neg Y \wedge \neg Z) \cdot (X \wedge Y \wedge \neg Z) \cdot (X \wedge Y \wedge Z) \in \Sigma^*$$

describes the following discrete interpretation

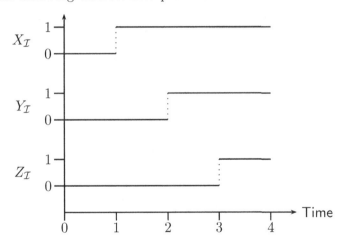

on the interval $[0, 4]$. ■

Following Zhou, Hansen, and Sestoft, we construct a language $\mathcal{L}(F)$. For this purpose, we need an auxiliary definition. Since each state assertion P of RDC can be transformed into an equivalent disjunctive normal form $\bigvee_{i=1}^{m} a_i$

with $a_i \in \Sigma$, we write $DNF(P)$ to denote the set of all basic conjuncts of this disjunctive normal form. Thus

$$DNF(P) = \{a_1, \ldots, a_m\} \subseteq \Sigma.$$

We can now define $\mathcal{L}(F)$ inductively:

$$\mathcal{L}(\lceil P \rceil) = DNF(P)^+,$$
$$\mathcal{L}(\neg F_1) = \Sigma^* \setminus \mathcal{L}(F_1),$$
$$\mathcal{L}(F_1 \vee F_2) = \mathcal{L}(F_1) \cup \mathcal{L}(F_2),$$
$$\mathcal{L}(F_1 \, ; F_2) = \mathcal{L}(F_1) \cdot \mathcal{L}(F_2).$$

For languages $L, L_1, L_2 \subseteq \Sigma^*$ we write $L_1 \cdot L_2$ to denote the *concatenation* and $L^+ = L \cdot L^*$ to denote the *non-empty iteration*.

Lemma 3.4

For all RDC formulas F, all discrete interpretations $\mathcal{I}$, all $n \geq 0$ and all words $w \in \Sigma^*$ which describe $\mathcal{I}$ on $[0, n]$ the following holds:

$$\mathcal{I}, [0, n] \models F \text{ iff } w \in \mathcal{L}(F).$$

Thus the words $w \in \mathcal{L}(F)$ describe the values of $\mathcal{I}$ for an initial part.

Proof:
We proceed by induction on the structure of F.

Induction basis: $F \stackrel{\text{def}}{\Longleftrightarrow} \lceil P \rceil$.

Suppose $w = a_1 \ldots a_n$ describes $\mathcal{I}$ on $[0, n]$. Then

$$\mathcal{I}, [0, n] \models F \text{ iff } \mathcal{I}, [0, n] \models \lceil P \rceil \text{ and } n \geq 1$$
$$\text{iff } n \geq 1 \text{ and } \forall j \in \{1, \ldots, n\} \bullet \mathcal{I}, [j - 1, j] \models \lceil P \rceil$$
$$\text{iff } n \geq 1 \text{ and } \forall j \in \{1, \ldots, n\} \bullet \mathcal{I}, [j - 1, j] \models \lceil P \rceil \wedge \lceil a_j \rceil$$
$$\wedge \, a_j \in DNF(P)$$
$$\text{iff } n \geq 1 \text{ and } \forall j \in \{1, \ldots, n\} \bullet a_j \in DNF(P)$$
$$\text{iff } w \in DNF(P)^+$$
$$\text{iff } w \in \mathcal{L}(F).$$

Induction hypothesis: Assume that the claim holds for F_1 and F_2.

Induction step: We distinguish three cases of which the first two are easy, but the third one needs some care.

Case $F \stackrel{\text{def}}{\Longleftrightarrow} \neg F_1$. Then

$$\mathcal{I}, [0, n] \models \neg F_1 \text{ iff } \mathcal{I}, [0, n] \not\models F_1$$
$$\text{iff} \quad \{\text{induction hypothesis}\}$$
$$w \notin \mathcal{L}(F_1)$$
$$\text{iff} \quad w \in \Sigma^* - \mathcal{L}(F_1)$$
$$\text{iff} \quad w \in \mathcal{L}(\neg F_1)$$
$$\text{iff} \quad w \in \mathcal{L}(F).$$

Case $F \stackrel{\text{def}}{\Longleftrightarrow} F_1 \vee F_2$. Then

$$\mathcal{I}, [0, n] \models F_1 \vee F_2 \text{ iff } \mathcal{I}, [0, n] \models F_1 \text{ or } \mathcal{I}, [0, n] \models F_2$$
$$\text{iff} \quad \{\text{induction hypothesis}\}$$
$$w \in \mathcal{L}(F_1) \text{ or } w \in \mathcal{L}(F_2)$$
$$\text{iff} \quad w \in \mathcal{L}(F_1) \cup \mathcal{L}(F_2)$$
$$\text{iff} \quad w \in \mathcal{L}(F_1 \vee F_2)$$
$$\text{iff} \quad w \in \mathcal{L}(F).$$

Case $F \stackrel{\text{def}}{\Longleftrightarrow} F_1 ; F_2$.
Suppose $w = a_1 \ldots a_n$ describes $\mathcal{I}$ on $[0, n]$. Then

$$\mathcal{I}, [0, n] \models F \text{ iff } \exists m \leq n \bullet (\mathcal{I}, [0, m] \models F_1 \text{ and } \mathcal{I}, [m, n] \models F_2)$$
$$\text{iff} \quad \{\text{consider the interpretation } \mathcal{I}_m \text{ which for}$$
$$\text{all observables } X \text{ satisfies the condition}$$
$$\mathcal{I}_m(X)(t) = \mathcal{I}(X)(t + m)\}$$
$$\exists m \leq n \bullet (\mathcal{I}, [0, m] \models F_1 \text{ and } \mathcal{I}_m, [0, n - m] \models F_2)$$
$$\text{iff} \quad \{\text{induction hypothesis:}$$
$$a_1 \ldots a_m \text{ describes } \mathcal{I} \text{ on } [0, m] \text{ and}$$
$$a_{m+1} \ldots a_n \text{ describes } \mathcal{I}_m \text{ on } [0, n - m]\}$$
$$\exists m \leq n \bullet (a_1 \ldots a_m \in \mathcal{L}(F_1) \text{ and } a_{m+1} \ldots a_n \in \mathcal{L}(F_2))$$
$$\text{iff} \quad w \in \mathcal{L}(F_1) \cdot \mathcal{L}(F_2)$$
$$\text{iff} \quad w \in \mathcal{L}(F).$$

This completes the proof of the lemma. $\qquad\qquad\qquad\qquad\qquad\qquad$ □

Zhou, Hansen, and Sestoft used the language $\mathcal{L}(F)$ to answer the question of satisfiability. First, they prove the following lemma:

Lemma 3.5

For all RDC formulas F the following holds:

$$F \text{ is satisfiable in discrete time}$$
$$\text{iff } \mathcal{L}(F) \text{ is non-empty.}$$

For a proof of this lemma we refer to [ZH04], Chapter 6. Since the regular language $\mathcal{L}(F)$ can be constructed effectively from F and emptiness of regular languages is decidable, the following theorem holds:

Theorem 3.6

The satisfiability problem for the Restricted Duration Calculus with discrete time is decidable.

We are interested in realisability rather than satisfiability. For this purpose, we need one further concept.

Definition 3.7 (Kernel)

The *prefix closed kernel* of a language $L \subseteq \Sigma$ is defined by

$$kern(L) = \{w \in \Sigma^* \mid w \in L \land \forall v \leq w \bullet v \in L\}.$$

Here $\leq$ denotes the *prefix relation* on words. Thus $kern(L)$ contains all those words of L whose prefixes are again in L.

It can be shown that for each regular language L also the language $kern(L)$ is regular (see Exercise 3.3). Moreover, the relations

$$kern(L) = L \setminus (\overline{L} \cdot \Sigma^*) \subseteq L$$

hold. Now we can prove the main result of this subsection.

Lemma 3.8

For all RDC formulas F the following holds:

$$F \text{ is realisable from 0 in discrete time}$$
$$\text{iff } kern(\mathcal{L}(F)) \text{ is infinite.}$$

Proof:

"*Only if*": Let $\mathcal{I}$ be a discrete interpretation such that $\mathcal{I}, [0, n] \models F$ holds for all $n \in \mathbb{N}$. By Lemma 3.4, for all $n \in \mathbb{N}$ there exists a word $w_n \in \Sigma^*$ of length n that describes $\mathcal{I}$ on $[0, n]$. Hence, $w_n \in \mathcal{L}(F)$. Since all prefixes of w_n are also of the form $w_j \in \mathcal{L}(F)$, we have $w_n \in kern(\mathcal{L}(F))$. Thus $kern(\mathcal{L}(F))$ is infinite.

"*If*": Since the alphabet Σ is finite, we can represent the infinite and prefix closed set $kern(\mathcal{L}(F))$ of words as an infinite, but finitely branching tree. By König's Lemma†, there exists an infinite path in this tree. This path represents a discrete interpretation $\mathcal{I}$ which realises F from 0 in discrete time. □

Since the regular language $kern(\mathcal{L}(F))$ can be constructed effectively from F and infinity of regular languages is decidable, we obtain the following result:

Theorem 3.9
The realisability problem for the Restricted Duration Calculus with discrete time is decidable.

3.1.2 Undecidability for continuous time

Zhou Chaochen, M.R. Hansen, and P. Sestoft also proved that in the case of continuous time the satisfiability problem of the Duration Calculus and certain subsets of it is undecidable [ZHS93]. To this end, they showed that the halting problem for two-counter machines can be *reduced* to the satisfiability problem of Duration Calculus in continuous time. Since two-counter machines are known to be as powerful as Turing machines, their halting problem is undecidable [Min67]. This implies the undecidability for the satisfaction problem. In the following we present the main idea of this reduction and apply it to obtain also the undecidability of the realisability problem.

Two-counter machines

A *two-counter machine* is a structure $\mathcal{M} = (\mathcal{Q}, q_0, q_{\text{fin}}, Prog)$ where

- $\mathcal{Q}$ is a finite set of *states* with *initial* state q_0 and *final* state q_{fin}.
- *Prog* is the *machine program* consisting of a finite set of commands of the form

$$q : inc_i : q' \quad \text{and} \quad q : dec_i : q', q''$$

with $i \in \{1, 2\}$. We assume that $\mathcal{M}$ is *deterministic*, i.e. for each state q there exists at most one command starting in q, and q_{fin} is the only state in which no command starts.

$\mathcal{M}$ manipulates *configurations* of the form $K = (q, n_1, n_2)$ where $q \in \mathcal{Q}$ is the current state and $n_1, n_2 \in \mathbb{N}$ are the current values of two counters. The *initial* configuration is $(q_0, 0, 0)$, i.e. both counters are initially set to 0. Executing a command of the machine program yields a *transition* $K \vdash K'$

---

† König's Lemma: Every finitely branching tree is either finite or it has an infinite path.

between configurations. The following table describes the semantics of the commands:

Command	Semantics: $K \vdash K'$
$q:\ inc_1\ :q'$	$(q, n_1, n_2)\ \vdash\ (q', n_1 + 1, n_2)$
$q:\ dec_1\ :q', q''$	$(q, 0, n_2)\ \vdash\ (q', 0, n_2)$
	$(q, n_1 + 1, n_2)\ \vdash\ (q'', n_1, n_2)$
$q:\ inc_2\ :q'$	$(q, n_1, n_2)\ \vdash\ (q', n_1, n_2 + 1)$
$q:\ dec_2\ :q', q''$	$(q, n_1, 0)\ \vdash\ (q', n_1, 0)$
	$(q, n_1, n_2 + 1)\ \vdash\ (q'', n_1, n_2)$

The *increment* commands increment the corresponding counter by 1 and change the state accordingly. The *decrement* commands first test whether the corresponding counter is 0. If this is the case the counter is left unchanged and the first successor state is taken. Otherwise the counter is decremented by 1 and the second successor state becomes the current state.

Since $\mathcal{M}$ is deterministic, it has exactly one *computation*, which is the maximal sequence of configurations obtained by successive transitions of $\mathcal{M}$ starting in $K_0 = (q_0, 0, 0)$. This sequence is either finite and of the form

$$K_0 = (q_0, 0, 0) \vdash \cdots \vdash (q_{\text{fin}}, n_1, n_2)$$

because q_{fin} is the only state without a starting command or it is infinite and of the form

$$K_0 = (q_0, 0, 0) \vdash K_1 \vdash K_2 \vdash \ldots$$

In the first case we say that $\mathcal{M}$ *halts* and otherwise we say that $\mathcal{M}$ *diverges*.

From the theory of computation it is known that it is *undecidable* whether a given deterministic two-counter machine $\mathcal{M}$ halts or diverges [Min67].

Reduction of two-counter machines to DC

We now describe the reduction of two-counter machines to the Duration Calculus. Let a two-counter machine $\mathcal{M}$ be given. The main issue is how to represent the configurations and transitions of $\mathcal{M}$ by suitable DC formulas.

Idea: Use a single observable **obs** ranging over the following data values: all states of $\mathcal{M}$ plus the four auxiliary values C_1, C_2, B, X. The values C_1 and C_2 are needed for the counters, and B and X serve as delimiters. A configuration $K = (q, n_1, n_2)$, say with $n_1 = 2$ and $n_2 = 3$, is represented by a formula of the following form:

$$
\begin{pmatrix} \lceil q \rceil \\ \wedge \\ \ell = 1 \end{pmatrix} ; \begin{pmatrix} \lceil B \rceil ; \lceil C_1 \rceil ; \lceil B \rceil ; \lceil C_1 \rceil ; \lceil B \rceil \\ \wedge \\ \ell = 1 \end{pmatrix} ; \begin{pmatrix} \lceil X \rceil \\ \wedge \\ \ell = 1 \end{pmatrix} ;
$$

$$
\begin{pmatrix} \lceil B \rceil ; \lceil C_2 \rceil ; \lceil B \rceil ; \lceil C_2 \rceil ; \lceil B \rceil ; \lceil C_2 \rceil ; \lceil B \rceil \\ \wedge \\ \ell = 1 \end{pmatrix} .
$$

The initial configuration $K_0 = (q_0, 0, 0)$ is represented by

$$
\begin{pmatrix} \lceil q_0 \rceil \\ \wedge \\ \ell = 1 \end{pmatrix} ; \begin{pmatrix} \lceil B \rceil \\ \wedge \\ \ell = 1 \end{pmatrix} ; \begin{pmatrix} \lceil X \rceil \\ \wedge \\ \ell = 1 \end{pmatrix} ; \begin{pmatrix} \lceil B \rceil \\ \wedge \\ \ell = 1 \end{pmatrix} ,
$$

more concisely written as

$$
\lceil q_0 \rceil^1 ; \lceil B \rceil^1 ; \lceil X \rceil^1 ; \lceil B \rceil^1 .
$$

It is important to notice that this representation exploits the continuous-time domain by encoding unboundedly large values of the counters by *unboundedly many changes* $\lceil C_1 \rceil ; \lceil B \rceil$ resp. $\lceil C_2 \rceil ; \lceil B \rceil$ on an interval of length 1. As a consequence, a configuration is represented by a formula that holds only on intervals of fixed length 4. Thus, a computation of $\mathcal{M}$ of the form $K_0 \vdash K_1 \vdash K_2 \vdash \dots$ can be represented as the concatenation of the formulas of the configurations:

$$
\underbrace{\boxed{\text{formula for } K_0}}_{\ell=4} ; \underbrace{\boxed{\text{formula for } K_1}}_{\ell=4} ; \underbrace{\boxed{\text{formula for } K_2}}_{\ell=4} \dots
$$

The two-counter machine $\mathcal{M}$ will be modelled by a conjunction of DC formulas which describe

- the initial configuration,
- the general form of configurations,
- the transitions between configurations,
- the handling of the final state.

The initial configuration is specified by the DC formula

$$
init_\mathcal{M} \stackrel{\text{def}}{\Longleftrightarrow} (\ell \geq 4 \Longrightarrow \lceil q_0 \rceil^1 ; \lceil B \rceil^1 ; \lceil X \rceil^1 ; \lceil B \rceil^1 ; \mathsf{true}).
$$

The sequence of configurations is enforced by:

$$
keep \stackrel{\text{def}}{\Longleftrightarrow} \square(\lceil Q \rceil^1 ; \lceil B \vee C_1 \rceil^1 ; \lceil X \rceil^1 ; \lceil B \vee C_2 \rceil^1 ; \ell = 4
$$
$$
\Longrightarrow \ell = 4; \lceil Q \rceil^1 ; \lceil B \vee C_1 \rceil^1 ; \lceil X \rceil^1 ; \lceil B \vee C_2 \rceil^1),
$$

where Q stands for $\neg(X \vee C_1 \vee C_2 \vee B)$.

Illustration:

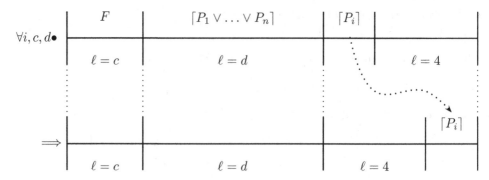

For each type of command we add four DC formulas to encode the correct behaviour of $\mathcal{M}$. For a better readability we define an auxiliary formula pattern *copy* expressing that the values of the observable are repeated exactly 4 time units later, i.e. in the next configuration:

$$copy(F, \{P_1, \ldots, P_n\}) \overset{\text{def}}{\Longleftrightarrow}$$
$$\forall c, d \bullet \Box((F \wedge \ell = c)\,;(\lceil P_1 \vee \ldots \vee P_n \rceil \wedge \ell = d)\,;\lceil P_1 \rceil\,;\ell = 4$$
$$\Longrightarrow \ell = c + d + 4\,;\lceil P_1 \rceil)$$
$$\vdots$$
$$\wedge \forall c, d \bullet \Box((F \wedge \ell = c)\,;(\lceil P_1 \vee \ldots \vee P_n \rceil \wedge \ell = d)\,;\lceil P_n \rceil\,;\ell = 4$$
$$\Longrightarrow \ell = c + d + 4\,;\lceil P_n \rceil),$$

where F is a DC formula and $P_1, \ldots, P_n$ are state assertions. This formula expresses that after each interval where in the first part F is true and in the second part $P_1 \vee \ldots \vee P_n$ is true the same pattern of $P_1, \ldots, P_n$ is repeated exactly 4 time units later. This copying process stops when a value is encountered that does not satisfy $P_1 \vee \ldots \vee P_n$ any more.

Illustration:

To express an increment command $q : inc_1 : q'$ we represent the following four activities in corresponding DC formulas:

(i) Change the state from q to q':

$$\square(\lceil q \rceil^1 \; ; \; \lceil B \vee C_1 \rceil^1 \; ; \; \lceil X \rceil^1 \; ; \; \lceil B \vee C_2 \rceil^1 \; ; \ell = 4$$
$$\Longrightarrow \ell = 4 ; \; \lceil q' \rceil^1 \; ; \text{true}).$$

Illustration:

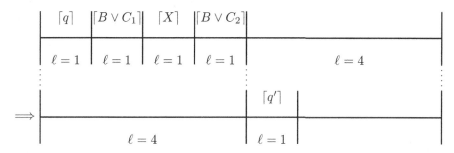

(ii) Increment the first counter by splitting the first B-interval into $B - C_1 - B$:

$$\forall d \bullet \square(\lceil q \rceil^1 \; ; \; \lceil B \rceil^d \; ; (\ell = 0 \vee \lceil C_1 \rceil \; ; \; \lceil \neg X \rceil) \lceil X \rceil^1 \; ; \; \lceil B \vee C_2 \rceil^1 \; ; \ell = 4$$
$$\Longrightarrow \ell = 4 ; \; \lceil q' \rceil^1 \; ; (\lceil B \rceil \; ; \; \lceil C_1 \rceil \; ; \; \lceil B \rceil \wedge \ell = d) \; ; \text{true}).$$

Illustration:

(iii) Keep the rest of the first counter unchanged:

$$copy(\lceil q \rceil^1 \; ; \; \lceil B \vee C_1 \rceil \; ; \; \lceil C_1 \rceil, \{B, C_1\}).$$

(iv) Leave the second counter unchanged:

$$copy(\lceil q \rceil^1 \; ; \; \lceil B \vee C_1 \rceil^1 \; ; \; \lceil X \rceil^1, \{B, C_2\}).$$

To express a decrement command $q : dec_1 : q', q''$ we represent the following four activities in corresponding DC formulas:

(i). If the first counter is zero change the state from q to q' and keep the value of the first counter:

$$\Box(\lceil q\rceil^1 \,;\, \lceil B\rceil^1 \,;\, \lceil X\rceil^1 \,;\, \lceil B \vee C_2\rceil^1 \,;\, \ell = 4$$
$$\Longrightarrow \ell = 4;\, \lceil q'\rceil^1 \,;\, \lceil B\rceil^1 \,;\, \text{true}).$$

(ii) If the first counter is not zero change the state from q to q'' and decrement the first counter by replacing the first $B - C_1$ sequence by a $B - interval$:

$$\forall d \bullet \Box(\lceil q\rceil^1 \,;\, (\lceil B\rceil \,;\, \lceil C_1\rceil \wedge \ell = d)\,;\, \lceil B\rceil \,;\, \lceil B \vee C_1\rceil \,;$$
$$\lceil X\rceil^1 \,;\, \lceil B \vee C_2\rceil^1 \,;\, \ell = 4$$
$$\Longrightarrow \ell = 4;\, \lceil q''\rceil^1 \,;\, \lceil B\rceil^d \,;\, \text{true}).$$

(iii) Leave the rest of the first counter unchanged:

$$copy(\lceil q\rceil^1 \,;\, \lceil B\rceil \,;\, \lceil C_1\rceil \,;\, \lceil B\rceil, \{B, C_1\}).$$

(iv) Leave the second counter unchanged:

$$copy(\lceil q\rceil^1 \,;\, \lceil B \vee C_1\rceil^1 \,;\, \lceil X\rceil^1, \{B, C_2\}).$$

Analogously, we express increment and decrement commands for the second counter.

Since no command starts in the final state q_{fin}, we force the observable obs to repeat the final configuration ad infinitum. This is expressed by the DC formula

$$copy(\lceil q_{\text{fin}}\rceil^1 \,;\, \lceil B \vee C_1\rceil^1 \,;\, \lceil X\rceil^1 \,;\, \lceil B \vee C_2\rceil^1, \{q_{\text{fin}}, B, X, C_1, C_2\}.$$

Let $encoding(\mathcal{M})$ denote the conjunction of all these DC formulas. Then $encoding(\mathcal{M})$ is a DC formula with one observable, obs, and without free global variables. It encodes the behaviour of the two-counter machine $\mathcal{M}$ in the following sense: each interpretation realising $encoding(\mathcal{M})$ from 0 represents the (diverging or halting) computation of $\mathcal{M}$ such that the following equivalence result holds:

$$\mathcal{M} \text{ diverges} \quad \text{iff} \quad \text{the DC formula}$$
$$encoding(\mathcal{M}) \wedge \neg\Diamond \lceil q_{\text{fin}}\rceil$$
$$\text{is realisable from 0.}$$

Since the divergence of two-counter machines is undecidable, not even semi-decidable, we obtain the following result:

Theorem 3.10
The realisability problem for the Duration Calculus with continuous time is undecidable, not even semi-decidable.

Following Zhou and Hansen [ZH04] we can also observe that

$$\mathcal{M} \text{ halts} \quad \text{iff} \quad \text{the DC formula} \qquad\qquad (3.1)$$
$$encoding(\mathcal{M}) \wedge \diamond \lceil q_{\text{fin}} \rceil$$
$$\text{is satisfiable.}$$

This yields the following theorem:

Theorem 3.11
The satisfiability problem for the Duration Calculus with continuous time is undecidable.

With a rather elaborate proof that is beyond the scope of this chapter it can be shown that the satisfiability problem for the Duration Calculus is semi-decidable. Further on, by taking the contraposition of equivalence (3.1), we obtain

$$\mathcal{M} \text{ diverges} \quad \text{iff} \quad \mathcal{M} \text{ does } not \text{ halt}$$
$$\text{iff} \quad \text{the DC formula}$$
$$encoding(\mathcal{M}) \wedge \diamond \lceil q_{\text{fin}} \rceil$$
$$\text{is } not \text{ satisfiable.}$$

Thus the problem of whether a DC formula is *not satisfiable* is undecidable, not even semi-decidable. Since by Remark 2.13, a DC formula F is valid iff $\neg F$ is not satisfiable, we obtain the following corollary of Theorem 3.11:

Corollary 3.12
The validity problem for the Duration Calculus with continuous time is undecidable, not even semi-decidable.

This corollary provides us with an alternative proof of Theorem 2.23: there is no sound and complete calculus $\mathcal{C}$ for DC formulas. *Suppose* there is such a calculus $\mathcal{C}$. By Lemma 2.22, it is semi-decidable whether a given DC formula F is a theorem in $\mathcal{C}$. By the soundness and completeness of $\mathcal{C}$, a formula F is a theorem in $\mathcal{C}$ iff F is valid. Thus it is semi-decidable whether a given DC formula F is valid. *Contradiction.*

Discussion

An analysis of the above reduction shows that we did not exploit all constructs of the Duration Calculus. In fact the subset of DC formulas defined by the following abstract syntax suffices for the reduction:

$$F ::= \lceil P \rceil \mid \neg F_1 \mid F_1 \vee F_2 \mid F_1 \,;\, F_2 \mid \ell = 1 \mid \ell = x \mid \forall x \bullet F_1,$$

where P is a state assertion involving observables ranging over a finite data domain and x is a global variable.

Note that in this subset further formulas used in the reduction can be expressed as abbreviations:

$$\ell = 4 \quad\Longleftrightarrow\quad \ell = 1 \,;\, \ell = 1 \,;\, \ell = 1 \,;\, \ell = 1,$$
$$\ell \geq 4 \quad\Longleftrightarrow\quad \ell = 4 \,;\, \mathsf{true},$$
$$\ell = x + y + 4 \quad\Longleftrightarrow\quad \ell = x \,;\, \ell = y \,;\, \ell = 4.$$

Of course, the logical connectives $\wedge, \Longrightarrow, \Longleftrightarrow$, and the quantifier $\exists$ can also be considered as abbreviations.

Even the formula $\ell = 1$ can be dropped in the above subset because instead of the unit length 1 we may use any positive time z. Thus we may replace the formula $encoding(\mathcal{M})$ by

$$\exists z \bullet encoding^z(\mathcal{M}),$$

where $encoding^z(\mathcal{M})$ results from $encoding(\mathcal{M})$ by first using the above abbreviations and then replacing every occurrence of $\ell = 1$ by $\ell = z$ for a fresh global variable z. Note that this subset is the Restricted Duration Calculus of Subsection 3.1.1 augmented by $\ell = x$ and $\forall x$, which we abbreviate by RDC + $\ell = x, \forall x$.

The following table gives an overview of the results on decidability and undecidability of the satisfiability problem for subsets of the Duration Calculus obtained by Zhou, Hansen, and Sestoft [ZHS93, ZH04]. We use suggestive abbreviations for the subsets. In the table r is a constant.

Subset	Discrete time	Continuous time
RDC	decidable*	decidable
RDC + $\ell = r$	decidable for $r \in \mathbb{N}$	undecidable for $r \in \mathbb{R}_{>0}$
RDC + $\int P_1 = \int P_2$	undecidable	undecidable
RDC + $\ell = x, \forall x$	undecidable	undecidable*

In this book we have shown the results marked *.

3.2 Implementables

In this section we introduce the notion of control automata which are closer
to implementations of real-time systems. Control automata are equipped
with a real-time semantics that is described by a collection of DC formulas
taken from the subset of so-called DC implementables due to A.P. Ravn.
Having a semantics in DC eases correctness proofs that control automata
satisfy their requirements, which are also given as DC formulas.

A *system of k control automata* describes the behaviour of k state variables
$X_1, \ldots, X_k$ ranging over finite data domains $D_1, \ldots, D_k$, respectively. A
state assertion of the ith control automaton that constrains the values of X_i
is called a phase. More precisely, a *basic phase of* X_i is a state assertion of
the form

$$X_i = d_i \text{ with } d_i \in D_i,$$

and a *phase of* X_i is a Boolean combination of basic phases of X_i.

Example 3.13
Let $d_{i_1}, d_{i_2} \in D_i$. Then $X_i = d_{i_1} \vee X_i = d_{i_2}$ is a phase of X_i. ∎

We use the following abbreviations for phases:

- If X_i is a Boolean state variable and thus $D_i = \{0, 1\}$ we write

$$X_i \quad \text{for the basic phase} \quad X_i = 1$$

  (as in Subsection 2.2.2). Hence, the following equivalences hold:

$$\neg X_i \iff \neg(X_i = 1) \iff X_i = 0.$$

- If D_i is disjoint from all D_j with $i \neq j$, we write

$$d_i \quad \text{for the basic phase} \quad X_i = d_i,$$

  where $d_i \in D_i$.

Example 3.14
We model a gas burner implementation as a system of four control automata,
represented by the following state variables:

- a Boolean state variable H representing *heat request*,
- a Boolean state variable F representing the *flame*,
- a state variable C ranging over $\{\mathsf{idle}, \mathsf{purge}, \mathsf{ignite}, \mathsf{burn}\}$ representing the
  controller, and
- a Boolean state variable G representing the *gas valve*.

The untimed transition behaviour of the state variables H, F, C, and G is given by the following transition diagrams of their basic phases:

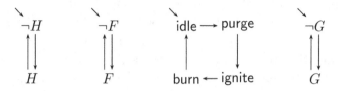

The initial phase of each control automaton is marked by an incoming edge. The four control automata behave independently from each other except for certain real-time constraints of these phases that will be specified in the sequel by DC implementables. From the viewpoint of the controller C, the state variables H and F are inputs and G is an output, i.e. controllable by C.   ■

Standard forms. DC implementables make use of so-called *standard forms* of the Duration Calculus, which we introduce now as abbreviations of certain patterns of formulas. In the following let F be a DC formula, P be a state assertion, and θ a *rigid* DC term.

- **Followed-by:**

$$F \longrightarrow \lceil P \rceil \overset{\text{def}}{\Longleftrightarrow} \neg\diamond(F\,;\lceil\neg P\rceil) \Longleftrightarrow \Box\neg(F\,;\lceil\neg P\rceil).$$

This definition uses a formula with a double negation, which is difficult to understand. It is equivalent to the following formula with a modal operator $\Box$ and a quantifier over a length restriction:

$$\forall x \bullet \Box((F \wedge \ell = x)\,;\ell > 0) \Longrightarrow$$
$$(F \wedge \ell = x)\,;\lceil P \rceil\,;\text{true})).$$

Thus $F \longrightarrow \lceil P \rceil$ holds on an interval $[b, e]$ if every subinterval (of length x) where F holds is followed by an interval where P holds.

Visualisation:

$$F \longrightarrow \lceil P \rceil$$

We use the followed-by operator to describe the transition behaviour of control automata. For instance, the formula

$$\lceil \mathsf{idle} \rceil \longrightarrow \lceil \mathsf{idle} \vee \mathsf{purge} \rceil$$

expresses that whenever the controller of Example 3.14 is in the idle phase, it subsequently stays in this phase or moves to the purge phase.

- **Followed-by-initially:**

$$F \longrightarrow_0 \lceil P \rceil \overset{\mathrm{def}}{\Longleftrightarrow} \neg(F \,; \lceil \neg P \rceil).$$

In contrast to $F \longrightarrow \lceil P \rceil$, no modal operator is used in the definition of this variant of the followed-by operator. It is equivalent to the following formula without modal operator $\Box$ but with a quantifier over a length restriction:

$$\forall x \bullet ((F \wedge \ell = x)\,;\ell > 0) \Longrightarrow$$
$$(F \wedge \ell = x)\,; \lceil P \rceil \,; \mathsf{true})).$$

It will be interpreted on initial intervals $[0, e]$. Thus $F \longrightarrow_0 \lceil P \rceil$ holds on $[0, e]$ if every initial subinterval (of length x) where F holds is followed by an interval where P holds.

Visualisation:

- **(Timed) leads-to:**

$$F \overset{\theta}{\longrightarrow} \lceil P \rceil \overset{\mathrm{def}}{\Longleftrightarrow} (F \wedge \ell = \theta) \longrightarrow \lceil P \rceil.$$

Intuitively, the formula $F \overset{\theta}{\longrightarrow} \lceil P \rceil$ holds on an interval $[b, e]$ if every subinterval where F holds for a duration of θ is followed by an interval where P holds.

Visualisation:

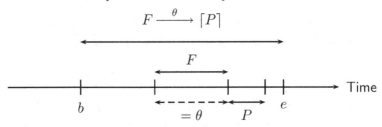

With the leads-to operator we can describe time restrictions for transitions of control automata. For instance, the formula

$$\lceil \mathsf{purge} \rceil \xrightarrow{\;30+\varepsilon\;} \lceil \neg\mathsf{purge} \rceil$$

requires the controller of Example 3.14 to leave the **purge** phase after at most $30 + \varepsilon$ time units. Similarly, we can express *synchronisation constraints* of different control automata. For instance, the formula

$$\lceil \mathsf{burn} \wedge (\neg H \vee \neg F) \rceil \xrightarrow{\;\varepsilon\;} \lceil \neg\mathsf{burn} \rceil$$

forces the controller to leave the **burn** phase if there is no heat request or no flame $(\neg H \vee \neg F)$ for a period of ε time units.

- **(Timed) up-to:**

$$F \xrightarrow{\;\leq\theta\;} \lceil P \rceil \overset{\text{def}}{\Longleftrightarrow} (F \wedge \ell \leq \theta) \longrightarrow \lceil P \rceil \,.$$

Intuitively, the formula $F \xrightarrow{\;\leq\theta\;} \lceil P \rceil$ holds on an interval $[b,e]$ if every subinterval where F holds for a duration of up to θ is followed by an interval where P holds.

Visualisation:

$$F \xrightarrow{\;\leq\theta\;} \lceil P \rceil$$

We shall use the up-to operator (in combination with the chop operator) to describe the *stability* of phases. For instance, the formula

$$\lceil \neg\mathsf{purge} \rceil \;;\; \lceil \mathsf{purge} \rceil \xrightarrow{\;\leq 30\;} \lceil \mathsf{purge} \rceil$$

expresses that the controller of Example 3.14 has to keep the **purge** phase stable for at least 30 time units. We stipulate that standard forms have the least priority. Thus ; binds stronger than $\xrightarrow{\leq 30}$ in this formula.

- **(Timed) up-to-initially:**

$$F \xrightarrow{\leq \theta}_0 \lceil P \rceil \overset{\text{def}}{\Longleftrightarrow} (F \wedge \ell \leq \theta) \longrightarrow_0 \lceil P \rceil .$$

Intuitively, the formula $F \xrightarrow{\leq \theta}_0 \lceil P \rceil$ holds on an initial interval $[0, e]$ if every initial subinterval where F holds for a duration of up to θ is followed by an interval where P holds.

Visualisation:

This variant of the up-to operator can be used to express initial stability requirements.

- **Initial phases:** To specify that P is the initial phase of a control automaton, we write

$$\lceil \rceil \vee \lceil P \rceil \text{ ; true.}$$

Recall that ; binds stronger than $\vee$. Intuitively, this formula holds on an initial interval $[0, e]$ if this interval is either empty or it starts with a non-empty subinterval where P holds.

Visualisation:

For instance, the formula

$$\lceil \rceil \vee \lceil \text{idle} \rceil \text{ ; true}$$

expresses that the controller of Example 3.14 has idle as its initial phase.

DC implementables. Equipped with these standard forms, we now introduce *DC implementables*, a subset of the Duration Calculus defined by A.P. Ravn. Implementables are certain patterns of DC formulas that are well suited for specifying the behaviour of control automata. In each of the following patterns the letters $\pi, \pi_1, \ldots, \pi_n$ with $n \geq 0$ denote phases of the *same* state variable X_i, the letter φ denotes a state assertion that does not depend on X_i, and the letter θ denotes a rigid DC term. Of course, different patterns can constrain different state variables.

- *Initialisation*:

$$\lceil\rceil \vee \lceil \pi \rceil \text{ ; true.}$$

This pattern expresses that initially, the control automaton is in phase π. Formally, each observation interval is either empty or starts with π.

- *Sequencing*:

$$\lceil \pi \rceil \longrightarrow \lceil \pi \vee \pi_1 \vee \ldots \vee \pi_n \rceil.$$

This pattern expresses that when the control automaton is in phase π it subsequently stays in π or moves to one of the phases $\pi_1, \ldots, \pi_n$.

- *Progress*:

$$\lceil \pi \rceil \xrightarrow{\theta} \lceil \neg\pi \rceil.$$

This pattern expresses that after the control automaton stayed for θ seconds in phase π, it subsequently leaves this phase and thus progresses.

- *Synchronisation*:

$$\lceil \pi \wedge \varphi \rceil \xrightarrow{\theta} \lceil \neg\pi \rceil.$$

This pattern expresses more generally that after the control automaton stayed for θ seconds in phase π, with the condition φ being true, it subsequently leaves this phase.

- *Bounded stability*:

$$\lceil \neg\pi \rceil \text{ ; } \lceil \pi \wedge \varphi \rceil \xrightarrow{\leq\theta} \lceil \pi \vee \pi_1 \vee \ldots \vee \pi_n \rceil.$$

This pattern expresses that when the control automaton changed its phase to π with the condition φ being true and the time since this change not exceeding θ seconds, it subsequently stays in π (i.e. π is stable) or it moves to one of the phases $\pi_1, \ldots, \pi_n$.

- *Unbounded stability*:

$$\lceil \neg\pi \rceil \text{ ; } \lceil \pi \wedge \varphi \rceil \longrightarrow \lceil \pi \vee \pi_1 \vee \ldots \vee \pi_n \rceil.$$

This pattern expresses that when the control automaton changed its phase to π with the condition φ being true, it subsequently stays in π or moves to one of the phases $\pi_1, \ldots, \pi_n$.

- *Bounded initial stability*:

$$\lceil \pi \wedge \varphi \rceil \xrightarrow{\leq \theta}_0 \lceil \pi \vee \pi_1 \vee \ldots \vee \pi_n \rceil .$$

This pattern expresses bounded stability of an initial phase π, i.e. when the control automaton initially is in phase π with the condition φ being true and the time since this change not exceeding θ seconds, it subsequently stays in π or moves to one of the phases $\pi_1, \ldots, \pi_n$.

- *Unbounded initial stability*:

$$\lceil \pi \wedge \varphi \rceil \longrightarrow_0 \lceil \pi \vee \pi_1 \vee \ldots \vee \pi_n \rceil .$$

This pattern expresses unbounded stability of an initial phase π, i.e. when the control automaton initially is in phase π with the condition φ being true, it subsequently stays in π or moves to one of the phases $\pi_1, \ldots, \pi_n$.

3.2.1 A controller for the gas burner

To specify the time-dependent behaviour of the control automata for C, H, F, and G we take a global variable ε representing a parameter for reaction time and introduce the implementables shown in Table 3.1.

Let GB-Ctrl denote the conjunction of all implementables above and the formula $\varepsilon > 0$:

$$\text{GB-Ctrl} \stackrel{\text{def}}{\Longleftrightarrow} \text{Init-1} \wedge \ldots \wedge \text{Stab-7} \wedge \varepsilon > 0.$$

Then GB-Ctrl is a DC formula with the free global variable ε and the observables C, H, F, and G. It specifies all interpretations $\mathcal{I}$ and valuations $\mathcal{V}$ of ε that realise GB-Ctrl from 0, i.e. with

$$\mathcal{I}, \mathcal{V} \models_0 \text{GB-Ctrl}.$$

Note that the implementables Init-1, $\ldots$, Seq-4 specify the (untimed) transition diagrams of the observables C, H, F, and G, as shown in Example 3.14. Informally, the specified behaviour of the controller C is as follows. Initially, the controller of the gas burner is in the idle phase (Init-1), and heat request, flame, and gas are all switched off ($\neg H, \neg F, \neg G$ due to Init-2, Init-3, Init-4). If no heat request occurs ($\neg H$), the controller stays in the idle phase (Stab-1 and Stab-1-Init). By Stab-5, Stab-5-Init and Stab-6, Stab-6-Init, the flame and the gas remain switched off in this phase. If a heat request occurs (H),

Init-1:	$\lceil\rceil \vee \lceil idle\rceil$; true,		
Init-2:	$\lceil\rceil \vee \lceil\neg H\rceil$; true,		
Init-3:	$\lceil\rceil \vee \lceil\neg F\rceil$; true,		
Init-4:	$\lceil\rceil \vee \lceil\neg G\rceil$; true,		
Seq-1:	$\lceil idle\rceil$	$\longrightarrow$	$\lceil idle \vee purge\rceil$,
Seq-2:	$\lceil purge\rceil$	$\longrightarrow$	$\lceil purge \vee ignite\rceil$,
Seq-3:	$\lceil ignite\rceil$	$\longrightarrow$	$\lceil ignite \vee burn\rceil$,
Seq-4:	$\lceil burn\rceil$	$\longrightarrow$	$\lceil burn \vee idle\rceil$,
Prog-1:	$\lceil purge\rceil$	$\xrightarrow{30+\varepsilon}$	$\lceil\neg purge\rceil$,
Prog-2:	$\lceil ignite\rceil$	$\xrightarrow{0.5+\varepsilon}$	$\lceil\neg ignite\rceil$,
Syn-1:	$\lceil idle \wedge H\rceil$	$\xrightarrow{\varepsilon}$	$\lceil\neg idle\rceil$,
Syn-2:	$\lceil burn \wedge (\neg H \vee \neg F)\rceil$	$\xrightarrow{\varepsilon}$	$\lceil\neg burn\rceil$,
Syn-3:	$\lceil G \wedge (idle \vee purge)\rceil$	$\xrightarrow{\varepsilon}$	$\lceil\neg G\rceil$,
Syn-4:	$\lceil\neg G \wedge (ignite \vee burn)\rceil$	$\xrightarrow{\varepsilon}$	$\lceil G\rceil$,
Stab-1:	$\lceil\neg idle\rceil$; $\lceil idle \wedge \neg H\rceil$	$\longrightarrow$	$\lceil idle\rceil$,
Stab-1-init:	$\lceil idle \wedge \neg H\rceil$	$\longrightarrow_0$	$\lceil idle\rceil$,
Stab-2:	$\lceil\neg purge\rceil$; $\lceil purge\rceil$	$\xrightarrow{\leq 30}$	$\lceil purge\rceil$,
Stab-3:	$\lceil\neg ignite\rceil$; $\lceil ignite\rceil$	$\xrightarrow{\leq 0.5}$	$\lceil ignite\rceil$,
Stab-4:	$\lceil\neg burn\rceil$; $\lceil burn \wedge H \wedge F\rceil$	$\longrightarrow$	$\lceil burn\rceil$,
Stab-5:	$\lceil F\rceil$; $\lceil\neg F \wedge \neg ignite\rceil$	$\longrightarrow$	$\lceil\neg F\rceil$,
Stab-5-init:	$\lceil\neg F \wedge \neg ignite\rceil$	$\longrightarrow_0$	$\lceil\neg F\rceil$,
Stab-6:	$\lceil G\rceil$; $\lceil\neg G \wedge (idle \vee purge)\rceil$	$\longrightarrow$	$\lceil\neg G\rceil$,
Stab-6-init:	$\lceil\neg G \wedge (idle \vee purge)\rceil$	$\longrightarrow_0$	$\lceil\neg G\rceil$,
Stab-7:	$\lceil\neg G\rceil$; $\lceil G \wedge (ignite \vee burn)\rceil$	$\longrightarrow$	$\lceil G\rceil$.

Table 3.1. *Implementables specifying the gas burner controller*

the controller leaves the idle phase (Syn-1). By Seq-1, the new phase is the purge phase. The design idea of the controller is that the purge phase takes some time, here 30 seconds due to Stab-2, to let gas evaporate. When 30 seconds are elapsed the controller can leave the purge phase. After at most $30 + \varepsilon$ seconds this transition has been performed (Prog-1). The summand ε takes care of the reaction time of the controller, which in reality is non-zero. By Seq-2, the new phase is the ignite phase. In this phase the gas valve is opened (Syn-4) and the flowing gas is ignited so that a flame appears. However, we cannot force the flame to appear because a flame failure may occur and thus gas may leak. To increase the chance for a proper ignition, the ignite phase takes some period, here 0.5 seconds due to Stab-3, and is left after at most $0.5 + \varepsilon$ seconds (Prog-2) to the burn phase (Seq-3). The burn phase is stable as long as the heat request and the flame continue to be on (Stab-4), and the gas valve is kept open in this phase (Stab-7). As soon as the heat request is switched off or the flame disappears the burn phase is left (Syn-2) for the idle phase (Seq-4). Here the controller cycle starts again. In both the idle phase and the purge phase the gas valve is closed (Syn-3).

3.2.2 Correctness proof

In this subsection we derive a sufficient condition for the reaction time ε which ensures that the controller for the gas burner is correct w.r.t. the safety requirement

$$\text{Req} \iff \Box(\ell \geq 60 \implies 20 \cdot \int L \leq \ell)$$

introduced in Subsection 2.3.1. Recall that the state assertion $L \overset{\text{def}}{\iff} G \wedge \neg F$ represents the gas leak. In Lemma 2.17 we proved

$$\models \text{Req-1} \implies \text{Req}$$

for the simplified requirement

$$\text{Req-1} \overset{\text{def}}{\iff} \Box(\ell \leq 30 \implies \int L \leq 1).$$

Here we show, for a certain condition $A(\varepsilon)$ on the values of ε, the validity

$$\models (\text{GB-Ctrl} \wedge A(\varepsilon)) \implies \text{Req-1}.$$

First, we prove upper bounds for the durations of the constituents G and $\neg F$ of L in the individual phases of the gas burner controller.

Lemma 3.15

$$\models \text{GB-Ctrl} \implies \Box \left(\begin{array}{ccc} (\lceil \text{idle} \rceil & \implies & \int G \leq \varepsilon) \\ \wedge \ (\lceil \text{purge} \rceil & \implies & \int G \leq \varepsilon) \\ \wedge \ (\lceil \text{ignite} \rceil & \implies & \ell \leq 0.5 + \varepsilon) \\ \wedge \ (\lceil \text{burn} \rceil & \implies & \int \neg F \leq 2 \cdot \varepsilon) \end{array} \right).$$

Proof:
Consider an interpretation $\mathcal{I}$, a valuation $\mathcal{V}$, and an interval $[b, e]$ with $\mathcal{I}, \mathcal{V}, [c, d] \models \text{GB-Ctrl}$. We have to show that for this choice of $\mathcal{I}, \mathcal{V}, [c, d]$ the right-hand side of the implication holds. To this end, take an arbitrary subinterval $[b, e]$ of $[c, d]$, i.e. with $c \leq b \leq e \leq d$. We distinguish four cases corresponding to the four phases of the controller.

Case 1: $\mathcal{I}, \mathcal{V}, [b, e] \models \lceil \text{idle} \rceil$.
Due to (Syn-3) and (Stab-6) we can conclude

$$\mathcal{I}, \mathcal{V}, [b, e] \models \Box(\lceil G \rceil \Longrightarrow \ell \leq \varepsilon)$$
$$\wedge \neg \Diamond(\lceil G \rceil \; ; \; \lceil \neg G \rceil \; ; \; \lceil G \rceil),$$

i.e. during an idle phase there is *at most one* G-phase and the duration of this G-phase is at most ε. Thus

$$\mathcal{I}, \mathcal{V}, [b, e] \models \int G \leq \varepsilon.$$

Case 2: $\mathcal{I}, \mathcal{V}, [b, e] \models \lceil \text{purge} \rceil$.
This case is shown analogously to Case 1, again by considering (Syn-3) and (Stab-6).

Case 3: $\mathcal{I}, \mathcal{V}, [b, e] \models \lceil \text{ignite} \rceil$.
With (Prog-2) we can conclude

$$\mathcal{I}, \mathcal{V}, [b, e] \models \ell \leq 0.5 + \varepsilon.$$

Case 4: $\mathcal{I}, \mathcal{V}, [b, e] \models \lceil \text{burn} \rceil$.
By (Syn-2) and (Stab-5), the following holds:

$$\mathcal{I}, \mathcal{V}, [b, e] \models \Box(\lceil \neg F \rceil \Longrightarrow \ell \leq \varepsilon)$$
$$\wedge \neg \Diamond(\lceil F \rceil \; ; \; \lceil \neg F \rceil \; ; \; \lceil F \rceil),$$

i.e. during a burn phase each $\neg F$-phase has a maximum duration of ε, and there are at most *two* $\neg F$-phases. Hence, we have

$$\mathcal{I}, \mathcal{V}, [b, e] \models \int \neg F \leq 2 \cdot \varepsilon$$

in this case. $\Box$

Now we can show the following lemma:

Lemma 3.16

$$\models \exists \varepsilon \bullet \text{GB-Ctrl} \Longrightarrow \text{Req-1}.$$

Proof:
Consider an interpretation $\mathcal{I}$, a valuation $\mathcal{V}$, and an interval $[b, e]$ with $\mathcal{I}, \mathcal{V}, [c, d] \models \text{GB-Ctrl}$. We shall derive a sufficient condition for ε such that $\mathcal{I}, \mathcal{V}, [c, d] \models \text{Req-1}$ holds. To this end, take a subinterval $[b, e]$ of $[c, d]$ of length $e - b \leq 30$. We have to show

$$\mathcal{I}, \mathcal{V}, [b, e] \models \int L \leq 1$$

for a suitable condition $A(\varepsilon)$ for ε. Due to the finite variability and the domain of the controller observable C it is clear that

$$\mathcal{I}, \mathcal{V}, [b, e] \models \quad \lceil\rceil$$
$$\vee \quad (\lceil \mathsf{idle} \rceil \; ; \mathsf{true} \quad \wedge \ell \le 30)$$
$$\vee \quad (\lceil \mathsf{purge} \rceil \; ; \mathsf{true} \quad \wedge \ell \le 30)$$
$$\vee \quad (\lceil \mathsf{ignite} \rceil \; ; \mathsf{true} \quad \wedge \ell \le 30)$$
$$\vee \quad (\lceil \mathsf{burn} \rceil \; ; \mathsf{true} \quad \wedge \ell \le 30)$$

holds. Following this disjunction we distinguish five cases, but proceed "backwards" by considering the phases in the order idle, burn, ignite, purge.

Case 0: $\mathcal{I}, \mathcal{V}, [b, e] \models \lceil\rceil$.
Then $\mathcal{I}, \mathcal{V}, [b, e] \models \int L \le 1$ is trivially true.

Case 1: $\mathcal{I}, \mathcal{V}, [b, e] \models \lceil \mathsf{idle} \rceil \; ; \mathsf{true} \wedge \ell \le 30$.
Due to (Seq-1) and (Stab-2), the following holds:

$$\mathcal{I}, \mathcal{V}, [b, e] \models \lceil \mathsf{idle} \rceil \vee \lceil \mathsf{idle} \rceil \; ; \lceil \mathsf{purge} \rceil \,.$$

By Lemma 3.15, we can conclude

$$\mathcal{I}, \mathcal{V}, [b, e] \models \int L \le \varepsilon \vee \int L \le \varepsilon \,; \int L \le \varepsilon,$$

which we can simplify to

$$\mathcal{I}, \mathcal{V}, [b, e] \models \int L \le 2 \cdot \varepsilon.$$

Therefore, $\boxed{\varepsilon \le 0.5}$ is sufficient for achieving Req-1 in this case.

Case 2: $\mathcal{I}, \mathcal{V}, [b, e] \models \lceil \mathsf{burn} \rceil \; ; \mathsf{true} \wedge \ell \le 30$.
By (Seq-4), the following holds:

$$\mathcal{I}, \mathcal{V}, [b, e] \models (\lceil \mathsf{burn} \rceil \vee (\lceil \mathsf{burn} \rceil \; ; \lceil \mathsf{idle} \rceil \; ; \mathsf{true})) \wedge \ell \le 30.$$

By Lemma 3.15 and the conclusions in Case 1, we can conclude

$$\mathcal{I}, \mathcal{V}, [b, e] \models (\int L \le 2 \cdot \varepsilon \vee (\int L \le 2 \cdot \varepsilon \,; \int L \le 2 \cdot \varepsilon)) \wedge \ell \le 30,$$

which we can simplify to

$$\mathcal{I}, \mathcal{V}, [b, e] \models \int L \le 4 \cdot \varepsilon.$$

Therefore, $\boxed{\varepsilon \le 0.25}$ is sufficient for achieving Req-1 in this case.

Case 3: $\mathcal{I}, \mathcal{V}, [b, e] \models \lceil \text{ignite} \rceil \,; \text{true} \wedge \ell \leq 30.$
Due to (Seq-3), the following holds:

$$\mathcal{I}, \mathcal{V}, [b, e] \models (\lceil \text{ignite} \rceil \vee (\lceil \text{ignite} \rceil \,; \lceil \text{burn} \rceil \,; \text{true})) \wedge \ell \leq 30.$$

By Lemma 3.15 and the conclusions in Case 2, we can conclude

$$\mathcal{I}, \mathcal{V}, [b, e] \models (\textstyle\int L \leq 0.5 + \varepsilon \vee (\textstyle\int L \leq 0.5 + \varepsilon \,; \textstyle\int L \leq 4 \cdot \varepsilon),$$

which we can simplify to

$$\mathcal{I}, \mathcal{V}, [b, e] \models \textstyle\int L \leq 0.5 + 5 \cdot \varepsilon.$$

Therefore, $\boxed{\varepsilon \leq 0.1}$ is a sufficient condition for achieving **Req-1** in this case.

Case 4: $\mathcal{I}, \mathcal{V}, [b, e] \models \lceil \text{purge} \rceil \,; \text{true} \wedge \ell \leq 30.$
By (Seq-2), the following holds:

$$\mathcal{I}, \mathcal{V}, [b, e] \models (\lceil \text{purge} \rceil \vee (\lceil \text{purge} \rceil \,; \lceil \text{ignite} \rceil \,; \text{true})) \wedge \ell \leq 30.$$

By Lemma 3.15 and the conclusions in Case 3, we can conclude

$$\mathcal{I}, \mathcal{V}, [b, e] \models \textstyle\int L \leq \varepsilon \vee (\textstyle\int L \leq \varepsilon \,; \textstyle\int L \leq 0.5 + 5 \cdot \varepsilon),$$

which we can simplify to

$$\mathcal{I}, \mathcal{V}, [b, e] \models \textstyle\int L \leq 0.5 + 6 \cdot \varepsilon.$$

Therefore, $\boxed{\varepsilon \leq \frac{1}{12}}$ is sufficient for achieving **Req-1** in this case.

The following diagram visualises the arguments of this proof. The phases of **GB-Ctrl** are shown with their lengths (if known) and with proven upper bounds of the duration $\int L$. Then in any observation interval $[b, e]$ of length $\ell \leq 30$ the overall duration $\int L$ is at most 1 provided $\varepsilon \leq \frac{1}{12}$ holds.

purge	ignite	burn	idle	purge
$\leftarrow \ell \geq 30 \rightarrow$	$\leftarrow \ell \geq 0.5 \rightarrow$			$\leftarrow \ell \geq 30 \rightarrow$
$\int L \leq \varepsilon$	$\int L \leq 0.5 + \varepsilon$	$\int L \leq 2 \cdot \varepsilon$	$\int L \leq \varepsilon$	$\int L \leq \varepsilon$

b $\longleftarrow \ell \leq 30 \longrightarrow$ e

$\int L \leq 0.5 + 6 \cdot \varepsilon \leq 1$

Altogether, we proved that the condition

$$A(\varepsilon) \stackrel{\text{def}}{\Longleftrightarrow} \varepsilon \leq \frac{1}{12}$$

is sufficient for establishing $\models$ (GB-Ctrl $\wedge$ $A(\varepsilon)$) $\implies$ Req-1. □

Combining Lemma 2.17 and (the proof of) Lemma 3.16 we obtain the following theorem:

Theorem 3.17
The correctness result

$$\models \left(\text{GB-Ctrl} \wedge \varepsilon \leq \frac{1}{12} \right) \implies \text{Req}$$

holds.

An immediate consequence of the theorem is that

$$\mathcal{I}, \mathcal{V} \models_0 \text{GB-Ctrl} \wedge \varepsilon \leq \frac{1}{12} \quad \text{implies} \quad \mathcal{I}, \mathcal{V} \models_0 \text{Req}$$

for all interpretations $\mathcal{I}$ and all valuations $\mathcal{V}$, i.e. all $\mathcal{I}$ and $\mathcal{V}$ that realise GB-Ctrl $\wedge$ $\varepsilon \leq \frac{1}{12}$ from 0 also realise Req from 0.

Discussion

In the correctness proof of GB-Ctrl we used only a subset of its implementables, i.e.

Seq-1, Seq-2, Seq-3, Seq-4,

Prog-2, Syn-2, Syn-3,

Stab-2, Stab-5, Stab-6.

Thus also a controller without the constraint Prog-1, forcing it to leave the purge phase, satisfies Req. Indeed, such a controller would switch off the gas in the idle phase and the purge phase within ε time and then never turn it on again. However, this controller would not satisfy a customer who wants a warm room. The implementable Prog-1 is needed as soon as we consider the utility requirement "Upon a heat request H, the controller should turn on the gas valve G" (see Exercise 3.8).

In Subsection 2.3.1 we introduced two design decisions Des-1 (every leak phase L lasts at most 1 second) and Des-2 (every non-leak phase $\neg L$ lasts more than 30 seconds), and showed that together they imply Req-1 and thus Req. The question arises whether they are implied by GB-Ctrl? Due to Remark 2.33 we know that Req-1 implies Des-1. Consequently, also GB-Ctrl implies Des-1. By contrast, GB-Ctrl *does not* imply Des-2. For example, GB-Ctrl does not prevent that during a burn phase a $\neg L$-phase ends. This happens when a *flame failure* occurs, where the flame suddenly vanishes.

3.3 Constraint Diagrams

When discussing and formalising the requirements of a system, application experts and computer science experts have to come to an agreement. The direct use of logic is often claimed to be an obstacle for engineers. Therefore graphical notations for specifying behavioural properties have been developed. In this section we present a graphical language which is inspired by timing diagrams that are used to describe the behaviour of hardware components (cf. Figure 1.6): the *Constraint Diagrams* (CDs for short) introduced by C. Kleuker for the specification of real-time requirements. Since the formal semantics of Constraint Diagrams is given in terms of the Duration Calculus, these diagrams can be integrated seamlessly into a design process based on the Duration Calculus. To give a first idea of Constraint Diagrams we discuss an example.

Example 3.18 (Watchdog)

A *watchdog* is a real-time system that observes a Boolean input signal S. If S does not hold for a period of 10 seconds, an alarm signal A should be raised within 1 second. To model this system we consider two Boolean observables S and A. The desired timing behaviour of these observables can be specified by the following Constraint Diagram:

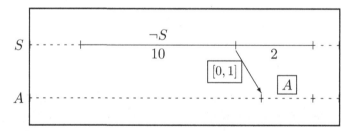

The two horizontal lines describe the behaviour of S and A in isolation. The arrow establishes a link between S and A. Semantically, a Constraint Diagram $\mathcal{C}$ represents an implication in an *assumption/commitment style*: if the *assumptions* of $\mathcal{C}$ hold then also the *commitments* of $\mathcal{C}$ hold. In the diagram above the assumption is that we see *no* signal ($\neg S$) for a duration of 10 seconds and wait 2 more seconds. Then the commitment is that an alarm is raised (A) at most 1 second after the 10 seconds where $\neg S$ holds. The extra 2 seconds in the assumption guarantee that we will observe the alarm A. The boxes around A and $[0, 1]$ indicate that these are commitments whereas the remaining parts are all assumptions. The dashed parts of the lines represent arbitrary behaviour of S and A.

Formally, the semantics of a Constraint Diagram will be defined in terms of the Duration Calculus. For the watchdog example, the intended implication is expressed by the following formula:

$$\forall \varepsilon \bullet (\ell = \varepsilon \,;\, (\lceil \neg S \rceil \wedge \ell = 10) \,;\, \ell = 2 \,;\, \mathsf{true} \tag{3.2}$$

$$\Longrightarrow \exists \delta \bullet (\ell = \delta \,;\, \lceil A \rceil \,;\, \mathsf{true} \tag{3.3}$$

$$\wedge\, \delta - (\varepsilon + 10) \in [0, 1])). \tag{3.4}$$

The formula uses two quantified global variables ε and δ as parameters for the unknown durations of the first phases of S and A. Line (3.2) formalises the assumption part: after ε seconds $\neg S$ holds for 10 seconds and at least 2 more seconds follow. The lines (3.3) and (3.4) formalise the commitment part of the diagram. Line (3.3) expresses that the alarm A is raised after δ seconds. In line (3.4) the meaning of the arrow is formalised by constraining the corresponding durations: the time δ (when the alarm is raised) is at most 1 second more than $\varepsilon + 10$ (when $\neg S$ holds for 10 seconds). The additional 2 seconds after $\neg S$ imply that $\varepsilon + 10 + 2 \geq \delta$ holds so that there is sufficient time to observe the alarm A.

For the watchdog we stipulate that initially S holds. This can be specified by the following Constraint Diagram:

Here the assumption is trivial, i.e. equivalent to true. The commitment is that the signal S is present initially. The semantics of this Constraint Diagram is equivalent to the formula $\lceil \rceil \vee \lceil S \rceil \,;\, \mathsf{true}$. ∎

3.3.1 Syntax and semantics

In this subsection we explain the general structure ("syntax") and semantics of Constraint Diagrams. Throughout, we consider observables $X_1, \ldots, X_k$ with $k \geq 1$ and global variables taken from the set GVar. Let X, Y be different elements of $\{X_1, \ldots, X_k\}$.

A Constraint Diagram $\mathcal{C}$ for $X_1, \ldots, X_k$ displays for each observable $X \in \{X_1, \ldots, X_k\}$ a sequence of phases $ph_1^X, ph_2^X, \ldots, ph_{\#(X)}^X$ with $\#(X) \geq 1$ where subsequent phases are delimited by small vertical bars. Arrows may link the phase sequences of different observables. Let $ar_{i,j}^{X,Y}$ denote an arrow from the *start* of phase ph_i^X of X to the *end* of phase ph_j^Y of Y.

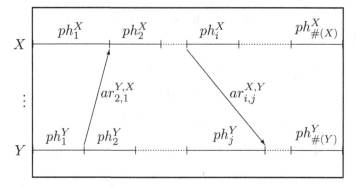

There are two mappings π and $\tilde{\pi}$ that assign to each phase ph_i^X:

- DC formulas $\pi(ph_i^X)$ and $\tilde{\pi}(ph_i^X)$ each of which is either true or a state assertion P about X, i.e.

$$P ::= 0 \mid 1 \mid X = d \mid \neg P \mid P_1 \wedge P_2,$$

where d belongs to the data type of X. For a Boolean observable X we abbreviate the basic property $X = 1$ to X. The other logical connectives $\vee$, $\Longrightarrow$, and $\Longleftrightarrow$ are considered as abbreviations. We write π_i^X and $\tilde{\pi}_i^X$ as shorthands for $\pi(ph_i^X)$ and $\tilde{\pi}(ph_i^X)$, respectively. The formula π_i^X represents an *assumption* and $\tilde{\pi}_i^X$ a *commitment*.

Furthermore, there are two mappings I and $\tilde{I}$ that assign to each phase ph_i^X and each arrow $ar_{i,j}^{X,Y}$:

- Non-empty time intervals $I(ph_i^X)$ and $\tilde{I}(ph_i^X)$ as well as $I(ar_{i,j}^{X,Y})$ and $\tilde{I}(ar_{i,j}^{X,Y})$. They may be open, half-open, or closed of the form (b, e) or $[b, e)$ with $b \in \mathsf{Time}$ and $e \in \mathsf{Time} \cup \{\infty\}$, and $(b, e]$ or $[b, e]$ with $b, e \in \mathsf{Time}$. Intervals (b, ∞) and $[b, \infty)$ denote the unbounded sets $\{t \in \mathsf{Time} \mid b < t\}$ and $\{t \in \mathsf{Time} \mid b \leq t\}$, respectively. The interval bounds b and e may also be given by rigid DC terms involving global variables. We write I_i^X and $I_{i,j}^{X,Y}$ as shorthands for $I(ph_i^X)$ and $I(ar_{i,j}^{X,Y})$, and $\tilde{I}_i^X$ and $\tilde{I}_{i,j}^{X,Y}$ as shorthands for $\tilde{I}(ph_i^X)$ and $\tilde{I}(ar_{i,j}^{X,Y})$, respectively. The intervals I_i^X and $I_{i,j}^{X,Y}$ represent timing *assumptions*, and $\tilde{I}_i^X$ and $\tilde{I}_{i,j}^{X,Y}$ timing *commitments*.

Graphically, a phase ph_i^X of X is represented as follows:

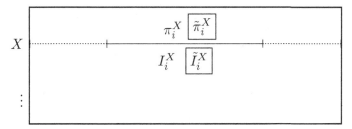

Unboxed state assertions describe *assumptions* whereas boxed state assertions are *commitments* constraining X. If $\pi_i^X = $ true this annotation is dropped and if $\tilde{\pi}_i^X = $ true this annotation together with the surrounding box are dropped. If $I_i^X = [0, \infty)$ the time interval is not shown and if $\tilde{I}_i^X = [0, \infty)$ the time interval and the surrounding box are not shown. If $\pi_i^X = $ true *and* $I_i^X = [0, \infty)$ both annotations are dropped and the phase ph_i^X is visualised as a *dashed line* (cf. the diagram of Example 3.18).

Graphically, an arrow $ar_{i,j}^{X,Y}$ is annotated with the interval $I_{i,j}^{X,Y}$ and the interval $\tilde{I}_{i,j}^{X,Y}$ inside a box.

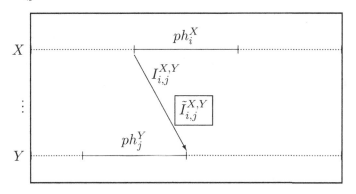

Unboxed intervals describe *assumptions* and boxed intervals *commitments*. If $I_{i,j}^{X,Y} = [0, \infty)$ the interval is not shown and if $\tilde{I}_{i,j}^{X,Y} = [0, \infty)$ the interval together with the surrounding box are not shown. Point intervals $[b, b]$ are abbreviated to the annotation b in the diagram.

The semantics of Constraint Diagrams will be expressed using two types of Duration Calculus formulas, called sequence and difference formulas.

Sequence formulas. The set of *sequence formulas*, with typical element *Sequ*, is defined by the following syntax:

$$Sequ ::= \ell = x \mid (\lceil P \rceil \wedge \ell = x) \mid Sequ_1 \, ; Sequ_2.$$

Here P is a state assertion and x is a global variable. A formula $(\lceil P \rceil \wedge \ell = x)$ represents a *(timed) phase*.

For sequence formulas we define the *prefix operator*, denoted by Pref, inductively as follows:

$$\mathsf{Pref}(\ell = x) \overset{\text{def}}{\Longleftrightarrow} \ell \leq x,$$

$$\mathsf{Pref}(\lceil P \rceil \wedge \ell = x) \overset{\text{def}}{\Longleftrightarrow} \lceil \rceil \vee (\lceil P \rceil \wedge \ell \leq x),$$

$$\mathsf{Pref}(Sequ_1 ; Sequ_2) \overset{\text{def}}{\Longleftrightarrow} \mathsf{Pref}(Sequ_1) \vee Sequ_1 ; \mathsf{Pref}(Sequ_2).$$

The application of the prefix operator weakens a sequence formula, as stated in the following remark.

Remark 3.19

For every sequence formula $Sequ$ the following holds:

$$\models Sequ \Longrightarrow \mathsf{Pref}(Sequ).$$

Difference formulas. A *difference formula* has the form

$$\left(\sum_{i=1}^{m} x_i - \sum_{j=1}^{n} y_j \right) \in I,$$

where x_i and y_j are global variables and I is an interval of the form described above. There are two special cases: if $I = [0,0]$ then the above difference formula is written as an equality

$$\sum_{i=1}^{m} x_i = \sum_{j=1}^{n} y_j$$

and if $I = [0, \infty)$ then it is written as an inequality

$$\sum_{i=1}^{m} x_i \geq \sum_{j=1}^{n} y_j.$$

We are now prepared to introduce the formal semantics of Constraint Diagrams.

Definition 3.20 (DC semantics of Constraint Diagrams)

The DC semantics of a Constraint Diagram $\mathcal{C}$ is given by the formula

$$\llbracket \mathcal{C} \rrbracket_{\mathrm{DC}} \overset{\text{def}}{\Longleftrightarrow} \forall AsmVar(\mathcal{C}) \bullet$$

$$(PSAsm(\mathcal{C}) \wedge TimeAsm(\mathcal{C})) \tag{3.5}$$

$$\Longrightarrow \exists ComVar(\mathcal{C}) \bullet$$

$$(PSCom(\mathcal{C}) \wedge TimeCom(\mathcal{C}) \wedge LenReq(\mathcal{C})). \tag{3.6}$$

The formula (3.5) describes the *assumption part* and (3.6) the *commitment part* of the diagram. $AsmVar(\mathcal{C})$ and $ComVar(\mathcal{C})$ are two lists of global variables used in these subformulas. The list $AsmVar(\mathcal{C})$ contains for each observable X and each phase i in the phase sequence of X a distinguished global variable ε_i^X, and the list $ComVar(\mathcal{C})$ contains for each observable X and each phase i in the phase sequence of X a distinguished global variable δ_i^X. These variables serve to describe the duration of the individual phases of X.

Next we define the various subformulas of (3.5) and (3.6). We distinguish phase sequence constraints $PSAsm(\mathcal{C})$ and $PSCom(\mathcal{C})$, time constraints $TimeAsm(\mathcal{C})$ and $TimeCom(\mathcal{C})$, and length requirements $LenReq(\mathcal{C})$.

Phase sequence constraints

Each phase sequence for a state variable X in $\mathcal{C}$

contributes to both assumptions and commitments.

- For the assumption part we define for X and $\mathcal{C}$:

$$PSAsm(X) \stackrel{\text{def}}{\Longleftrightarrow} \left(\lceil \pi_1^X \rceil \wedge \ell = \varepsilon_1^X\right) ; \ldots ; \left(\left\lceil \pi_{\#(X)}^X \right\rceil \wedge \ell = \varepsilon_{\#(X)}^X\right),$$

$$PSAsm(\mathcal{C}) \stackrel{\text{def}}{\Longleftrightarrow} \bigwedge_{X \in \{X_1, \ldots, X_k\}} PSAsm(X).$$

- For the commitment part we define for X and $\mathcal{C}$:

$$PSCom(X) \stackrel{\text{def}}{\Longleftrightarrow} \mathsf{Pref}\left(\left(\lceil \pi_1^X \wedge \tilde{\pi}_1^X \rceil \wedge \ell = \delta_1^X\right) ; \ldots ; \right.$$
$$\left. \left(\left\lceil \pi_{\#(X)}^X \wedge \tilde{\pi}_{\#(X)}^X \right\rceil \wedge \ell = \delta_{\#(X)}^X\right)\right),$$

$$PSCom(\mathcal{C}) \stackrel{\text{def}}{\Longleftrightarrow} \bigwedge_{X \in \{X_1, \ldots, X_k\}} PSCom(X).$$

Note that in the definitions of $PSAsm(X)$ and $PSCom(X)$ subformulas of the form $(\lceil \text{true} \rceil \wedge \ell = \varepsilon_i^X)$ or $(\lceil \text{true} \wedge \text{true} \rceil \wedge \ell = \delta_i^X)$ can occur which have to be read as $(\ell = \varepsilon_i^X)$ or $(\ell = \delta_i^X)$, respectively. Note that the prefix operator is applied in the commitment part. We shall explain the effect of this in Example 3.21.

Time constraints

Each phase ph_i^X of a state variable X in $\mathcal{C}$ and each arrow $ar_{m,n}^{X,Y}$ from the start of phase ph_m^X to the end of phase ph_n^Y of two different state variables X and Y in $\mathcal{C}$ as shown in

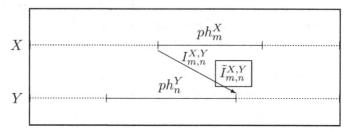

contribute time constraints to both assumptions and commitments.

- For the assumption part we define for phases and arrows:

$$TimeAsm(ph_i^X) \stackrel{\text{def}}{\Longleftrightarrow} \varepsilon_i^X \in I_i^X,$$

$$TimeAsm(ar_{m,n}^{X,Y}) \stackrel{\text{def}}{\Longleftrightarrow} \left(\sum_{j=1}^{n} \varepsilon_j^Y - \sum_{i=1}^{m-1} \varepsilon_i^X \right) \in I_{m,n}^{X,Y}.$$

The time constraint in the assumption part of the diagram $\mathcal{C}$ is the conjunction of these formulas taken over all phases and arrows:

$$TimeAsm(\mathcal{C}) \stackrel{\text{def}}{\Longleftrightarrow} \bigwedge_{\substack{X \in \{X_1, \ldots, X_k\} \\ 1 \leq i \leq \#(X)}} TimeAsm(ph_i^X)$$

$$\wedge \bigwedge_{\text{all arrows } ar_{m,n}^{X,Y} \text{ present in } \mathcal{C}} TimeAsm(ar_{m,n}^{X,Y}).$$

The sub- and superscripts of the arrows $ar_{m,n}^{X,Y}$ are constrained as follows: $X, Y \in \{X_1, \ldots, X_k\}$ with $X \neq Y$ and $1 \leq m \leq \#(X)$ and $1 \leq n \leq \#(Y)$.

- For the commitment part we define for phases and arrows:

$$TimeCom(ph_i^X) \stackrel{\text{def}}{\Longleftrightarrow} \delta_i^X \in I_i^X \cap \tilde{I}_i^X,$$

$$TimeCom(ar_{m,n}^{X,Y}) \stackrel{\text{def}}{\Longleftrightarrow} \left(\sum_{j=1}^{n} \delta_j^Y - \sum_{i=1}^{m-1} \delta_i^X \right) \in I_{m,n}^{X,Y} \cap \tilde{I}_{m,n}^{X,Y}.$$

The time constraint in the commitment part of the diagram $\mathcal{C}$ is the conjunction of these formulas taken over all phases and arrows:

$$TimeCom(\mathcal{C}) \stackrel{\text{def}}{\Longleftrightarrow} \bigwedge_{\substack{X \in \{X_1, \ldots, X_k\} \\ 1 \leq i \leq \#(X)}} TimeCom(ph_i^X)$$

$$\wedge \bigwedge_{\text{all arrows } ar_{m,n}^{X,Y} \text{ present in } \mathcal{C}} TimeCom(ar_{m,n}^{X,Y}).$$

The sub- and superscripts of the arrows $ar_{m,n}^{X,Y}$ are constrained as above.

Length requirements

To connect the global variables ε_i^X and δ_i^X used in assumptions and commitments we formulate additional length requirements in the commitment part of the semantics. These requirements are expressed in terms of *specified parts*, consisting of phases with formulas $\neq$ true or time intervals $\neq [0, \infty)$ as assumptions, and their surrounding *unspecified parts*.

Let us first consider a simple case as shown in the diagram

with $\pi_m^X \neq$ true and $\pi_{m+1}^X \neq$ true but $\pi_{m-1}^X =$ true and $\pi_{m+2}^X =$ true. Here the specified part is $sp = ph_m^X, ph_{m+1}^X$ and the corresponding length requirement is given by the formula

$$LenReq(sp) \stackrel{\text{def}}{\Longleftrightarrow} \sum_{i=1}^{m-1} \delta_i^X \leq \sum_{i=1}^{m-1} \varepsilon_i^X \tag{3.7}$$

$$\wedge \sum_{i=1}^{m} \delta_i^X = \sum_{i=1}^{m} \varepsilon_i^X \tag{3.8}$$

$$\wedge \sum_{i=1}^{m+1} \delta_i^X \geq \sum_{i=1}^{m+1} \varepsilon_i^X. \tag{3.9}$$

The purpose of these (special cases of difference) formulas is to ensure that the lengths of the phases ph_m^X and ph_{m+1}^X in the assumption part are properly connected to those in the commitment part. The formula (3.8) ensures that the chop point between phase ph_m^X and ph_{m+1}^X (inside the specified part) in the assumption part occurs at the same time as the corresponding chop point in the commitment part, and the formulas (3.7) and (3.9) ensure that the margins to unspecified parts in the assumption part may expand in the commitment part in the direction of the unspecified parts.

In general, a *specified part* of an observable X is a segment

$$sp_{r,s}^X = ph_r^X, \ldots, ph_s^X$$

of the phase sequence of X with $1 \leq r \leq s \leq \#(X)$ and maximal length $s - r$ such that for each $m \in \{r, \ldots, s\}$ either $\pi_m^X \neq \text{true}$ or $I_m^X \neq [0, \infty)$ holds. The parts of the phase sequence of X surrounding $sp_{r,s}^X$ are called *unspecified*. This is illustrated by the following diagram:

The length requirement for a specified part is defined as follows:

$$LenReq(sp_{r,s}^X) \overset{\text{def}}{\Longleftrightarrow} \sum_{i=1}^{r-1} \delta_i^X \leq \sum_{i=1}^{r-1} \varepsilon_i^X \tag{3.10}$$

$$\wedge \bigwedge_{m \in \{r, \ldots, s-1\}} \left(\sum_{i=1}^{m} \delta_i^X = \sum_{i=1}^{m} \varepsilon_i^X \right) \tag{3.11}$$

$$\wedge \sum_{i=1}^{s} \delta_i^X \geq \sum_{i=1}^{s} \varepsilon_i^X. \tag{3.12}$$

Formula (3.10) states that in the commitment part the left margin of a specified part can be expanded to the left and formula (3.12) states that in the commitment part the right margin of a specified part can be expanded to the right. Formula (3.11) states that inside a specified part the lengths of the assumption part are preserved in the commitment part. The length requirement of the diagram $\mathcal{C}$ is the conjunction of these formulas taken over all specified parts:

$$LenReq(\mathcal{C}) \overset{\text{def}}{\Longleftrightarrow} \bigwedge_{\substack{X \in \{X_1, \ldots, X_k\} \\ 1 \leq r \leq s \leq \#(X) \\ sp_{r,s}^X \text{ is a specified part of } X}} LenReq(sp_{r,s}^X).$$

This completes the definition of all constituents of the semantics $[\![\mathcal{C}]\!]_{\text{DC}}$.

In an application a Constraint Diagram $\mathcal{C}$ is used to specify the set of all interpretations $\mathcal{I}$ that realise from 0 the DC formula $[\![\mathcal{C}]\!]_{\mathrm{DC}}$ representing its semantics. The meaning of several Constraint Diagrams is given by the set of interpretations that satisfy all of them. This corresponds to the conjunction of the DC formulas representing the semantics of the Constraint Diagrams.

Example 3.21 (Watchdog, continued)
Thanks to the prefix operator in the commitment part of the DC semantics of Constraint Diagrams, we can simplify the specification of the watchdog by dropping the assumption of a phase of duration 2 after the $\neg S$-phase. The simplified Constraint Diagram looks as follows:

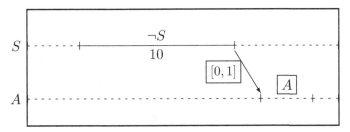

Literally, the DC semantics of this Constraint Diagram yields the formula

$$\forall \varepsilon_1^S, \varepsilon_2^S, \varepsilon_3^S, \varepsilon_1^A, \varepsilon_2^A, \varepsilon_3^A \bullet \left(\begin{array}{l} \ell = \varepsilon_1^S \,;\, (\lceil \neg S \rceil \wedge \ell = \varepsilon_2^S) \,;\, \ell = \varepsilon_3^S \\ \wedge \quad \ell = \varepsilon_1^A \,;\, \ell = \varepsilon_2^A \,;\, \ell = \varepsilon_3^A \\ \wedge \quad \varepsilon_2^S \in [10, 10] \end{array} \right)$$

$$\Longrightarrow \exists \delta_1^S, \delta_2^S, \delta_3^S, \delta_1^A, \delta_2^A, \delta_2^A \bullet$$

$$\left(\begin{array}{l} \mathsf{Pref}(\ell = \delta_1^S \,;\, (\lceil \neg S \rceil \wedge \ell = \delta_2^S) \,;\, \ell = \delta_3^S) \\ \wedge \quad \mathsf{Pref}(\ell = \delta_1^A \,;\, (\lceil A \rceil \wedge \ell = \delta_2^A) \,;\, \ell = \delta_3^A) \\ \wedge \quad \delta_2^S \in [10, 10] \\ \wedge \quad \delta_1^A - (\delta_1^S + \delta_2^S) \in [0, 1] \\ \wedge \quad \delta_1^S \leq \varepsilon_1^S \\ \wedge \quad (\delta_1^S + \delta_2^S) \geq (\varepsilon_1^S + \varepsilon_2^S) \end{array} \right).$$

The formulas $\varepsilon_2^S \in [10, 10]$ and $\delta_2^S \in [10, 10]$ result from $TimeAsm(ph_2^S)$ and $TimeCom(ph_2^S)$, respectively. They imply $\varepsilon_2^S = \delta_2^S = 10$. The difference formula $\delta_1^A - (\delta_1^S + \delta_2^S) \in [0, 1]$ is the time commitment $TimeCom(ar_{3,1}^{S,A})$. The last two subformulas represent the length requirement $LenReq(sp_{2,2}^S)$. Since $\varepsilon_2^S = \delta_2^S = 10$ holds, they imply $\varepsilon_1^S = \delta_1^S$. Hence, with a change of the bound variables, the DC semantics can be simplified to

$$\forall \varepsilon \bullet (\ell = \varepsilon \,;\, (\lceil \neg S \rceil \wedge \ell = 10) \,;\, \mathsf{true})$$

$$\implies \exists \delta \bullet \left(\begin{array}{c} \mathsf{Pref}(\ell = \delta \,;\, \lceil A \rceil \,;\, \mathsf{true}) \\ \wedge \quad \delta - (\varepsilon + 10) \in [0,1] \end{array} \right),$$

where the prefix operator yields

$$\mathsf{Pref}(\ell = \delta \,;\, \lceil A \rceil \,;\, \mathsf{true}) \iff \ell \leq \delta \vee (\ell = \delta \,;\, \lceil A \rceil \,;\, \mathsf{true}).$$

This ensures that in the commitment part A is required only if in the assumption part there is sufficient time after the $\neg S$-phase. If this is not the case the interval of the assumption part is matched with the first disjunct of the prefix operator, i.e. with $\ell \leq \delta$. ∎

3.3.2 Generalised railroad crossing revisited

To specify the railroad crossing, we introduced in Section 1.3 the observables

- Track ranging over {empty, appr, cross} representing the state of the track,
- g ranging over the interval $[0, 90]$ representing the gate angle,

and the following abbreviations for state assertions:

$$E \stackrel{\mathrm{def}}{=} \mathsf{Track} = \mathsf{empty},$$
$$A \stackrel{\mathrm{def}}{=} \mathsf{Track} = \mathsf{appr},$$
$$Cr \stackrel{\mathrm{def}}{=} \mathsf{Track} = \mathsf{cross},$$
$$O \stackrel{\mathrm{def}}{=} g = 90,$$
$$Cl \stackrel{\mathrm{def}}{=} g = 0.$$

Using Constraint Diagrams, we can capture the requirements for the generalised railroad crossing in a very intuitive way.

Safety. The safety requirement is formalised by the following diagram:

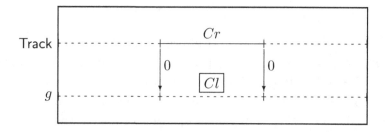

This diagram expresses that whenever a train is in the crossing (assumption Cr) the gate should be closed (commitment Cl). The arrows annotated with 0 express simultaneity, i.e. the commitment has to occur without delay. The DC semantics of this diagram is equivalent to the formula $\Box(\lceil Cr \rceil \Longrightarrow \lceil Cl \rceil)$.

Utility. The utility requirement is formalised by the following diagram:

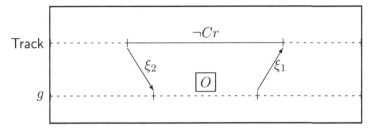

This diagram is an excellent example to demonstrate the conciseness of Constraint Diagrams. It expresses that whenever for a certain time interval there is *no* train in the crossing (assumption $\neg Cr$) the gate should be open ξ_2 seconds after the beginning of that interval and stay open until ξ_1 seconds before the end of the interval (commitment O). Recall that the parameters ξ_2 and ξ_1 represent the time it takes to open the gate and to close the gate, respectively. The DC semantics of this Constraint Diagram is equivalent to the formula

$$\forall \varepsilon_1, \varepsilon_2 \bullet (\ell = \varepsilon_1 \,;\, (\lceil \neg Cr \rceil \wedge \ell = \varepsilon_2) \,;\, \mathsf{true})$$
$$\wedge\, \varepsilon_2 > \xi_1 + \xi_2$$
$$\Longrightarrow \ell = \varepsilon_1 + \xi_2 \,;\, (\lceil O \rceil \wedge \ell = \varepsilon_2 - \xi_1 - \xi_2) \,;\, \mathsf{true}.$$

It is also possible to use Constraint Diagrams to specify assumptions about the behaviour of the observable Track.

Initial value. The commitment is that initially the track is empty (E).

Similarly to Example 3.21, we can simplify the DC semantics of this diagram to the formula $\lceil \rceil \vee \lceil E \rceil \,;\, \mathsf{true}$.

State changes. If the track is empty (E) it remains empty or a train approaches (A). We can specify this by the following Constraint Diagram:

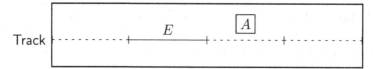

Analogously, we require that an approaching train cannot leave the track without passing the crossing:

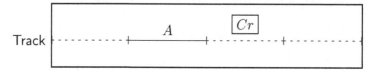

Note that we do not need a diagram to specify the state changes when a train crosses. There are two choices and both are legal: either the track is empty after the train has crossed or there is another train already approaching. Hence, all values of the observable track have been covered.

Let us analyse the DC semantics of the last Constraint Diagram in more detail. After a simplification we obtain the following DC formula:

$$\forall \varepsilon_1, \varepsilon_2 \bullet \ell = \varepsilon_1 \,;\, (\lceil A \rceil \wedge \ell = \varepsilon_2) \,;\, \text{true}$$

$$\Longrightarrow \exists \delta_1, \delta_2 \bullet \left(\begin{array}{c} \text{Pref}(\ell = \delta_1 \,;\, (\lceil A \rceil \wedge \ell = \delta_2) \,;\, \lceil Cr \rceil \,;\, \text{true}) \\ \wedge \quad \delta_1 \le \varepsilon_1 \wedge \varepsilon_1 + \varepsilon_2 \le \delta_1 + \delta_2 \end{array} \right),$$

where the prefix operator yields

$$\text{Pref}(\ell = \delta_1 \,;\, (\lceil A \rceil \wedge \ell = \delta_2) \,;\, \lceil Cr \rceil \,;\, \text{true}) \iff$$
$$\ell \le \delta_1$$
$$\vee\, (\ell = \delta_1 \,;\, (\lceil A \rceil \wedge \ell \le \delta_2))$$
$$\vee\, (\ell = \delta_1 \,;\, (\lceil A \rceil \wedge \ell = \delta_2) \,;\, \lceil Cr \rceil \,;\, \text{true}).$$

This ensures that in the commitment part Cr is required only if in the assumption part there is sufficient time after the A-phase. If this is not the case the interval of the assumption part is matched with the second disjunct of the prefix operator. In other words, Cr is the only possible successor state of A but it is not assured that state A will be left. Formally, the Constraint Diagram describes exactly the same property as the DC implementable $\lceil A \rceil \longrightarrow \lceil A \vee Cr \rceil$.

3.3.3 A real-time filter

This application considers a *fault-tolerance* problem that occurs when using sensors. It is taken from an industrial case study performed in collaboration with a company designing software for railway control. The full context of this application will be explained in Chapter 5.

Suppose an *entry sensor ES* has to detect whether a train has entered a certain line segment of a track. A technical problem is that sensors may *stutter*, i.e. issue (for a limited period of time) more than one output signal when in reality only a single train has passed the sensor. We assume here that the sensor hardware guarantees that after 4 seconds any stuttering of the sensor has ceased. We also assume that successive trains are at least 6 seconds apart. To avoid wrong data in the drive controller for the trains a suitable *filter* is needed for each sensor. The idea is that the filter exploits the timing assumptions to achieve fault-tolerance.

We consider here a filter *FES* reading input values *no_tr* (*no train is passing*), *tr* (*train is passing*), and *Error* (*erroneous sensor value*) issued by the (possibly stuttering) entry sensor *ES* and transforming them into (reliable) output values N (*no train detected*), T (*train detected*), and X (*exception*). To model the filter we introduce the observables

- *in* ranging over $\{no\_tr, tr, Error\}$,
- *out* ranging over $\{N, T, X\}$,

and a global variable ρ as a parameter for the reaction time of the filter.

The desired real-time behaviour is shown in the timing diagram in Figure 3.1. When an input *tr* is issued by the sensor *ES* the filter *FES* should (after a reaction time of at most ρ) output T (*train detected*). In the sub-

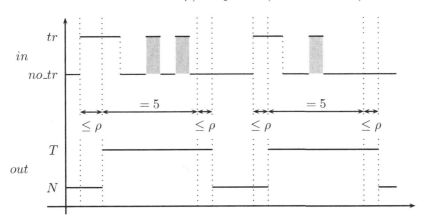

Fig. 3.1. Timing diagrams for the filter

sequent 5 seconds the filter should ignore any further stuttering of inputs *no_tr* or *tr* from the sensor and stay with output T. After 5 seconds, when by our assumption any stuttering of the sensor has ceased and the next train has not yet arrived, the input is *no_tr* and the filter (after a reaction time of at most ρ) can return to output N. Afterwards any further input *tr* will be treated as signalling that a new train approaches, causing output T again. There is one input though which the filter *FES* must not ignore: the input *Error* indicating an erroneous sensor value. Then the filter should proceed as fast as possible and (after a reaction time of at most ρ) output X.

These informal requirements can be formalised using Constraint Diagrams. In the sequel we show CDs for the most important aspects of the desired filter behaviour.

Initial state. The commitment is that initially the output is N.

Filtering inputs for 5 seconds. Assuming that input *tr* is present for ρ seconds while output is N, the filter is committed to change its output to T. Note that if the input *tr* is present for less than ρ seconds, nothing is required from the filter. The assumption of *tr* being present for some duration of time anticipates that hardware cannot react arbitrarily fast.

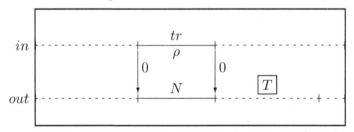

The filter should keep the output T for up to 5 seconds provided only *no_tr* or *tr* (i.e. no *Error*) occurs as input during that period.

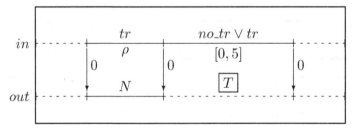

Reset after 5 seconds. Assuming that after a period of 5 seconds of output T an input *no_tr* is present for ρ seconds while output is still T, the filter is committed to change its output to N.

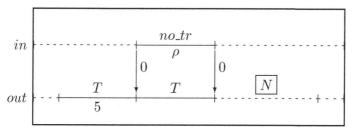

Error handling. Assuming the input *Error* is present for ρ seconds, the filter is committed to output X after this time.

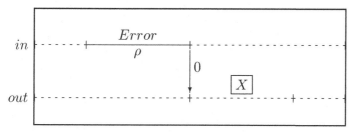

Exceptional state is kept. Assuming the filter is in X it is committed to stay in this state.

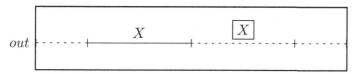

3.3.4 Expressiveness

C. Kleuker showed that conjunctions of Constraint Diagrams are Turing powerful. The proof exploits the density of the continuous-time domain Time = $\mathbb{R}_{\geq 0}$ and proceeds by giving Constraint Diagrams for all the DC formulas used in the proof of Zhou Chaochen, Hansen, and Sestoft that the DC can express the behaviour of any given two-counter machine (see Subsection 3.1.2). As a consequence, it is not decidable whether a given set of Constraint Diagrams represents a satisfiable or realisable real-time specification.

C. Kleuker also proved the following specific result on expressiveness of the DC implementables introduced in Section 3.2:

Theorem 3.22 (Expressiveness)
The DC implementables can be expressed by Constraint Diagrams.

Sketch of proof:
We show how Constraint Diagrams can be used to express the implementable patterns graphically. Let X be an observable and let $\pi, \pi_1, \ldots, \pi_n$ with $n \geq 0$ be state assertions (phases) over X. We assume that $\mathcal{Y}$ is a finite set of observables with $X \notin \mathcal{Y}$ and φ is a state assertion over $\mathcal{Y}$. Further on, let θ be a rigid DC term.

Then the following Constraint Diagrams express the DC implementables.

- *Initialisation.* The CD

  expresses the implementable

$$\lceil\rceil \vee \lceil \pi \rceil \; ; \text{true}.$$

- *Sequencing.* The CD

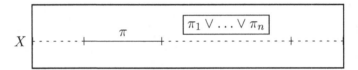

  expresses the implementable

$$\lceil \pi \rceil \longrightarrow \lceil \pi \vee \pi_1 \vee \ldots \vee \pi_n \rceil .$$

  By the prefix operator in the semantics of its commitment $\pi_1 \vee \ldots \vee \pi_n$, this Constraint Diagram implicitly allows the system to stay in the π-phase as it is explicitly stated in the sequencing implementable. This enables the equivalence proof for this case.

- *Progress.* The CD

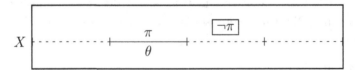

  expresses the implementable

$$\lceil \pi \rceil \xrightarrow{\;\theta\;} \lceil \neg\pi \rceil .$$

- *Synchronisation.* The CD

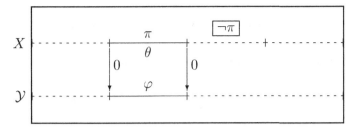

expresses the implementable

$$\lceil \pi \wedge \varphi \rceil \xrightarrow{\;\theta\;} \lceil \neg \pi \rceil \,.$$

Here we use the *set* of observables $\mathcal{Y}$ in the lower line of the Constraint Diagram and the state assertion φ. This can be conceived as an abbreviation for the Cartesian product of the observables and a corresponding transformation of φ in a state assertion over this Cartesian product.

- *Unbounded stability.* The CD

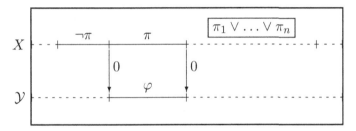

expresses the implementable

$$\lceil \neg \pi \rceil \,;\, \lceil \pi \wedge \varphi \rceil \longrightarrow \lceil \pi \vee \pi_1 \vee \ldots \vee \pi_n \rceil \,.$$

- *Bounded stability.* The CD

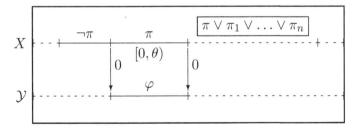

expresses the implementable

$$\lceil \neg \pi \rceil \,;\, \lceil \pi \wedge \varphi \rceil \xrightarrow{\;\leq \theta\;} \lceil \pi \vee \pi_1 \vee \ldots \vee \pi_n \rceil \,.$$

Note that in the stability formula θ appears as an upper time bound of the sequence $\lceil \neg \pi \rceil$; $\lceil \pi \wedge \varphi \rceil$. Hence, a positive amount of time is spent in the $\lceil \neg \pi \rceil$-phase. However, in the Constraint Diagram we constrain only the phase $\lceil \pi \wedge \varphi \rceil$. Therefore we use the half-open interval $[0, \theta)$ to keep the equivalence between implementable and Constraint Diagram.

- *Unbounded initial stability.* The CD

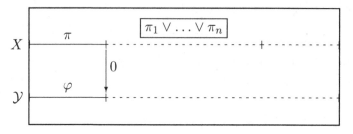

expresses the implementable

$$\lceil \pi \wedge \varphi \rceil \longrightarrow_0 \lceil \pi \vee \pi_1 \vee \ldots \vee \pi_n \rceil .$$

- *Bounded initial stability.* The CD

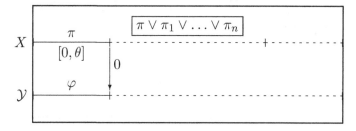

expresses the implementable

$$\lceil \pi \wedge \varphi \rceil \xrightarrow{\leq \theta}_0 \lceil \pi \vee \pi_1 \vee \ldots \vee \pi_n \rceil .$$

This concludes the sketch of the proof. We leave the calculation that the semantics of the Constraint Diagrams shown above are equivalent to the corresponding implementables as an exercise.   □

3.4 Exercises

Exercise 3.1 (Decidability)
Explain how to decide whether a regular language is

(a) empty,
(b) infinite.

Exercise 3.2 (Discrete DC)

Construct automata accepting the languages $\mathcal{L}(\Diamond\lceil P\rceil)$ and $kern(\mathcal{L}(\Diamond\lceil P\rceil))$. Use these automata to decide whether the formula $\Diamond\lceil P\rceil$ is

(a) satisfiable,
(b) realisable from 0.

Exercise 3.3 (Kernel)

(a) Prove that for a regular language L the language $kern(L)$ is also regular. Show how to modify a finite automaton $\mathcal{A}$ accepting L to an automaton $kern(\mathcal{A})$ accepting $kern(L)$.

(b) Prove that Lemma 3.8 is wrong if $\mathcal{L}(F)$ instead of $kern(\mathcal{L}(F))$ is considered.

Exercise 3.4 (Standard forms)

Consider an interpretation of P as shown in the timing diagram below. Give interpretations of Q and Q' so that

(a) $\lceil P\rceil \longrightarrow \lceil Q\rceil$,
(b) $\lceil P\rceil \xrightarrow{2} \lceil Q'\rceil$

are satisfied.

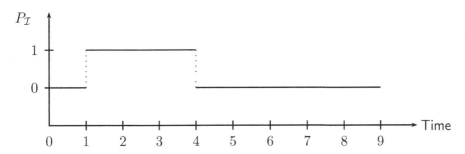

Exercise 3.5 (Standard forms)

Let P, Q, R be state assertions and θ_1, θ_2 be rigid terms. Prove the validity of the following implications:

(a) $(\lceil P\rceil \longrightarrow \lceil Q\rceil) \wedge (\lceil Q\rceil \longrightarrow \lceil R\rceil) \Longrightarrow (\lceil P\rceil \longrightarrow \lceil R\rceil)$,
(b) $(\lceil P\rceil \xrightarrow{t_1} \lceil Q\rceil) \wedge (\lceil Q\rceil \xrightarrow{t_2} \lceil R\rceil) \Longrightarrow (\lceil P\rceil \xrightarrow{t_1+t_2} \lceil R\rceil)$.

Exercise 3.6 (Stability)

Discuss the difference of the stability pattern $\lceil\neg\pi\rceil \,;\, \lceil\pi\rceil \xrightarrow{\leq\theta} \lceil\pi\rceil$ and the following pattern: $\lceil \pi \rceil \xrightarrow{\leq \theta} \lceil \pi \rceil$. As an example take the constraint **Stab-2** of the gas burner controller in Subsection 3.2.1:

$$\lceil \neg \mathsf{purge} \rceil \; ; \; \lceil \mathsf{purge} \rceil \xrightarrow{\leq 30} \lceil \mathsf{purge} \rceil \,.$$

What does $\lceil \mathsf{purge} \rceil \xrightarrow{\leq 30} \lceil \mathsf{purge} \rceil$ specify?

Exercise 3.7 (Inboard light)

Consider the control of an inboard light of a car that switches the light inside the car on or off depending on the state of the doors. The light should be switched on if one of the doors is open. If the last door is closed the light should continue to shine for t_{stable} time units and then go off.

Let the state of the doors be described by an observable ranging over two values O ("one door open") and Cl ("all doors closed"). Let the state of a control automaton for the light be described by an observable ranging over three values off, light, and wait, and let its untimed transition behaviour be given by the following diagram:

In the state wait the control automaton should stay for t_{stable} time after closing the last door and the light should continue to shine. Further on, assume that the reaction time of the controller to changes of the doors' state is t_{react}.

Specify the intended timed behaviour of the control automaton by DC implementables. Check whether the specification indeed satisfies the informal requirements for the inboard light.

Exercise 3.8 (Gas burner)

Reconsider the controller for the gas burner in Subsection 3.2.1. A utility requirement is that a customer gets a warm room when the heat request is turned on. However, since we cannot exclude flame failures, we guarantee only that upon a heat request the gas valve is switched on and the burn phase is reached within some period of time. Also, a customer does not want overheating. Thus when the heat request is switched off, the gas valve should be closed.

(a) Prove that

$$\models \mathsf{GB\text{-}Crtl} \wedge \varepsilon \leq 0.5 \Longrightarrow \Box(\lceil \mathsf{burn} \rceil \Longrightarrow \lceil G \rceil)$$

holds and keep track which of the implementables are needed in the proof.

(b) Prove that

$$\models \mathsf{GB\text{-}Crtl} \wedge \varepsilon \leq 0.5 \Longrightarrow \lceil \neg G \wedge H \rceil \xrightarrow{\;t_1\;} \lceil G \rceil$$

for $t_1 = 30 + 3 \cdot \varepsilon$ and keep track which of the implementables are needed in the proof.

(c) Prove that

$$\models \mathsf{GB\text{-}Crtl} \Longrightarrow \lceil \neg \mathsf{burn} \wedge H \rceil \xrightarrow{\;t_2\;} \lceil \mathsf{burn} \rceil$$

for $t_2 = 30.5 + 3 \cdot \varepsilon$ and keep track which of the implementables are needed in the proof.

(d) Prove that

$$\models \mathsf{GB\text{-}Crtl} \Longrightarrow \lceil \neg H \rceil \xrightarrow{\;t_3\;} \lceil \neg G \rceil$$

for $t_3 = 30.5 + 4 \cdot \varepsilon$ and keep track which of the implementables are needed in the proof.

Exercise 3.9 (Constraint Diagrams)
Specify the implementables of the gas burner in Subsection 3.2.1 graphically in terms of Constraint Diagrams.

Exercise 3.10 (Constraint Diagrams)
Specify the following requirements for a Boolean observable X formally in terms of CDs:

(a) Whenever $\neg X$ holds it lasts for at least 2 seconds.
(b) If $\neg X$ holds for more than 5 seconds the subsequent X-phase lasts at least 10 seconds.
(c) Each X-phase with a duration of less than 1 second has a preceding $\neg X$-phase with at most 3 seconds.

Exercise 3.11 (Constraint Diagrams)
The following CD describes a stability property:

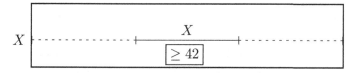

(a) Construct the DC semantics of this CD.

(b) Explain why the length requirements are necessary here to meet the intended meaning of the CD.

Exercise 3.12 (Expressiveness proof)
Complete the proof of Theorem 3.22 by showing that in each case the semantics of the Constraint Diagram shown is indeed equivalent to the implementable.

3.5 Bibliographic remarks

The results on decidability and undecidability of the satisfiability (and thus of the validity) problem of the Duration Calculus are due to Zhou Chaochen, M.R. Hansen, and P. Sestoft [ZHS93]. They are also explained in the monograph [ZH04]. Thus we cannot expect an automatic verification of real-time systems with respect to properties expressed in full Duration Calculus. However, for subsets of the Duration Calculus this is possible as shown by M. Fränzle and M.R. Hansen [Frä04, FH07] and in [MFR06]. Exercise 3.3 is due to M. Lettrari, who gave an example showing that the kernel operation is needed in Lemma 3.8.

The decidability for the case of discrete time has been exploited by P.K. Pandya in the construction of a tool DCVALID [Pan01] based on second-order monadic logic. For the case of continuous-time Duration Calculus, J.U. Skakkebæk provided interactive proof support via an embedding of the calculus into the logic of the PVS system [Ska94]. Similar work was done by S. Heilmann on the basis of the interactive theorem prover Isabelle [Hei99]. The tool Moby/DC provides a semi-decision procedure for a subset of (continuous-time) Duration Calculus [DT03], and the tool Moby/RT offers model checking of PLC-Automata against specifications written in this subset [OD03].

The subset of DC implementables was introduced by A.P. Ravn in [Rav95]. In [Die97] it is shown that the name "implementable" is justified because every consistent set of DC implementables can indeed be implemented by a PLC-Automaton, which in turn can be translated into a program to be executed on a simple hardware platform (PLC). For more details see Section 5.5. The correctness proof of the gas burner implementables against the safety specification in Subsection 3.2.2 is similar to the one in [RRH93].

Constraint Diagrams were developed as a graphical language for specifying real-time requirements by C. Dietz/Kleuker [Die96]. They are fully described in [Kle00] where also graphic refinement rules for Constraint Diagrams are introduced. The diagrams were inspired by the *Symbolic Timing*

Diagrams of W. Damm and R. Schlör, a graphical specification language for the temporal behaviour of reactive systems [SD93]. The term *symbolic* indicates that with these diagrams only qualitative time can be expressed.

The first formal treatment of the case study "Generalised Railroad Crossing" [HL94] in terms of the Duration Calculus appeared in [ORS96]. There the two requirements, Safety and Utility, were specified in the Duration Calculus and systematically refined via a controller design expressed by standard forms (cf. Section 3.2) down to a program specification. The refinement steps were checked with the verification assistant due to [Ska94]. A graphic counterpart of this specification in terms of Constraint Diagrams (as shown in Subsection 3.3.2) together with a graphic correctness proof of the refinements steps appeared in [DD97, Kle00].

The informal requirements of the real-time filter in Subsection 3.3.3 are due to the company Elpro, Berlin, with whom we cooperated within the project UniForM [KPOB99]. The Constraint Diagrams for the filter appeared in the overview paper [Old99].

The Shape Calculus by A. Schäfer is a multi-dimensional extension of the Duration Calculus for the specification and verification of objects moving in space and time [Sch05, Sch06]. Like the Duration Calculus, the Shape Calculus has an undecidable satisfiability problem for continuous time. Satisfiability is even undecidable for the case of discrete time and at least one spatial dimension. However, for subsets of the Shape Calculus with discrete space and time the validity and the satisfiability problem are decidable [Sch06, Sch07]. Inspired by the work on DCVALID [Pan01], an automatic verification method has been developed for a restricted Shape Calculus and discrete space and time on the basis of the tool MONA [KM01] for second-order monadic logic [QS06].

4

Timed automata

Timed automata were introduced by R. Alur and D. Dill as an operational model of real-time systems. In their simplest form timed automata extend classical finite automata, having only finitely many control states, by clock variables ranging over the non-negative real numbers (continuous time). Constraints on the values of the clock variables serve as guards of the transitions and as invariants in the control states. Timed automata can be combined into networks by using parallel composition and restriction operators of process algebras like CCS or CSP. One of the most important results on timed automata is that it is decidable whether a given control state is reachable. This led to the development of several tools for the automatic verification of behavioural properties of timed automata. Here we shall present in more detail the tool UPPAAL.

4.1 Timed automata

Timed automata engage in transitions from locations to locations when certain timing conditions are satisfied. These transitions either perform input and output actions on channels that will synchronise with other timed automata working in parallel or they perform internal actions that are invisible from the outside.

As a first contact with timed automata let us look at an example.

Example 4.1 (Light controller)
We wish to model a light controller with the following behaviour. Initially, the light is off. When the switch is pressed once, the light goes on (into a dim mode). If the switch is pressed twice quickly the light gets bright. Otherwise, if the switch is pressed only after a while the light goes off again. Let us try to model this behaviour with an automaton with three locations called

off, *light*, and *bright*. The initial location is *off*. There are four transitions marked with a symbol *press?* where the question mark expresses that the transition is waiting for an input (pressing the switch) by the environment (the user). Graphically, the automaton is depicted as follows:

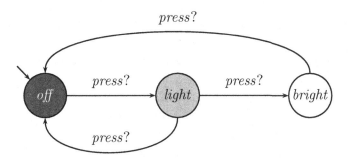

A problem with this model is that the time-related concepts "quickly" and "after a while" are not represented. Instead, the automaton exhibits nondeterminism in the location *light*: when the switch is pressed it can go either to the location *bright* or the location *off*.

Here timed automata can help. They extend ordinary automata with clocks for continuous time. Initially, clocks start with the value 0. Then the values of the clocks grow continuously. Transitions can depend on the current values of the clocks. Also, they can reset clocks to 0.

For the light controller we take one clock named x and extend the above automaton to the following timed automaton due to K.G. Larsen:

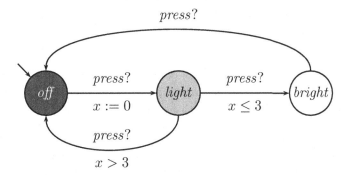

When the switch is pressed first the clock is reset by the assignment $x := 0$. Only if the second pressing of the switch occurs within 3 seconds after the first one (represented by the timing condition $x \leq 3$ at the transition) does the light get bright. If it occurs later than 3 seconds (represented by the timing condition $x > 3$) the light goes off again. This is also the case when the switch is pressed in the location *bright*. Note that the disjoint timing conditions have removed the nondeterminism at the location *light*.   ∎

To define timed automata formally, we need the following sets of symbols:

- A set Chan of *channel names* or simply *channels*, with typical elements a, b or suggestive names like *press* in Example 4.1.
- For each channel a there are two *visible actions*: $a?$ denotes an *input* and $a!$ the corresponding *output* on the channel a, where $a?, a! \notin$ Chan.
- $\tau \notin$ Chan represents an *internal action*, not visible from outside.
- $Act = \{a? \mid a \in \text{Chan}\} \cup \{a! \mid a \in \text{Chan}\} \cup \{\tau\}$ is the set of all *actions*, with typical elements α, β.
- $Lab = \text{Time} \cup Act$ is the set of all *labels*, with typical element λ, that can occur at transitions of timed automata.
- *Alphabets* B are sets of channels: $B \subseteq$ Chan.
- For each alphabet B we define the corresponding action set $B_{?!}$ by

$$B_{?!} = \{a? \mid a \in B\} \cup \{a! \mid a \in B\} \cup \{\tau\}.$$

Note that $B_{?!} \subseteq Act = \text{Chan}_{?!}$ holds. Input and output are *complementary* actions that can synchronise when timed automata work in parallel. It is convenient to introduce an operation of *complementation* on actions. Formally,

$$\overline{\cdot} : Act \longrightarrow Act$$

is defined by $\overline{a!} = a?$ and $\overline{a?} = a!$ and $\overline{\tau} = \tau$. Note that $\overline{\overline{\alpha}} = \alpha$ holds for all $\alpha \in Act$. Also we introduce an operation yielding the *underlying channel name* of an input or output:

$$\text{chan} : Act \xrightarrow{part} \text{Chan}$$

is defined by $\text{chan}(a!) = \text{chan}(a?) = a$. Note that $\text{chan}(\tau)$ is undefined.

Also, we need to define what clock constraints may appear as guards of transitions and as invariants of locations in timed automata.

Definition 4.2 (Clock constraints)

Let $\mathbb{X}$ be a set of clock variables, with typical elements x, y. The set $\Phi(\mathbb{X})$ of *clock constraints over* $\mathbb{X}$, with typical element φ, is defined by the following syntax:

$$\varphi ::= x \sim c \mid x - y \sim c \mid \varphi_1 \wedge \varphi_2$$

where $x, y \in \mathbb{X}$, $c \in \mathbb{Q}_{\geq 0}$, and $\sim \in \{<, >, \leq, \geq\}$. Constraints of the form $x - y \sim c$ are called *difference constraints*.

The restriction to rational time constants c is needed to obtain decidability results (see Section 4.3). Note that further clock constraints like true or $x = c$ are expressible by the operators in the definition of $\Phi(\mathbb{X})$.

We now introduce the "syntax" of timed automata, i.e. their structural components.

Definition 4.3 (Timed automaton)

A (*pure*) *timed automaton* $\mathcal{A}$ is a structure $\mathcal{A} = (L, B, \mathbb{X}, I, E, \ell_{\mathrm{ini}})$ where:

- L is a finite set of *locations* or *control states*, with typical element ℓ.

- $B \subseteq$ Chan is a finite alphabet of *channels*, with typical elements α, β.

- $\mathbb{X}$ is a finite set of *clocks*, with typical elements x, y.

- $I : L \to \Phi(\mathbb{X})$ is a mapping that assigns to each location a clock constraint, its *invariant*.

- $E \subseteq L \times B_{?!} \times \Phi(\mathbb{X}) \times \mathcal{P}(\mathbb{X}) \times L$ is the set of directed *edges*. An element $(\ell, \alpha, \varphi, Y, \ell') \in E$ describes an edge from location ℓ to location ℓ' labelled with the action α, the *guard* φ, and the set Y of clocks that will be *reset*.

- $\ell_{\mathrm{ini}} \in L$ is the *initial location*.

A timed automaton can be represented graphically. Each location ℓ is drawn as a circle inscribed with ℓ and the location invariant $I(\ell)$; the initial location is marked by an ingoing arc:

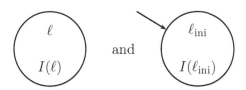

An edge $(\ell, \alpha, \varphi, Y, \ell') \in E$ can be represented graphically as an arrow from location ℓ to location ℓ' labelled with α, φ, and assignments of the form $y := 0$ for all clocks $y \in Y$. This is illustrated by the following example:

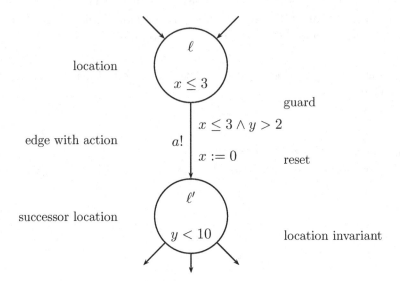

This diagram represents the edge $(\ell, a!, x \leq 3 \wedge y > 2, \{x\}, \ell')$. The constraints in the locations ℓ and ℓ' represent the invariants $I(\ell) \stackrel{\text{def}}{\Longleftrightarrow} x \leq 3$ and $I(\ell') \stackrel{\text{def}}{\Longleftrightarrow} y < 10$. Constraints equivalent to true are not shown in the graphical representation.

A location ℓ is called *isolated* if there is no chain of directed edges from ℓ_{ini} to ℓ. Since isolated locations are not reachable in the operational semantics (see Definition 4.4), they and all edges directly connected to them are usually not shown in the graphical representation.

For the semantics of a timed automaton we need valuations of clocks. A *valuation ν of clocks* in $\mathbb{X}$ is a mapping

$$\nu : \mathbb{X} \longrightarrow \text{Time}$$

assigning to each clock $x \in \mathbb{X}$ a time value, the current time. We write

$$\nu \models \varphi,$$

if ν *satisfies* the clock constraint φ, which is defined inductively:

$$
\begin{aligned}
\nu &\models x \sim c & \text{iff} \quad & \nu(x) \sim c, \\
\nu &\models x - y \sim c & \text{iff} \quad & \nu(x) - \nu(y) \sim c, \\
\nu &\models \varphi_1 \wedge \varphi_2 & \text{iff} \quad & \nu \models \varphi_1 \text{ and } \nu \models \varphi_2.
\end{aligned}
$$

Two clock constraints φ_1 and φ_2 are called (*logically*) *equivalent* if for all valuations ν the following holds: $\nu \models \varphi_1$ iff $\nu \models \varphi_2$. In that case we write

$$\models \varphi_1 \iff \varphi_2 .$$

Further on, we need two operations on valuations. The first one increases all clocks uniformly by a given amount of time and the second one modifies the value of a given set of clocks to t but leaves all other clocks unchanged.

- *Time-shift.* For a clock valuation ν for $\mathbb{X}$ and $t \in \mathsf{Time}$ we write $\nu + t$ to denote the valuation with

$$(\nu + t)(x) = \nu(x) + t$$

  for all $x \in \mathbb{X}$.
- *Modification.* For a clock valuation ν for $\mathbb{X}$, a set $Y \subseteq \mathbb{X}$ of clocks, and $t \in \mathsf{Time}$ we write $\nu[Y := t]$ to denote the valuation with

$$\nu[Y := t](x) = \begin{cases} t, & \text{if } x \in Y, \\ \nu(x), & \text{otherwise.} \end{cases}$$

The operational semantics of a timed automaton is defined by a transition system in the sense of G.D. Plotkin. It performs transitions between so-called configurations that combine control (here the locations) with data (here the valuations of the clock variables). The transitions are labelled either by time values or by actions.

Definition 4.4 (Operational semantics)
The *operational semantics* of a timed automaton $\mathcal{A} = (L, B, \mathbb{X}, I, E, \ell_{\text{ini}})$ is defined by the (labelled) transition system

$$T(\mathcal{A}) = (\mathit{Conf}(\mathcal{A}), \mathsf{Time} \cup B_{?!}, \{\xrightarrow{\lambda} \mid \lambda \in \mathsf{Time} \cup B_{?!}\}, C_{\text{ini}}),$$

where the following hold:

- $\mathit{Conf}(\mathcal{A}) = \{\langle \ell, \nu \rangle \mid \ell \in L \wedge \nu : \mathbb{X} \longrightarrow \mathsf{Time} \wedge \nu \models I(\ell)\}$ is the set of *configurations* of $\mathcal{A}$.
- The set $\mathsf{Time} \cup B_{?!}$ contains all labels that may appear at transitions.
- For each $\lambda \in \mathsf{Time} \cup B_{?!}$ the transition relation $\xrightarrow{\lambda} \subseteq \mathit{Conf}(\mathcal{A}) \times \mathit{Conf}(\mathcal{A})$ has one of the following two types:
  - In a *time* or *delay transition* some time $t \in \mathsf{Time}$ elapses, but the location is left unchanged. Formally,

$$\langle \ell, \nu \rangle \xrightarrow{t} \langle \ell, \nu + t \rangle$$

    iff $\nu + t' \models I(\ell)$ holds for all $t' \in [0, t]$.

– In an *action* or *discrete transition* an action $\alpha \in B_{?!}$ occurs and some clocks may be reset, but time does not advance. Formally,

$$\langle \ell, \nu \rangle \xrightarrow{\alpha} \langle \ell', \nu' \rangle$$

iff there exists an edge $(\ell, \alpha, \varphi, Y, \ell') \in E$ with $\nu \models \varphi$ and $\nu' = \nu[Y := 0]$ and $\nu' \models I(\ell')$.

• $C_{\text{ini}} = \{\langle \ell_{\text{ini}}, \nu_{\text{ini}} \rangle\} \cap \text{Conf}(\mathcal{A})$ with $\nu_{\text{ini}}(x) = 0$ for all clocks $x \in \mathbb{X}$ is the set of *initial* configurations.

Thus a configuration is a pair $\langle \ell, \nu \rangle$ consisting of a location ℓ and a valuation ν of the clocks that satisfies the invariant of ℓ. Although there are only finitely many locations, the set $\text{Conf}(\mathcal{A})$ of configurations is *infinite* due to infinitely many clock valuations. In fact, this set is *uncountable*, i.e. of a larger cardinality than the set $\mathbb{N}$ of natural numbers because we consider $\text{Time} = \mathbb{R}_{\geq 0}$.

Note that a delay transition in a location ℓ is only possible as long as the location invariant $I(\ell)$ holds. Therefore location invariants can be used to model *progress* in timed automata. Before the invariant $I(\ell)$ ceases to hold, the location ℓ has to be left by an action transition. There are two special cases. First, if the invariant $I(\ell)$ is equivalent to true the timed automaton can stay in ℓ forever. Second, if neither a delay transition is possible in ℓ nor an action transition can be taken to leave ℓ, the timed automaton is *ill-defined* because it would prevent time from advancing. We come back to this problem when defining computation paths and runs.

The set C_{ini} of initial configurations contains at most one element, the configuration $\langle \ell_{\text{ini}}, \nu_{\text{ini}} \rangle$ where the valuation ν_{ini} assigns 0 to all clocks. The set is *empty* if ν_{ini} does not satisfy the invariant $I(\ell_{\text{ini}})$. In that case the timed automaton is ill-defined as well because it cannot even start.

Since all the transitions $\xrightarrow{\lambda}$ are binary relations on the set $\text{Conf}(\mathcal{A})$ of configurations, we may apply *relational composition*. Thus

$$\xrightarrow{\lambda_1} \circ \xrightarrow{\lambda_2}$$

is the binary relation on $\text{Conf}(\mathcal{A})$ defined by first applying $\xrightarrow{\lambda_1}$ and then $\xrightarrow{\lambda_2}$. At the level of configurations this means: for all $\langle \ell_1, \nu_1 \rangle, \langle \ell_2, \nu_2 \rangle \in \text{Conf}(\mathcal{A})$

$$\langle \ell_1, \nu_1 \rangle \xrightarrow{\lambda_1} \circ \xrightarrow{\lambda_2} \langle \ell_2, \nu_2 \rangle$$

iff there exists some $\langle \ell', \nu' \rangle \in \mathit{Conf}(\mathcal{A})$ with

$$\langle \ell_1, \nu_1 \rangle \xrightarrow{\lambda_1} \langle \ell', \nu' \rangle \text{ and } \langle \ell', \nu' \rangle \xrightarrow{\lambda_2} \langle \ell_2, \nu_2 \rangle \,.$$

Remark 4.5 (Time-additivity)
For all $t_1, t_2 \in \mathsf{Time}$ the following property of *time-additivity* holds:

$$\xrightarrow{t_1} \circ \xrightarrow{t_2} \;=\; \xrightarrow{t_1+t_2} \,.$$

This property relies on the requirement that $I(\ell)$ holds invariantly while time is progressing.

A *transition sequence* is any finite or infinite sequence of the form

$$\langle \ell_0, \nu_0 \rangle \xrightarrow{\lambda_1} \langle \ell_1, \nu_1 \rangle \xrightarrow{\lambda_2} \langle \ell_2, \nu_2 \rangle \xrightarrow{\lambda_3} \ldots$$

with $\langle \ell_0, \nu_0 \rangle \in C_{\mathrm{ini}}$ showing all the intermediate configurations of the transitions taken. Thus if $C_{\mathrm{ini}} = \varnothing$ there does not exist any transition sequence. A *configuration* $\langle \ell, \nu \rangle$ is *reachable* iff there is a transition sequence of the form

$$\langle \ell_0, \nu_0 \rangle \xrightarrow{\lambda_1} \ldots \xrightarrow{\lambda_n} \langle \ell, \nu \rangle.$$

A *location* ℓ is *reachable* iff a configuration of the form $\langle \ell, \nu \rangle$ is reachable. Note that an isolated location is not reachable.

Example 4.6 (Light controller, continued)
Look at a timed automaton $\mathcal{L}$ for the light controller of Example 4.1:

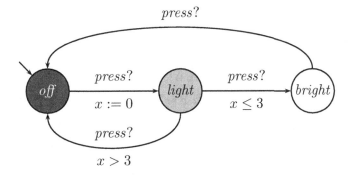

A finite transition sequence of the corresponding transition system $T(\mathcal{L})$ is

$$\langle \mathit{off}, x = 0 \rangle \xrightarrow{2.5} \langle \mathit{off}, x = 2.5 \rangle \xrightarrow{1.7} \langle \mathit{off}, x = 4.2 \rangle$$

$$\xrightarrow{\mathit{press?}} \langle \mathit{light}, x = 0 \rangle \xrightarrow{2.1} \langle \mathit{light}, x = 2.1 \rangle$$

$$\xrightarrow{\mathit{press?}} \langle \mathit{bright}, x = 2.1 \rangle \xrightarrow{10} \langle \mathit{bright}, x = 12.1 \rangle$$

$$\xrightarrow{\mathit{press?}} \langle \mathit{off}, x = 12.1 \rangle.$$

Here and in the following examples we write $x = t$ for a valuation ν with $\nu(x) = t$. This sequence shows that all three control locations of $\mathcal{L}$ are reachable. ∎

Since clocks can be reset in action transitions, a configuration $\langle \ell, \nu \rangle$ does not tell us how much time has elapsed since the start of the transition sequence. To record this information, we consider *time-stamped configurations* of the form

$$\langle \ell, \nu \rangle, t$$

where the time stamp $t \in \mathsf{Time}$ corresponds to the value of a special clock that is never reset. We extend the two types of labelled transitions accordingly:

- In a *time-stamped delay transition* the time stamp advances by some value $t' \in \mathsf{Time}$, but the location is left unchanged. Formally,

$$\langle \ell, \nu \rangle, t \xrightarrow{t'} \langle \ell, \nu + t' \rangle, t + t'$$

where $\langle \ell, \nu \rangle \xrightarrow{t'} \langle \ell, \nu + t' \rangle$ is a (normal) delay transition.

- In a *time-stamped action transition* an action $\alpha \in B_{?!}$ occurs and some clocks may be reset, but time does not advance. Formally,

$$\langle \ell, \nu \rangle, t \xrightarrow{\alpha} \langle \ell', \nu' \rangle, t$$

where $\langle \ell, \nu \rangle \xrightarrow{\alpha} \langle \ell', \nu' \rangle$ is a (normal) action transition.

Definition 4.7 (Computation path)

A *computation path* (or simply *path*) of $\mathcal{A}$ starting in the time-stamped configuration $\langle \ell_0, \nu_0 \rangle, t_0$ is a sequence

$$\xi : \langle \ell_0, \nu_0 \rangle, t_0 \xrightarrow{\lambda_1} \langle \ell_1, \nu_1 \rangle, t_1 \xrightarrow{\lambda_2} \langle \ell_2, \nu_2 \rangle, t_2 \xrightarrow{\lambda_3} \cdots$$

of time-stamped configurations of $\mathcal{A}$ which is either infinite or maximally finite, i.e. the sequence cannot be extended any further by some time-stamped transition. A *computation path* (or simply *path*) of $\mathcal{A}$ is a computation path starting in $\langle \ell_0, \nu_0 \rangle, 0$ where $\langle \ell_0, \nu_0 \rangle \in C_{\text{ini}}$.

Intuitively, each computation path should be infinite because time should be able to progress beyond any given bound. However, it is easy to construct timed automata that violate this property.

Example 4.8 (Zeno behaviour)
Consider the following timed automaton $\mathcal{A}$:

$\mathcal{A}:$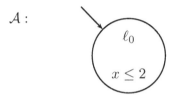

The clock invariant $x \leq 2$ tells us that the initial location ℓ_0 must be left after 2 seconds. However, there is no outgoing edge. Thus in any computation path of $\mathcal{A}$ time cannot progress beyond 2. Note that there are both finite and infinite computation paths satisfying this property. For instance, a finite computation path is

$$\xi_{\text{fin}} : \langle \ell_0, x = 0 \rangle, 0 \xrightarrow{2} \langle \ell_0, x = 2 \rangle, 2,$$

and an infinite computation path is

$$\xi_\infty : \langle \ell_0, x = 0 \rangle, 0 \xrightarrow{1/2} \langle \ell_0, x = 1/2 \rangle, \frac{1}{2} \xrightarrow{1/4} \langle \ell_0, x = 3/4 \rangle, \frac{3}{4}$$
$$\cdots \xrightarrow{1/2^n} \langle \ell_0, x = (2^n - 1)/2^n \rangle, \frac{2^n - 1}{2^n} \cdots \quad (\text{for all } n \in \mathbb{N}).$$

In ξ_{fin} a *timelock* occurs, i.e. time is stopped. In ξ_∞ time progresses with each transition but in smaller and smaller quantities. Such a computation path is known as a *Zeno behaviour*, named after the Greek philosopher Zeno of Elea. ∎

Such computation paths are deficient. In a "realistic" path the time stamps should constitute a real-time sequence in the sense of the following definition:

Definition 4.9 (Real-time sequence)

A *real-time sequence* is an infinite sequence

$$t_0, t_1, t_2, t_3, \ldots$$

of values $t_i \in$ Time for $i \in \mathbb{N}$ with the following properties:

(1) *Monotonicity*: $\forall i \in \mathbb{N} \bullet\ t_i \leq t_{i+1}$.

(2) *Non-Zeno behaviour* or *unboundedness*: $\forall t \in$ Time $\exists i \in \mathbb{N} \bullet\ t < t_i$.

Now we define a *run* as a computation path where the time stamps enjoy these properties.

Definition 4.10 (Run)

A *run of $\mathcal{A}$ starting in the time-stamped configuration* $\langle \ell_0, \nu_0 \rangle, t_0$ is an infinite computation path of $\mathcal{A}$

$$\xi : \langle \ell_0, \nu_0 \rangle, t_0 \xrightarrow{\lambda_1} \langle \ell_1, \nu_1 \rangle, t_1 \xrightarrow{\lambda_2} \langle \ell_2, \nu_2 \rangle, t_2 \xrightarrow{\lambda_3} \ldots,$$

where $t_0, t_1, t_2, t_3, \ldots$ is a real-time sequence. If $\langle \ell_0, \nu_0 \rangle \in C_{\text{ini}}$ and $t_0 = 0$ we call ξ a *run* of $\mathcal{A}$.

While monotonicity holds by definition for any infinite computation path, unboundedness need not hold as shown in Example 4.8. We give an example of a run.

Example 4.11 (Watchdog)

A *watchdog* can be specified by the following timed automaton $\mathcal{W}$ with the alphabet $\{a, s\}$ and a clock x:

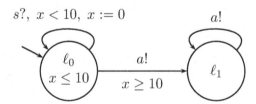

Intuitively, $\mathcal{W}$ checks whether an input signal $s?$ arrives before every 10 seconds. If the signal $s?$ is absent for at least 10 seconds an alarm $a!$ is raised. A run of $\mathcal{W}$ is

$$\langle \ell_0, x = 0 \rangle, 0 \xrightarrow{3.5} \langle \ell_0, x = 3.5 \rangle, 3.5 \xrightarrow{1.5} \langle \ell_0, x = 5 \rangle, 5 \xrightarrow{s?} \langle \ell_0, x = 0 \rangle, 5$$

$$\xrightarrow{6} \langle \ell_0, x = 6 \rangle, 11 \xrightarrow{s?} \langle \ell_0, x = 0 \rangle, 11$$

$$\xrightarrow{4.1} \langle \ell_0, x = 4.1 \rangle, 15.1 \xrightarrow{5.9} \langle \ell_0, x = 10 \rangle, 21$$

$$\xrightarrow{a!} \langle \ell_1, x = 10 \rangle, 21$$

$$\cdots$$

$$\xrightarrow{7} \langle \ell_1, x = 10 + 7 \cdot n \rangle, 21 + 7 \cdot n$$

$$\xrightarrow{a!} \langle \ell_1, x = 10 + 7 \cdot n \rangle, 21 + 7 \cdot n \quad \text{(for all } n \in \mathbb{N})$$

$$\cdots$$

The location invariant in ℓ_0 forces $\mathcal{W}$ to leave ℓ_0 once the clock x shows 10 seconds and thus raise the alarm $a!$. Note that all computation paths of $\mathcal{W}$ are infinite, but not all of them are runs. For instance, among the computation paths is the Zeno path ξ_∞ shown in Example 4.8; it is not a run because the time stamps of ξ_∞ are not unbounded. In fact, the automaton $\mathcal{A}$ of Example 4.8 does not have any runs. It can thus be considered as an ill-defined timed automaton. ∎

4.2 Networks of timed automata

Real-time systems mostly consist of a number of components that work in parallel but also interact with each other from time to time. To model such systems, we consider networks of timed automata built up from single timed automata by two composition operators: parallel composition and restriction. Any notion of parallel composition of process algebra can be taken to combine timed automata. Here we choose the setting of R. Milner's Calculus of Communicating Systems (CCS) because this is implemented in the tool UPPAAL that we use for the automatic verification of properties of timed automata. The idea of CCS is that parallel processes, or in our case timed automata, communicate in a one-to-one fashion via handshake communication. To this end, complementary actions $a!$ and $a?$ of two parallel automata can synchronise to yield the internal action τ but they can also be performed individually to be prepared for a later synchronisation. This is important for parallel composition to be an associative binary operator on timed automata. To enforce synchronisation the channel a has to be declared as a local channel.

Definition 4.12 (Parallel composition)

The *parallel composition* $\mathcal{A}_1 \parallel \mathcal{A}_2$ of two timed automata

$$\mathcal{A}_i = (L_i, B_i, \mathbb{X}_i, I_i, E_i, \ell_{\mathrm{ini},i}),$$

$i = 1, 2$, with disjoint sets of clocks $\mathbb{X}_1$ and $\mathbb{X}_2$ yields the timed automaton

$$\mathcal{A}_1 \parallel \mathcal{A}_2 \stackrel{\mathrm{def}}{=} (L_1 \times L_2, B_1 \cup B_2, \mathbb{X}_1 \cup \mathbb{X}_2, I, E, (\ell_{\mathrm{ini},1}, \ell_{\mathrm{ini},2}))$$

where the following hold:

- Conjunction of location invariants: $I(\ell_1, \ell_2) \stackrel{\mathrm{def}}{\Longleftrightarrow} I_1(\ell_1) \wedge I_2(\ell_2)$.
- The transition relation E is constructed by the following rules:

  - Handshake communication: synchronising $a!$ with $a?$ yields τ (internal action), i.e. if $(\ell_1, \alpha, \varphi_1, Y_1, \ell_1') \in E_1$ and $(\ell_2, \overline{\alpha}, \varphi_2, Y_2, \ell_2') \in E_2$ with $\{a!, a?\} = \{\alpha, \overline{\alpha}\}$ then also

    $$((\ell_1, \ell_2), \tau, \varphi_1 \wedge \varphi_2, Y_1 \cup Y_2, (\ell_1', \ell_2')) \in E.$$

  - Asynchrony: if $(\ell_1, \alpha, \varphi_1, Y_1, \ell_1') \in E_1$ then for all $\ell_2 \in L_2$ also

    $$((\ell_1, \ell_2), \alpha, \varphi_1, Y_1, (\ell_1', \ell_2)) \in E$$

    and conversely, if $(\ell_2, \alpha, \varphi_2, Y_2, \ell_2') \in E_2$ then for all $\ell_1 \in L_1$ also

    $$((\ell_1, \ell_2), \alpha, \varphi_2, Y_2, (\ell_1, \ell_2')) \in E.$$

Definition 4.13 (Restriction)

A local channel b is introduced by the *restriction operator* chan $b \bullet \mathcal{A}$ which, for a timed automaton $\mathcal{A} = (L, B, \mathbb{X}, I, E, \ell_{\mathrm{ini}})$, yields the timed automaton

$$\text{chan } b \bullet \mathcal{A} \stackrel{\mathrm{def}}{=} (L, B \setminus \{b\}, \mathbb{X}, I, E', \ell_{\mathrm{ini}}),$$

where the following holds:

- Restriction: if $(\ell, \alpha, \varphi, Y, \ell') \in E$ and $\alpha \notin \{b!, b?\}$ then $(\ell, \alpha, \varphi, Y, \ell') \in E'$.

For lists of channels we introduce the abbreviation

$$\text{chan } b_1 \ldots b_m \bullet \mathcal{A} \stackrel{\mathrm{def}}{=} \text{chan } b_1 \bullet \ldots \text{chan } b_m \bullet \mathcal{A}.$$

When comparing timed automata we are often not interested in the exact names of locations but only in the structure of the edges modulo logical equivalence of the clock constraints. To this end, we introduce the following notion of isomorphism:

Definition 4.14 (Isomorphism)

Two timed automata $\mathcal{A}_i = (L_i, B_i, \mathbb{X}_i, I_i, E_i, \ell_{\text{ini},i})$, with $i = 1, 2$, are called *isomorphic*, abbreviated $\mathcal{A}_1 \simeq \mathcal{A}_2$, if $B_1 = B_2$ and $\mathbb{X}_1 = \mathbb{X}_2$, and there exist two bijections $\beta_L : L_1 \to L_2$ and $\beta_E : E_1 \to E_2$ satisfying the following conditions:

- If $\ell \in L_1$ then $\models I_1(\ell) \iff I_2(\beta_L(\ell))$.
- If $(\ell, \alpha, \varphi_1, Y, \ell') \in E_1$ then $\beta_E(\ell, \alpha, \varphi_1, Y, \ell') = (\beta_L(\ell), \alpha, \varphi_2, Y, \beta_L(\ell'))$ for some constraint φ_2 with $\models \varphi_1 \iff \varphi_2$.
- $\beta_L(\ell_{\text{ini},1}) = \ell_{\text{ini},2}$.

The bijection β_L is called a *location isomorphism* between $\mathcal{A}_1$ and $\mathcal{A}_2$.

Thus in $\mathcal{A}_2$ each location ℓ of $\mathcal{A}_1$ is renamed into $\beta(\ell)$. The location invariants of ℓ and $\beta(\ell)$ are required to be logically equivalent. For each edge in $\mathcal{A}_1$ there is a corresponding edge in $\mathcal{A}_2$ between the renamed locations which is guarded by a logically equivalent clock constraint. It is easy to see that $\simeq$ is an equivalence relation on timed automata.

Proposition 4.15 (Algebraic laws)

Up to isomorphism, parallel composition of timed automata is commutative and associative:

$$\mathcal{A}_1 \parallel \mathcal{A}_2 \simeq \mathcal{A}_2 \parallel \mathcal{A}_1,$$
$$\mathcal{A}_1 \parallel (\mathcal{A}_2 \parallel \mathcal{A}_3) \simeq (\mathcal{A}_1 \parallel \mathcal{A}_2) \parallel \mathcal{A}_3.$$

The chan operator is idempotent and the order of applications of the chan operator is irrelevant:

$$\text{chan } b \bullet \text{chan } b \bullet \mathcal{A} = \text{chan } b \bullet \mathcal{A},$$
$$\text{chan } b_1 \bullet \text{chan } b_2 \bullet \mathcal{A} = \text{chan } b_2 \bullet \text{chan } b_1 \bullet \mathcal{A}.$$

Here equality of the automata holds.

Proof:

To show the commutativity law of parallel composition consider the location isomorphism that maps each location (ℓ_1, ℓ_2) of $\mathcal{A}_1 \parallel \mathcal{A}_2$ to the location (ℓ_2, ℓ_1) of $\mathcal{A}_2 \parallel \mathcal{A}_1$, and use the fact that set union and logical conjunction are commutative. To show the associativity law of parallel composition consider the location isomorphism that maps each location $(\ell_1, (\ell_2, \ell_3))$ of $\mathcal{A}_1 \parallel (\mathcal{A}_2 \parallel \mathcal{A}_3)$ to the location $((\ell_1, \ell_2), \ell_3)$ of $(\mathcal{A}_1 \parallel \mathcal{A}_2) \parallel \mathcal{A}_3$, and use the fact that set union and logical conjunction are associative. The laws of the chan operator follow immediately from its definition. $\square$

In applications one often considers *networks* $\mathcal{N}$ of timed automata working in parallel and communicating over channels, some of which are local:

$$\mathcal{N} = \text{chan } b_1, \dots, b_m \bullet (\mathcal{A}_1 \ || \ \dots \ || \ \mathcal{A}_n).$$

Since both parallel composition of timed automata and the restriction operator again yield timed automata, Definition 4.4 can be applied to obtain the operational semantics of such networks. In a network $\mathcal{N}$ each component automaton $\mathcal{A}_i$ has its own control location ℓ_i. Hence, for the whole network a *control vector* $\vec{\ell} = (\ell_1, \dots, \ell_n)$ collects the control locations of the components. We denote a change of the ith component's location from ℓ_i to ℓ_i' by $\vec{\ell}[\ell_i := \ell_i']$. The following lemma calculates the operational semantics $\mathcal{T}(\mathcal{N})$:

Lemma 4.16 (Operational semantics of networks)
For timed automata $\mathcal{A}_i = (L_i, B_i, \mathbb{X}_i, I_i, E_i, \ell_{\text{ini},i})$ with $i = 1, \dots, n$ and pairwise disjoint sets $\mathbb{X}_i$ of clocks consider the network

$$\mathcal{N} = \text{chan } b_1, \dots, b_m \bullet (\mathcal{A}_1 \ || \ \dots \ || \ \mathcal{A}_n).$$

Then the operational semantics of $\mathcal{N}$ yields the labelled transition system

$$\mathcal{T}(\mathcal{N}) = (\mathit{Conf}(\mathcal{N}), \mathsf{Time} \cup B_{?!}, \{ \xrightarrow{\lambda} \ | \ \lambda \in \mathsf{Time} \cup B_{?!}\}, C_{\text{ini}})$$

where:

- $\mathbb{X} = \bigcup_{k=1}^{n} \mathbb{X}_k$ and $B = (\bigcup_{k=1}^{n} B_k) \setminus \{b_1, \dots, b_m\}$.
- $\mathit{Conf}(\mathcal{N}) = \{\langle \vec{\ell}, \nu \rangle \ | \ \ell_i \in L_i \wedge \nu : \mathbb{X} \longrightarrow \mathsf{Time} \wedge \nu \models \bigwedge_{k=1}^{n} I_k(\ell_k)\}$.
- *For each $\lambda \in \mathsf{Time} \cup B_{?!}$ the transition relation $\xrightarrow{\lambda} \subseteq \mathit{Conf}(\mathcal{N}) \times \mathit{Conf}(\mathcal{N})$ has one of the following three types:*

  (i) *A local transition $\langle \vec{\ell}, \nu \rangle \xrightarrow{\alpha} \langle \vec{\ell}', \nu' \rangle$ occurs if for some $i \in \{1, \dots, n\}$ there is an edge $(\ell_i, \alpha, \varphi, Y, \ell_i') \in E_i$ with $\alpha \in B_{?!}$ in the ith automaton such that*

     $- \nu \models \varphi$, *i.e. the guard is satisfied,*
     $- \vec{\ell}' = \vec{\ell}[\ell_i := \ell_i']$,
     $- \nu' = \nu[Y := 0]$ *and* $\nu' \models I_i(\ell_i')$.

  (ii) *A synchronisation transition $\langle \vec{\ell}, \nu \rangle \xrightarrow{\tau} \langle \vec{\ell}', \nu' \rangle$ occurs if for some $i, j \in \{1, \dots, n\}$ with $i \neq j$ and some channel $b \in B_i \cap B_j$ there are edges $(\ell_i, b!, \varphi_i, Y_i, \ell_i') \in E_i$ and $(\ell_j, b?, \varphi_j, Y_j, \ell_j') \in E_j$, i.e. the ith and the jth automaton can synchronise their output and input on the channel b, such that*

     $- \nu \models \varphi_i \wedge \varphi_j$, *i.e. both guards are satisfied,*

$-\ \vec{\ell}' = \vec{\ell}\,[\ell_i := \ell_i'][\ell_j := \ell_j'],$

$-\ \nu' = \nu[Y_i \cup Y_j := 0]$ and $\nu' \models I_i(\ell_i') \wedge I_j(\ell_j').$

(iii) A delay transition $\langle \vec{\ell}, \nu \rangle \xrightarrow{\ t\ } \langle \vec{\ell}, \nu + t \rangle$ occurs if $\nu + t' \models \bigwedge_{k=1}^{n} I_k(\ell_k)$ for all $t' \in [0, t]$, i.e. all invariants are satisfied during the passage of time.

- $C_{\mathrm{ini}} = \{\langle \overrightarrow{\ell_{\mathrm{ini}}}, \nu_{\mathrm{ini}} \rangle\} \cap \mathit{Conf}(\mathcal{N})$ with $\overrightarrow{\ell_{\mathrm{ini}}} = (\ell_{\mathrm{ini},1}, \dots, \ell_{\mathrm{ini},n})$ and $\nu_{\mathrm{ini}}(x) = 0$ for all clocks $x \in \mathbb{X}.$

Proof:

By the definition of parallel composition and restriction, the locations of $\mathcal{N}$ are of the form $\vec{\ell} = (\ell_1, \dots, \ell_n)$, where $\ell_i \in L_i$, and have $\bigwedge_{k=1}^{n} I_k(\ell_k)$ as their location variant. The labelled transition system $\mathcal{T}(\mathcal{N})$ contains delay transitions $\langle \vec{\ell}, \nu \rangle \xrightarrow{\ t\ } \langle \vec{\ell}, \nu + t \rangle$ and discrete transitions $\langle \vec{\ell}, \nu \rangle \xrightarrow{\ \alpha\ } \langle \vec{\ell}', \nu' \rangle$. By Definition 4.4, applied to $\mathcal{T}(\mathcal{N})$, the delay transitions are exactly as claimed for transitions of type (iii) in the lemma.

For a discrete transition $\langle \vec{\ell}, \nu \rangle \xrightarrow{\ \alpha\ } \langle \vec{\ell}', \nu' \rangle$, Definition 4.4 requires that there is an edge $(\vec{\ell}, \alpha, \varphi, Y, \vec{\ell}') \in E$, the set of edges in $\mathcal{N}$, such that

- $\nu \models \varphi,$
- $\nu' = \nu[Y := 0],$
- $\nu' \models I(\vec{\ell}')$, i.e. $\nu' \models \bigwedge_{k=1}^{n} I_k(\ell_k').$

By Definition 4.12 of parallel composition and Definition 4.13 of restriction, the edge $(\vec{\ell}, \alpha, \varphi, Y, \vec{\ell}') \in E$ can have two forms.

(i) *Asynchrony:* $\alpha \in B_{?!}$ and for some $i \in \{1, \dots, n\}$ there is an edge of the form $(\ell_i, \alpha, \varphi, Y, \ell_i') \in E_i$ such that

- $\vec{\ell}' = \vec{\ell}\,[\ell_i := \ell_i'].$

Since $Y \subseteq \mathbb{X}_i$, the disjointness of the sets of clocks yields $Y \cap \mathbb{X}_k = \varnothing$ for $k \neq i$. Thus the claim (i) of the lemma follows since $\nu' \models \bigwedge_{k=1}^{n} I_k(\ell_k')$ iff $\nu' \models I_i(\ell_i').$

(ii) *Synchronisation:* $\alpha = \tau$ and for some $i, j \in \{1, \dots, n\}$ with $i \neq j$ and some $b \in B_i \cap B_j$ there are edges $(\ell_i, b!, \varphi_i, Y_i, \ell_i') \in E_i$ and $(\ell_j, b?, \varphi_j, Y_j, \ell_j') \in E_j$ such that

- $\varphi = \varphi_i \wedge \varphi_j,$
- $Y = Y_i \cup Y_j,$
- $\vec{\ell}' = \vec{\ell}\,[\ell_i := \ell_i'][\ell_j := \ell_j'].$

Since $Y_i \subseteq \mathbb{X}_i$ and $Y_j \subseteq \mathbb{X}_j$, the disjointness of the sets of clocks yields $Y \cap \mathbb{X}_k = \varnothing$ for $k \neq i, j$. Thus the claim (ii) of the lemma follows since $\nu' \models \bigwedge_{k=1}^{n} I_k(\ell_k')$ iff $\nu' \models I_i(\ell_i') \wedge I_j(\ell_j').$

This completes the proof of the lemma. □

A network $\mathcal{N} = $ chan $b_1, \ldots, b_m \bullet (\mathcal{A}_1 \parallel \ldots \parallel \mathcal{A}_n)$ is called *closed* if all channels of the automata are local, i.e. if $\{b_1, \ldots, b_m\}$ is the set of all channels used in one of the $\mathcal{A}_i$. Since then $B = \varnothing$ holds in Lemma 4.16, the operational semantics of closed networks has only transitions labelled with the internal action τ or with a delay time $t \in$ Time. Let us now consider some examples.

Example 4.17 (Timed buffers)

The following timed automata $\mathcal{P}$ and $\mathcal{Q}$ model two different timed one-place buffers. When $\mathcal{P}$ has been engaged in an input action on channel a it has to perform the corresponding output action on channel b in less than 2 seconds. For $\mathcal{Q}$ the following behaviour is specified. Initially, $\mathcal{Q}$ has to wait for more than 1 second before the first input action on channel b can occur. Once a corresponding output action on channel c has occurred, the next input on b can only happen more than 1 second later.

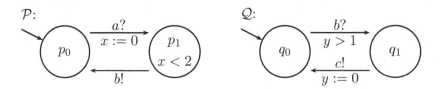

The parallel composition of $\mathcal{P}$ and $\mathcal{Q}$ yields the timed automaton $\mathcal{P} \parallel \mathcal{Q}$:

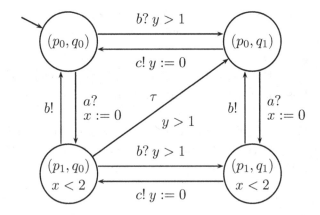

In $\mathcal{P} \parallel \mathcal{Q}$ the first τ-transition is possible only more than 1 second after the start (due to the guard $y > 1$ of the τ-transition) and less than 2 seconds after the initial a?-transition (due to the reset of the clock x at the initial a?-transition and the invariant $x < 2$ in the location (p_0, q_0)). All subsequent

τ-transitions are possible only more than 1 second after the last $c!$-transition (due to the reset of the clock y at the $c!$-transitions and the guard $y > 1$ at the τ-transition) and less than 2 seconds after the last $a?$-transition (due to the reset of the clock x at the $a?$-transitions and the invariant $x < 2$ in the location (p_0, q_0)).

Restricting the communications on the channel b yields chan $b \bullet (P \parallel Q)$ as a network. In the corresponding timed automaton all transitions labelled with $b!$ and $b?$ are removed:

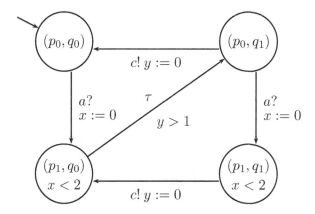

Thus restriction enforces synchronisation between $\mathcal{P}$ and $\mathcal{Q}$ along the common channel b yielding an internal τ-transition. ∎

Example 4.18 (Generalised railroad crossing)
Consider the following two timed automata $\mathcal{T}$ and $\mathcal{G}$ modelling the track and the gate of the generalised railroad crossing introduced in Section 1.3.

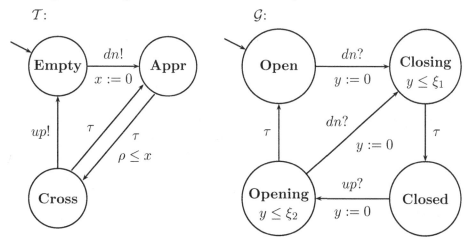

Initially, the track is empty and the gate is open. When a train is approaching, the track automaton communicates *dn* (for "down") to the gate automaton which then starts closing the gate. By the invariant $y \leq \xi_1$ in the location **Closing**, this location will be left to the safe location **Closed** within ξ_1 time. The train automaton models that each train takes at least ρ time to reach the crossing. Provided that ξ_1 and ρ are suitably constrained, the gate will be closed before the train reaches the crossing. After the train leaves the crossing, either a new train approaches or the track is empty. In the latter case the track automaton communicates *up* to the gate, which then starts opening within ξ_2 time.

The timed automata for the closed network

$$\mathcal{N} = \mathsf{chan}\ up, dn \bullet (\mathcal{T} \parallel \mathcal{G})$$

has $3 \cdot 4 = 12$ locations but six of them are isolated. With all isolated locations removed, the automaton looks as follows:

$\mathcal{N}$:

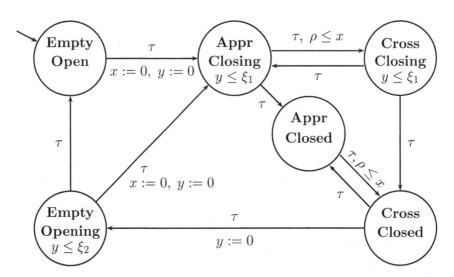

An example of an isolated combined location is **Appr/Open**. In $\mathcal{T} \parallel \mathcal{G}$ this location is connected to the combined initial location **Empty/Open** only via an edge with the action *dn*! which is removed when applying the operator $\mathsf{chan}\ up, dn$ to $\mathcal{T} \parallel \mathcal{G}$. This leaves **Appr/Open** isolated in $\mathcal{N}$, so it is not shown in the timed automaton above.

Note that the combined location **Cross/Closing** represents an unsafe location: a train is in the crossing while the gate is still closing. However, by assuming $\xi_1 < \rho$, i.e. the fastest train takes longer to approach the crossing than the closing of the gate, we can show that this unsafe location is not reachable. Indeed, in the combined location **Appr/Closing** the clocks x and y show the same time $t \in$ Time:

$$\langle\textbf{Empty/Open}, x = y = 0\rangle \xrightarrow{\tau} \circ \xrightarrow{t} \langle\textbf{Appr/Closing}, x = y = t\rangle.$$

By the location invariant $y \leq \xi_1$, this location has to be left by time ξ_1, at which the guard $\rho \leq x$ of transition to **Cross/Closing** is not yet enabled. Thus under the assumption $\xi_1 < \rho$ the network $\mathcal{N}$ is safe: the only combined location with a train being in the crossing is **Cross/Closed** where the gate is closed.   ∎

4.3 Reachability is decidable

In this section we show that for timed automata the reachability of configurations is decidable. More precisely, we consider two variants of reachability.

4.3.1 Location reachability

First we consider the following *location reachability problem*.

Given: A timed automaton $\mathcal{A}$ and one of its control locations ℓ.
Question: Is ℓ reachable, i.e. is there a transition sequence of the form

$$\langle\ell_{\mathrm{ini}}, \nu_{\mathrm{ini}}\rangle \xrightarrow{\lambda_1} \ldots \xrightarrow{\lambda_n} \langle\ell, \nu\rangle$$

in the labelled transition system $\mathcal{T}(\mathcal{A})$?

A key result on timed automata due to R. Alur and D. Dill is the decidability of this question. This is remarkable because the clocks range over real numbers and thus yield infinitely many configurations that need to be checked. To explain this result, we proceed in several steps.

First, we assume without loss of generality that in $\mathcal{A}$ only time conditions $\varphi \in \Phi(\mathbb{X})$ with constants $c \in \mathbb{N}$ appear. For a timed automaton $\mathcal{A}$ with time constants $c \in \mathbb{Q}_{\geq 0}$, we define the *scaling factor*

$$t \stackrel{\mathrm{def}}{=} \text{ least common multiple of the denominators}$$
$$\text{of all time constants that appear in } \mathcal{A}.$$

Let $t \cdot \mathcal{A}$ be the timed automaton $\mathcal{A}$ where all time constants are multiplied by t. Then the following hold:

- In $t \cdot \mathcal{A}$ all time constants are in $\mathbb{N}$.
- A location ℓ is reachable in $t \cdot \mathcal{A}$ iff ℓ is reachable in $\mathcal{A}$.

Hence, we can assume without loss of generality that $\mathcal{A}$ uses only time constants in $\mathbb{N}$. Second, we introduce the time-abstract transition relation.

Definition 4.19 (Time-abstract transition system)

For a timed automaton $\mathcal{A}$ the *time-abstract transition system* $\mathcal{U}(\mathcal{A})$ is obtained from the transition system $\mathcal{T}(\mathcal{A})$ of Definition 4.4 by taking

$$\mathcal{U}(\mathcal{A}) \stackrel{\text{def}}{=} (\mathit{Conf}(\mathcal{A}), B_{?!}, \{ \stackrel{\alpha}{\Longrightarrow} \mid \alpha \in B_{?!} \}, C_{\text{ini}})$$

where $\{ \stackrel{\alpha}{\Longrightarrow} \mid \alpha \in B_{?!} \}$ is a family of labelled *time-abstract transition relations*

$$\stackrel{\alpha}{\Longrightarrow} \subseteq \mathit{Conf}(\mathcal{A}) \times \mathit{Conf}(\mathcal{A})$$

defined as follows: for configurations $\langle \ell, \nu \rangle, \langle \ell', \nu' \rangle$ of $\mathcal{A}$ and actions $\alpha \in B_{?!}$

$$\langle \ell, \nu \rangle \stackrel{\alpha}{\Longrightarrow} \langle \ell', \nu' \rangle$$

iff there exists some $t \in \mathrm{Time}$ with

$$\langle \ell, \nu \rangle \stackrel{t}{\longrightarrow} \circ \stackrel{\alpha}{\longrightarrow} \langle \ell', \nu' \rangle.$$

Thus a time-abstract transition combines two steps of $\mathcal{A}$: first time passes and then an action transition is taken. The following lemma shows that it suffices to consider $\mathcal{U}(\mathcal{A})$ instead of $\mathcal{T}(\mathcal{A})$ when solving the reachability problem:

Lemma 4.20

For all locations ℓ of a given timed automaton $\mathcal{A}$ the following holds:

$$\ell \text{ is reachable in } \mathcal{T}(\mathcal{A}) \text{ iff } \ell \text{ is reachable in } \mathcal{U}(\mathcal{A}).$$

Proof:

"Only if": Let ℓ be reachable in $\mathcal{T}(\mathcal{A})$. Then there exists a transition sequence of the form

$$\langle \ell_{\text{ini}}, \nu_{\text{ini}} \rangle \xrightarrow{t_{0,1}} \circ \; \ldots \; \circ \xrightarrow{t_{0,n_0}} \qquad \circ \xrightarrow{\alpha_1} \langle \ell_1, \nu_1 \rangle$$

$$\vdots \qquad \qquad \ddots \qquad \qquad \vdots$$

$$\xrightarrow{t_{k-1,1}} \circ \; \ldots \; \circ \xrightarrow{t_{k-1,n_{k-1}}} \qquad \circ \xrightarrow{\alpha_k} \langle \ell_k, \nu_k \rangle$$

$$\xrightarrow{t_{k,1}} \circ \; \ldots \; \circ \xrightarrow{t_{k,n_k}} \qquad \qquad \langle \ell, \nu \rangle$$

with $\ell = \ell_k$. By Remark 4.5 on time-additivity, we have

$$\langle \ell_{\text{ini}}, \nu_{\text{ini}} \rangle \xrightarrow{\sum_{i=1}^{n_0} t_{0,i}} \circ \xrightarrow{\alpha_1} \langle \ell_1, \nu_1 \rangle \; \ldots \; \xrightarrow{\sum_{i=1}^{n_{k-1}} t_{k-1,i}} \circ \xrightarrow{\alpha_k} \langle \ell_k, \nu_k \rangle = \langle \ell, \nu_k \rangle.$$

By the definition of the time-abstract transition relations,

$$\langle \ell_{\text{ini}}, \nu_{\text{ini}} \rangle \stackrel{\alpha_1}{\Longrightarrow} \langle \ell_1, \nu_1 \rangle \; \ldots \; \stackrel{\alpha_k}{\Longrightarrow} \langle \ell_k, \nu_k \rangle = \langle \ell, \nu_k \rangle.$$

Thus ℓ is reachable in $\mathcal{U}(\mathcal{A})$.

"*If*": Expand the definition of the time-abstract transition relation $\overset{\alpha}{\Longrightarrow}$.

$\square$

Note that $\mathcal{U}(\mathcal{A})$ has still infinitely (even uncountably) many configurations. The third step is therefore to collapse these configurations into *finitely many* so-called regions, which are equivalence classes of a suitably defined equivalence relation on clock valuations. For this equivalence to be respected by the abstract transition relations, it should be a bisimulation.

Definition 4.21 (Bisimulation)

An equivalence relation $\cong$ on valuations is a *(strong) bisimulation* iff whenever

$$\nu_1 \cong \nu_2 \quad \text{and} \quad \langle \ell, \nu_1 \rangle \overset{\alpha}{\Longrightarrow} \langle \ell', \nu_1' \rangle$$

holds then there exists a valuation ν_2' with

$$\nu_1' \cong \nu_2' \quad \text{and} \quad \langle \ell, \nu_2 \rangle \overset{\alpha}{\Longrightarrow} \langle \ell', \nu_2' \rangle.$$

This can be visualised by the following commuting diagram:

$$
\begin{array}{ccc}
\langle \ell, \nu_1 \rangle & \overset{\nu_1 \cong \nu_2}{- - - - - - -} & \langle \ell, \nu_2 \rangle \\
\alpha \Big\Downarrow & & \Big\Downarrow \alpha \\
\langle \ell', \nu_1' \rangle & \underset{\nu_1' \cong \nu_2'}{- - - - - - -} & \langle \ell', \nu_2' \rangle
\end{array}
$$

Then we can lift the transition relation on the equivalence classes and know that this is well-defined. Now we are interested in the coarsest equivalence relation $\cong$ on clock valuations that has this property. These equivalence classes are called *clock regions*. Let us first study an example.

Example 4.22

Let $\mathcal{A}_0$ be the timed automaton with the alphabet $B = \{a, b, c, d\}$ and the clocks x and y shown in the following diagram:

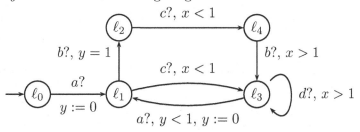

$\blacksquare$

For each location $\ell \in \{\ell_0, \ell_1, \ell_2, \ell_3, \ell_4\}$ the set of configurations $\langle \ell, \nu \rangle$ can be visualised as a point in a two-dimensional space with the coordinates $(\nu(x), \nu(y))$, as illustrated by the following diagram:

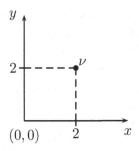

In the following we investigate which clock valuations *cannot* be distinguished by a timed automaton and hence belong to the same equivalence class $\cong$.

The regions depend on the number of clocks and, for each clock x, on the maximum c_x of the time constants with which x is compared in the timed automaton.

Definition 4.23 (Maximal constant)

For a timed automaton $\mathcal{A} = (L, B, \mathbb{X}, I, E, \ell_{\text{ini}})$ and a clock $x \in \mathbb{X}$ let $c_x \in \mathbb{N}$ be the maximum of the time constants c that appear in constraints of the form $x \sim c$ or difference constraints of the form $x - y \sim c$ or $y - x \sim c$ in $\mathcal{A}$.

In case of one clock x it is clear that all valuations ν_1 and ν_2 with $\nu_i(x) > c_x$ cannot be distinguished by the automaton because there is no such comparison beyond c_x. Each valuation ν with $\nu(x) \in \{0, 1, \ldots, c_x\}$ builds an equivalence class because it is possible for the timed automaton to distinguish valuations with $\nu(x) = k$ and $\nu(x) \neq k$ if $k \in \mathbb{N}$ and $k \leq c_x$. Furthermore, it is clear that valuations ν_1 and ν_2 with $\nu_i(x) \in (k, k+1)$, the open interval with lower bound k and upper bound $k+1$, belong to the same class if $k \in \{0, \ldots, c_x - 1\}$. Hence, for $c_x \geq 1$ we get the following set of equivalence classes:

$$\{\{0\}, (0, 1), \{1\}, (1, 2), \ldots, \{c_x\}, (c_x, \infty)\}.$$

For instance, $c_x = 1$ yields four equivalence classes. In general, we have $2c_x + 2$ equivalence classes.

In case of two clocks x and y it is *not* sufficient to take the Cartesian product of the corresponding equivalence relations for the individual clocks

x and y as shown in Figure 4.1, part (a). Additionally, the difference constraints $x - y \sim c$ and $y - x \sim c$ come into play; they yield the diagonal regions as shown in Figure 4.1, part (b).

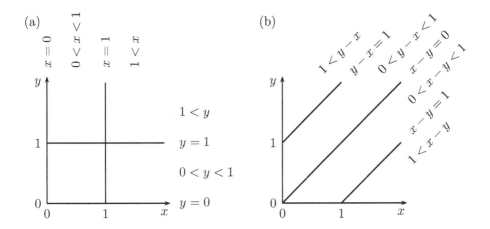

Fig. 4.1. Regions for individual clocks and clock differences

Altogether, the regions for two clocks x and y with $c_x = c_y = 1$ are depicted in Figure 4.2. Instead of $4 \times 4 = 16$ regions we see 32 regions. Why are all these regions needed? Suppose the valuations in the grey square $(0, 1) \times (0, 1)$ were all equivalent. Then the successor relation would not satisfy the bisimulation property. For example, if at a location ℓ there exists an edge $(\ell, a, \text{true}, \varnothing, \ell)$, which is always enabled and leaves both clocks unchanged, we would get for the valuations $(0.5, 0.4)$, $(0.5, 0.5)$, and $(0.4, 0.5)$ different equivalences classes as successors when exactly 0.5 seconds elapse. Hence, the grey square is split into three regions because there are three different successor regions when time passes.

We can generalise this observation to more than two clocks. This leads us to the final definition of the equivalence $\cong$ on clock valuations. From mathematical calculus it is known that each real number $q \in \mathbb{R}_{\geq 0}$ can be split in a unique way into an integer part $\lfloor q \rfloor$, the *floor* of q, and a fraction $frac(q)$. Formally,

$$q = \lfloor q \rfloor + frac(q), \text{ where } \lfloor q \rfloor \in \mathbb{N} \text{ and } 0 \leq frac(q) < 1.$$

Definition 4.24 (Equivalence on valuations)

Let $\mathbb{X}$ be a set of clocks and the constant $c_x \in \mathbb{N}$ be given for each clock $x \in \mathbb{X}$. Then we define a relation $\cong$ on the set of valuations for $\mathbb{X}$ as follows:

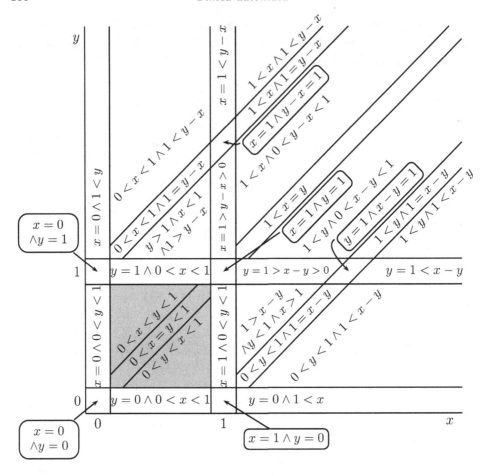

Fig. 4.2. Regions for two clocks x and y with $c_x = c_y = 1$

for valuations ν and ν' for $\mathbb{X}$

$$\nu \cong \nu'$$

holds iff the following four conditions are satisfied:

(1) For all $x \in \mathbb{X}$ the following holds:

$$\lfloor \nu(x) \rfloor = \lfloor \nu'(x) \rfloor$$
$$\text{or both } \nu(x) > c_x \text{ and } \nu'(x) > c_x.$$

(2) For all $x \in \mathbb{X}$ with $\nu(x) \le c_x$ the following holds:

$$frac(\nu(x)) = 0 \text{ iff } frac(\nu'(x)) = 0.$$

(3) For all $x, y \in \mathbb{X}$ the following holds:

$$\lfloor \nu(x) - \nu(y) \rfloor = \lfloor \nu'(x) - \nu'(y) \rfloor$$
$$\text{or both } |\nu(x) - \nu(y)| > c \text{ and } |\nu'(x) - \nu'(y)| > c$$

where $c = \max\{c_x, c_y\}$.

(4) For all $x, y \in \mathbb{X}$ with $-c \le \nu(x) - \nu(y) \le c$ the following holds:

$$frac(\nu(x) - \nu(y)) = 0 \text{ iff } frac(\nu'(x) - \nu'(y)) = 0$$

where $c = \max\{c_x, c_y\}$.

While conditions (1) and (2) deal with individual clocks, conditions (3) and (4) deal with clock differences as illustrated by the following example.

Example 4.25
For the valuations $\nu_1 = (0.5, 0.4)$, $\nu_2 = (0.5, 0.5)$, and $\nu_3 = (0.4, 0.5)$ we calculate

- $\nu_1 \not\cong \nu_2$ because $frac(\nu_1(x) - \nu_1(y)) = 0.1$ and $frac(\nu_2(x) - \nu_2(y)) = 0$,
- $\nu_2 \not\cong \nu_3$ because $frac(\nu_2(y) - \nu_2(x)) = 0$ and $frac(\nu_3(y) - \nu_3(x)) = 0.1$,
- $\nu_1 \not\cong \nu_3$ because $\lfloor \nu_1(x) - \nu_1(y) \rfloor = 0$ and $\lfloor \nu_3(x) - \nu_3(y) \rfloor = -1$.

∎

It is easy to check that $\cong$ is an equivalence relation on valuations. In fact, the following lemma holds. The proof is left as an exercise.

Lemma 4.26 (Bisimulation)
The equivalence relation $\cong$ is a strong bisimulation.

Definition 4.27 (Region)
For a given valuation ν we denote by $[\nu]$ the equivalence class of ν. We call equivalence classes of $\cong$ *regions*.

As shown in Figure 4.2, we can describe regions by a clock constraint φ over the given clocks. Hence, we also use the notation $[\varphi]$ for the region $[\nu]$ that is characterised by φ, i.e. with $\nu' \models \varphi$ iff all $\nu' \cong \nu$. For example, the lower triangle region of the shaded area in Figure 4.2 is given by $[0 < y < x < 1]$.

Lemma 4.28 (Number of regions)
Let $\mathbb{X}$ be the set of clocks, $c_x \in \mathbb{N}$ be the maximal constant for each $x \in \mathbb{X}$, and $c = \max\{c_x \mid x \in \mathbb{X}\}$. Then

$$(2c + 2)^{|\mathbb{X}|} \cdot (4c + 3)^{\frac{1}{2}|\mathbb{X}| \cdot (|\mathbb{X}| - 1)}$$

is an upper bound of the number of regions.

Proof:

We calculate the upper bound of the number of regions as follows:

- Considering individual clocks yields the left-hand factor of the product. Since $c_x \leq c$, we get at most $2c+2$ intervals for the values of a given clock x that can be distinguished by the timed automaton. These intervals can be characterised by the following constraints:

$$[x = 0], [0 < x < 1], [x = 1], [1 < x < 2], \ldots, [x = c], [x > c].$$

  Considering all clocks $x \in \mathbb{X}$ together thus yields at most $(2c + 2)^{|\mathbb{X}|}$ regions.

- Considering clock differences yields the right-hand factor of the product. Extending the argument from above, it is easy to see that for each two-element set $\{x, y\}$ of clocks x and y we have $4c+3$ intervals for the values of clock differences $x - y$ that can be distinguished by the timed automaton. These intervals can be characterised by the following constraints:

$$[x - y < -c], [x - y = -c], \ldots, [-1 < x - y < 0],$$
$$[x - y = 0], [0 < x - y < 1], \ldots, [x - y = c], [x - y > c].$$

  The constraints with negative constants $-c$ can be rewritten into equivalent ones with positive constants c, which are in the set $\Phi(\mathbb{X})$ of clock constraints. For instance, $x - y < -c$ is equivalent to $y - x > c$. Thus when we exchange the role of x and y, we get constraints equivalent to the ones above. Therefore we need to count only all two-element sets $\{x, y\}$ instead of all ordered pairs (x, y) of clocks x and y. The number of two-element sets of clocks from the set $\mathbb{X}$ is $\frac{1}{2}|\mathbb{X}| \cdot (|\mathbb{X}| - 1)$.

This completes our calculations. □

In particular, the lemma proves that there is a *finite* number of regions. We note that it is possible to find tighter bounds than the one presented. In our example we have $|\mathbb{X}| = 2$ and $c_x = c_y = 1$. So the bound calculated by the lemma is $4^2 \cdot 7^1 = 112$ whereas in reality there are (only) 32 regions as shown in Figure 4.2.

Definition 4.29 (Region automaton)

For a timed automaton $\mathcal{A} = (L, B, \mathbb{X}, I, E, \ell_{\text{ini}})$ the *region automaton* $\mathcal{R}(\mathcal{A})$ is defined as the labelled transition system

$$\mathcal{R}(\mathcal{A}) \stackrel{\text{def}}{=} (Conf(\mathcal{R}(\mathcal{A})), B_{?!}, \{ \stackrel{\alpha}{\longrightarrow}_{\mathcal{R}(\mathcal{A})} \mid \alpha \in B_{?!}\}, C_{\text{ini}})$$

where:

- $Conf(\mathcal{R}(\mathcal{A})) = \{\langle \ell, [\nu] \rangle \mid \ell \in L \wedge \nu : \mathbb{X} \longrightarrow \text{Time} \wedge \nu \models I(\ell)\}$ is the set of (*region*) *configurations*, where $[\nu]$ is the region of ν constructed in accordance with the maximal constants c_x for the clocks $x \in \mathbb{X}$.
- For each $\alpha \in B_{?!}$ the transition relation

$$\xrightarrow{\alpha}_{\mathcal{R}(\mathcal{A})} \subseteq Conf(\mathcal{R}(\mathcal{A})) \times Conf(\mathcal{R}(\mathcal{A}))$$

defined as follows:

$$\langle \ell, [\nu] \rangle \xrightarrow{\alpha}_{\mathcal{R}(\mathcal{A})} \langle \ell', [\nu'] \rangle \quad \text{iff} \quad \langle \ell, \nu \rangle \xRightarrow{\alpha} \langle \ell', \nu' \rangle$$

holds in the time-abstract transition system $\mathcal{U}(\mathcal{A})$ of Definition 4.19.

- $C_{\text{ini}} = \{\langle \ell_{\text{ini}}, [\nu_{\text{ini}}] \rangle\} \cap Conf(\mathcal{R}(\mathcal{A}))$ with $\nu_{\text{ini}}(x) = 0$ for all clocks $x \in \mathbb{X}$ is the set of *initial* (region) configurations.

By Lemma 4.28, the set $Conf(\mathcal{R}(\mathcal{A}))$ of region configurations is *finite*. The bisimulation Lemma 4.26 implies that the transition relation $\longrightarrow_{\mathcal{R}(\mathcal{A})}$ is *well-defined*, i.e. independent of the choice of the representative ν of a region $[\nu]$. If $\nu_{\text{ini}} \models I(\ell_{\text{ini}})$ then C_{ini} consists of $\langle \ell_{\text{ini}}, [\nu_{\text{ini}}] \rangle$ as the unique initial region configuration, otherwise $C_{\text{ini}} = \varnothing$.

Remark 4.30
In a configuration $\langle \ell, [\nu] \rangle$ of $\mathcal{R}(\mathcal{A})$ the region $[\nu]$ represents the clock valuations that hold when the location ℓ is *just entered*. For the initial configuration $\langle \ell_{\text{ini}}, [\nu_{\text{ini}}] \rangle$ the region $[\nu_{\text{ini}}]$ is characterised by the initial constraint $\bigwedge_{x \in \mathbb{X}} x = 0$. The clock values obtained when staying longer in a location are *not* represented by the regions of $\mathcal{R}(\mathcal{A})$.

Example 4.31
The region automaton for the timed automaton $\mathcal{A}_0$ of Example 4.22, restricted to the reachable configurations, is shown in Figure 4.3. The initial configuration is $\langle \ell_0, [x = y = 0] \rangle$. We see that the locations $\ell_1, \ell_2,$ and ℓ_3 are reachable from this configuration, but the location ℓ_4 is not reachable (and thus not shown in Figure 4.3). $\blacksquare$

By the following lemma, it suffices to consider $\mathcal{R}(\mathcal{A})$ instead of $\mathcal{U}(\mathcal{A})$ when solving the reachability problem:

Lemma 4.32 (Correctness)
For all locations ℓ of a given timed automaton $\mathcal{A}$ the following holds:

$$\ell \text{ is reachable in } \mathcal{U}(\mathcal{A}) \quad \text{iff} \quad \ell \text{ is reachable in } \mathcal{R}(\mathcal{A}).$$

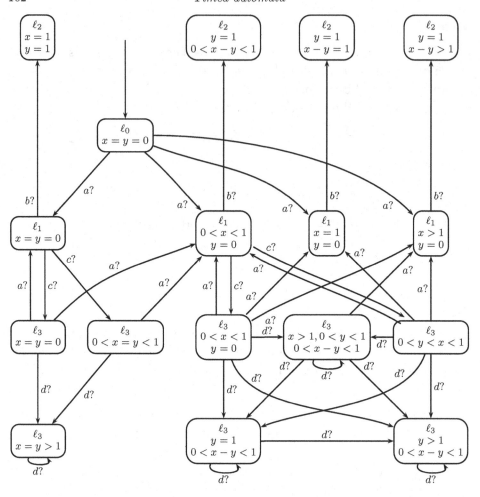

Fig. 4.3. Region automaton for $\mathcal{A}_0$ of Example 4.22

Proof:

The claim follows from the definitions: ℓ is reachable in $\mathcal{U}(\mathcal{A})$ iff there exists a time-abstract transition sequence in $\mathcal{U}(\mathcal{A})$ of the form

$$\langle \ell_{\mathrm{ini}}, \nu_{\mathrm{ini}} \rangle \xrightarrow{\alpha_1} \ldots \xrightarrow{\alpha_k} \langle \ell, \nu \rangle$$

iff there exists a transition sequence in $\mathcal{R}(\mathcal{A})$ of the form

$$\langle \ell_{\mathrm{ini}}, [\nu_{\mathrm{ini}}] \rangle \xrightarrow{\alpha_1}_{\mathcal{R}(\mathcal{A})} \cdots \xrightarrow{\alpha_k}_{\mathcal{R}(\mathcal{A})} \langle \ell, [\nu] \rangle$$

iff ℓ is reachable in $\mathcal{R}(\mathcal{A})$. $\square$

Since the region automaton $\mathcal{R}(\mathcal{A})$ can be constructed effectively from $\mathcal{A}$ and has only finitely many configurations, we obtain the following main theorem:

Theorem 4.33 (Decidability)
The location reachability problem for timed automata is decidable.

4.3.2 Constraint reachability

Now we consider a more demanding variant of the reachability problem, the *constraint reachability problem*.

Given: A timed automaton $\mathcal{A}$, one of its control locations ℓ, and a clock constraint φ.

Question: Is a configuration reachable with the location ℓ and the clock valuation satisfying φ, i.e. is there a transition sequence of the form

$$\langle \ell_{\text{ini}}, \nu_{\text{ini}} \rangle \xrightarrow{\lambda_1} \ldots \xrightarrow{\lambda_n} \langle \ell, \nu \rangle \quad \text{with} \quad \nu \models \varphi$$

in the labelled transition system $\mathcal{T}(\mathcal{A})$?

For a clock region $[\nu]$ we introduce a delay operation

$$delay[\nu] = \{\nu' + t \mid \nu' \cong \nu \text{ and } t \in \text{Time}\}.$$

We remark that $delay[\nu]$ can be represented as a finite union of regions. For example, in Figure 4.2 we have

$$delay[x = y = 0] = [x = y = 0] \cup [0 < x = y < 1] \cup [x = y = 1] \cup [1 < x = y].$$

These regions are obtained from Figure 4.2 by pursuing the diagonal in the x–y-area starting at $x = y = 0$.

Theorem 4.34 (Decidability)
The constraint reachability problem for timed automata is decidable.

Proof:
Let a timed automaton $\mathcal{A}$, a location ℓ, and a clock constraint φ be given. First construct $\mathcal{R}_\varphi(\mathcal{A})$, the region automaton of $\mathcal{A}$ but modified so that the constraint φ is taken into account in the definition of the maximal constants c_x for each clock variable x appearing in $\mathcal{A}$ or φ.

Then check whether there exist a configuration $\langle \ell, [\nu] \rangle$ in $\mathcal{R}_\varphi(\mathcal{A})$ and a region in the finite union forming $delay[\nu]$, say characterised by the constraint $[\varphi_0]$, such that the formula

$$\varphi_0 \wedge I(\ell) \wedge \varphi \tag{4.1}$$

is satisfiable. The conjunct $I(\ell)$ checks whether the location invariant of ℓ is preserved while time is progressing as described by φ_0. The formula (4.1) can be effectively constructed and it can be represented as a finite disjunction of region formulas taken from $R_\varphi(\mathcal{A})$. The formula (4.1) is satisfiable if and only if this disjunction is non-empty. Since this can easily be checked, satisfiability of (4.1) is decidable. This proves the theorem. □

Example 4.35

Consider the timed automaton $\mathcal{A}_0$ of Example 4.22. Note that in this automaton all location invariants are true. So we can drop the conjunct $I(\ell)$ when checking formula (4.1).

First, we pose the question: is the location ℓ_3 reachable with $\varphi \iff y \geq 2$? Due to the new constant 2 in φ we have to construct the modified region automaton $R_\varphi(\mathcal{A}_0)$ for $c_x = 1$ and $c_y = 2$. The regions are sketched in Figure 4.4, with the area marked grey where φ is satisfied. We do not present the automaton $R_\varphi(\mathcal{A}_0)$ in detail, but remark that in $R_\varphi(\mathcal{A}_0)$, the reachable configuration $\langle \ell_3, [x = y > 1] \rangle$ of $R(\mathcal{A}_0)$ is split into three configurations, namely

$$\langle \ell_3, [1 < x = y < 2] \rangle, \langle \ell_3, [x = y = 2] \rangle, \text{ and } \langle \ell_3, [x = y > 2] \rangle.$$

Take $\langle \ell_3, [x = y = 2] \rangle$. By looking at the region diagram in Figure 4.4, we see the black area representing

$$delay[x = y = 2] = [x = y = 2] \cup [x = y > 2].$$

Thus formula (4.1) amounts to

$$(x = y = 2 \vee x = y > 2) \wedge y \geq 2 \iff x = y = 2 \vee x = y > 2,$$

which is a non-empty disjunction of regions. So the answer to our question is: *yes*.

Second, consider the question: is the location ℓ_2 reachable with $x = 0$? For this constraint it suffices to consider the region automaton $R(\mathcal{A}_0)$ in Figure 4.3. It contains four (reachable) configurations with location ℓ_2:

$$\langle \ell_2, [x = 1 \wedge y = 1] \rangle, \qquad\qquad \langle \ell_2, [y = 1 \wedge 0 < x - y < 1] \rangle,$$
$$\langle \ell_2, [y = 1 \wedge x - y = 1] \rangle, \qquad\qquad \langle \ell_2, [y = 1 \wedge x - y > 1] \rangle.$$

By looking at the region diagram in Figure 4.2, we see that applying the *delay* operator to the four clock regions of these configurations yields a triangle formed by eight regions within the area $x \geq 1 \wedge y \geq 1$ marked grey in Figure 4.5. However, the constraint $x = 0$ in question is represented

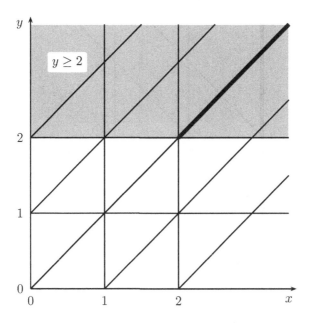

Fig. 4.4. Reachable constraint $y \geq 2$ in location ℓ_3

by four regions, all with $x = 0$ and marked black in Figure 4.5. We see
that the grey and black areas in Figure 4.5 do not intersect. Formally, the
conjunction of the regions representing the delays of the ℓ_2-regions with the
regions representing $x = 0$ in formula (4.1) yields false, i.e. is represented by
the empty disjunctions of regions. So the answer to the second question is:
no.   ■

4.4 The model checker UPPAAL

UPPAAL is a tool for modelling, simulating, and verifying real-time systems. The name is an acronym for the universities of *Upp*sala, Sweden and
*Aal*borg, Denmark, where the tool was developed under the guidance of
K.G. Larsen and Wang Yi. The tool is designed for real-time systems that
can be modelled as networks of timed automata. To increase the applica-
bility of this system model, UPPAAL extends the "pure" timed automata
introduced in Definition 4.3 by supporting

(1) data variables,
(2) high-level structuring facilities,
(3) concepts for restricting the nondeterminism, and

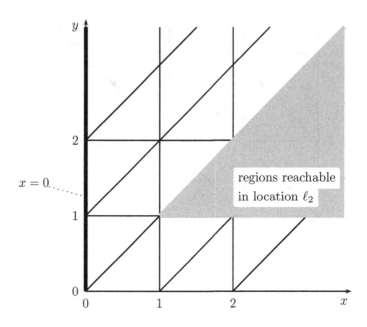

Fig. 4.5. Non-reachable constraint $x = 0$ in location ℓ_2

(4) a logic for specifying behavioural properties.

4.4.1 Data variables

Data variables range over finite subsets of integers with finite range and may be grouped into arrays. Just as clock variables, also data variables may appear in the guards of edges. The values of these variables can be changed by assignments that are executed when a transition fires. UPPAAL provides expressions with all standard integer operations, and their syntax and semantics are as usual. We do not give full details of the expressions here because we only need a tiny subset of them in this book.

Definition 4.36

Let V be a set of data variables, with typical element v.

- The set $\Psi(V)$ of *integer expressions over* V, with typical element ψ_{int}, is defined by the usual syntax, using variables in V and the operator symbols $+, -, \ldots$
- The set $\Phi(V)$ of *integer constraints* or *data constraints over* V, with typical element φ_{int}, is defined as the set of Boolean expressions with the usual

syntax, using variables in V, the operator symbols $+, -, \ldots$, and the predicate symbols $=, <, >, \leq, \geq$.

- Let $\mathbb{X}$ be a set of clock variables, with typical element x. The set $\Phi(\mathbb{X}, V)$ of *guards*, with typical element φ, is defined by the following syntax:

$$\varphi ::= \varphi_{\text{clk}}|\; \varphi_{\text{int}} \mid \varphi_1 \wedge \varphi_2,$$

where $\varphi_{\text{clk}} \in \Phi(\mathbb{X})$ is a clock constraint and $\varphi_{\text{int}} \in \Phi(V)$ is an integer constraint.

Valuations ν now assign values to both clocks and data variables. The satisfaction relation $\nu \models \varphi$ between valuations and guards extends the definition in Section 4.1 for data constraints in the straightforward way.

For the extended definition of valuations we adapt the operations of time-shift and modification. The *time-shift* operator $\nu + t$ for $t \in \mathsf{Time}$ is now defined for clocks x and data variables v:

$$(\nu + t)(x) = \nu(x) + t,$$
$$(\nu + t)(v) = \nu(v).$$

As before, the value of each clock x is increased by the time t; the values of the data variables v remain unchanged.

A *modification* or *reset operation* is an assignment to a clock $x \in \mathbb{X}$

$$x := 0$$

or an assignment to a data variable $v \in V$ of the form

$$v := \psi_i$$

where $\psi_i \in \Psi(V)$. Let $R(\mathbb{X}, V)$ denote the set of these reset operations, with typical element r. The modification of a valuation ν under a reset operation r is denoted by $\nu[r]$ and defined as follows:

$$\nu[x := 0](v') = \begin{cases} 0, & \text{if } v' = x, \\ \nu(v'), & \text{otherwise}, \end{cases}$$

$$\nu[v := \psi_i](v') = \begin{cases} \nu(\psi_i), & \text{if } v' = v, \\ \nu(v'), & \text{otherwise}. \end{cases}$$

By $\vec{r}$ we denote a finite list of reset operations on clocks and data variables, $\vec{r} = \langle r_1, \ldots, r_n \rangle$, and we extend the definition of modification appropriately:

$$\nu[\langle r_1, \ldots, r_n \rangle] = \nu[r_1] \ldots [r_n].$$

We use $R(\mathbb{X}, V)^*$ to denote the set of these lists of reset operations and $\langle \, \rangle$ to denote the empty list of reset operations. Note that we omit the brackets in the graphical representation of extended timed automata.

Remark 4.37

It is possible to construct data constraints or assignments to data variables
that lead to exceptions like division by zero, violation of array bounds, etc. If
UPPAAL encounters such an exception during the evaluation of a transition
it considers this transition as disabled. In this book we assume that such
exceptions do not occur, by construction of the extended timed automata.

4.4.2 Structuring facilities

UPPAAL provides several structuring facilities for networks of automata.

- Global *declarations* of clocks, data variables, channels, and constants can
  be introduced. Channels for binary synchronisation are declared as chan c
  and have a semantics as defined in Section 4.2. Thus at each moment a
  sender can only interact with one receiver, and a send action $c!$ is only
  possible if simultaneously a corresponding receive action $c?$ is executed.

  UPPAAL also offers *broadcast channels* declared as broadcast chan b.
  On a broadcast channel one sender $b!$ can synchronise with an arbitrary
  number of receivers $b?$. Any receiver that can synchronise in its current
  state must do so. If there are no receivers available the sender can still
  execute the $b!$ action. Thus unlike binary synchronisation, broadcast send-
  ing is never blocking. Figure 4.6 gives a graphic impression of a network
  of timed automata with channels a, c, d for binary synchronisation and a
  broadcast channel b. The picture suggests that only the automata $\mathcal{A}_1$ and
  $\mathcal{A}_3$ listen to the sender $\mathcal{A}_4$ during its broadcast. However, in this book we
  shall not treat broadcast channels in more detail.
- *Templates* are timed automata equipped with lists of formal parameters of
  types like int or chan and with local declarations of clocks, data variables,
  channels, and constants.
- *Process assignments* instantiate the templates by substituting actual parameters for the formal ones. An instantiated template is called a *process*.
- A *system definition* consists of a list of processes.

4.4.3 Restricting nondeterminism

To restrict the nondeterminism arising from the interleaving semantics of
parallel composition, UPPAAL extends networks of timed automata by
the following concepts:

- *Urgent locations.* In an urgent location time is not allowed to pass.

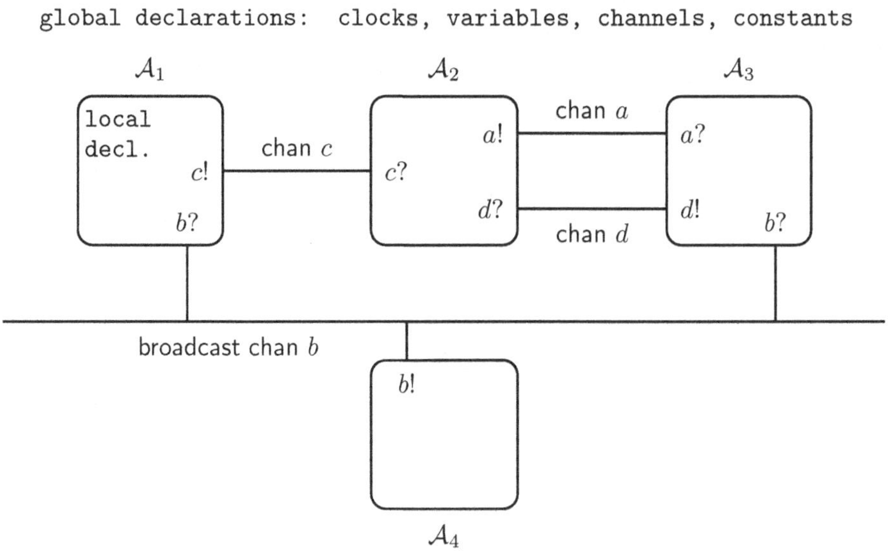

global declarations: clocks, variables, channels, constants

Fig. 4.6. Network of timed automata in UPPAAL

- *Committed locations.* A committed location restricts the possible transition sequences even further. If at least one automaton of a network is in a committed location, time is not allowed to pass and the next transition must involve an outgoing edge of at least one of the committed locations. Committed locations serve to model *atomic regions* consisting of several transitions that should be executed without interference by transitions of any other automaton.
- *Urgent channels.* Once a synchronisation between two automata along an urgent channel is enabled, a transition must happen without delay. Note that this transition does not necessarily synchronise over the urgent channel.

Let us look at an example.

Example 4.38 (Urgency and commitments)
For the three timed automata $\mathcal{P}$, $\mathcal{Q}$, and $\mathcal{R}$ shown in Figure 4.7, consider the network $\mathcal{N} = $ chan $b \bullet (\mathcal{P} \ || \ \mathcal{Q} \ || \ \mathcal{R})$. There are two clocks x and y, and two data variables v and w, all initialised to 0. In $\mathcal{N}$ the component automata $\mathcal{P}, \mathcal{Q}, \mathcal{R}$ can *wait arbitrarily long* in all locations because there is no location invariant requiring progress. At the start, each component automaton can take its initial τ-transition. The τ-transition of $\mathcal{P}$ enables the $b?$-transition,

which can be taken only together with the complementary $b!$-transition of $\mathcal{Q}$, which in turn is enabled by the initial τ-transition of $\mathcal{Q}$. Whenever $\mathcal{Q}$ fires a transition it changes the value of the data variable v. When $\mathcal{R}$ executes its τ-transition it copies the current value of v into the data variable w.

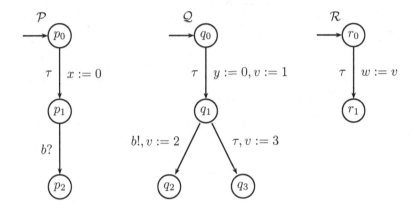

Fig. 4.7. Urgent locations and channels, committed locations

We now discuss three variants of the network $\mathcal{N}$.

Variant 1. If q_1 is declared as an *urgent location* the automaton $\mathcal{Q}$ is no longer allowed to wait in q_1, i.e. the clock y must stay at 0. However, it is possible that the τ-transition in $\mathcal{P}$ or $\mathcal{R}$ is taken because this does not take any time. Once these τ-transitions have occurred, $\mathcal{Q}$ must leave the location q_1, either by taking the $b!$-transition synchronising with the $b?$-transition of $\mathcal{P}$ or by taking its own τ-transition to location q_3.

Variant 2. If q_1 is declared as a *committed location* the automaton $\mathcal{Q}$ is forced to take a transition leaving q_1 as its next step. Thus staying in q_1 is not allowed any more, not even a τ-transition may be performed by $\mathcal{P}$ or $\mathcal{R}$. Again, the process $\mathcal{Q}$ has two alternatives to leave q_1 described above.

Variant 3. Suppose now that b is declared as an *urgent channel*. Then once a synchronisation along channel b is enabled it must happen without delay. However, other transitions may occur before the synchronisation because transitions do not take time. In this example, the τ-transition in $\mathcal{P}$ or $\mathcal{R}$ can be taken. With urgent channels a *conditional* urgent location can be modelled, which becomes urgent only if an outgoing communication along the urgent channel is enabled.

Note that $\mathcal{N}$ and its variants above all have distinct semantics. This can be demonstrated by the following three properties.

Property 1. *It is possible that the variable w is assigned the value 1.*
This can only happen if the τ-transition of $\mathcal{R}$ can be fired while $\mathcal{Q}$ stays in q_1. This property is satisfied except for Variant 2 where q_1 is committed.

Property 2. *Whenever $\mathcal{Q}$ is in location q_1 the clock x has the value 0.*
This property says that time cannot progress as soon as $\mathcal{Q}$ has reached location q_1. This is only true if q_1 is urgent or even committed.

Property 3. *Whenever $\mathcal{Q}$ enters the location q_1 while $\mathcal{P}$ is in location p_1 the clock y has the value 0 as long as $\mathcal{Q}$ stays in q_1.*
Consider the case that $\mathcal{P}$ has already executed the τ-transition to p_1. If then $\mathcal{Q}$ enters q_1 we know that y has been reset to 0 after x has been reset, i.e. $x \geq y$ holds. Moreover, the synchronisation via channel b is enabled. The property now requires that time cannot pass. This is only true if q_1 is either committed or urgent or b is declared as an urgent channel.

These differences are summarised in the following table:

	Property 1	Property 2	Property 3
	w can become 1	$y \leq 0$ holds when $\mathcal{Q}$ is in q_1	$x \geq y \Rightarrow y \leq 0$ holds when $\mathcal{P}$ is in p_1 and $\mathcal{Q}$ is in q_1
$\mathcal{N}$	✓	wrong	wrong
V.1 $\mathcal{N}$, q_1 urgent	✓	✓	✓
V.2 $\mathcal{N}$, q_1 committed	wrong	✓	✓
V.3 $\mathcal{N}$, b urgent	✓	wrong	✓

Here V.1–V.3 refer to the three variants of $\mathcal{N}$, and ✓ denotes that the corresponding property is satisfied.   ∎

The semantics of urgent locations can easily be expressed by a transformation. Replace a given urgent location with an ordinary location ℓ, take a new clock z that is reset on all edges pointing to ℓ, and add $z = 0$ as an invariant for ℓ (see Figure 4.8). Because of this transformation we shall not introduce urgent locations explicitly in the following Definition 4.39, but restrict ourselves to committed locations and urgent channels.

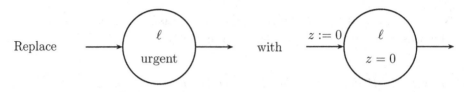

Fig. 4.8. Transformation eliminating urgent locations

For efficiency reasons, UPPAAL restricts location invariants to conjunctions of constraints

$$x \preceq n \quad \text{with } \preceq \in \{<, \leq\} \text{ and } n \in \mathbb{N}.$$

With this restriction, location invariants $I(\ell)$ are *downward closed*, i.e. whenever $\nu + t \models I(\ell)$ then also $\nu + t' \models I(\ell)$ for all $t' \in [0, t]$.

Summarising, UPPAAL uses the following notion of an extended timed automaton:

Definition 4.39 (Extended timed automaton)

An *extended timed automaton* $\mathcal{A}_e$ is a structure

$$\mathcal{A}_e = (L, C, B, U, \mathbb{X}, V, I, E, \ell_{\text{ini}})$$

where $L, B, \mathbb{X}, I, \ell_{\text{ini}}$ are defined as in Definition 4.3 of pure timed automata (but I is restricted as just explained) and where:

- $C \subseteq L$ is the set of *committed locations*.
- $U \subseteq B$ is the set of *urgent channels*.
- V is a set of *data variables*, with typical element v.
- $E \subseteq L \times B_{?!} \times \Phi(\mathbb{X}, V) \times R(\mathbb{X}, V)^* \times L$ is the set of directed edges. An element $(\ell, \alpha, \varphi, \vec{r}, \ell') \in E$ describes an edge from location ℓ to ℓ' with action α, guard φ, and a list $\vec{r}$ of reset operations.
- If $(\ell, \alpha, \varphi, r, \ell') \in E$ and $\text{chan}(\alpha) \in U$ then $\varphi = \text{true}$. This condition prevents that urgent actions are prohibited by guards.

Referring to Definition 4.3 for I means that it assigns to each location ℓ an invariant $I(\ell) \in \Phi(\mathbb{X}) = \Phi(\mathbb{X}, \varnothing)$. Thus location invariants constrain only clocks but not data variables. Extended timed automata specialise to pure timed automata if $C = U = V = \varnothing$ and if all clock resets are of the form $x := 0$. Then a list of such resets can be replaced by a set of resets as used in Definition 4.3.

In the graphic representation of extended timed automata we shall indicate that a location ℓ is committed by writing $c : \ell$ inside the location circle:

Urgent channels will be declared so in the running text.

4.4.4 Operational semantics of networks

Both pure and extended timed automata serve as building blocks for networks of such automata. However, semantically there is a major difference. Whereas the semantics of a network of pure timed automata can be reduced to the semantics of a single timed automaton by two composition operators (parallel composition and restriction), this is no longer possible for extended timed automata. The reason is that the meaning of committed locations and urgent channels can be defined only in the presence of *all* automata in the network. To make this difference explicit, we write

$$C(\mathcal{A}_1, \ldots, \mathcal{A}_n)$$

for a *closed* network of extended timed automata $\mathcal{A}_1, \ldots, \mathcal{A}_n$ with disjoint sets of clocks. In case of pure timed automata we would express this as

$$\mathsf{chan}\ b_1, \ldots, b_m \bullet (\mathcal{A}_1 \parallel \ldots \parallel \mathcal{A}_n),$$

where $\{b_1, \ldots, b_m\}$ is the set of *all* channels used in one of the $\mathcal{A}_i$. In a network $C(\mathcal{A}_1, \ldots, \mathcal{A}_n)$ each component automaton $\mathcal{A}_i$ has its own control location ℓ_i. Hence, for the whole network a *control vector* $\vec{\ell} = (\ell_1, \ldots, \ell_n)$ collects the control locations of the components. As before, we denote a change of the ith component's location from ℓ_i to ℓ_i' by $\vec{\ell}[\ell_i := \ell_i']$.

Definition 4.40 (Semantics of extended timed automata)
For extended timed automata $\mathcal{A}_e = (L_i, C_i, B_i, U_i, \mathbb{X}_i, V_i, I_i, E_i, \ell_{\mathrm{ini},i})$ with $i = 1, \ldots, n$ and pairwise disjoint sets $\mathbb{X}_i$ of clocks consider the closed network $C(\mathcal{A}_1, \ldots, \mathcal{A}_n)$. Then its operational semantics is defined by the labelled transition system

$$\mathcal{T}_e(C(\mathcal{A}_1, \ldots, \mathcal{A}_n)) = (\mathit{Conf}, \mathsf{Time} \cup \{\tau\}, \{\xrightarrow{\lambda} \mid \lambda \in \mathsf{Time} \cup \{\tau\}\}, C_{\mathrm{ini}})$$

where:

- $\mathbb{X} = \bigcup_{k=1}^n \mathbb{X}_k$ and $V = \bigcup_{k=1}^n V_k$.
- $\mathit{Conf} = \{\langle \vec{\ell}, \nu \rangle \mid \ell_i \in L_i \wedge \nu : \mathbb{X} \longrightarrow \mathsf{Time} \wedge \nu \models \bigwedge_{k=1}^n I_k(\ell_k)\}$ is the set of *configurations* of $C(\mathcal{A}_1, \ldots, \mathcal{A}_n)$.

- For each $\lambda \in \text{Time} \cup \{\tau\}$ the transition relation $\xrightarrow{\lambda} \subseteq Conf \times Conf$ has one of the following three types:

(i) An *internal transition* $\langle \vec{\ell}, \nu \rangle \xrightarrow{\tau} \langle \vec{\ell}', \nu' \rangle$ occurs if for some $i \in \{1, \ldots, n\}$ there is a τ-edge $(\ell_i, \tau, \varphi, \vec{r}, \ell_i') \in E_i$ in the ith automaton such that

- $\nu \models \varphi$, i.e. the guard is satisfied,
- $\vec{\ell}' = \vec{\ell}[\ell_i := \ell_i']$,
- $\nu' = \nu[\vec{r}]$ and $\nu' \models I_i(\ell_i')$,
- (♣) if $\ell_k \in C_k$ for some $k \in \{1, \ldots, n\}$ then $\ell_i \in C_i$, i.e. if there is a committed location in ℓ then the ith automaton is in such a location.

(ii) A *synchronisation transition* $\langle \vec{\ell}, \nu \rangle \xrightarrow{\tau} \langle \vec{\ell}', \nu' \rangle$ occurs if for some $i, j \in \{1, \ldots, n\}$ with $i \neq j$ and some channel $b \in B_i \cap B_j$ there are edges $(\ell_i, b!, \varphi_i, \vec{r}_i, \ell_i') \in E_i$ and $(\ell_j, b?, \varphi_j, \vec{r}_j, \ell_j') \in E_j$, i.e. the ith and the jth automaton can synchronise their output and input on the channel b, such that

- $\nu \models \varphi_i \wedge \varphi_j$, i.e. both guards are satisfied,
- $\vec{\ell}' = \vec{\ell}[\ell_i := \ell_i'][\ell_j := \ell_j']$,
- $\nu' = \nu[\vec{r}_i][\vec{r}_j]$ and $\nu' \models I_i(\ell_i') \wedge I_j(\ell_j')$,
- (♣) if $\ell_k \in C_k$ for some $k \in \{1, \ldots, n\}$ then $\ell_i \in C_i$ or $\ell_j \in C_j$, i.e. if there is a committed location in ℓ the ith or the jth automaton is in such a location.

(iii) A *delay transition* $\langle \vec{\ell}, \nu \rangle \xrightarrow{t} \langle \vec{\ell}, \nu + t \rangle$ occurs if

- $\nu + t \models \bigwedge_{k=1}^{n} I_k(\ell_k)$ holds, i.e. all invariants are satisfied at the *end of the delay*,
- (♣) there are *no* $i, j \in \{1, \ldots, n\}$ and $b \in U$ with $(\ell_i, b!, \varphi_i, \vec{r}_i, \ell_i') \in E_i$ and $(\ell_j, b?, \varphi_j, \vec{r}_j, \ell_j') \in E_j$, i.e. there is no urgent action enabled,
- (♣) there is *no* $i \in \{1, \ldots, n\}$ with $\ell_i \in C_i$, i.e. no automaton is in a committed location.

- $C_{\text{ini}} = \{\langle \overrightarrow{\ell_{\text{ini}}}, \nu_{\text{ini}} \rangle\} \cap Conf$, where the vector $\overrightarrow{\ell_{\text{ini}}}$ consists of the initial locations of all component automata $\mathcal{A}_i$ and the valuation ν_{ini} assigns 0 to all clocks and data (here: integer) variables in the set $\mathbb{X} \cup V$, is the set of *initial configurations*.

Whereas clocks of different component automata $\mathcal{A}_i$ are required to be disjoint, data variables may be *shared* by several component automata. Since $\mathcal{C}(\mathcal{A}_1, \ldots, \mathcal{A}_n)$ is a closed network, each transition is either labelled by the internal action τ or by a delay time $t \in \text{Time}$. Observe that the reset operations of synchronisation transitions are executed *sequentially*. First the reset operations r_i of the (output) $b!$-transition are executed and afterwards the reset operations r_j of the (input) b?-transition. This way, a *data flow* from output to input is modelled. For the delay transition the downward closure of the invariants $I_k(\ell_k)$ guarantees that $\nu + t \models I_k(\ell_k)$ implies $\nu + t' \models I_k(\ell_k)$ for all $t' \in [0, t]$. Thus checking the invariant at the end of the delay implies that it holds for all smaller values as well. The meaning of committed locations and urgent channels is specified in the conditions marked (♣). Note that these conditions are formulated *negatively* (e.g. if *no* urgent action is enabled). Thus they can be evaluated only if all automata in the network are known because they may become invalid if we add one more automaton.

The notions of *transition sequence, computation path*, and *run* introduced for pure timed automata (see Definitions 4.7 and 4.10) apply also to networks $\mathcal{C}(\mathcal{A}_1, \ldots, \mathcal{A}_n)$ of extended timed automata since these notions rely only on sequences of (time-stamped) configurations, here taken from the transition system $\mathcal{T}_e(\mathcal{C}(\mathcal{A}_1, \ldots, \mathcal{A}_n))$.

We now relate the semantics of closed networks of extended and pure timed automata.

Theorem 4.41 (Semantics of extended and pure timed automata)
If $\mathcal{A}_1, \ldots, \mathcal{A}_n$ specialise to pure timed automata as in Definition 4.3 the operational semantics of $\mathcal{C}(\mathcal{A}_1, \ldots, \mathcal{A}_n)$ and

$$\mathcal{N} = \text{chan } b_1, \ldots, b_m \bullet (\mathcal{A}_1 \mid\mid \ldots \mid\mid \mathcal{A}_n),$$

where $\{b_1, \ldots, b_m\}$ is the set of all channels used in one of the $\mathcal{A}_i$, coincide. Formally,

$$\mathcal{T}_e(\mathcal{C}(\mathcal{A}_1, \ldots, \mathcal{A}_n)) = \mathcal{T}(\mathcal{N}).$$

Proof:
If $\mathcal{A}_1, \ldots, \mathcal{A}_n$ are pure timed automata, the conditions in Definition 4.40 marked (♣), which deal with committed locations and urgent channels, do not apply. We compare the remaining clauses with those describing the transitions of $\mathcal{T}(\mathcal{N})$, as established in Lemma 4.16. Since $\mathcal{N}$ is closed, all local transitions of $\mathcal{N}$ are labelled by τ. Thus the only remaining differences between the clauses in Definition 4.40 and Lemma 4.16 are as follows.

First, for a synchronisation transition $\langle \vec{\ell}, \nu \rangle \xrightarrow{\tau} \langle \vec{\ell'}, \nu' \rangle$ the new valuation ν' is obtained for extended timed automata by two *sequential* reset operations $\nu' = \nu[\vec{r_i}][\vec{r_j}]$ and for pure timed automata by the *simultaneous* modification $\nu' = \nu[Y_i \cup Y_j := 0]$. Since the clocks in Y_i and Y_j are all reset to 0, both definitions of ν' coincide. An analogous but simpler argument applies if $\langle \vec{\ell}, \nu \rangle \xrightarrow{\tau} \langle \vec{\ell'}, \nu' \rangle$ is a local, hence internal transition.

Second, for a delay transition $\langle \vec{\ell}, \nu \rangle \xrightarrow{t} \langle \vec{\ell}, \nu + t \rangle$ the location invariant $I_i(\ell_i)$ is checked only for the final valuation $\nu + t$ in case of extended timed automata and for all valuations $\nu + t'$ with $t' \in [0, t]$ in case of timed automata. The simplified check for extended timed automata is justified because by syntactic restrictions the invariants are *downward closed*, and this property is inherited when extended timed automata specialise to pure timed automata. □

In case of pure timed automata $\mathcal{A}_1, \ldots, \mathcal{A}_n$ we continue to use the more informative notation

$$\mathcal{N} = \mathsf{chan}\ b_1, \ldots, b_m \bullet (\mathcal{A}_1 \mid\mid \ldots \mid\mid \mathcal{A}_n),$$

instead of $\mathcal{C}(\mathcal{A}_1, \ldots, \mathcal{A}_n)$ for closed networks.

4.4.5 *The logic of* UPPAAL

The logic of UPPAAL is a subset of the Timed Computation Tree Logic, tailored towards an efficient model-checking procedure. Informally, this logic allows us to express that the following properties φ of configurations should hold along the computation paths of a given network

$$\mathcal{C}(\mathcal{A}_1, \ldots, \mathcal{A}_n) \tag{4.2}$$

of extended timed automata:

- $\exists \Diamond\, \varphi$ expresses that there exists a computation path along which eventually φ holds.
- $\forall \Box\, \varphi$ expresses that along all computation paths φ always holds.
- $\exists \Box\, \varphi$ expresses that there exists a computation path along which φ always holds.
- $\forall \Diamond\, \varphi$ expresses that along all computation paths φ eventually holds.
- $\varphi_1 \longrightarrow \varphi_2$ expresses that each occurrence of φ_1 eventually leads to an occurrence of φ_2.

The following diagrams illustrate the semantics of path formulas by representing the set of computation paths as a computation tree and highlighting the node(s) where any of the formulas φ, φ_1, or φ_2 hold.

∃◇φ : there exists a computation path along which eventually φ holds:

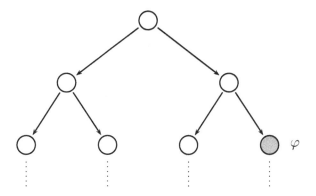

∀□φ : along all computation paths φ always holds:

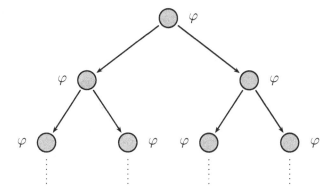

∃□φ : there exists a computation path along which φ always holds:

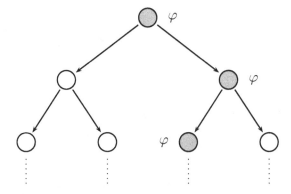

$\forall \Diamond \varphi$: along all computation paths φ eventually holds:

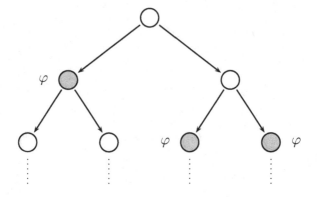

$\varphi_1 \longrightarrow \varphi_2$: each occurrence of φ_1 eventually leads to an occurrence of φ_2:

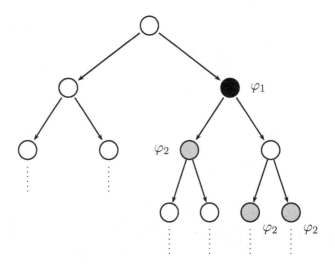

Formally, the logic comprises *basic formulas BF*, *configuration formulas CF*, and *path formulas PF*, divided into *existential* path formulas *EPF* and *universal* path formulas *APF*, and is defined by the following syntax:

$$
\begin{aligned}
BF \quad &::= \quad \mathcal{A}_i.\ell \mid \varphi, \\
CF \quad &::= \quad BF \mid \neg CF \mid CF_1 \wedge CF_2, \\
EPF \quad &::= \quad \exists \Diamond\, CF \mid \exists \Box\, CF, \\
APF \quad &::= \quad \forall \Box\, CF \mid \forall \Diamond\, CF \mid CF_1 \longrightarrow CF_2, \\
PF \quad &::= \quad EPF \mid APF.
\end{aligned}
$$

The basic formula $\mathcal{A}_i.\ell$ expresses that the automaton $\mathcal{A}_i$ of the network $\mathcal{C}(\mathcal{A}_1, \ldots, \mathcal{A}_n)$ is at location ℓ, and basic formula φ is a constraint on the clock and data values. In configuration formulas CF the logical connectives $\vee, \Longrightarrow$, and $\Longleftrightarrow$ are considered as abbreviations. In path formulas PF the quantifiers $\exists$ and $\forall$ express existential and universal quantification over computation paths, respectively, and the modalities $\diamond$ and $\square$ express existential and universal quantification over configurations, respectively. For example,

$$\exists \diamond \mathcal{A}_i.\ell$$

expresses that there exists a computation path on which there exists a configuration where the automaton $\mathcal{A}_i$ is at location ℓ. In other words, the location ℓ is reachable in $\mathcal{A}_i$.

We need one more notation for the formal definition of the semantics of the logic. Given a path ξ of $\mathcal{C}(\mathcal{A}_1, \ldots, \mathcal{A}_n)$ starting in the time-stamped configuration $\langle \vec{\ell}_0, \nu_0 \rangle, t_0$ of the form

$$\xi : \langle \vec{\ell}_0, \nu_0 \rangle, t_0 \xrightarrow{\lambda_1} \langle \vec{\ell}_1, \nu_1 \rangle, t_1 \xrightarrow{\lambda_2} \langle \vec{\ell}_2, \nu_2 \rangle, t_2 \xrightarrow{\lambda_3} \ldots$$

and a value $t \in \mathsf{Time}$ we denote by $\xi(t)$ the *set of configurations at time* t, defined as follows:

$$\xi(t) = \{ \langle \vec{\ell}, \nu \rangle \mid \exists i \in \mathbb{N} \bullet (t_i \leq t \leq t_{i+1} \wedge$$
$$\vec{\ell} = \vec{\ell}_i \wedge \nu = \nu_i + t - t_i) \}.$$

Note that $\xi(t)$ is defined as a *set* because in ξ a sequence of transitions can occur at the same time. This set may be empty if the time stamps $t_0, t_1, t_2, t_3, \ldots$ do not form a real-time sequence, i.e. do not grow unboundedly. In that case there may be no index i with $t_i \leq t \leq t_{i+1}$.

Formally, we introduce a binary *satisfaction relation* $\models$ between time-stamped configurations $\langle \vec{\ell}_0, \nu_0 \rangle, t_0$ of the network (4.2) and formulas F of the UPPAAL logic, written as

$$\langle \vec{\ell}_0, \nu_0 \rangle, t_0 \models F$$

and defined inductively as follows:

$$\langle \vec{\ell}_0, \nu_0 \rangle, t_0 \models \mathcal{A}_i.\ell \qquad \text{iff} \quad \ell_{0,i} = \ell, \text{ i.e. the } i\text{th component of the location vector } \vec{\ell}_0 \text{ is } \ell,$$

$$\langle \vec{\ell}_0, \nu_0 \rangle, t_0 \models \varphi \qquad \text{iff} \quad \nu_0 \models \varphi,$$

$$\langle \vec{\ell}_0, \nu_0 \rangle, t_0 \models \neg CF \qquad \text{iff} \quad \langle \vec{\ell}_0, \nu_0 \rangle, t_0 \not\models \neg CF,$$

$$\langle \vec{\ell}_0, \nu_0 \rangle, t_0 \models CF_1 \wedge CF_2 \quad \text{iff} \quad \langle \vec{\ell}_0, \nu_0 \rangle, t_0 \models CF_1 \text{ and } \langle \vec{\ell}_0, \nu_0 \rangle, t_0 \models CF_2,$$

$$\langle \vec{\ell_0}, \nu_0 \rangle, t_0 \models \exists \Diamond\, CF \qquad \text{iff} \quad \exists\ \text{path}\ \xi\ \text{of (4.2) starting in}\ \langle \vec{\ell_0}, \nu_0 \rangle, t_0$$
$$\exists t \in \mathsf{Time}, \langle \vec{\ell}, \nu \rangle \in Conf \bullet t_0 \leq t$$
$$\wedge \langle \vec{\ell}, \nu \rangle \in \xi(t) \wedge \langle \vec{\ell}, \nu \rangle, t \models CF,$$

$$\langle \vec{\ell_0}, \nu_0 \rangle, t_0 \models \forall \Box\, CF \qquad \text{iff} \quad \forall\ \text{path}\ \xi\ \text{of (4.2) starting in}\ \langle \vec{\ell_0}, \nu_0 \rangle, t_0$$
$$\forall t \in \mathsf{Time}, \langle \vec{\ell}, \nu \rangle \in Conf \bullet t_0 \leq t$$
$$\wedge \langle \vec{\ell}, \nu \rangle \in \xi(t) \Longrightarrow \langle \vec{\ell}, \nu \rangle, t \models CF,$$

$$\langle \vec{\ell_0}, \nu_0 \rangle, t_0 \models \exists \Box\, CF \qquad \text{iff} \quad \exists\ \text{path}\ \xi\ \text{of (4.2) starting in}\ \langle \vec{\ell_0}, \nu_0 \rangle, t_0$$
$$\forall t \in \mathsf{Time}, \langle \vec{\ell}, \nu \rangle \in Conf \bullet t_0 \leq t$$
$$\wedge \langle \vec{\ell}, \nu \rangle \in \xi(t) \Longrightarrow \langle \vec{\ell}, \nu \rangle, t \models CF,$$

$$\langle \vec{\ell_0}, \nu_0 \rangle, t_0 \models \forall \Diamond\, CF \qquad \text{iff} \quad \forall\ \text{path}\ \xi\ \text{of (4.2) starting in}\ \langle \vec{\ell_0}, \nu_0 \rangle, t_0$$
$$\exists t \in \mathsf{Time}, \langle \vec{\ell}, \nu \rangle \in Conf \bullet t_0 \leq t$$
$$\wedge \langle \vec{\ell}, \nu \rangle \in \xi(t) \wedge \langle \vec{\ell}, \nu \rangle, t \models CF,$$

$$\langle \vec{\ell_0}, \nu_0 \rangle, t_0 \models CF_1 \longrightarrow CF_2 \quad \text{iff} \quad \forall\ \text{path}\ \xi\ \text{of (4.2) starting in}\ \langle \vec{\ell_0}, \nu_0 \rangle, t_0$$
$$\forall t \in \mathsf{Time}, \langle \vec{\ell}, \nu \rangle \in Conf \bullet t_0 \leq t$$
$$\wedge \langle \vec{\ell}, \nu \rangle \in \xi(t) \wedge \langle \vec{\ell}, \nu \rangle, t \models CF_1$$
$$\text{implies}\ \langle \vec{\ell}, \nu \rangle, t \models \forall \Diamond\, CF_2.$$

We lift the satisfaction relation $\models$ to networks $\mathcal{C}(\mathcal{A}_1, \ldots, \mathcal{A}_n)$, existential path formulas EPF, and universal path formulas APF as follows:

$$\mathcal{C}(\mathcal{A}_1, \ldots, \mathcal{A}_n) \models EPF \quad \text{iff} \quad \langle \vec{\ell_0}, \nu_0 \rangle, 0 \models EPF\ \text{for some}\ \langle \vec{\ell_0}, \nu_0 \rangle \in C_{\mathrm{ini}},$$

$$\mathcal{C}(\mathcal{A}_1, \ldots, \mathcal{A}_n) \models APF \quad \text{iff} \quad \langle \vec{\ell_0}, \nu_0 \rangle, 0 \models APF\ \text{for all}\ \langle \vec{\ell_0}, \nu_0 \rangle \in C_{\mathrm{ini}},$$

where C_{ini} is the set of initial configurations in $\mathcal{T}_e(\mathcal{C}(\mathcal{A}_1, \ldots, \mathcal{A}_n))$, the transition system of the network.

Recall that C_{ini} contains at most one element. If $C_{\mathrm{ini}} = \varnothing$ the formula EPF is never satisfied whereas APF is trivially satisfied. If $\langle \vec{\ell}_{\mathrm{ini}}, \nu_{\mathrm{ini}} \rangle \in C_{\mathrm{ini}}$ both definitions agree on all path formulas PF and simplify to

$$\mathcal{C}(\mathcal{A}_1, \ldots, \mathcal{A}_n) \models PF \quad \text{iff} \quad \langle \vec{\ell}_{\mathrm{ini}}, \nu_{\mathrm{ini}} \rangle, 0 \models PF.$$

Let us now look at some examples.

Example 4.42 (Light controller and user)

The following two pure timed automata represent the light controller $\mathcal{L}$ of Example 4.6 together with a user $\mathcal{U}$:

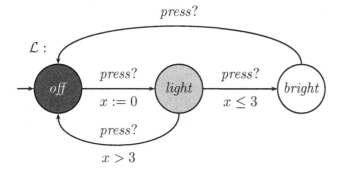

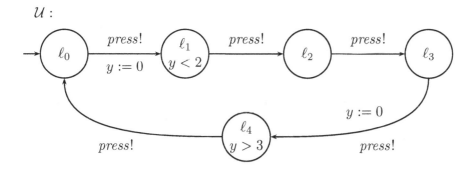

Let $\mathcal{N}$ be the closed network chan $press \bullet (\mathcal{L} \,||\, \mathcal{U})$. Then the *liveness property*

$$\mathcal{N} \models \exists \Diamond \mathcal{L}.bright$$

holds as the following initial segment of a path of $\mathcal{N}$ shows:

$$\langle (off, \ell_0), x = y = 0 \rangle \xrightarrow{2.5} \langle (off, \ell_0), x = y = 2.5 \rangle$$
$$\xrightarrow{1.7} \langle (off, \ell_0), x = y = 4.2 \rangle$$
$$\xrightarrow{\tau} \langle (light, \ell_1), x = y = 0 \rangle$$
$$\xrightarrow{1.9} \langle (light, \ell_1), x = y = 1.9 \rangle$$
$$\xrightarrow{\tau} \langle (bright, \ell_2), x = y = 1.9 \rangle$$
$$\xrightarrow{10} \langle (bright, \ell_2), x = y = 11.9 \rangle$$
$$\xrightarrow{\tau} \langle (off, q0), x = y = 11.9 \rangle \dots$$

On the other hand, $\mathcal{N} \not\models \forall \Diamond \mathcal{L}.bright$ because the network $\mathcal{N}$ can stay in the initial location vector (off, ℓ_0) for ever. Since in (off, ℓ_0) time may progress unboundedly, staying there is even possible for a *run* of $\mathcal{N}$.   ■

Example 4.43 (Generalised railroad crossing)

For the pure timed automata $\mathcal{T}$ and $\mathcal{G}$ of Example 4.18 consider once more the closed network $\mathcal{N} = $ chan $up, dn \bullet (\mathcal{T} \parallel \mathcal{G})$. If the constraint $\xi_1 < \rho$ is satisfied the desired *safety property*

$$\mathcal{N} \models \forall \square (\mathcal{T}.\text{Cross} \implies \mathcal{G}.\text{Closed})$$

holds.   .   ■

Example 4.44 (Fischer's protocol)

Fischer's protocol exploits time to achieve mutual exclusion of the critical sections cs_1 and cs_2 accessed by two processes. The processes are modelled by the following two extended timed automata $\mathcal{A}_1$ and $\mathcal{A}_2$ with clocks x and y, respectively, which use a *shared data variable id* ranging over the values 0, 1, and 2, but have no common channel for synchronisation:

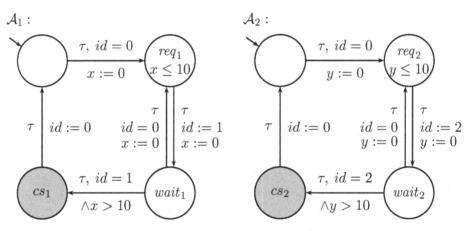

The variable id has the value 0 when none of the processes wishes to enter their critical sections. If $\mathcal{A}_1$ wishes to enter its critical section cs_1 it sets id to 1, and likewise for $\mathcal{A}_2$. Altogether, the following *mutual exclusion* property holds:

$$\mathcal{C}(\mathcal{A}_1, \mathcal{A}_2) \models \forall \square \neg (A1.cs_1 \land A2.cs_2).$$

Let us now consider the property of *alternating entry*, i.e. none of the processes $\mathcal{A}_1$ and $\mathcal{A}_2$ may access the critical section twice in a row. To check this property, we introduce two channels p_1 and p_2 and extend the automata $\mathcal{A}_1$ and $\mathcal{A}_2$ by outputs $p_1!$ and $p_2!$, respectively, notifying their entry of the critical section. These outputs have to synchronise with a separate *test automaton* $\mathcal{T}$, which has a distinguished location called *bad*.

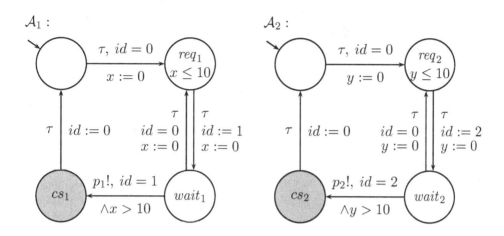

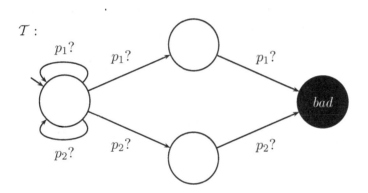

The automaton $\mathcal{T}$ is constructed in such a way that the alternating entry property is *violated* iff

$$\mathcal{C}(\mathcal{A}_1, \mathcal{A}_2, \mathcal{T}) \models \exists \Diamond \, \mathcal{T}.bad$$

holds, i.e. iff $\mathcal{T}$ can reach its "bad" location. For Fischer's protocol this is indeed the case.   ∎

4.5 Exercises

Exercise 4.1 (Traffic lights)

Consider traffic lights for cars and pedestrians wishing to cross a road, informally described as follows. The lights $\mathcal{LC}$ for the cars proceed through the following cycle of phases: *Idle* (showing no light), *Yellow, Red,* and *Red–Yellow* (showing both a red and a yellow light). The initial phase is *Idle*, it should last at least 20 seconds (to let cars pass) and otherwise can be arbitrarily long (if no pedestrians wish to cross). The phase *Yellow* should take 5 seconds, the phase *Red* 15 seconds, and the phase *Red–Yellow* 5 seconds.

The lights $\mathcal{LP}$ for the pedestrians have the following phases: *idle* (showing no light), *red1, red2* (both showing a red light), and *green*. The initial phase *idle* lasts as long as no pedestrian pushes a button at the traffic light. When a button is pushed the phase *red1* is entered and held for 35 seconds, afterwards the phase *green* is entered and held for 10 seconds. Then the phase *red2* is entered for at most 5 seconds. If a button is pushed during this phase the phase *red1* is re-entered, otherwise the light controller returns to the phase *idle* and the light is switched off. Pushing a button during the phases *red1* and *green* has no effect.

Model $\mathcal{LC}$ and $\mathcal{LP}$ as well as the pedestrian $\mathcal{P}$ as a network $\mathcal{N}$ of three timed automata working in parallel and synchronising on suitable channels. The pedestrian's behaviour is modelled only as far as it is noticeable at the button, i.e. the timed automaton should be able to engage at any moment in an output $b!$ on a channel b (representing the *button*). The corresponding input $b?$ is used in the timed automaton for $\mathcal{LP}$. To synchronise $\mathcal{LC}$ and $\mathcal{LP}$ appropriately, the timed automata should use a further common channel s.

Argue why the following safety properties hold:

- Whenever the pedestrian's light is in the phase *green* the light for the cars is in the phase *Red*.
- Whenever the light for the cars is in the phase *Idle* the pedestrian's light is *not* in the phase *green*.

Exercise 4.2 (Compositionality)

Show that parallel composition of (pure) timed automata behaves *compositionally* over labelled transition systems. For this purpose, define an appropriate parallel operator $\|_T$ directly on labelled transition systems as used for the operational semantics of timed automata and prove for all timed automata $\mathcal{A}_1$ and $\mathcal{A}_2$ the following *compositionality* result:

$$\mathcal{T}(\mathcal{A}_1 \| \mathcal{A}_2) = \mathcal{T}(\mathcal{A}_1) \|_T \mathcal{T}(\mathcal{A}_2).$$

Exercise 4.3 (Shared clocks)

In Definitions 4.12 and 4.40 we required that the components of a parallel composition have disjoint clocks. Generalise these definitions by removing this constraint, thus introducing *shared clocks*. Discuss the impact on compositionality and the consequences for Lemma 4.16 and Theorem 4.41.

Exercise 4.4 (Clock differences)

Let $\mathcal{A} = (L, B, \mathbb{X}, I, E, \ell_{\text{ini}})$ be a timed automaton. Prove that there exists a timed automaton $\mathcal{A}' = (L', B, \mathbb{X}, I', E', \ell'_{\text{ini}})$ *without* clock differences (of the form $x - y \sim c$) that satisfies the following property. For each transition sequence

$$\langle \ell_0, \nu_0 \rangle \xrightarrow{\lambda_1} \langle \ell_1, \nu_1 \rangle \xrightarrow{\lambda_2} \langle \ell_2, \nu_2 \rangle \xrightarrow{\lambda_3} \cdots$$

of $\mathcal{A}$ there exists a transition sequence of $\mathcal{A}'$ of the form

$$\langle \ell'_0, \nu_0 \rangle \xrightarrow{\lambda_1} \langle \ell'_1, \nu_1 \rangle \xrightarrow{\lambda_2} \langle \ell'_2, \nu_2 \rangle \xrightarrow{\lambda_3} \cdots$$

and vice versa.

Hints:

- It suffices to construct an automaton $\mathcal{A}'$ where only a single clock difference is removed.
- Consider what happens to clock differences when time passes.

Exercise 4.5 (Bisimulation)

Prove Lemma 4.26.

Exercise 4.6 (Equivalence relation)

Consider a timed automaton of the form $k \cdot \mathcal{A}$ with $k \geq 2$.

(a) Show that there is a coarser equivalence relation than $\cong$ of Definition 4.24.

(b) Improve the upper bound of the number of regions given in Lemma 4.28.

Exercise 4.7 (Region construction)

Consider the following timed automaton $\mathcal{A}$:

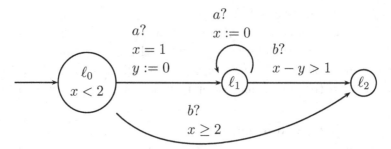

(a) Construct the region automaton $\mathcal{R}(\mathcal{A})$ and give a graphic representation of the clock regions.

(b) Determine whether the location ℓ_2 of $\mathcal{A}$ is reachable.

(c) Is there a non-Zeno computation path in $\mathcal{A}$?

Exercise 4.8 (Constraint reachability)
Show that constraint reachability for timed automata is decidable by a reduction of this problem to a suitable instance of the location reachability problem.

Hint: Add a dedicated location and appropriate transitions to the given automaton.

Exercise 4.9 (Determining the winner)
For $i \in \{1, 2\}$ consider the following schema of a timed automaton $\mathcal{A}_i$ where $l_i, u_i \in \mathbb{Q}_{\geq 0}$ are two constants with $l_i < u_i$:

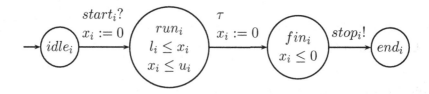

Construct a (possibly extended) timed automaton $\mathcal{R}$ modelling a *referee* that starts $\mathcal{A}_1$ and $\mathcal{A}_2$ simultaneously and determines by reaching one of the three locations win_1, win_2, and $draw$ which of the following three situations has occurred:

- win_1 means that $\mathcal{A}_1$ finished before $\mathcal{A}_2$,
- win_2 means that $\mathcal{A}_2$ finished before $\mathcal{A}_1$,

- *draw* means that $\mathcal{A}_1$ and $\mathcal{A}_2$ finished simultaneously.

To this end, $\mathcal{R}$ should interact with $\mathcal{A}_1$ and $\mathcal{A}_2$ in a network by synchronising over the channels $start_1, start_2, stop_1,$ and $stop_2$.

Hint: Think of using committed locations and urgent channels.

Exercise 4.10 (Expressing properties)
The logic of UPPAAL is somewhat restricted in its expressiveness. First, to express timing properties appropriate clocks need to be present in the system of timed automata under test. Second, negation is not allowed at the level of path formulas. To express properties involving such features the given system of timed automata has to be extended either by adding suitable clocks with corresponding invariants and guards or by adding a separate test automaton with a distinguished location indicating violation of the property and extra communications with the system under test, as shown in Example 4.44.

Formalise the following properties in the logic of UPPAAL, possibly preparing the system under test as outlined above:

- (i) The location ℓ is never visited for more than 5 seconds.
- (ii) The data variable v never has the value 3.
- (iii) There exists a path in which first the location ℓ_1 and then the location ℓ_2 is visited.
- (iv) There is *no* path in which first the location ℓ_1 and then the location ℓ_2 is visited.
- (v) There exists a path in which first the location ℓ_1 is visited for 2 seconds and then the location ℓ_2 for 3 seconds.

4.6 Bibliographic remarks
Originally, R. Alur and D. Dill defined timed automata as an extension of Büchi automata by real-valued clocks [AD94]. Büchi automata are finite-state automata equipped with an acceptance condition for infinite words [Tho90]. Alur and Dill's timed automata were acceptors of timed languages consisting of infinite real-time words. The Büchi acceptance condition was used to enforce progress. Their main results were the decidability of important properties like the emptiness problem for timed languages and the reachability problem for locations [ACD93, AD94]. These results have triggered the development of tools for the automatic verification of properties of timed automata, in particular UPPAAL [LPW97], KRONOS[Yov97], and HyTech [HHW97].

A simplified definition of timed automata, originally called *timed safety automata* in [HNSY94], dropped the Büchi acceptance condition and introduced instead location invariants to enforce progress. This version is now widespread [Alu98] and forms the basis of tools for the verification of properties of timed automata like UPPAAL [LPW97] and KRONOS [Yov97]. Therefore we introduced this definition in this chapter.

The main obstacle for verification of timed automata is that the number of regions grows exponentially with the number of clocks. Hence, for an efficient tool support suitable data structures for regions are needed. UPPAAL uses *Difference Bounded Matrices* (DBMs, [Bel57, BY03]) to represent so-called *zones*, which are convex unions of regions that can be characterised by clock constraints [Alu98, CGP00].

The notion of a transition system is due to R.M. Keller [Kel76]. The systematic and structured use of transition systems for the definition of the semantics of programming and specification languages was advocated by G.D. Plotkin [Plo81, Plo04].

The parallel composition and the local channel operator of Section 4.2 was introduced by R. Milner [Mil89] in the context of his process algebra CCS (Calculus of Communicating Systems) and further developed for the π-calculus [Mil99]. Also the notion of bisimulation was developed in the context of the process algebra CCS. An alternative is the parallel composition operator of CSP (Communicating Sequential Processes) that allows (multiple) synchronisation of events with the same name [Hoa85]. This is also used for timed automata [Alu98].

In Subsection 4.4.1 we introduced data variables ranging over (finite subsets) of integers for UPPAAL. Recent extensions of UPPAAL permit C-like data types and operations in the extended timed automata. However, the model-checking algorithms build on an explicit-state representation of all non-clock components and thus limit data objects to small finite domains. Timed Computation Tree Logic (abbreviated TCTL) was introduced in [ACD93]. Here we considered only the subset that is supported by UPPAAL. An overview of the implementation details of UPPAAL is given in [BBD+02]. The examples of the light controller and of Fischer's protocol are taken from a tutorial for UPPAAL [Lar02]. More information on the model checker UPPAAL can be found on the website http://www.uppaal.com.

5

PLC-Automata

In industrial automation the aim is to control and optimise production processes and to provide high-quality and reliable products and services by minimising material, cost, and energy waste. Automation systems rely on smart sensors, actuators, and other industrial equipment like robotic and mechatronic components. Open and standardised communication networks are employed for the communication as well as configuration and control of the various automation components. The standard architecture consists of PLCs (Programmable Logic Controllers) or DCS (Distributed Control Systems), fieldbus systems, and PCs serving as man/machine interfaces as well as intelligent sensors and actuators (e.g. frequency converters). The fieldbus systems gather the signals from the process level or the sensors and actuators with fieldbus interfaces, and are directly connected to distributed or centralised control devices, such as PLCs.

The standard IEC 61131-3 of the International Electrotechnical Commission provides a range of programming notations suitable for implementation on PLCs. It comprises basic notations close to those in electrical engineering like contact plans, instruction lists, and function plans as well as graphical and textual programming notations called sequential function charts and structured text. Currently, the development of software in automation technology proceeds step by step along the life cycle using the notations of this standard and different tools provided by different PLC vendors.

A problem is that different PLC vendors use their own variants of the standard with different syntax, semantics, and tool sets. Also, the approaches based on the standard are not well suited for the development of distributed applications and applications with hard real-time requirements. An attempt to overcome this shortcoming is the standard IEC 61499, which embeds IEC 61131-3 and allows distributed systems to be described. However, the semantics remains formally ambiguous. This hampers the integration of formal methods and tools for verification.

As a contribution to overcome these problems, we present in this chapter a formal model of the computational essence of PLCs, called PLC-Automata. These automata enjoy the following important properties:

- *Implementability.* PLC-Automata can be automatically compiled into real-time programs (source code) that are executable on Programmable Logic Controllers and other hardware platforms (see Section 5.3).
- *Semantics.* A formal semantics of PLC-Automata in terms of the Duration Calculus describes how the PLC hardware behaves when the compiled code is executed (see Section 5.4). An alternative operational semantics in terms of timed automata is given later in Chapter 6.
- *Verifiability.* In the Duration Calculus, proofs can be conducted that a given PLC-Automaton satisfies a given real-time requirement (see Subsection 5.4.1). Assuming the correctness of the compiler such a proof implies that the source code generated from the PLC-Automaton satisfies the requirement. Alternatively, using the timed automata semantics, automatic verification of real-time properties is possible (see Chapter 6).

5.1 Programmable Logic Controllers

Programmable Logic Controllers (PLCs for short) are often used in industry to control real-time systems. Typical application areas of PLCs are production lines and traffic control systems. The hardware is constructed in a robust manner to resist environmental influences like heat, cold, dust, and vibration. A reason for the relevance of PLCs in real-time applications is that each PLC has a built-in real-time operating system. For safety reasons it cannot be disturbed by application programs to guarantee a minimal functionality in case of a program failure.

Given an application program, the operating system executes the following cycle consisting of three phases:

Polling. In this first phase input busses are read and the results are copied to a reserved area in the memory of the PLC. This phase is executed autonomously by the operating system and cannot be manipulated by the application program.

Computing. In this phase the operating system executes the application program *once*. The program itself is allowed to do arbitrary computations and has access to both the saved values of the input busses and the designated values for the output busses.

To handle time the program can use *timers*. The timers are implemented by the operating system and the program may set, read, and reset them. Setting a timer defines a time span for how long the timer should run. Reading a timer returns a Boolean value that signals whether the given time span has elapsed. Resetting a timer is a prerequisite for a new set operation.

Updating. The last phase of the cycle sets the values of the output busses by copying values from the reserved memory location. This is the moment where the environment would observe a change of outputs.

The following timing diagram shows possible changes of input and output values (here indicated by white and grey) together with three PLC cycles, each one consisting of the three phases just explained. Arrows indicate when input values are read and when output values are written, respectively. Notice that only at the end of each cycle does the effect of the computing phase become visible by a corresponding update of the output values. Notice also that input changes in between two polling phases cannot be observed by the PLC. For example, the grey value during the first cycle is not observed.

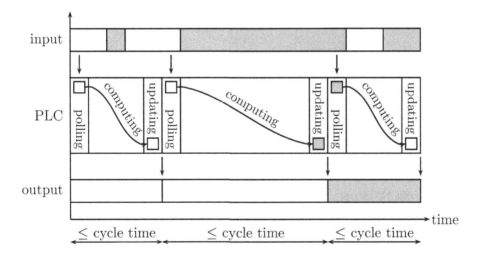

The time consumption of a cycle is influenced by several factors. The time needed for the polling and updating phases depends on the number of busses. The time consumption of the computing phase depends on the application program and may vary from cycle to cycle.

> We want to stress that each computing device which is equipped with a clock can be programmed to behave like a PLC. Hence, the exposition in this chapter is *not restricted to PLCs* as an implementation platform.

5.2 PLC-Automata

In this section we motivate and introduce the model of PLC-Automata by examples taken from a case study of an industrial project partner engaged in the application domain of railway control: the safe control of a *single-track line segment* (SLS) for trams shown in Figure 5.1. Single-track line segments can occur in case of repair work along one of the tracks and represent a possible danger for the traffic.

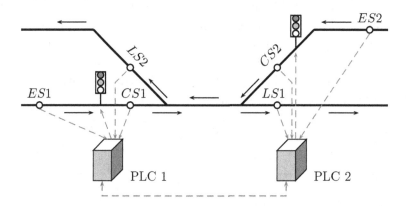

Fig. 5.1. Single-track line segment

The task of a controller for the SLS is to safely guide trams driving in opposite directions through a single-track line segment so that no collision can occur on this segment. To this end, suitable sensors and traffic lights are installed along the track. For each direction $i \in \{1, 2\}$ of the trams there are three sensors called *ESi* (entry sensor), *CSi* (critical sensor), and *LSi* (leave sensor) as shown in Figure 5.1. From the values of these sensors the control under development has to compute the signals for the traffic lights of both directions. For each direction there are three possible signals: *Go, Stop,* and *Ack*, an acknowledgement for the tram drivers requesting to pass the single-track segment. The controller for the SLS should satisfy the following informal requirements:

- *Safety.* No collision should occur on the single-track segment, i.e. this critical segment should be used in *mutual exclusion*.

- *Utility.* Trams operate according to several *driving policies*. One such policy requires that first all trams from one direction are guided through the single-track segment and then all trams from the other direction. Another policy gives the right of way alternatively to one tram from one direction and then one from the other direction.
- *Target hardware.* The control software should run on Programmable Logic Controllers (PLCs).

Here we concentrate on a further requirement concerning *fault tolerance*. In physical devices along the track subtle faults can occur. For example, the purpose of the sensors *ESi*, *CSi*, and *LSi* is to enable counting how many trams are in the corresponding track segments. A sensor at the track should detect the passage of trains by outputting the values no_tr ("no passing train") or tr ("a train is passing"). A change from no_tr to tr signals the arrival of a train at the sensor's position on the track.

Stuttering problem. However, the sensor's signal may *stutter* when a train passes, i.e. it may alternate several times between no_tr and tr. This is potentially dangerous because the control could misinterpret a stuttering sensor's signal and assume that several trains are on the track.

Suppose the sensor hardware guarantees that stuttering ceases after 4 seconds. Further on, suppose the minimal time distance between trains is 6 seconds. Given these assumptions the problem is to construct a system that filters the stuttering reliably.

The idea is that the filter should ignore the possible stuttering of the sensor for a short period of time, say 5 seconds. This requirement indicates that the whole control software is indeed a real-time software. A possible solution to this problem could be the following design:

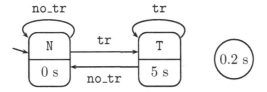

This is an automaton consisting of two states with output N ("no train") and T ("train"). It reacts to an input signal with values no_tr and tr according to the transitions given in the picture. The state T should be stable for at least 5 seconds. To implement such an automaton on a PLC we assume that during each cycle the system reacts at most once to a read input value. In case of a delay as in state T the executing PLC ignores the input value as long as the delay time has not been exceeded.

Hence, a PLC implementing this automaton should behave as follows:

- Initially, it is in state N.
- If it is in state N and the read input value is tr, it takes the transition to state T. Otherwise, it will stay in state N.
- In state T the system will stay for at least 5 seconds regardless of the polled input value. After that period it will stay in this state as long as tr is polled. Otherwise, it will change to N.

A sample behaviour is shown in the following timing diagram:

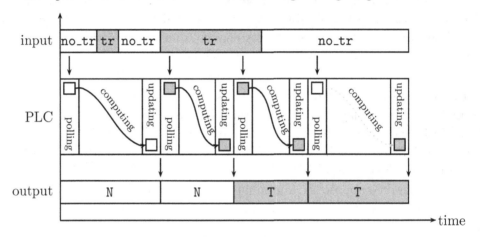

Solid arrows in the computing phase stand for fired transitions while dotted arrows symbolise a computing phase where the given transition was not taken due to the delay constraint. In the timing diagram above the fourth cycle did not fire a transition due to the delay constraint of 5 seconds. Note that otherwise the system would have changed to output N. The transition of the third cycle can be taken regardless of whether the delay has elapsed or not because it does not change the current state.

The picture of the automaton contains a circle with the inscription "0.2 s". This specifies the upper bound for the worst case execution time (WCET) of a complete cycle "polling–computing–updating". In the example the time distance between trains is at least 6 seconds. Due to the upper bound of 0.2 seconds we ensure that the system will be in the state with output N when the next train arrives. Otherwise, it would be possible for the system to filter the signals of a real train as stuttering of the sensor.

The automaton above is a very simple PLC-Automaton. Further extensions are motivated by the following example:

Example 5.1
Consider the filter of the previous example again but assume now that the
track sensor can also send a signal **Error**. This should inform the system
that the sensor has a technical problem. We want to extend our filtering
automaton such that it reacts to the **Error** signal immediately by outputting
a value **X** ("exception").   ■

A solution could be the following automaton:

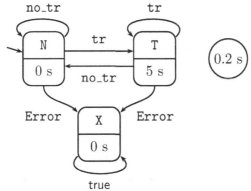

However, the problem of this solution is that the **Error** signal could arise
just after a change to the state with output **T**. Then it would take about
5 seconds to observe the desired output **X** due to the delay constraint. To
solve this problem we extend the delay annotation by a *set of inputs* for
which the delay should hold:

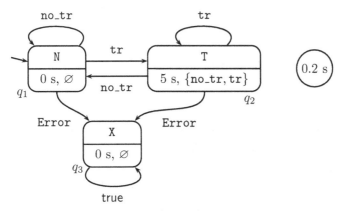

Fig. 5.2. Filtering PLC-Automaton (final version)

The idea of this annotation is that the **Error**-transition from T to X can be fired without checking whether the delay time of 5 seconds has elapsed. By contrast, the transition from T to N has to check the delay time.† The effect of this construction is that the T state can only be left by changing to X during the first 5 seconds. In case of the N and X states the set of *delayed inputs* is meaningless since there is no delay. Hence, we took the empty set there.

The following timing diagram shows a sample behaviour of the extended automaton:

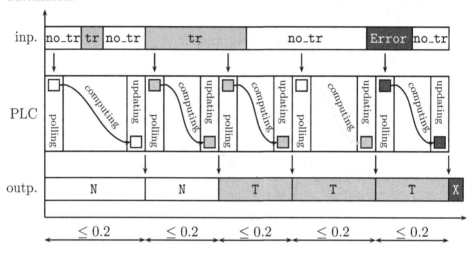

Note that during the first cycle there is a short phase where input **tr** holds but this value is not read by the system. To ensure that a physical signal will be read eventually we have to know the minimal duration for which the signal will be stable and specify the upper time bound for the execution of a cycle accordingly.

Having motivated all components of PLC-Automata, we present the formal definition:

Definition 5.2 (PLC-Automaton)
A *PLC-Automaton* is a structure $\mathcal{A} = (Q, \Sigma, \delta, q_0, \varepsilon, S_t, S_e, \Omega, \omega)$ where:

- Q is a non-empty, finite set of *states*, with q as typical element;
- Σ is a non-empty, finite set of *inputs*, with σ as typical element;
- δ is a *transition function* of type $Q \times \Sigma \longrightarrow Q$;
- $q_0 \in Q$ is the *initial state*;
- $\varepsilon > 0$ is an *upper time bound* for the execution of a cycle;

---

† It is easy to see that we do not need to define whether the self-loop with input **tr** has to obey the delay time. It would not change the behaviour of the system.

- S_t is a function of type $Q \longrightarrow \mathbb{R}_{\geq 0}$ that assigns a *delay time* to each state;
- S_e is a function of type $Q \longrightarrow 2^\Sigma$ that assigns a *set of delayed inputs* to each state;
- Ω is a non-empty, finite set of *outputs*; and
- ω is a function of type $Q \longrightarrow \Omega$ that assigns an *output* to each state.

Note that this definition gives only the "syntax" of PLC-Automata, i.e. their structural components. The semantics was explained informally in this section. It will be made more precise in the next section by a translation into programs. A formal semantics in terms of Duration Calculus will be presented in Section 5.4.

As shown in this section, a PLC-Automaton can be represented graphically. Each state q is drawn as a box (sometimes annotated with the letter q) with two compartments. The upper compartment displays the output value $\omega(q)$. The lower compartment exhibits the delay time $S_t(q)$ and the set $S_e(q)$ of delayed outputs. A transition $\delta(q, \sigma) = q'$ is represented as an arrow from state q to state q' labelled with the input value σ. The time bound for the cycle is shown in a separate circle.

5.3 Translation into PLC source code

This section presents a translation of PLC-Automata into programs that are executable on PLCs. The translation puts the informal description of the expected behaviour of PLC-Automata into practice. As a programming language we use ST, which stands for "Structured Text", a Pascal-like imperative programming language that is defined in the IEC 61131-3 standard for Programmable Logic Controllers.

The PLC operating system implements the cyclic behaviour of the PLC with an *implicit* non-terminating WHILE loop repeating the three phases Polling, Computing, and Updating in each cycle:

```
WHILE TRUE DO
    • input from sensors (* Polling Phase *)
    • perform state transformation
      depending on timers (* Computing Phase *)
    • output to actuators (* Updating Phase *)
END
```

The translation of a PLC-Automaton has only to produce the state transformation implementing the Computing phase of this loop. To this end, we use one outer IF statement to distinguish the states and additional inner IF statements to distinguish the currently polled input values. Together, these statements identify the unique transition that can fire in a given computing phase. The only thing that remains to be checked is whether or not a delay time has elapsed and thus an appropriate action is required.

To illustrate this approach, we consider the final version of the filtering PLC-Automaton in Figure 5.2. It is translated into the following ST code:

```
 1: PROGRAM PLC_PRG_FILTER
 2: VAR
 3:     state  : INT := 0; (* 0:=N, 1:=T, 2:=X *)
 4:     tmr    : TP;
 5: ENDVAR
 6:
 7: IF state=0 THEN
 8:          %output:=N;
 9:          IF %input = tr THEN
10:                    state:=1;
11:                    %output:=T;
12:          ELSIF %input = Error THEN
13:                    state:=2;
14:                    %output:=X;
15:          ENDIF
16: ELSIF state=1 THEN
17:          tmr(IN:=TRUE,PT:=t#5.0s);
18:          IF (%input = no_tr AND NOT tmr.Q) THEN
19:                    state:=0;
20:                    %output:=N;
21:                    tmr(IN:=FALSE,PT:=t#0.0s);
22:          ELSIF %input = Error THEN
23:                    state:=2;
24:                    %output:=X;
25:                    tmr(IN:=FALSE,PT:=t#0.0s);
26:          ENDIF
27: ENDIF
```

We comment on this ST program by referring to its line numbers:

1–5: These lines constitute the program header, which declares two variables: an *integer* variable called state, storing the current state of the PLC-Automaton and initialised with 0, and a *timer* variable called tmr, indicated by the standard type TP. In the program, states are coded as integers (here 0, 1, and 2). In the comments below we shall also identify them with their output values N, T, and X, respectively. The timer tmr can be set to a certain time value d. Once set, the timer output tmr.Q holds the value true for d time units. Afterwards the output tmr.Q switches to false and stays there until the next set operation. The handling of the timer is explained in the comment on line 17.

7: Here an IF statement begins that distinguishes the current state of the PLC-Automaton.

8: For the initial state (here 0) we set the initial output value (to N). For all other states we will update the output value when we change the state. The symbol % is used to address reserved areas of the PLC's memory. In the pseudo code the names %input and %output are used to represent the program interface to sensors and actuators, respectively. These names are implicitly declared and can be used as ordinary variables.

9: Here we test the polled input value in the state (with output) N. Only those values which cause a state change have to be tested. In this state these are tr and Error. For the self-loop with input value no_tr no code needs to be generated.

10–11: The PLC is in state N and has polled the input value tr. By the transition function of the PLC-Automaton, the system assigns 1 to the state variable and sets the output value to T.

16–26: This part deals with the state that has output T.

17: Since this state has a delay time of 5 seconds, we start the timer tmr. This is done by calling a corresponding procedure

$$\texttt{tmr(IN:=TRUE,PT:=t\#5.0s)}$$

with two parameters. The parameter IN represents a start flag and the parameter PT the desired duration. Only if the operating system observes a *rising edge* at the start flag will it start the timer with the value of the duration parameter. Otherwise, this call has no effect. In other words, the timer is set only if this call has a start flag true and the previous call had start flag false. Initially, the start flag is treated as being false.

18: In this line we test whether the transition to N can be fired. This is the case only if the polled input value is no_tr and the timer tmr has elapsed. The latter condition is represented by the timer output tmr.Q. This output is true as long as the duration d of the last setting has not been exceeded, and false afterwards.

19–21: The transition from T to N can be fired. Therefore, the variables
state and %output are set appropriately. In line 21 we reset the
start flag of the timer in order to enable later setting. Recall that
the operating system starts a timer only if it observes a rising edge
at this flag.

22–25: In case that the system is in state 1 and Error was polled it does
not need to test the value of the timer.

We conclude with some further remarks. Note that the above program does
not handle state 2 with output X in its outer IF statement. Indeed, there
is no need for this because state 2 is never left by any transition. Also, as
stated for line 9, no code needs to be generated for self-loops like the loop
with input value tr at state T.

Further on, there is *no* statement implementing the upper time bound
(here 0.2 seconds) of the PLC cycle. Indeed, this bound represents the
assumption that the PLC hardware is fast enough to stay within the bound
in each cycle. There are two ways to discharge this assumption:

(1) One can compute the *Worst Case Execution Time* of the ST code on the
given PLC hardware (by a so-called WCET analysis) and check whether
it does not exceed the upper time bound for the execution of a cycle of
the PLC-Automaton. Since the generated code is relatively simple, this
is feasible.

(2) One can inform the operating system of a PLC about the upper time
bound. If it detects a violation of this bound at runtime it changes to
an error state and signals this by appropriate output values.

The program above uses only one timer to implement the intended behaviour of the filtering PLC-Automaton. It turns out that a *single* timer is
sufficient in the translation of *any* PLC-Automaton of Definition 5.2. This
is because in each state of a PLC-Automaton at most one delay time needs
to be observed. As soon as the state is left its delay time becomes irrelevant.
Thus a single timer can be reused when implementing several states with
delayed inputs.

PLC-Automata are not only useful when PLCs serve as implementation
platforms. They can be implemented on any hardware platform that performs a non-terminating loop consisting of inputting sensor values, updating
the state in accordance with timer values, and outputting actuator values.

5.4 Duration Calculus semantics

In this section we formally describe the real-time behaviour of a system that executes a PLC-Automaton and satisfies the upper time bound for the execution of a cycle. For the formal description we choose Duration Calculus. The idea of this formal semantics is not to describe *exactly* how the system behaves, but to give only a safe approximation. That is, all observable behaviours of the real physical system belong to the semantics but the semantics might contain behaviours that are not possible in the physical world:

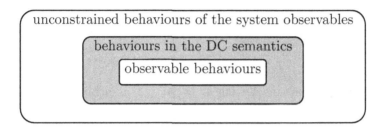

Let $\mathcal{A} = (Q, \Sigma, \delta, q_0, \varepsilon, S_t, S_e, \Omega, \omega)$ be a PLC-Automaton. Then the DC semantics of $\mathcal{A}$ (in symbols: $[\![\mathcal{A}]\!]_{DC}$) defines a subset of all interpretations of the three observables

$$
\begin{aligned}
&\mathsf{In}_{\mathcal{A}} &&\text{ranging over } \Sigma \text{ representing the input,}\\
&\mathsf{St}_{\mathcal{A}} &&\text{ranging over } Q \text{ representing the state,}\\
&\mathsf{Out}_{\mathcal{A}} &&\text{ranging over } \Omega \text{ representing the output.}
\end{aligned}
$$

We describe this set of interpretations by formulas that have to be realised from 0 by these interpretations. First we require that the PLC-Automaton starts in its initial state q_0:

$$\lceil\,\rceil \vee \lceil q_0 \rceil \,; \mathsf{true}. \tag{DC-1}$$

Read $\lceil q_0 \rceil$ as an abbreviation for $\lceil \mathsf{St}_{\mathcal{A}} = q_0 \rceil$. Then we specify which states are reachable from a given state q of the automaton. This depends on the inputs and we model two phenomena:

- The system can only poll input values which were observable since q holds.
- If state q is left this must be caused by an input value that was observable at most ε seconds ago.

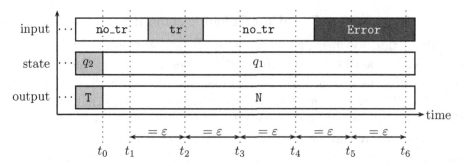

Fig. 5.3. A behaviour of the filter satisfying the requirements (DC-2) and (DC-3)

We can specify these properties in DC as follows:

$$\lceil \neg q \rceil ; \lceil q \wedge A \rceil \longrightarrow \lceil q \vee \delta(q, A) \rceil, \tag{DC-2}$$

$$\lceil q \wedge A \rceil \xrightarrow{\ \varepsilon\ } \lceil q \vee \delta(q, A) \rceil. \tag{DC-3}$$

In these formulas the set A with $\varnothing \neq A \subseteq \Sigma$ is arbitrary. Read $\lceil q \wedge A \rceil$ as $\lceil \mathsf{St}_{\mathcal{A}} = q \wedge \mathsf{In}_{\mathcal{A}} \in A \rceil$ and the expression $\delta(q, A)$ as $\mathsf{St}_{\mathcal{A}} \in \{\delta(q, a) | a \in A\}$. The idea of quantifying all non-empty subsets A of the input alphabet is to gain a maximum of knowledge for a given interval about the possible behaviour.

Figure 5.3 exhibits a possible behaviour of the filter in Figure 5.2. Due to (DC-2) we can draw some conclusions for intervals that begin at t_0:

$\lceil q_1 \wedge A \rceil$ holds in	with input	After	state	output
$[t_0, t_1]$	$A = \{\texttt{no\_tr}\}$	t_1	$\{q_1\}$	$\{\texttt{N}\}$
$[t_0, t_2]$	$A = \{\texttt{no\_tr}, \texttt{tr}\}$	t_2	$\{q_1, q_2\}$	$\{\texttt{N}, \texttt{T}\}$
$[t_0, t_3]$	$A = \{\texttt{no\_tr}, \texttt{tr}\}$	t_3	$\{q_1, q_2\}$	$\{\texttt{N}, \texttt{T}\}$
$[t_0, t_4]$	$A = \{\texttt{no\_tr}, \texttt{tr}\}$	t_4	$\{q_1, q_2\}$	$\{\texttt{N}, \texttt{T}\}$
$[t_0, t_5]$	$A = \{\texttt{no\_tr}, \texttt{tr}, \texttt{Error}\}$	t_5	$\{q_1, q_2, q_3\}$	$\{\texttt{N}, \texttt{T}, \texttt{X}\}$
$[t_0, t_6]$	$A = \{\texttt{no\_tr}, \texttt{tr}, \texttt{Error}\}$	t_6	$\{q_1, q_2, q_3\}$	$\{\texttt{N}, \texttt{T}, \texttt{X}\}$

With (DC-3) we can ensure the following:

$\lceil q_1 \wedge A \rceil$ holds in	with input	After	state	output
$[t_1, t_2]$	$A = \{\texttt{no\_tr}, \texttt{tr}\}$	t_2	$\{q_1, q_2\}$	$\{\texttt{N}, \texttt{T}\}$
$[t_2, t_3]$	$A = \{\texttt{no\_tr}, \texttt{tr}\}$	t_3	$\{q_1, q_2\}$	$\{\texttt{N}, \texttt{T}\}$
$[t_3, t_4]$	$A = \{\texttt{no\_tr}\}$	t_4	$\{q_1\}$	$\{\texttt{N}\}$
$[t_4, t_5]$	$A = \{\texttt{no\_tr}, \texttt{Error}\}$	t_5	$\{q_1, q_3\}$	$\{\texttt{N}, \texttt{X}\}$
$[t_5, t_6]$	$A = \{\texttt{Error}\}$	t_6	$\{q_1, q_3\}$	$\{\texttt{N}, \texttt{X}\}$

In case of $S_t(q) > 0$ the assertions made by (DC-2) and (DC-3) may be too weak because for the first $S_t(q)$ seconds the system stays in state q. The

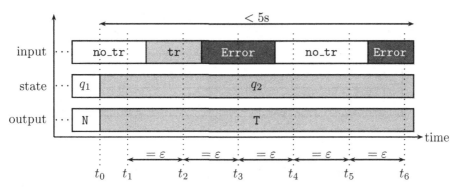

Fig. 5.4. A behaviour of the filter satisfying the requirements (DC-4) and (DC-5)

formulas do not take the delay feature into account. To make this knowledge available in the semantics, we add the following formulas:

$$S_t(q) > 0 \Longrightarrow \lceil \neg q \rceil ; \lceil q \wedge A \rceil \xrightarrow{\leq S_t(q)} \lceil q \vee \delta(q, A \setminus S_e(q)) \rceil, \qquad \text{(DC-4)}$$

$$S_t(q) > 0 \Longrightarrow \lceil \neg q \rceil ; \lceil q \rceil ; \lceil q \wedge A \rceil^{\varepsilon} \xrightarrow{\leq S_t(q)} \lceil q \vee \delta(q, A \setminus S_e(q)) \rceil. \qquad \text{(DC-5)}$$

By (DC-4), we arrive at the following conclusions for the behaviour shown in Figure 5.4:

$\lceil q_2 \wedge A \rceil$ holds in	with input		After	state	output
$[t_0, t_1]$	$A = \{\texttt{no\_tr}\}$		t_1	$\{q_2\}$	$\{\texttt{T}\}$
$[t_0, t_2]$	$A = \{\texttt{no\_tr}, \texttt{tr}\}$		t_2	$\{q_2\}$	$\{\texttt{T}\}$
$[t_0, t_3]$	$A = \{\texttt{no\_tr}, \texttt{tr}, \texttt{Error}\}$		t_3	$\{q_2, q_3\}$	$\{\texttt{T}, \texttt{X}\}$
$[t_0, t_4]$	$A = \{\texttt{no\_tr}, \texttt{tr}, \texttt{Error}\}$		t_4	$\{q_2, q_3\}$	$\{\texttt{T}, \texttt{X}\}$
$[t_0, t_5]$	$A = \{\texttt{no\_tr}, \texttt{tr}, \texttt{Error}\}$		t_5	$\{q_2, q_3\}$	$\{\texttt{T}, \texttt{X}\}$
$[t_0, t_6]$	$A = \{\texttt{no\_tr}, \texttt{tr}, \texttt{Error}\}$		t_6	$\{q_2, q_3\}$	$\{\texttt{T}, \texttt{X}\}$

With (DC-5) we can ensure:

$\lceil q_2 \wedge A \rceil$ holds in	with input		After	state	output
$[t_1, t_2]$	$A = \{\texttt{no\_tr}, \texttt{tr}\}$		t_2	$\{q_2\}$	$\{\texttt{T}\}$
$[t_2, t_3]$	$A = \{\texttt{tr}, \texttt{Error}\}$		t_3	$\{q_2, q_3\}$	$\{\texttt{T}, \texttt{X}\}$
$[t_3, t_4]$	$A = \{\texttt{no\_tr}, \texttt{Error}\}$		t_4	$\{q_2, q_3\}$	$\{\texttt{T}, \texttt{X}\}$
$[t_4, t_5]$	$A = \{\texttt{no\_tr}\}$		t_5	$\{q_2\}$	$\{\texttt{T}\}$
$[t_5, t_6]$	$A = \{\texttt{no\_tr}, \texttt{Error}\}$		t_6	$\{q_2, q_3\}$	$\{\texttt{T}, \texttt{X}\}$

By (DC-2)–(DC-5), we can draw conclusions on the set of possible successor states, but not when the current state *must* be left. For a state q without delay ($S_t(q) = 0$) we know that there has to be a state change after

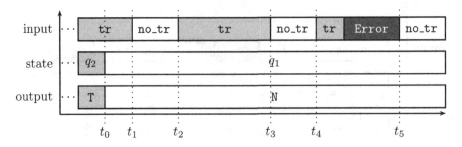

Fig. 5.5. A behaviour of the filter satisfying the requirements (DC-6) and (DC-7)

a complete cycle in which only inputs A could be observed that cause a state change, i.e. $q \notin \delta(q, A)$.

From the external observer's point of view we can ensure two properties for a state q without delay and a set A of inputs that cause a state change:

- It cannot happen that there is an interval of length 2ε in which $\lceil q \wedge A \rceil$ holds because within this interval there is at least one complete cycle of the system.
- If we observe a state change leading to state q, we also gain the information that a new cycle starts. This new cycle has to end within ε seconds. If in this period only inputs in A are observable, we know that there has to be a state change.

We can express these properties in DC as follows:

$$S_t(q) = 0 \wedge q \notin \delta(q, A) \Longrightarrow \square(\lceil q \wedge A \rceil \Longrightarrow \ell < 2\varepsilon), \qquad \text{(DC-6)}$$
$$S_t(q) = 0 \wedge q \notin \delta(q, A) \Longrightarrow \lceil \neg q \rceil \,;\, \lceil q \wedge A \rceil^\varepsilon \longrightarrow \lceil \neg q \rceil. \qquad \text{(DC-7)}$$

Figure 5.5 exhibits another behaviour of the filter. Due to (DC-6) we are able to conclude that $t_5 - t_4 < 2\varepsilon$ and $t_3 - t_2 < 2\varepsilon$ must hold. With (DC-7) we also know that $t_1 - t_0 < \varepsilon$ is true because otherwise the formulas would require a change of the output.

Having described when changes have to happen in states without delay, we now consider the states with delays. First, we collect some observations:

- If we observe that state q holds for $S_t(q)$ seconds and afterwards there is a period where $\lceil q \wedge A \rceil$ with $q \notin \delta(q, A)$, then it is clear that the latter period cannot exceed 2ε seconds. The reason is that we know the delay time has already passed and a period of at least 2ε seconds ensures at least one complete cycle.
- There cannot be an interval of length 2ε in which $\lceil q \wedge A \rceil$ holds with $q \notin \delta(q, A)$ and $A \cap S_e(q) = \varnothing$. The reason is that otherwise at least one

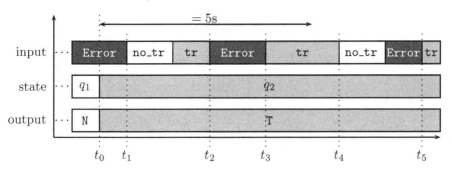

Fig. 5.6. A behaviour of the filter satisfying the requirements (DC-8)–(DC-10)

complete cycle can be found in that interval where an input in A is polled and a state change must happen.

- In the moment where the system enters state q it also starts a new cycle that ends within ε seconds. If in this period only inputs in A with $q \notin \delta(q, A)$ and $A \cap S_e(q) = \varnothing$ hold we know that a state change must happen.

Now, we formalise these properties as follows:

$$S_t(q) > 0 \wedge q \notin \delta(q, A) \Longrightarrow$$
$$\Box(\lceil q \rceil^{S_t(q)} ; \lceil q \wedge A \rceil \Longrightarrow \ell < S_t(q) + 2\varepsilon), \qquad \text{(DC-8)}$$
$$S_t(q) > 0 \wedge A \cap S_e(q) = \varnothing \wedge q \notin \delta(q, A)$$
$$\Longrightarrow \Box(\lceil q \wedge A \rceil \Longrightarrow \ell < 2\varepsilon), \qquad \text{(DC-9)}$$
$$S_t(q) > 0 \wedge A \cap S_e(q) = \varnothing \wedge q \notin \delta(q, A)$$
$$\Longrightarrow \lceil \neg q \rceil ; \lceil q \wedge A \rceil^{\varepsilon} \longrightarrow \lceil \neg q \rceil . \qquad \text{(DC-10)}$$

Consider the behaviour of the filter shown in Figure 5.6. By (DC-10), it is clear that $t_1 - t_0 < \varepsilon$ must be true. With (DC-9) we can derive that $t_3 - t_2 < 2\varepsilon$ holds and finally (DC-8) allows us to conclude $t_5 - t_4 < 2\varepsilon$.

All formulas above do not constrain the behaviour of the Out observable. The idea of the semantics is that it describes only the external behaviour and considers the hardware as a black box behaving like a PLC. Hence, there should be no means to distinguish the changes of the St observable and the changes of the Out observable. In other words: the externally observed changes happen synchronously. This is covered by the following formula:

$$\Box(\lceil q \rceil \Longrightarrow \lceil \omega(q) \rceil). \qquad \text{(DC-11)}$$

The formulas above handle all phenomena that we want to cover. However, some formulas depend on a state change and this is expressed by a subformula like $\lceil \neg q \rceil ; \lceil q \wedge A \rceil$. The subformula is not applicable at time 0, when the system starts its computation. Hence, we need to handle these initial intervals separately by the following formulas:

$$\lceil q_0 \wedge A \rceil \longrightarrow_0 \lceil q_0 \vee \delta(q_0, A) \rceil, \quad \text{(DC-2')}$$

$$S_t(q_0) > 0 \Longrightarrow \lceil q_0 \wedge A \rceil \xrightarrow[\;0\;]{<S_t(q_0)} \lceil q_0 \vee \delta(q_0, A \setminus S_e(q_0)) \rceil, \quad \text{(DC-4')}$$

$$S_t(q_0) > 0 \Longrightarrow \lceil q_0 \rceil ; \lceil q_0 \wedge A \rceil^\varepsilon \xrightarrow[\;0\;]{<S_t(q_0)} \lceil q_0 \vee \delta(q_0, A \setminus S_e(q_0)) \rceil, \quad \text{(DC-5')}$$

$$S_t(q_0) = 0 \wedge q_0 \notin \delta(q_0, A) \Longrightarrow \lceil q_0 \wedge A \rceil^\varepsilon \longrightarrow_0 \lceil \neg q_0 \rceil, \quad \text{(DC-7')}$$

$$S_t(q_0) > 0 \wedge A \cap S_e(q_0) = \varnothing \wedge q_0 \notin \delta(q_0, A) \Longrightarrow$$
$$\lceil q_0 \wedge A \rceil^\varepsilon \longrightarrow_0 \lceil \neg q_0 \rceil. \quad \text{(DC-10')}$$

Each of these formulas corresponds to a previous one, as indicated by the primed numbers.

We now conjoin all formulas introduced above.

Definition 5.3 (Duration Calculus semantics of PLC-Automata)
The Duration Calculus semantics of a PLC-Automaton $\mathcal{A}$ is defined by the following DC formula:

$$[\![\mathcal{A}]\!]_{\mathrm{DC}} \overset{\mathrm{def}}{\Longleftrightarrow} \bigwedge_{\substack{q \in Q, \\ \varnothing \neq A \subseteq \Sigma}} \left(\bigwedge_{j=1}^{11} (\mathrm{DC}\text{-}j) \begin{array}{l} \wedge\, (\mathrm{DC}\text{-}2') \wedge (\mathrm{DC}\text{-}4') \wedge (\mathrm{DC}\text{-}5') \\ \wedge\, (\mathrm{DC}\text{-}7') \wedge (\mathrm{DC}\text{-}10') \end{array} \right).$$

This is a formula in the observables $\mathsf{In}_\mathcal{A}, \mathsf{St}_\mathcal{A}, \mathsf{Out}_\mathcal{A}$ and without global variables. It represents the set of all interpretations $\mathcal{I}$ of these observables that realise $[\![\mathcal{A}]\!]_{\mathrm{DC}}$ from 0, i.e. with $\mathcal{I} \models_0 [\![\mathcal{A}]\!]_{\mathrm{DC}}$. The DC semantics can be used to prove that an implementation meets its requirement by showing that the DC semantics *implies* the requirement. To simplify this task it is useful to find theorems tailored to prove frequently used requirement patterns.

5.4.1 Reaction times

As a first application of the DC semantics we present a theorem estimating upper bounds of the reaction times of PLC-Automata. For example, we might wish to establish for such an automaton $\mathcal{A}$ with a state set Q that

$$\lceil \mathsf{St}_\mathcal{A} \in Q \wedge \mathsf{In}_\mathcal{A} = \text{emergency signal} \rceil \xrightarrow{0.1} \lceil \mathsf{St}_\mathcal{A} = \text{motor switched off} \rceil$$

holds, i.e. in case of an emergency signal the motor is switched off after at most 0.1 seconds, independent of the state in which the emergency occurred.

In general, let

$$\Pi \subseteq Q \quad \text{be a set of start states,}$$
$$A \subseteq \Sigma \quad \text{be a set of inputs,}$$
$$c \in \text{Time} \quad \text{be a time bound, and}$$
$$\Pi_{\text{target}} \subseteq Q \quad \text{be a set of target states.}$$

Then we wish to prove statements of the form

$$\lceil St_A \in \Pi \wedge In_A \in A \rceil \xrightarrow{\; c \;} \lceil St_A \in \Pi_{\text{target}} \rceil,$$

abbreviated by

$$\lceil \Pi \wedge A \rceil \xrightarrow{\; c \;} \lceil \Pi_{\text{target}} \rceil.$$

The point is that we consider only sets of target states of a special form. To this end, we extend the transition function δ to sets:

$$\delta(\Pi, A) = \{\delta(q, a) \mid q \in \Pi \wedge a \in A\}.$$

Note that δ satisfies the following *monotonicity* property:

Proposition 5.4
If $\Pi \subseteq \Pi' \subseteq Q$ and $A \subseteq A' \subseteq \Sigma$ then $\delta(\Pi, A) \subseteq \delta(\Pi', A')$.

Next we define inductively for $n \in \mathbb{N}$ the set $\delta^n(\Pi, A)$ of all states that can be reached from Π in n steps using only A-transitions:

$$\delta^0(\Pi, A) \stackrel{\text{def}}{=} \Pi,$$
$$\delta^{n+1}(\Pi, A) \stackrel{\text{def}}{=} \delta(\delta^n(\Pi, A), A).$$

To estimate the reaction times we stipulate that

$$\delta(\Pi, A) \subseteq \Pi$$

holds. By Proposition 5.4, this implies

$$\delta^{n+1}(\Pi, A) \subseteq \delta^n(\Pi, A) \subseteq \cdots \subseteq \delta(\Pi, A) \subseteq \Pi.$$

Thus applying δ repeatedly yields a *contraction* as illustrated by the following diagram:

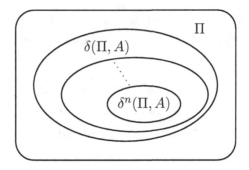

Example 5.5

We consider the filter in Figure 5.2 and identify its states with the corresponding outputs N, T, and X. Then

$$\delta^0(\{N, T\}, \{no\_tr\}) = \{N, T\}$$
$$\delta(\{N, T\}, \{no\_tr\}) = \{N\} \subseteq \{N, T\}$$
$$\delta^n(\{N, T\}, \{no\_tr\}) = \{N\} \text{ for } n \geq 1$$

and

$$\delta^0(\{N, T, X\}, \{Error\}) = \{N, T, X\}$$
$$\delta(\{N, T, X\}, \{Error\}) = \{X\} \subseteq \{N, T, X\}$$
$$\delta^n(\{N, T, X\}, \{Error\}) = \{X\} \text{ for } n \geq 1$$

are examples for contractions, whereas

$$\delta(\{T\}, \{no\_tr\}) = \{N\} \not\subseteq \{T\}$$

is not a contraction.   ∎

We first state a special case of the announced theorem on reaction times, with $\Pi_{\text{target}} = \delta(\Pi, A)$.

Theorem 5.6

Let $\mathcal{A} = (Q, \Sigma, \delta, q_0, \varepsilon, S_e, S_t, \Omega, \omega)$ be a *PLC-Automaton*, $\Pi \subseteq Q$ and $A \subseteq \Sigma$ with

$$\delta(\Pi, A) \subseteq \Pi.$$

Then the following holds:

$$\lceil \Pi \wedge A \rceil \xrightarrow{\ c\ } \lceil \delta(\Pi, A) \rceil \, ,$$

where

$$c \stackrel{\text{def}}{=} \varepsilon + \max(\{0\} \cup \{s(\pi, A) \mid \pi \in \Pi \setminus \delta(\Pi, A)\}) \qquad (5.1)$$

and

$$s(\pi, A) \overset{\text{def}}{=} \begin{cases} S_t(\pi) + 2\varepsilon, & \text{if } S_t(\pi) > 0 \text{ and } A \cap S_e(\pi) \neq \emptyset, \\ \varepsilon, & \text{otherwise.} \end{cases}$$

Note that $c = \varepsilon$ if $\Pi = \delta(\Pi, A)$ holds in (5.1) because then the max-operator yields 0.

Example 5.7

We apply this theorem to estimate the reaction times of the filter in Figure 5.2.

(1) We estimate $\lceil\{N, T\} \wedge \{no\_tr\}\rceil \xrightarrow{5+3\varepsilon} \lceil N\rceil$ as the following calculation shows. By Example 5.5, we have

$$\delta(\{N, T\}, \{no\_tr\}) = \{N\}$$

and thus Theorem 5.6 yields

$$\lceil\{N, T\} \wedge \{no\_tr\}\rceil \xrightarrow{c} \lceil N\rceil,$$

where c is calculated as follows:

$$\begin{aligned} c &= \varepsilon + \max(\{0\} \cup \{s(\pi, \{no\_tr\}) \mid \pi \in \{N, T\} \setminus \{N\}\}) \\ &= \varepsilon + \max(\{0\} \cup \{s(T, \{no\_tr\})\}) \\ &= \varepsilon + 5 + 2\varepsilon \\ &= 5 + 3\varepsilon. \end{aligned}$$

(2) We have the following reaction $\lceil\{N, T, X\} \wedge \{Error\}\rceil \xrightarrow{2\varepsilon} \lceil X\rceil$ as the following calculation shows. By Example 5.5, we have

$$\delta(\{N, T, X\}, \{Error\}) = \{X\}$$

and thus Theorem 5.6 yields

$$\lceil\{N, T, X\} \wedge \{Error\}\rceil \xrightarrow{c} \lceil X\rceil,$$

where c is calculated as follows:

$$\begin{aligned} c &= \varepsilon + \max(\{0\} \cup \{s(\pi, \{Error\}) \mid \pi \in \{N, T, X\} \setminus \{X\}\}) \\ &= \varepsilon + \max(\{0\} \cup \{s(N, \{Error\}), s(T, \{Error\})\}) \\ &= \varepsilon + \varepsilon \\ &= 2\varepsilon. \end{aligned}$$

(3) We have the following reaction $\lceil\{\mathtt{N},\mathtt{T}\} \wedge \{\mathtt{no\_tr}, \mathtt{tr}\}\rceil \xrightarrow{\varepsilon} \lceil\mathtt{N},\mathtt{T}\rceil$ as the following calculation shows. By Example 5.5, we have

$$\delta(\{\mathtt{N},\mathtt{T}\}, \{\mathtt{no\_tr}, \mathtt{tr}\}) = \{\mathtt{N},\mathtt{T}\}$$

and thus Theorem 5.6 yields

$$\lceil\{\mathtt{N},\mathtt{T}\} \wedge \{\mathtt{no\_tr}, \mathtt{tr}\}\rceil \xrightarrow{c} \lceil\mathtt{N},\mathtt{T}\rceil ,$$

where c is calculated as follows:

$$\begin{aligned}
c &= \varepsilon + \max(\{0\} \cup \{s(\pi, \{\mathtt{Error}\}) \mid \pi \in \{\mathtt{N},\mathtt{T}\} \setminus \{\mathtt{N},\mathtt{T}\}\}) \\
&= \varepsilon + \max(\{0\} \cup \varnothing) \\
&= \varepsilon + 0 \\
&= \varepsilon.
\end{aligned}$$

The set $\{0\}$ prevents that the max-operator is applied to the empty set.

∎

We conclude this section by formulating the general theorem on reaction times, with $\Pi_{\mathrm{target}} = \delta^n(\Pi, A)$.

Theorem 5.8
Let $\mathcal{A} = (Q, \Sigma, \delta, q_0, \varepsilon, S_e, S_t, \Omega, \omega)$ be a PLC-Automaton, $\Pi \subseteq Q$ and $A \subseteq \Sigma$ with

$$\delta(\Pi, A) \subseteq \Pi.$$

Then the following holds for all $n \in \mathbb{N}$:

$$\lceil \Pi \wedge A \rceil \xrightarrow{c_n} \lceil \delta^n(\Pi, A) \rceil ,$$

where

$$c_n \stackrel{\mathrm{def}}{=} \varepsilon + \max \left(\{0\} \cup \left\{ \sum_{i=1}^{k} s(\pi_i, A) \; \middle| \; \begin{array}{l} 1 \le k \le n \wedge \\ \exists\, \pi_1, \ldots, \pi_k \in \Pi \setminus \delta^n(\Pi, A) \; \bullet \\ \forall j \in \{1, \ldots, k-1\} \; \bullet \\ \pi_{j+1} \in \delta(\pi_j, A) \end{array} \right\} \right)$$

and where $s(\pi, A)$ is defined as in Theorem 5.6.

For $n = 1$ this theorem specialises to the previous Theorem 5.6. Intuitively, this general theorem states a worst-case estimate of the reaction times on all possible paths from Π to $\delta^n(\Pi, A)$ as illustrated by the following diagram:

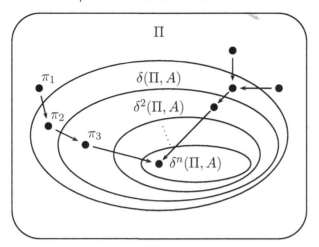

Sketch of proof:
Proof by contradiction:

$$\neg(\lceil \Pi \wedge A \rceil \xrightarrow{c_n} \lceil \delta^n(\Pi, A) \rceil)$$
$$\Longleftrightarrow \neg(\neg(\text{true}; \lceil \Pi \wedge A \rceil^{c_n} ; \lceil \neg \delta^n(\Pi, A) \rceil ; \text{true}))$$
$$\Longleftrightarrow \text{true}; \lceil \Pi \wedge A \rceil^{c_n} ; \lceil \neg \delta^n(\Pi, A) \rceil ; \text{true}.$$

Due to the finite variability we can find a partitioning such that the following holds:

$$\Longrightarrow \exists m \in \mathbb{N}, \pi_0, \ldots, \pi_m \in \Pi \bullet \forall 0 \le i < m \bullet \pi_i \ne \pi_{i+1}$$
$$\wedge \text{true}; (\lceil A \rceil^{c_n} \wedge \lceil \pi_0 \rceil ; \ldots ; \lceil \pi_m \rceil); \lceil \neg \delta^n(\Pi, A) \rceil ; \text{true}.$$

By (DC-2), we have $\pi_2 \in \delta(\pi_1, A), \ldots, \pi_m \in \delta(\pi_{m-1}, A)$. Thus

$$\Longrightarrow \exists m \in \mathbb{N}, \pi_0, \ldots, \pi_m \in \Pi \bullet \forall 0 \le i < m \bullet \pi_i \ne \pi_{i+1}$$
$$\wedge \text{true}; (\lceil A \rceil^{c_n} \wedge \lceil \pi_0 \rceil ; \ldots ; \lceil \pi_m \rceil); \lceil \neg \delta^n(\Pi, A) \rceil ; \text{true}$$
$$\wedge \forall i \in \{2, \ldots, m\} \bullet \pi_i \in \delta^{i-1}(\pi_1, A).$$

We can conclude that $\pi_m \notin \delta^n(\Pi, A)$ holds due to $c_n \ge \varepsilon$ and (DC-3). Moreover, we have $m \le n$ and $\pi_i \notin \delta(\pi_i, A)$ for all $i \ge 1$. Hence

$$\Longrightarrow \exists m \in \{0, \ldots, n\}, \pi_0, \ldots, \pi_m \in \Pi \bullet \forall 0 \le i < m \bullet \pi_i \ne \pi_{i+1}$$
$$\wedge \text{true}; (\lceil A \rceil^{c_n} \wedge \lceil \pi_0 \rceil ; \ldots ; \lceil \pi_m \rceil); \lceil \neg \delta^n(\Pi, A) \rceil ; \text{true}$$
$$\wedge \pi_m \notin \delta^n(\Pi, A) \wedge \forall i \in \{2, \ldots, m\} \bullet \pi_i \in \delta^{i-1}(\pi_1, A)$$
$$\wedge \forall i \in \{1, \ldots, m\} \bullet \pi_i \notin \delta(\pi_i, A).$$

Now we can find upper time bounds for π_i with $i \ge 1$ due to (DC-7), (DC-8), and (DC-10):

$$\implies \exists m \in \{0, \ldots, n\}, \pi_0, \ldots, \pi_m \in \Pi \bullet \forall 0 \le i < m \bullet \pi_i \ne \pi_{i+1}$$
$$\land \text{ true}; (\lceil A \rceil^{c_n} \land \lceil \pi_0 \rceil; \lceil \pi_1 \rceil^{\le s(\pi_1, A)}; \ldots; \lceil \pi_m \rceil^{\le s(\pi_m, A)});$$
$$\lceil \neg \delta^n(\Pi, A) \rceil; \text{ true}$$
$$\land \pi_m \notin \delta^n(\Pi, A) \land \forall i \in \{2, \ldots, m\} \bullet \pi_i \in \delta^{i-1}(\pi_1, A)$$
$$\land \forall i \in \{1, \ldots, m\} \bullet \pi_i \notin \delta(\pi_i, A).$$

If the $\lceil \pi_0 \rceil$-phase is shorter than ε seconds, we can derive a contradiction because the sum of durations would be shorter than c_n. For the remaining case we can exploit (DC-3) to conclude that $\pi_1 \in \delta(\pi_0, A)$ holds. Therefore we conclude by (DC-6), (DC-8), and (DC-9) that the $\lceil \pi_0 \rceil$-phase lasts at most $\varepsilon + s(\pi_0, A)$ seconds. □

5.5 Synthesis from DC implementables

In Chapter 3 we introduced DC implementables as a sublanguage of the Duration Calculus. In this section we investigate how to implement a specification given as a set of DC implementables by a PLC-Automaton. To this end, we consider the following *synthesis problem*:

Given: A set Spec of DC implementables.
Task: Generate a PLC-Automaton $\mathcal{A}$ that implements Spec.

We will present an algorithm that synthesises a PLC-Automaton from Spec provided this specification is *consistent*. We will explain what consistency means in this setting.

Formally, we stipulate that Spec constrains the values of two observables: an input observable† $\text{In}_{\mathcal{A}}$ ranging over a set Σ and an output observable $\text{Out}_{\mathcal{A}}$ ranging over a set Ω. The synthesised PLC-Automaton $\mathcal{A}$ should then determine an observable $\text{St}_{\mathcal{A}}$ ranging over a set of states Q. In particular, the synthesis should generate the set Q from $\text{In}_{\mathcal{A}}$ and $\text{Out}_{\mathcal{A}}$. As notation we use the following typical letters, possibly decorated by indices:

$$\sigma \in \Sigma, \quad \varphi \subseteq \Sigma, \quad \pi \in \Omega, \quad q \in Q.$$

Inside DC implementables we use the following abbreviations:

$$\sigma \quad \text{abbreviates} \quad \text{In}_{\mathcal{A}} = \sigma,$$
$$\varphi \quad \text{abbreviates} \quad \text{In}_{\mathcal{A}} \in \varphi,$$
$$\pi \quad \text{abbreviates} \quad \text{Out}_{\mathcal{A}} = \pi.$$

---

† Several input observables can be handled by taking their Cartesian product.

In the specification Spec the following patterns of DC implementables may appear (cf. Section 3.2):

- Initialisation:

$$\lceil\,\rceil \vee \lceil \pi_0 \rceil \text{ ; true.}$$

- Sequencing:

$$\lceil \pi \rceil \longrightarrow \lceil \pi \vee \pi_1 \vee \ldots \vee \pi_n \rceil \quad (n \geq 0).$$

- Unbounded stability:

$$\lceil \neg\pi \rceil \,;\, \lceil \pi \wedge \varphi \rceil \longrightarrow \lceil \pi \vee \pi_1 \vee \ldots \vee \pi_n \rceil \quad (n \geq 0).$$

- Bounded stability:

$$\lceil \neg\pi \rceil \,;\, \lceil \pi \wedge \varphi \rceil \xrightarrow{\leq t} \lceil \pi \vee \pi_1 \vee \ldots \vee \pi_n \rceil \quad (n \geq 0).$$

- Synchronisation:

$$\lceil \pi \wedge \varphi \rceil \xrightarrow{t} \lceil \neg\pi \rceil .$$

Note that by taking $\varphi = \Sigma$ this synchronisation pattern specialises to the progress pattern $\lceil \pi \rceil \xrightarrow{t} \lceil \neg\pi \rceil$.

To each unbounded stability of the above form we implicitly add the following initial requirement:

- Unbounded initial stability:

$$\lceil \pi \wedge \varphi \rceil \longrightarrow_0 \lceil \pi \vee \pi_1 \vee \ldots \vee \pi_n \rceil \quad (n \geq 0).$$

Analogously, to each bounded stability of the above form we implicitly add the following initial requirement:

- Bounded initial stability:

$$\lceil \pi \wedge \varphi \rceil \xrightarrow{\leq t}_0 \lceil \pi \vee \pi_1 \vee \ldots \vee \pi_n \rceil \quad (n \geq 0).$$

Example 5.9

A *two-tier watchdog* should supervise input values n, m, s with the following intuition:

$$n \text{ stands for a normal value,}$$
$$m \text{ signals a major problem,}$$
$$s \text{ signals a small problem.}$$

The output values are as follows:

N stands for Normal,

W stands for Warning,

A stands for Alarm.

The watchdog starts in a state with output N. It stays there as long as it reads n as input value. If the watchdog discovers a (small or major) problem, it issues a warning W. If after 5 seconds it still senses the major problem m, the watchdog outputs an alarm A. In case of a small problem s the watchdog waits for 15 seconds to see whether it disappears on its own. If this is not the case, it will also output an alarm A.

We specify this desired behaviour with the help of DC implementables:

$$\text{Init}: \quad \lceil\rceil \vee \lceil N \rceil \; ; \text{true},$$

$$\text{Sequ-1}: \quad \lceil N \rceil \longrightarrow \lceil N \vee W \rceil,$$

$$\text{Sequ-2}: \quad \lceil A \rceil \longrightarrow \lceil A \rceil,$$

$$\text{Unb.Stab-1}: \quad \lceil \neg N \rceil \; ; \lceil N \wedge n \rceil \longrightarrow \lceil N \rceil,$$

$$\text{Unb.Stab-2}: \quad \lceil \neg W \rceil \; ; \lceil W \wedge n \rceil \longrightarrow \lceil W \vee N \rceil,$$

$$\text{Unb.Stab-3}: \quad \lceil \neg W \rceil \; ; \lceil W \wedge \{ms\} \rceil \longrightarrow \lceil W \vee A \rceil,$$

$$\text{Bd.Stab-1}: \quad \lceil \neg W \rceil \; ; \lceil W \wedge \{m, s\} \rceil \xrightarrow{\leq 5} \lceil W \rceil,$$

$$\text{Bd.Stab-2}: \quad \lceil \neg W \rceil \; ; \lceil W \wedge \{s\} \rceil \xrightarrow{\leq 15} \lceil W \rceil,$$

$$\text{Syn-1}: \quad \lceil N \wedge \{m, s\} \rceil \xrightarrow{0.1} \lceil \neg N \rceil,$$

$$\text{Syn-2}: \quad \lceil W \wedge n \rceil \xrightarrow{0.2} \lceil \neg W \rceil,$$

$$\text{Syn-3}: \quad \lceil W \wedge m \rceil \xrightarrow{5.1} \lceil \neg W \rceil,$$

$$\text{Syn-4}: \quad \lceil W \wedge s \rceil \xrightarrow{15.1} \lceil \neg W \rceil.$$

Our aim is now to synthesise a PLC-Automaton that implements these requirements. To this end, we introduce a synthesis algorithm and illustrate its steps with the watchdog as a running example.   ■

5.5.1 Synthesis algorithm

The synthesis algorithm constructs a PLC-Automaton from Spec in a sequence of steps:

(1) *Computing the state space.* The idea is that for each output $\pi \in \Omega$ a set

of states $\{q_{\pi,t_1}, \ldots, q_{\pi,t_n}\}$ is computed where $t_1 < \cdots < t_n$ are the time
bounds that appear in bounded stabilities for π. We refer to this set
of states when ordered according to the time bounds as the π-*cascade*.
Intuitively, a state q_{π,t_i} in the cascade represents the knowledge that π
holds for at least t_{i-1} seconds and at most $t_i + 2i \cdot \varepsilon$ seconds where ε is
the (to be determined) cycle time of the (to be synthesised) PLC-Au-
tomaton.

Formally, for each output value $\pi \in \Omega$ we compute the set

$$bounds(\pi) \stackrel{\text{def}}{=} \{t \in \mathsf{Time} \mid \exists \text{ bounded stability}$$

$$\lceil \neg \pi \rceil \; ; \; \lceil \pi \wedge \varphi \rceil \xrightarrow{\leq t} \lceil \pi \vee \pi_1 \vee \ldots \vee \pi_n \rceil$$

$$\in \mathsf{Spec}\}.$$

The state space Q is then defined as

$$Q \stackrel{\text{def}}{=} \{q_{\pi,0} \mid \pi \in \Omega \wedge bounds(\pi) = \varnothing\} \cup \{q_{\pi,t} \mid \pi \in \Omega \wedge t \in bounds(\pi)\}.$$

In our example we get the following sets of bounds:

$$bounds(\mathbb{N}) = \varnothing,$$
$$bounds(\mathbb{W}) = \{5, 15\},$$
$$bounds(\mathbb{A}) = \varnothing.$$

This yields the state space $Q = \{q_{\mathbb{N},0}, q_{\mathbb{W},5}, q_{\mathbb{W},15}, q_{\mathbb{A},0}\}$.

(2) *Initial Δ-table.* The synthesis algorithm manipulates an over-approxi-
mation of the possible transitions as a function

$$\Delta : Q \times \Sigma \longrightarrow \mathcal{P}(\Omega)$$

represented as a so-called Δ-*table* that contains for each state $q_{\pi,t} \in Q$
and each input value $\sigma \in \Sigma$ a *set of output values* that are not yet
forbidden by the specification. In the Δ-table, the sets are represented
as *lists* of output values:

Δ	$\cdots$	$q_{\pi,t}$	$\cdots$
$\vdots$	$\ddots$	$\vdots$	
σ	$\cdots$	$\pi_1, \ldots, \pi_m$	$\cdots$
$\vdots$		$\vdots$	$\ddots$

Initially, nothing is forbidden and hence each entry of the Δ-table contains all output values. From the final Δ-table the transition function δ
of the PLC-Automaton is derived.

The initial Δ-table of the watchdog specification is

Δ	$q_{N,0}$	$q_{W,5}$	$q_{W,15}$	$q_{A,0}$
n	N, W, A	N, W, A	N, W, A	N, W, A
m	N, W, A	N, W, A	N, W, A	N, W, A
s	N, W, A	N, W, A	N, W, A	N, W, A

In the following steps we will examine the various types of implementables and manipulate the Δ-table accordingly.

(3) *Sequencing requirements.* For each sequencing formula

$$\lceil \pi \rceil \longrightarrow \lceil \pi \vee \pi_1 \vee \ldots \vee \pi_n \rceil$$

in Spec we intersect all entries in $q_{\pi,t}$-columns with $\{\pi, \pi_1, \ldots, \pi_n\}$.

Processing the two sequencing formulas Sequ-1 and Sequ-2 of our example yields the following Δ-table:

Δ	$q_{N,0}$	$q_{W,5}$	$q_{W,15}$	$q_{A,0}$
n	N, W	N, W, A	N, W, A	A
m	N, W	N, W, A	N, W, A	A
s	N, W	N, W, A	N, W, A	A

(4) *Unbounded stabilities.* Now we consider all unbounded stabilities. If

$$\lceil \neg \pi \rceil \; ; \; \lceil \pi \wedge \varphi \rceil \longrightarrow \lceil \pi \vee \pi_1 \vee \ldots \vee \pi_n \rceil$$

is in Spec we take all entries that are in a $q_{\pi,t}$-column *and* in a σ-row where σ satisfies φ and intersect these entries with $\{\pi, \pi_1, \ldots, \pi_n\}$.

In our example there are three unbounded stabilities. Processing the formula Unb.Stab-1 yields

Δ	$q_{N,0}$	$q_{W,5}$	$q_{W,15}$	$q_{A,0}$
n	N	N, W, A	N, W, A	A
m	N, W	N, W, A	N, W, A	A
s	N, W	N, W, A	N, W, A	A

Next we take Unb.Stab-2 and obtain

Δ	$q_{N,0}$	$q_{W,5}$	$q_{W,15}$	$q_{A,0}$
n	N	N, W	N, W	A
m	N, W	N, W, A	N, W, A	A
s	N, W	N, W, A	N, W, A	A

The remaining unbounded stability Unb.Stab-3 leads to the following

Δ-table as the final result of this step:

Δ	$q_{N,0}$	$q_{W,5}$	$q_{W,15}$	$q_{A,0}$
n	N	N, W	N, W	A
m	N, W	W, A	W, A	A
s	N, W	W, A	W, A	A

(5) *Bounded stabilities.* If there are bounded stabilities of the form

$$\lceil \neg\pi \rceil \; ; \; \lceil \pi \wedge \varphi \rceil \xrightarrow{\leq t} \lceil \pi \vee \pi_1 \vee \ldots \vee \pi_n \rceil$$

in Spec, we intersect all entries of $q_{\pi,t'}$-columns where $t' < t$ holds and φ-rows with the set $\{\pi, \pi_1, \ldots, \pi_n\}$. Thus the outputs are restricted only to those states $q_{\pi,t'}$ where the waiting time t' has not yet exceeded the time bound t.

In our example the bounded stability Bd.Stab-2 yields

Δ	$q_{N,0}$	$q_{W,5}$	$q_{W,15}$	$q_{A,0}$
n	N	N, W	N, W	A
m	N, W	W, A	W, A	A
s	N, W	W	W, A	A

(6) *Synchronisation requirements.* Synchronisations and progress formulas (which are special cases of synchronisations with $\varphi = \Sigma$) of the form

$$\lceil \pi \wedge \varphi \rceil \xrightarrow{t} \lceil \neg\pi \rceil$$

are handled as follows: we remove π in each entry of a φ-row and $q_{\pi,t'}$-column provided that either $t \leq t'$ or $t' < t$ such that there is no $q_{\pi,t''}$-column with $t' < t'' < t$. The latter condition ensures that the output π is changed as late as possible before the deadline t.

Our example has four synchronisation formulas. Processing the formula Syn-1 yields

Δ	$q_{N,0}$	$q_{W,5}$	$q_{W,15}$	$q_{A,0}$
n	N	N, W	N, W	A
m	W	W, A	W, A	A
s	W	W	W, A	A

Processing Syn-2 yields

Δ	$q_{N,0}$	$q_{W,5}$	$q_{W,15}$	$q_{A,0}$
n	N	N	N	A
m	W	W, A	W, A	A
s	W	W	W, A	A

Processing Syn-3 yields

Δ	$q_{N,0}$	$q_{W,5}$	$q_{W,15}$	$q_{A,0}$
n	N	N	N	A
m	W	A	A	A
s	W	W	W, A	A

Processing Syn-4 finally yields

Δ	$q_{N,0}$	$q_{W,5}$	$q_{W,15}$	$q_{A,0}$
n	N	N	N	A
m	W	A	A	A
s	W	W	A	A

(7) *Determining delayed inputs.* We define the S_e-function of the PLC-Automaton as follows:

$$S_e(q_{\pi,t}) \overset{\text{def}}{=} \Sigma \setminus \{\sigma \in \Sigma \mid \exists \lceil \pi \wedge \varphi \rceil \xrightarrow{t'} \lceil \neg \pi \rceil \in \mathsf{Spec} \bullet t' \le t \wedge \sigma \in \varphi\}.$$

Informally, the reaction is delayed for all inputs for which there is no explicit requirement for an output change *before* the delay time t.

In the example we obtain:

$$S_e(q_{W,5}) = \{n, m, s\} \setminus \{n\} = \{m, s\} \text{ by Syn-2,}$$
$$S_e(q_{W,15}) = \{n, m, s\} \setminus \{n, m\} = \{s\} \text{ by Syn-2 and Syn-3.}$$

(8) *Estimating the cycle time.* In this step we calculate upper bounds for the cycle time ε. Each synchronisation formula

$$\lceil \pi \wedge \varphi \rceil \xrightarrow{t} \lceil \neg \pi \rceil \in \mathsf{Spec}$$

yields one upper time bound. Let the set of predecessor states be

$$Pred(\pi, t) \overset{\text{def}}{=} \{q_{\pi,t'} \mid 0 < t' < t\}.$$

Then the upper time bound for ε induced by $\lceil \pi \wedge \varphi \rceil \xrightarrow{t} \lceil \neg \pi \rceil$ is given by

$$\varepsilon \le \begin{cases} \frac{t}{2}, & \text{if } Pred(\pi, t) = \varnothing, \\ \frac{t - \max\{t' \mid q_{\pi,t'} \in Pred(\pi,t)\}}{2 \cdot |Pred(\pi,t)|}, & \text{otherwise.} \end{cases}$$

In the first case we take into account that it takes at most two cycles for a PLC-Automaton to react to an input φ (cf. (DC-6) of the DC semantics in Section 5.4). In the second case we take the quotient of the time difference to the *last* predecessor in the π-cascade and the worst-case estimate that in each predecessor in the π-cascade two cycles could be consumed.

In our example the four synchronisation formulas yield the following upper time bounds for ε:

$$\varepsilon \ \leq \ \tfrac{0.1}{2} = 0.05 \qquad \text{due to Syn-1,}$$

$$\varepsilon \ \leq \ \tfrac{0.2}{2} = 0.1 \qquad \text{due to Syn-2,}$$

$$\varepsilon \ \leq \ \tfrac{5.1-5}{2\cdot 1} = 0.05 \qquad \text{due to Syn-3,}$$

$$\varepsilon \ \leq \ \tfrac{15.1-15}{2\cdot 2} = 0.025 \quad \text{due to Syn-4.}$$

For Syn-3 we calculate $Pred(\mathtt{W}, 5.1) = \{q_{\mathtt{W},5}\}$ and thus $|Pred(\mathtt{W}, 5.1)| = 1$, and in case of Syn-4 we obtain $Pred(\mathtt{W}, 15.1) = \{q_{\mathtt{W},5}, q_{\mathtt{W},15}\}$ and thus $|Pred(\mathtt{W}, 15.1)| = 2$.

(9) *Eliminating contradictions.* We have to *remove outputs* π for which there is a bounded stability $\lceil \neg \pi \rceil \;;\; \lceil \pi \wedge \varphi \rceil \overset{\leq t}{\longrightarrow} \lceil \pi \vee \pi_1 \vee \ldots \vee \pi_n \rceil$ in the specification *and* a time bound $t' \leq t$ with $\varphi \not\subseteq S_e(q_{\pi,t'})$. The reason is the existence of an input $\sigma \in \varphi \setminus S_e(q_{\pi,t'})$ for which the delay time t' is not relevant $(\notin S_e(q_{\pi,t'}))$ although the bounded stability requires the system to stay in π for at least t seconds provided σ holds from the beginning of π. For instance, consider two formulas in Spec of the form

$$\lceil \neg \pi \rceil \;;\; \lceil \pi \wedge \varphi \rceil \overset{\leq t}{\longrightarrow} \lceil \pi \rceil \ \text{ and } \ \lceil \pi \wedge \varphi' \rceil \overset{t'}{\longrightarrow} \lceil \neg \pi \rceil$$

where $\varphi \cap \varphi' \neq \varnothing$ and $t' \leq t$ holds. Then a problem arises if the system changes the output to π and subsequently reads only inputs from $\varphi \cap \varphi'$. In that case the system on the one hand has to stay in π for at least t seconds and on the other hand has to leave π after t' seconds. This is realisable only for $t < t'$.†

Now we consider the Δ-table again and remove all states for which an empty entry exists. That means if for output π there is a t and an input $\sigma \in \Sigma$ such that the entry in column $q_{\pi,t}$ and row σ is empty, then we can conclude that the given specification contains formulas that in conjunction imply that π should never be observable. As a consequence we remove all columns with output π and remove all π's in the remaining entries.

We have to repeat step (9) as long as states are found that have to be removed.

† Even the case $t = t'$ is a problem because then the specification requires perfect timing, which is not realisable in practice.

In our example no output has to be removed because there is no empty entry in the Δ-table and the sets of delayed inputs $S_e(q_{W,5})$ and $S_e(q_{W,15})$ are not in conflict with the bounded stabilities Bd.Stab-1 and Bd.Stab-2.

(10) *Consistency check.* In this step we determine whether the synthesis was successful or not. To this end, we perform the following *consistency check* depending on Spec and the final Δ-table:

> The specification Spec contains *at most* one initialisation formula $\bigcap \vee \lceil \pi_0 \rceil$; true. If $\bigcap \vee \lceil \pi_0 \rceil$; true is in Spec then there exists a state of the form $q_{\pi_0,t}$ in the final Δ-table (which was not removed in step (9)).

In case this consistency check is successful, we proceed with step (11) and construct a PLC-Automaton that meets Spec. Otherwise the synthesis algorithm stops without producing any automaton.

In our example, the consistency check is successful because the initial constraint $\bigcap \vee \lceil N \rceil$; true is in the specification and the state $q_{N,0}$ is in the final Δ-table of step (6).

(11) *Construction of the PLC-Automaton.* We need two auxiliary functions. For an output value π and $t \in$ Time we introduce

$$first(\pi) \stackrel{\text{def}}{=} \min(\{t \in \text{Time} \mid q_{\pi,t} \in Q\})$$

to determine the time stamp of the *first* state in the π-cascade, and

$$next(\pi, t) \stackrel{\text{def}}{=} \begin{cases} \min(\{t' \in \text{Time} \mid & t' > t \wedge q_{\pi,t'} \in Q\}) \\ & \text{if } \{t' \in \text{Time} \mid t' > t \wedge q_{\pi,t'} \in Q\} \neq \varnothing, \\ t, & \text{otherwise} \end{cases}$$

to determine the time stamp of the *next* state after time t in the π-cascade.

Then the PLC-Automaton synthesised from the specification Spec is defined by

$$\mathcal{A}(\text{Spec}) = (Q, \Sigma, \delta, q_0, \varepsilon, S_t, S_e, \Omega, \omega)$$

where the following holds:

- Q is as defined in step (1) and possibly reduced in step (9).
- Σ is the data type of the input observable.
- The transition function $\delta : Q \times \Sigma \longrightarrow Q$ is determined as follows. For

each state $q_{\pi,t} \in Q$ and each input $\sigma \in \Sigma$ choose an arbitrary output π' from the corresponding entry in the Δ-table and define

$$\delta(q_{\pi,t}, \sigma) \stackrel{\text{def}}{=} \begin{cases} q_{\pi', \text{first}(\pi')}, & \text{if } \pi \neq \pi', \\ q_{\pi, \text{next}(\pi,t)}, & \text{otherwise.} \end{cases}$$

- The initial state is

$$q_0 = \begin{cases} q_{\pi_0, \text{first}(\pi_0)}, & \text{if } \lceil\,\rceil \vee \lceil \pi_0 \rceil \text{ ; true} \in SPEC, \\ q_{\pi, \text{first}(\pi)}, & \text{for an arbitrary } \pi \text{ otherwise.} \end{cases}$$

- The cycle time ε is chosen to satisfy the bounds given in step (8).

- The delay time $S_t(q_{\pi,\tilde{t}})$ of inputs in a state $q_{\pi,\tilde{t}}$ is calculated as follows:

$$S_t(q_{\pi,\tilde{t}}) = \begin{cases} \tilde{t} - \max\{t' \mid q_{\pi,t'} \in Q \text{ and } t' < \tilde{t}\} \\ \qquad \text{if } \{t' \mid q_{\pi,t'} \in Q \text{ and } t' < \tilde{t}\} \neq \varnothing, \\ \tilde{t}, \qquad \text{otherwise.} \end{cases}$$

In the first case the time difference to the *last* state before time $\tilde{t}$ in the π-cascade is taken as the delay time.

- The set of delayed inputs $S_e(q_{\pi,t})$ in a state $q_{\pi,t}$ is defined as in step (7).

- Ω is the data type of the output observable.

- The output function ω is given by $\omega(q_{\pi,t}) = \pi$ for each state $q_{\pi,t}$.

For our running example let us look at the cases of the transition function δ where a state in the W-cascade $\{q_{W,5}, q_{W,15}\}$ is entered:

$$\delta(q_{N,0}, \mathtt{m}) = q_{W, \text{first}(W)} = q_{W,5},$$

$$\delta(q_{N,0}, \mathtt{s}) = q_{W, \text{first}(W)} = q_{W,5},$$

$$\delta(q_{W,5}, \mathtt{s}) = q_{W, \text{next}(W,5)} = q_{W,15}.$$

All other cases are straightforward to extract from the final Δ-table at the end of step (6). For instance, $\delta(q_{N,0}, \mathtt{n}) = q_{N,0}$. Altogether, we have synthesised the following PLC-Automaton:

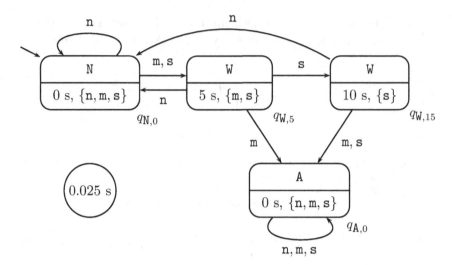

To discuss step (9) of the synthesis algorithm further, consider as an alternative to Syn-3 the synchronisation constraint

$$\text{Syn-3}': \qquad \lceil W \wedge m \rceil \xrightarrow{\;4.5\;} \lceil \neg W \rceil .$$

This constraint is inconsistent with

$$\text{Bd.Stab-1}: \qquad \lceil \neg W \rceil \; ; \; \lceil W \wedge \{m, s\} \rceil \xrightarrow{\;\leq 5\;} \lceil W \rceil .$$

How would the synthesis algorithm have discovered this inconsistency? Until step (6) the algorithm would proceed as above. However, in step (7) we would have obtained

$$S_e(q_{W,5}) = \{n, m, s\} \setminus \{n, m\} = \{s\}.$$

In this set of delayed inputs m is missing, which should be ignored for 5 seconds due to constraint Bd.Stab-1. Step (9) would thus have deleted the output W from the Δ-table obtained in step (6). As a consequence also the columns corresponding to the states $q_{W,5}$, $q_{W,15}$, and (in the next iteration) $q_{N,0}$ have to be deleted. Thus only the column for state $q_{A,0}$ remains. In step (10) the algorithm would then have noticed that the initial state $q_{N,0}$ is missing. Thus the synthesis would have been unsuccessful.

It is possible to define the notion of consistency used in the synthesis algorithm purely at the specification level.

Definition 5.10 (Consistency)

Let Spec be a set of DC implementables constraining an output observable Out_A (ranging over Ω) dependent on an input observable In_A (ranging over Σ). We call Spec *consistent* if there is a non-empty subset $\Omega' \subseteq \Omega$ with the following properties:

- There is at most one initialisation formula $\lceil \rceil \vee \lceil \pi_0 \rceil$; true in Spec and if there is one $\pi_o \in \Omega'$ holds.
- For all synchronisation formulas $\lceil \pi \wedge \varphi \rceil \xrightarrow{s} \lceil \neg \pi \rceil$ with $\pi \in \Omega'$ and all $\sigma \in \Sigma$ satisfying φ there is a $\pi' \in \Omega'$ with

(i) $\pi' \neq \pi$,

(ii) for all $\lceil \pi \wedge \varphi \rceil \longrightarrow \lceil \pi \vee \pi_1 \vee \ldots \vee \pi_n \rceil$ in Spec it is $\pi' \in \{\pi_1, \ldots, \pi_n\}$,

(iii) for all $\lceil \neg \pi \rceil$; $\lceil \pi \wedge \varphi' \rceil \longrightarrow \lceil \pi \vee \pi_1 \vee \ldots \vee \pi_n \rceil$ in Spec with σ satisfying φ' it is $\pi' \in \{\pi_1, \ldots, \pi_n\}$, and

(iv) for all $\lceil \neg \pi \rceil$; $\lceil \pi \wedge \varphi' \rceil \xrightarrow{\leq t} \lceil \pi \vee \pi_1 \vee \ldots \vee \pi_n \rceil$ in Spec with σ satisfying φ' and $s \leq t$ it is $\pi' \in \{\pi_1, \ldots, \pi_n\}$.

Otherwise Spec is called *inconsistent*.

Intuitively, Ω' is a set of outputs for which no problems with the specification can occur. The definition requires that the initial output (if specified) must be in this set and that – whenever an output change is required by the specification – there must be a successor output in Ω' that is not forbidden by the specification. It is possible to show that inconsistent specifications restrict the admissible interpretations of the *input* observable, i.e. the system environment, which is not desirable (see Exercise 5.6).

Theorem 5.11 (Correctness and completeness)

  (i) *If the synthesis terminates with a PLC-Automaton $\mathcal{A}(\mathsf{Spec})$ then the implication $[\![\mathcal{A}(\mathsf{Spec})]\!]_{\mathrm{DC}} \Longrightarrow \bigwedge \mathsf{Spec}$ is valid.†*

  (ii) *The synthesis terminates with a PLC-Automaton iff the specification is consistent.*

Proof idea:
The first statement claims the partial correctness of the algorithm. In the proof it is shown that each implementable is handled by the synthesis such that the resulting PLC-Automaton cannot violate the constraint. For example, for a sequencing formula the algorithm removes some output values in the Δ-table. As a consequence the resulting PLC-Automaton cannot execute output changes which would violate the sequencing formula.

It is easy to see that the algorithm always terminates but not necessarily successfully, yielding a PLC-Automaton. The second statement says that for *each consistent* specification the algorithm terminates successfully

† Here $\bigwedge \mathsf{Spec}$ denotes the conjunction of all formulas in the set Spec.

with a PLC-Automaton and for inconsistent specifications it is not success-ful. In other words, the synthesis algorithm is a decision procedure for the consistency of Spec. It is rather obvious that the algorithm produces a PLC-Automaton for a consistent specification because the definition of consistency requires the existence of a subset of outputs where no contra-dicting requirements appear. For inconsistent specifications it can be shown that the algorithm subsequently removes outputs from the Δ-table until no output remains or the initial output (if specified) is removed.

The details of the proof can be found in [Die99].   □

The semantics $[\![\mathcal{A}(\mathsf{Spec})]\!]_{\mathrm{DC}}$ of the synthesised automaton is a DC formula in the observables $\mathsf{In}_A, \mathsf{St}_A, \mathsf{Out}_A$ whereas Spec is a DC formula in the ob-servables In_A and Out_A only. None of the formulas contains a global variable. Thus property (i) of the correctness theorem implies that all interpretations $\mathcal{I}$ of the three observables $\mathsf{In}_A, \mathsf{St}_A, \mathsf{Out}_A$ that realise $[\![\mathcal{A}(\mathsf{Spec})]\!]_{\mathrm{DC}}$ from 0 also realise Spec from 0, in symbols:

$$\mathcal{I} \models_0 [\![\mathcal{A}(\mathsf{Spec})]\!]_{\mathrm{DC}} \quad \text{implies} \quad \mathcal{I} \models_0 \bigwedge \mathsf{Spec}.$$

We conclude with a further application of the synthesis algorithm.

Example 5.12

Consider as a specification of the filter as shown in Figure 5.2 the set Spec consisting of the following DC implementables:

$$
\begin{aligned}
\text{Init}: & \quad \lceil\rceil \vee \lceil \mathtt{N} \rceil \text{ ; true}, \\
\text{Sequ}: & \quad \lceil \mathtt{X} \rceil \longrightarrow \lceil \mathtt{X} \rceil, \\
\text{Unb.Stab-1}: & \quad \lceil \neg \mathtt{N} \rceil \text{ ; } \lceil \mathtt{N} \wedge \mathtt{no\_tr} \rceil \longrightarrow \lceil \mathtt{N} \rceil, \\
\text{Unb.Stab-2}: & \quad \lceil \neg \mathtt{N} \rceil \text{ ; } \lceil \mathtt{N} \wedge \neg \mathtt{Error} \rceil \longrightarrow \lceil \mathtt{N} \vee \mathtt{T} \rceil, \\
\text{Unb.Stab-3}: & \quad \lceil \neg \mathtt{T} \rceil \text{ ; } \lceil \mathtt{T} \wedge \mathtt{tr} \rceil \longrightarrow \lceil \mathtt{T} \rceil, \\
\text{Unb.Stab-4}: & \quad \lceil \neg \mathtt{T} \rceil \text{ ; } \lceil \mathtt{T} \wedge \neg \mathtt{Error} \rceil \longrightarrow \lceil \mathtt{T} \vee \mathtt{N} \rceil, \\
\text{Bd.Stab}: & \quad \lceil \neg \mathtt{T} \rceil \text{ ; } \lceil \mathtt{T} \wedge \neg \mathtt{Error} \rceil \xrightarrow{\leq 5} \lceil \mathtt{T} \rceil, \\
\text{Syn-1}: & \quad \lceil \mathtt{N} \wedge \neg \mathtt{no\_tr} \rceil \xrightarrow{0.1} \lceil \neg \mathtt{N} \rceil, \\
\text{Syn-2}: & \quad \lceil \mathtt{T} \wedge \mathtt{no\_tr} \rceil \xrightarrow{5.1} \lceil \neg \mathtt{T} \rceil, \\
\text{Syn-3}: & \quad \lceil \mathtt{T} \wedge \mathtt{Error} \rceil \xrightarrow{0.1} \lceil \neg \mathtt{T} \rceil.
\end{aligned}
$$

Here $\mathtt{no\_tr}, \mathtt{tr}, \mathtt{Error}$ are the values of the input observable In_A and $\mathtt{N}, \mathtt{T}, \mathtt{X}$ are the values of the output observable Out_A.

(1) We calculate the following sets of bounds:

$$bounds(\mathrm{N}) = \varnothing,$$
$$bounds(\mathrm{T}) = \{5\},$$
$$bounds(\mathrm{X}) = \varnothing.$$

This yields the state space $Q = \{q_{\mathrm{N},0}, q_{\mathrm{T},5}, q_{\mathrm{X},0}\}$, without any cascade.

(2) The synthesis starts with the full Δ-table:

Δ	$q_{\mathrm{N},0}$	$q_{\mathrm{T},5}$	$q_{\mathrm{X},0}$
no_tr	N, T, X	N, T, X	N, T, X
tr	N, T, X	N, T, X	N, T, X
Error	N, T, X	N, T, X	N, T, X

(3) The sequencing formula Sequ reduces this table to

Δ	$q_{\mathrm{N},0}$	$q_{\mathrm{T},5}$	$q_{\mathrm{X},0}$
no_tr	N, T, X	N, T, X	X
tr	N, T, X	N, T, X	X
Error	N, T, X	N, T, X	X

(4) In our example there are four unbounded stabilities. Processing the stability formula Unb.Stab-1 yields

Δ	$q_{\mathrm{N},0}$	$q_{\mathrm{T},5}$	$q_{\mathrm{X},0}$
no_tr	N	N, T, X	X
tr	N, T, X	N, T, X	X
Error	N, T, X	N, T, X	X

Next we take Unb.Stab-2 and obtain

Δ	$q_{\mathrm{N},0}$	$q_{\mathrm{T},5}$	$q_{\mathrm{X},0}$
no_tr	N	N, T, X	X
tr	N, T	N, T, X	X
Error	N, T, X	N, T, X	X

The remaining unbounded stabilities Unb.Stab-3 and Unb.Stab-4 lead to the following Δ-table as the final result of this step:

Δ	$q_{\mathrm{N},0}$	$q_{\mathrm{T},5}$	$q_{\mathrm{X},0}$
no_tr	N	N, T	X
tr	N, T	T	X
Error	N, T, X	N, T, X	X

(5) Now look at the bounded stability Bd.Stab. Since there is no $q_{T,t}$-column in the Δ-table with $t < 5$, nothing needs to be done in this step.

(6) The example provides three synchronisation formulas. Processing the formula Syn-1 yields

Δ	$q_{N,0}$	$q_{T,5}$	$q_{X,0}$
no_tr	N	N, T	X
tr	T	T	X
Error	T, X	N, T, X	X

Processing Syn-2 yields

Δ	$q_{N,0}$	$q_{T,5}$	$q_{X,0}$
no_tr	N	N	X
tr	T	T	X
Error	T, X	N, T, X	X

Processing Syn-3 finally yields the following Δ-table:

Δ	$q_{N,0}$	$q_{T,5}$	$q_{X,0}$
no_tr	N	N	X
tr	T	T	X
Error	T, X	N, X	X

(7) The sets of delayed inputs S_e are computed as follows:

$$S_e(q_{N,0}) = \{\texttt{no\_tr}, \texttt{tr}, \texttt{Error}\},$$
$$S_e(q_{T,5}) = \{\texttt{no\_tr}, \texttt{tr}\},$$
$$S_e(q_{X,0}) = \{\texttt{no\_tr}, \texttt{tr}, \texttt{Error}\}.$$

(8) The synchronisation constraints generate the following inequalities as upper time bounds for the cycle time ε:

$$\varepsilon \leq \tfrac{0.1}{2} = 0.05 \qquad \text{due to Syn-1 and Syn-3,}$$
$$\varepsilon \leq \tfrac{5.1-5}{2 \cdot 1} = 0.05 \quad \text{due to Syn-2.}$$

(9) Now we examine the final Δ-table of step (6) again. No output has to be removed because there is no empty entry in the table and for the only bounded stability Bd.Stab we have $\neg\texttt{Error} \subseteq S_e(q_{T,5})$.

(10) We see that the synthesis is successful because the initial constraint $\lceil\rceil \vee \lceil N \rceil$; true is in Spec and the state $q_{N,0}$ is in the final Δ-table.

(11) From the specification Spec the algorithm can synthesise the PLC-Automaton of Figure 5.2, but with $\varepsilon = 0.05$ as its cycle time.

However, this is not the only choice the algorithm has because the final Δ-table contains two entries with two elements. The reason is that Spec specifies that both N and T have to be left when the **Error** signal holds for longer than 0.1 seconds, but there is no formula specifying to which state the system should change.

■

5.6 Extensions of PLC-Automata

The definition of PLC-Automata presented so far can be extended either to increase the expressiveness or to allow for more convenient specifications. In this section we present three extensions of PLC-Automata. First, we increase the expressiveness by introducing hierarchical states. Then, we simplify the handling of the discrete state space by introducing data variables, similarly to extended timed automata. Finally, we discuss networks of PLC-Automata formed by two composition operators.

5.6.1 Hierarchical PLC-Automata

The PLC-Automata introduced so far are restricted in their expressiveness. An indication for this is that the PLC source code for a PLC-Automaton uses only a *single* timer. However, there are cases where states need several simultaneously active timers.

Example 5.13
Consider the stuttering problem of Section 5.2 again. Assume now that there is the possibility of *glitches* in the **Error** signal. These are **Error** signals that appear for a short period of time even if there is no real error. We require that the filter is able to handle this problem and output X only if the **Error** signal was not a glitch. More precisely, we want the filter to interpret an **Error** signal lasting for less than 0.2 seconds as a glitch and an **Error** signal lasting for at least 0.4 seconds as a real **Error** signal. ■

An attempt to implement this by a PLC-Automaton is the automaton in Figure 5.7. Unfortunately, this automaton has a problem. Consider the case where it detects a train and changes from state q_1 to q_2. By this transition, a timer is started that runs for 5 seconds. If 3 seconds after starting the timer a glitch occurs, the system will enter state q_4 and return to q_2 again. However, this returning transition will start the timer with 5 seconds again. Hence, the system has "forgotten" the initial time period in which stuttering is filtered and it assumes now that a new phase begins in which stuttering has to be filtered. This can result in a failure to detect a newly arriving train because the system might consider the change from no_tr to tr as stuttering instead of a real train.

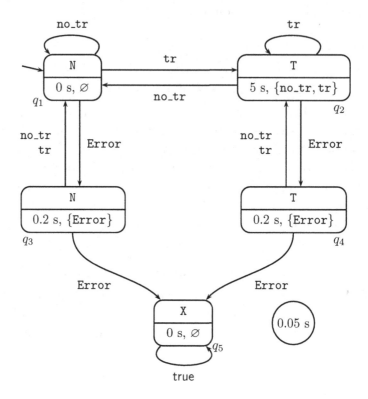

Fig. 5.7. Attempt to implement the problem given in Example 5.13

The core of the problem is that the system is restricted to one timer per state while it should have more than one. Since PLC-Automata can be translated into source code using only one timer, they are not able to solve this problem. Instead, we will extend the previous definition of PLC-Automata to cope with systems that need more than one timer. The basic idea of this extension is the notion of *hierarchy*. By grouping states together into a "superstate" we can structure the state space of large automata. We will also exploit hierarchy to introduce additional timers by adding the timing annotations to both states and superstates.

A hierarchical PLC-Automaton for Example 5.13 could have the structure as shown in Figure 5.8. We have extended the previous automaton by a superstate s_1 containing q_2 and q_4. As before, the state q_4 handles the

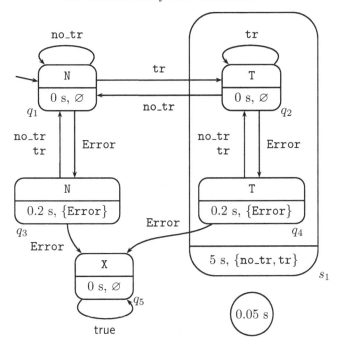

Fig. 5.8. Hierarchical filter

detection of **Error** glitches. The handling of the stuttering period is now done by the superstate s_1 instead of q_2, which is undelayed. The meaning of the delay annotation of s_1 is that the system has to stay for 5 seconds in s_1 unless it can leave s_1 via an **Error** transition. In other words: the **Error** transition from q_4 to q_5 can be fired without checking the stutter time whereas the transition from q_2 to q_1 can only be fired if s_1 is stable for at least 5 seconds. Note that in state q_4 the two system timers are active.

The following definition formalises these ideas:

Definition 5.14 ($\mathcal{H}$PLC-Automaton)
A *hierarchical* PLC-Automaton (abbreviated $\mathcal{H}$PLC-Automaton) is a structure $\mathcal{H} = (Q, S, Tr, \Sigma, \delta, q_0, \varepsilon, S_t, S_e, \Omega, \omega)$ where:

- Q, Σ, δ, q_0, ε, Ω, and ω are as in Definition 5.2.
- S is a finite set of so-called *superstates* with $Q \cap S = \varnothing$.
- $Tr = (V, E)$ is the so-called *hierarchy tree* with the set $V = \{r\} \cup Q \cup S$ of vertices, the root $r \notin Q \cup S$, and the set $E \subseteq (V \setminus Q) \times (V \setminus \{r\})$ of directed edges. The set of leaves of Tr is exactly Q.

- S_t is a function of type $Q \cup S \longrightarrow \mathbb{R}_{\geq 0}$ that assigns a *delay time* to each state and superstate.
- S_e is a function of type $Q \cup S \longrightarrow 2^\Sigma$ that assigns a *set of delayed inputs* to each state and superstate.

Example 5.15

The hierarchical PLC-Automaton above has the following hierarchy tree:

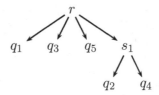

Here s_1 is the only superstate. The normal states are q_1, q_2, q_3, q_4, q_5, and r is the root.   ■

Since hierarchy trees can have an arbitrary depth, an arbitrary nesting of superstates is possible in (the graphic representation of) $\mathcal{H}$PLC-Automata. This implies that in a state q with n ancestors in the hierarchy tree, n timers may be active.

5.6.2 *Data and timer variables*

A PLC-Automaton has only one input variable and one output variable. This simplifies the formal definition but is unnecessarily restrictive when more complex specifications have to be developed. For example, an implementation of the gas burner controller should have two input variables: H for heat request and F for flame. Although this could be handled by a PLC-Automaton using a single input variable ranging over the Cartesian product of the values of H and F, it is clearer to declare H and F separately.

In this subsection we informally present *generalised PLC-Automata*, extending PLC-Automata with data and timer variables. The declaration of a *data variable* consists of a name, a direction (input or output), a data type, and an initial value in case of an output variable. The declaration of a Boolean *timer variable* consists of a name, the indication "Timer", a time constant (the *timer period*), and an *activity set*, which is a set of states in which the timer is active. A timer variable is initialised to false. The idea is that a timer variable *tmr* is set to true when a state of its activity set is entered by a transition. The timer value stays true as long as the timer period has not elapsed *and* the automaton is in one of the states in the activity set of *tmr*. When the timer period has elapsed or the activity set is left the value of the timer variable switches back to false. Both data and timer variables can appear in the guards of transitions. This concept of timer variables corresponds to the timers that are available in the programming language ST (Structured Text) for PLCs (cf. Section 5.3).

An example of a generalised PLC-Automaton is shown in Figure 5.9. It is intended to implement the gas burner controller **GB-Ctrl** specified in Subsection 3.2.1. This PLC-Automaton declares two Boolean input variables

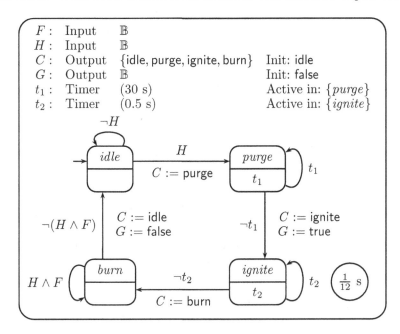

Fig. 5.9. Gas burner controller as a PLC-Automaton with data variables

H and F for heat request and flame, respectively. Moreover, two output variables are declared: G with Boolean type stands for an open gas valve and is initialised with false. The second output variable C mirrors the internal state of the PLC-Automaton so that it becomes visible from outside. Further on, there are two timer variables t_1 and t_2, each with a singleton activity set.

The four states of the PLC-Automaton are called *idle*, *purge*, *ignite*, and *burn*. The transitions are annotated with guards over data and timer variables and with assignments to the output variables which are executed when the transition fires. For example, the variable G is set to true when the transition from *purge* to *ignite* is fired and reset to false when *idle* is entered.

Note that the transition from *purge* to *ignite* is only possible if the timer variable t_1 is false. This is the case when the controller has been for 30 seconds in *purge* because entering the activity set of t_1, i.e. entering *purge*, starts the timer t_1 and it keeps the value true for the given time period.

In a generalised PLC-Automaton, a state q can be a member of the activity sets of several timers. Graphically, the state q is then annotated with the *set* of timers that are active in q. Thus as in hierarchical PLC-Automata, several timers may be active in a state of a generalised PLC-Automaton. Moreover, activity sets may overlap without being contained in each other. For example, consider a system with three states q_1, q_2, and q_3. To specify that *outside* q_1 the system should wait for 3 seconds and *outside* q_3 it should wait for 5 seconds one may introduce two timers t_1 and t_2, where q_1, q_2 are in the activity set of a timer t_1 and q_2, q_3 are in the activity set of a timer t_2. This is not possible with hierarchical PLC-Automata.

5.6.3 Networks of PLC-Automata

In more complex applications a real-time system will be specified by a collection of, say, k PLC-Automata that have to be implemented on, say, n computing devices, which may be PLCs or other suitable hardware platforms. The point is that in general $k \neq n$ holds so that some PLC-Automata may have to be implemented on the *same* computing device and others are *distributed* over several computing devices.

In this subsection we informally present two composition operators on PLC-Automata: a *parallel composition* describing the effect of a distributed implementation and a *sequential composition* describing the effect of an implementation on the same computing device. The parallel composition is parameterised with the specification of a *transmission medium* between the composed PLC-Automata. With these two operators, networks of PLC-Automata can be specified. Figure 5.10 illustrates a parallel composition of two computing devices linked by a medium m, which in turn are sequentially composed of PLC-Automata $\mathcal{A}_1 ; \mathcal{A}_2$ and $\mathcal{A}_3 ; \mathcal{A}_4 ; \mathcal{A}_5$, respectively.

Parallel composition

The parallel composition depends on the transmission medium. Such media can introduce transmission delays or errors. We present a uniform approach to model the transmission of information between different PLCs. Abstractly, the transmission between two PLC-Automata is a relation between the output of the first automaton and the input of the second one. We describe this relation by DC formulas speaking about both observables.

For the parallel composition of two PLC-Automata $\mathcal{A}$ and $\mathcal{B}$ connected via the medium m we write

$$\mathcal{A}\,[m]\,\mathcal{B}.$$

The DC semantics of $\mathcal{A}\,[m]\,\mathcal{B}$ is defined as follows:

$$[\![\mathcal{A}\,[m]\,\mathcal{B}]\!]_{\mathrm{DC}} \overset{\mathrm{def}}{\Longleftrightarrow} [\![\mathcal{A}]\!]_{\mathrm{DC}} \wedge [\![\mathcal{B}]\!]_{\mathrm{DC}} \wedge [\![m]\!]_{\mathcal{A},\mathcal{B}},$$

where $[\![\mathcal{A}]\!]_{\mathrm{DC}}$ and $[\![\mathcal{B}]\!]_{\mathrm{DC}}$ are the DC semantics of $\mathcal{A}$ and $\mathcal{B}$ and where $[\![m]\!]_{\mathcal{A},\mathcal{B}}$ is a DC formula specifying a relation between the interpretations of the input and output observables of $\mathcal{A}$ and $\mathcal{B}$.

Note that this definition of transmission is not very restrictive. For instance, it is possible to interpret a PLC-Automaton as a medium because it represents a relation between its input and output. Typically, we are interested in the delay time of the transmission. For this purpose, we introduce a *standard medium sm* that is parameterised by a delay time t. Its semantics defines a relation between the input and output observables $\mathcal{I}$ and $\mathcal{O}$ of type D as follows:

$$[\![sm(t)]\!]_{\mathcal{I}}^{\mathcal{O}} \overset{\mathrm{def}}{=} \bigwedge_{\varnothing \neq A \subseteq D} (\lceil \mathcal{I} \in A \rceil \xrightarrow{\ t\ } \lceil \mathcal{O} \in A \rceil).$$

Informally speaking, the possible outputs of $sm(t)$ at time $t_0 \in \mathsf{Time}$ are the inputs that were valid during $(\max(0, t_0 - t), t_0)$.

We return to the gas burner controller of Figure 5.9. Suppose its implementation has to be distributed over two computing devices. The first device should not manipulate the gas valve directly, but compute the internal state only and communicate it to the second device. The first device is modelled by the generalised PLC-Automaton $\mathcal{G}_1$ shown in Figure 5.11. The output C of $\mathcal{G}_1$ is input by another generalised PLC-Automaton $\mathcal{G}_2$ which controls the gas valve. This one is depicted in Figure 5.12.

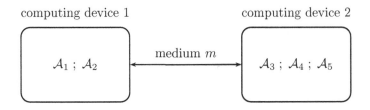

Fig. 5.10. Example for a composition of PLC-Automata

$\mathcal{G}_1$:

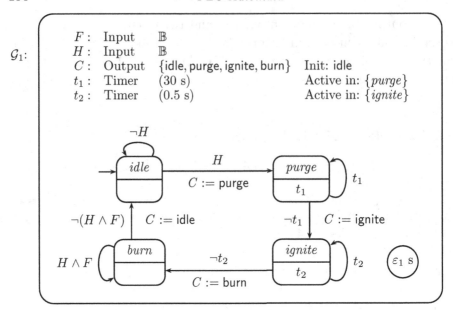

Fig. 5.11. A distributed implementation of the gas burner: the automaton $\mathcal{G}_1$

$\mathcal{G}_2$:

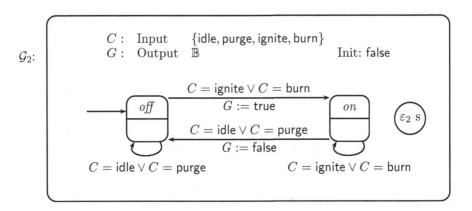

Fig. 5.12. A distributed implementation of the gas burner: the automaton $\mathcal{G}_2$

Assuming that both PLC-Automata $\mathcal{G}_\infty$ and $\mathcal{G}_\in$ are connected using a standard medium $sm(t)$ we have the following system:

$$\mathcal{G}_1\,[sm(t)]\,\mathcal{G}_2.$$

Since neither $\mathcal{G}_1$ nor $\mathcal{G}_2$ uses the features of hierarchy or timer variables, we can apply Theorem 5.8 on reaction times (adapted to PLC-Automata of data variables only) to conclude that the following properties hold:

$$\mathcal{G}_1 : \lceil \neg H \rceil \xrightarrow{\varepsilon_1 + 30 + 2\varepsilon_1 + 0.5 + 2\varepsilon_1 + \varepsilon_1} \lceil C_{\mathcal{G}_1} = \text{idle} \rceil,$$

$$\mathcal{G}_2 : \lceil C_{\mathcal{G}_2} = \text{idle} \rceil \xrightarrow{2\varepsilon_2} \lceil \textit{off} \rceil.$$

Further on, the standard medium $sm(t)$ ensures the property

$$sm(t) : \lceil C_{\mathcal{G}_1} = \text{idle} \rceil \xrightarrow{t} \lceil C_{\mathcal{G}_2} = \text{idle} \rceil.$$

By Exercise 3.5, these formulas imply the following timed leads-to property of the parallel composition $\mathcal{G}_1 \left[sm(t) \right] \mathcal{G}_2$:

$$\lceil \neg H \rceil \xrightarrow{30.5 + 6\varepsilon_1 + t + 2\varepsilon_2} \lceil \textit{off} \rceil.$$

Sequential composition

Sequential composition assumes that two (or more) PLC-Automata are to be implemented on the same computing device. This could be modelled by a parallel composition with an "internal transmission" of data between the automata, but we can do better by exploiting the information of a shared implementation.

- We know that the result computed by the first automaton during a cycle can be immediately used in the same cycle by the second automaton as input. That is, every output of the first automaton will be readable by the second one. If both automata change their state in the same cycle, an external observer will notice these changes simultaneously.
- In case the PLC-Automata are implemented on the same computing device they share the cyclic behaviour and the input values. Then we can benefit from the knowledge that during each cycle the same input value is read by both automata.

Suppose that we have to implement two PLC-Automata $\mathcal{A}$ and $\mathcal{B}$ on the same computing device, and $\mathcal{A}$ has to be executed before $\mathcal{B}$. We stipulate that a *connector relation* f between the data variables of $\mathcal{A}$ and $\mathcal{B}$ is given describing which input variable of $\mathcal{B}$ is driven by an output variable of $\mathcal{A}$, and vice versa. Formally, f consists of pairs $(in_{\mathcal{B}}, out_{\mathcal{A}})$ or $(in_{\mathcal{A}}, out_{\mathcal{B}})$ where the elements of the pairs describe type-consistent data variables of the automata.

For the sequential composition of two PLC-Automata $\mathcal{A}$ and $\mathcal{B}$ using the connector f we write

$$\mathcal{A} ;_f \mathcal{B}.$$

The semantics of sequential composition can be defined by a transformation of $\mathcal{A};_f \mathcal{B}$ into a single PLC-Automaton, for which the DC semantics is defined. We skip this formal definition here but present the result of the transformation for two sequential compositions of the separated gas burner controllers $\mathcal{G}_1$ and $\mathcal{G}_2$. With the connector $f = \{(C_{\mathcal{G}_2}, C_{\mathcal{G}_1})\}$ the automata for

$$\mathcal{G}_1;_f \mathcal{G}_2 \qquad \text{and} \qquad \mathcal{G}_2;_f \mathcal{G}_1$$

are shown in Figures 5.13 and 5.14, respectively.

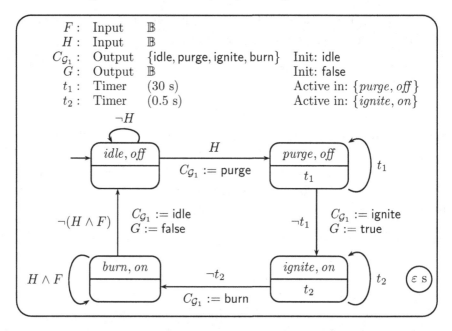

Fig. 5.13. Semantics of the sequential composition $\mathcal{G}_1;_f \mathcal{G}_2$

The upper time bound for the execution of a cycle in the sequential composition $\mathcal{G}_1;_f \mathcal{G}_2$ is the *minimum* of both upper time bounds ε_1 of $\mathcal{G}_1$ and ε_2 of $\mathcal{G}_2$, i.e. $\varepsilon = \min(\varepsilon_1, \varepsilon_2)$. The examples in Figures 5.13 and 5.14 show that sequential composition is not commutative. In the second variant the computation of the output G happens one cycle after the computation of the gas burner's state because $\mathcal{G}_2$ is executed first and hence it operates with the C value of the previous cycle.

Finally, we mention that an implementation of the sequential composition $\mathcal{A};_f \mathcal{B}$ can be obtained by compiling the following code sequence:

1. The declaration part. It has to contain uniquely named variables for both automata.

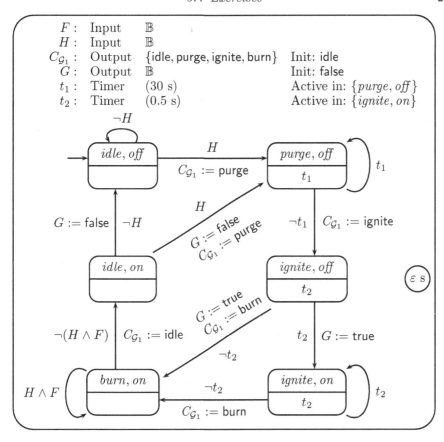

Fig. 5.14. Semantics of the sequential composition $\mathcal{G}_2;_f \mathcal{G}_1$

2. Connector assignments for inputs of $\mathcal{A}$. Each pair $(in_\mathcal{A}, out_\mathcal{B}) \in f$ yields an assignment of the form $in_\mathcal{A} := out_\mathcal{B}$.
3. The body of $\mathcal{A}$. It has to precede the body of $\mathcal{B}$.
4. Connector assignments for inputs of $\mathcal{B}$. Each pair $(in_\mathcal{B}, out_\mathcal{A}) \in f$ yields an assignment of the form $in_\mathcal{B} := out_\mathcal{A}$.
5. The body of $\mathcal{B}$.

5.7 Exercises

Exercise 5.1 (Semantics)

Let $\mathcal{A}_\varepsilon$ be a PLC-Automaton with the upper bound ε for its cycle time and let $\mathcal{A}_{\varepsilon'}$ be the same automaton except for a smaller bound $\varepsilon' \leq \varepsilon$. Prove that $[\![\mathcal{A}_{\varepsilon'}]\!]_{\mathrm{DC}} \Longrightarrow [\![\mathcal{A}_\varepsilon]\!]_{\mathrm{DC}}$ is valid.

Hint: Conduct the proof by showing the implications of the corresponding formulas in the DC semantics of $\mathcal{A}_\varepsilon$ and $\mathcal{A}_{\varepsilon'}$.

Exercise 5.2 (PLC-Automata are input-open)

Consider a PLC-Automaton $\mathcal{A}$ and a function $\mathcal{I}_0 :$ Time $\longrightarrow \Sigma$. Show that there exists an interpretation $\mathcal{I}$ with $\mathcal{I}(\mathsf{In}_\mathcal{A}) = \mathcal{I}_o$ and $\mathcal{I} \models_0 [\![\mathcal{A}]\!]_{\mathrm{DC}}$. In other words, a PLC-Automaton cannot reject any input behaviour.

Exercise 5.3 (Reaction time)

Consider the following PLC-Automaton $\mathcal{A}$ with states q_0, q_1, q_2, q_3, input values $\mathtt{x}, \mathtt{y}$, output values $\mathtt{A}, \mathtt{B}, \mathtt{C}$, and a cycle time $\varepsilon = 0.5$ seconds:

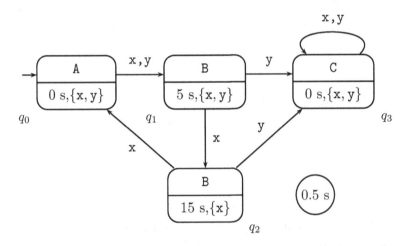

Calculate an upper bound of the reaction time c with

$$\lceil \mathsf{St}_\mathcal{A} \in \{q_0, q_1, q_2, q_3\} \wedge \mathsf{In}_\mathcal{A} = \mathtt{y}\rceil \xrightarrow{\;\;c\;\;} \lceil \mathsf{St}_\mathcal{A} = q_3 \rceil .$$

Exercise 5.4 (Synthesis)

Consider a traffic light for pedestrians wishing to cross a street. The light reacts to the two input values $\mathtt{b}$ ("button depressed") and $\mathtt{n}$ ("button not depressed") with one of the following three output values: $\mathtt{I}$ ("idle", i.e. no light shown), $\mathtt{R}$ ("red light" shown to pedestrians), $\mathtt{G}$ ("green light" shown to pedestrians). The intended timed behaviour is specified by the set Spec

consisting of the following implementables:

$$
\begin{aligned}
\text{Init-1}: &\quad \lceil\rceil \vee \lceil\text{I}\rceil \;; \mathsf{true}\,, \\
\text{Sequ-1}: &\quad \lceil\text{I}\rceil \longrightarrow \lceil\text{I} \vee \text{R}\rceil\,, \\
\text{Sequ-2}: &\quad \lceil\text{R}\rceil \longrightarrow \lceil\text{R} \vee \text{G}\rceil\,, \\
\text{Sequ-3}: &\quad \lceil\text{G}\rceil \longrightarrow \lceil\text{G} \vee \text{I}\rceil\,, \\
\text{Unb.Stab-1}: &\quad \lceil\neg\text{I}\rceil \;; \lceil\text{I} \wedge \text{n}\rceil \longrightarrow \lceil\text{I}\rceil\,, \\
\text{Bd.Stab-1}: &\quad \lceil\neg\text{R}\rceil \;; \lceil\text{R}\rceil \xrightarrow{\leq 30} \lceil\text{R}\rceil\,, \\
\text{Bd.Stab-2}: &\quad \lceil\neg\text{G}\rceil \;; \lceil\text{G}\rceil \xrightarrow{\leq 60} \lceil\text{G}\rceil\,, \\
\text{Syn-1}: &\quad \lceil\text{I} \wedge \text{b}\rceil \xrightarrow{0.5} \lceil\neg\text{I}\rceil\,, \\
\text{Syn-2}: &\quad \lceil\text{R}\rceil \xrightarrow{30.5} \lceil\neg\text{R}\rceil\,, \\
\text{Syn-3}: &\quad \lceil\text{G}\rceil \xrightarrow{60.5} \lceil\neg\text{G}\rceil\,.
\end{aligned}
$$

Synthesise a PLC-Automaton satisfying Spec.

Exercise 5.5 (Synthesis)
Consider Example 5.12 again. Extend the specification by implementables such that the result of the synthesis algorithm is deterministic.

Exercise 5.6 (Consistency)
Consider a specification Spec that is *inconsistent* in the sense of Definition 5.10. Prove that in this case there exists a function $\mathcal{I}_0 : \mathsf{Time} \longrightarrow \Sigma$ such that for all interpretations $\mathcal{I}$

$$
\mathcal{I}(\mathsf{In}_A) = \mathcal{I}_0 \quad \text{implies} \quad \mathcal{I} \not\models \bigwedge \mathsf{Spec}.
$$

In other words, there exists an input behaviour that is rejected by Spec.

Exercise 5.7 (Hierarchical PLC-Automaton)
Translate the $\mathcal{H}$PLC-Automaton shown in Figure 5.8 into ST code.

Hint: Extend the translation scheme of Section 5.3 appropriately.

Exercise 5.8 (Hierarchical PLC-Automaton)
Generalise the DC semantics of PLC-Automata to $\mathcal{H}$PLC-Automata.

Hint: Note that a $\mathcal{H}$PLC-Automaton has the same observables as a PLC-Automaton. Generalise the DC formulas (DC-1)–(DC-11) appropriately if necessary.

Exercise 5.9 (Hierarchical PLC-Automaton)

Translate the PLC-Automaton given in Figure 5.9 into ST code. Assume that ST provides all standard data types.

5.8 Bibliographic remarks

The standard IEC 61131-3 of the International Electrotechnical Commission provides a range of programming notations suitable for implementation on PLCs and is defined in [IEC93]. A more popular description can be found in [Lew95]. An investigation of the software development in automation technology is conducted in [FVH02]. The authors of [BE02] pointed out that different PLC vendors use their own variants of the standard with different syntax and ambiguous semantics. This hampers the integration of formal methods and tools for verification.

To avoid these problems, PLC-Automata as a formal model of the computational essence of PLCs were proposed by H. Dierks in [Die00a]. The work on PLC-Automata was motivated by a collaborative research project with industry called UniForM (Universal Workbench for Formal Methods, 1995–1998) [KPOB99]. The industrial partner in this project was developing tramway control systems based on PLCs and looking for a formal method supporting this activity. The informal description of the filter example in this chapter stems from this partner.

PLC-Automata are not only useful when PLCs serve as implementation platforms. In fact, they can be implemented on any hardware platform that performs a non-terminating loop consisting of inputting sensor values, updating the state in accordance with timer values, and outputting actuator values. For instance, at the University of Oldenburg a compiler has been developed that generates C code from PLC-Automata. It is used in student labs where the C code is executed on the experimental robot platform of LEGO Mindstorms [LEG01]. The advantage is that real-time properties of the PLC-Automata can be verified before the code is executed on the robots.

The synthesis algorithm from DC implementables to PLC-Automata was first published in [Die97]. The idea of using hierarchy to structure large state spaces of automata, here employed in the definition of Hierarchical PLC-Automata, is due to D. Harel, who introduced it in the definition of statecharts [Har87]. Generalised PLC-Automata with the operators for parallel and sequential composition as outlined in Section 5.6 are defined and studied in [Die00b, Die06].

6

Automatic verification

In this chapter we present an approach to the automatic verification of behavioural properties of PLC-Automata. The properties are specified by Constraint Diagrams. Since both PLC-Automata and Constraint Diagrams have a semantics in the Duration Calculus, it is well-defined when a PLC-Automaton satisfies a given Constraint Diagram (cf. Section 2.3). However, tool support for the Duration Calculus with continuous time is not very much developed. Therefore our approach to an automatic verification is to translate both PLC-Automata and Constraint Diagrams into (semantically equivalent) timed automata, for which tool support is very well developed (cf. Chapter 4). As a first step we define an alternative semantics of both Constraint Diagrams and PLC-Automata in terms of timed automata. Later we describe a tool MOBY/RT, which incorporates these semantics and exploits the model-checking facilities of UPPAAL for an automatic verification. To illustrate this approach we will use the generalised railroad crossing (GRC) as a running example.

6.1 The approach

Our aim is to show that a real-time system S *satisfies* or *is correct w.r.t* a requirement P, abbreviated

$$S \models_1 P. \tag{6.1}$$

In this chapter, S will be given by a PLC-Automaton and P by a Constraint Diagram. In that case both S and P have a semantics in the Duration Calculus so that $\models_1$ can be defined by logical implication between the DC formulas expressing the semantics of S and P:

$$S \models_1 P \quad \text{iff} \quad \models [\![S]\!]_{DC} \implies [\![P]\!]_{DC}. \tag{6.2}$$

241

Our approach is automatic verification based on (extended) timed automata (using the model checker UPPAAL). To this end, we proceed in three steps:

(I) Represent $\mathcal{S}$ as a network $\mathcal{C}(\mathcal{A}_1, \ldots, \mathcal{A}_n)$ of (extended) timed automata.

(II) Represent P as a formula $\mathcal{F}(P)$ (in the logic of UPPAAL) such that the following equivalence holds:

$$\mathcal{S} \models_1 P \qquad \text{iff} \qquad \mathcal{C}(\mathcal{A}_1, \ldots, \mathcal{A}_n) \models \mathcal{F}(P) \qquad (6.3)$$

where $\models$ is the satisfaction relation defined in Subsection 4.4.5.

(III) Check $\mathcal{C}(\mathcal{A}_1, \ldots, \mathcal{A}_n) \models \mathcal{F}(P)$ using the model checker UPPAAL.

However, the logic of UPPAAL may be too weak to express P as a formula $\mathcal{F}(P)$ satisfying (6.3). Recall that for efficiency reasons the model checker UPPAAL covers only a subset of the Timed Computation Tree Logic (TCTL). To overcome this problem, we modify the steps (II) and (III) as follows:

(II*) Represent P as a *test automaton* $\mathcal{T}(P)$ together with a formula $\mathcal{F}(P)$ (in the logic of UPPAAL). The purpose of a test automaton is to act as an observer of the system. The test automaton should react to the observed system's behaviour such that the following equivalence holds:

$$\mathcal{S} \models_1 P \qquad \text{iff} \qquad \mathcal{C}(\mathcal{A}'_1, \ldots, \mathcal{A}'_n, \mathcal{T}(P)) \models \mathcal{F}(P). \qquad (6.4)$$

The automata $\mathcal{A}'_1, \ldots, \mathcal{A}'_n$ may differ somewhat from $\mathcal{A}_1, \ldots, \mathcal{A}_n$ to allow for a communication with the test automaton $\mathcal{T}(P)$. These changes must not change the behaviour of the system as far as P is concerned.

(III*) Check $\mathcal{C}(\mathcal{A}'_1, \ldots, \mathcal{A}'_n, \mathcal{T}(P)) \models \mathcal{F}(P)$ using the model checker UPPAAL.

An example of a test automaton appeared already in Example 4.44. In our setting, the test automaton $\mathcal{T}(P)$ will have a distinguished *bad location* called q_{bad} such that the formula $\mathcal{F}(P)$ is defined as follows:

$$\mathcal{F}(P) \stackrel{\text{def}}{\Longleftrightarrow} \forall \Box \, \neg \mathcal{T}(P).q_{\text{bad}}. \qquad (6.5)$$

Thus combining (6.4) with (6.5) yields: $\mathcal{S} \models_1 P$ iff in the context of the network $\mathcal{C}(\mathcal{A}'_1, \ldots, \mathcal{A}'_n, \mathcal{T}(P))$ the test automaton $\mathcal{T}(P)$ never reaches its bad location.

Moreover, $\mathcal{T}(P)$ will have edges labelled with the input action *step?* that have to synchronise with corresponding output actions *step!* which are added in a transformation of $\mathcal{A}_i$ into $\mathcal{A}'_i$. More precisely, $\mathcal{A}'_i$ differs from $\mathcal{A}_i$ by an additional communication *step!* without passage of time after each discrete transition. This modification is done by introducing for each location ℓ of $\mathcal{A}_i$ an auxiliary committed location ℓ^c and redirecting all edges with target ℓ to ℓ^c. An unconstrained *step!* edge from ℓ^c to ℓ is then the only ingoing edge of ℓ. This transformation of $\mathcal{A}_i$ into $\mathcal{A}'_i$ is shown in Figure 6.1. As indicated in this figure, a self-loop at ℓ in $\mathcal{A}_i$ becomes an edge from ℓ to ℓ^c in $\mathcal{A}'_i$. If ℓ is the initial location of $\mathcal{A}_i$ then ℓ^c becomes the new initial location of $\mathcal{A}'_i$.

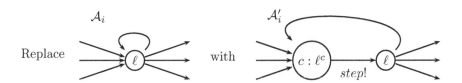

Fig. 6.1. Transformation of $\mathcal{A}_i$ into $\mathcal{A}'_i$ by adding a *step!* edge

In the remainder of this chapter we begin with step (II*) and discuss how to represent requirements given by Constraint Diagrams as test automata, both for the running example GRC and in general. Then we turn to step (I) and explain how to represent design specification given by PLC-Automata as timed automata, both for the running example and in general. Afterwards we consider step (III*) and discuss for the running example how to verify automatically that the GRC design specification satisfies its requirements.

Further on, we address the questions of how to represent assumptions on the system environment and how to represent a more realistic system model with plant, sensors, and actuators. Finally, we give an overview of the tool MOBY/RT that supports the verification steps.

Convention. Throughout this chapter we shall drop the internal action τ in the graphical representation of (extended) timed automata.

6.2 Requirements

In a top-down development of a system one first fixes the requirements in an informal way. When using formal methods these informal requirements are then formalised.

6.2.1 Railroad crossing

In case of the GRC we dealt with this problem already in Subsection 1.3.2 where we formalised the requirements **Safety** and **Utility** using notations of predicate logic. To simplify this step we introduced Constraint Diagrams (CDs) in Section 3.3 as graphical notation for real-time properties. In Subsection 3.3.2 the following Constraint Diagrams were proposed.

Safety:

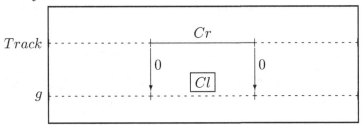

This diagram requires – as marked by the box around Cl – that the gate is closed during intervals in which a train is crossing (Cr). We will refer to this diagram as $CD_{\mathbf{S}}$. The following constraint diagram – called $CD_{\mathbf{U}}$ – captures the **Utility** requirement for the GRC.

Utility:

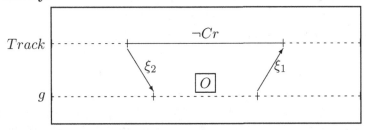

This diagram restricts the behaviour of the gate in case there is a period of at least $\xi_1 + \xi_2$ time units in which no train crosses ($\neg Cr$). For such periods it requires the gate to be open at latest ξ_2 time units after the beginning and it has to stay open until at least ξ_1 time units before the end of the non-crossing period.

6.2.2 Constructing test automata

The GRC has two CDs with a Duration Calculus semantics. For the purpose of automatic verification we have to construct test automata that capture the desired property. For this construction we assume that the test automaton has access to those variables of the system that represent the observables appearing in the CD.

Safety

In case of safety it is easy to construct an appropriate test automaton (cf. Figure 6.2). The construction of the automaton assumes that the timed automata model of the system informs without a delay the test automata about discrete transitions via a new channel *step*. It is important that the test automaton never blocks this communication to avoid interference with the behaviour of the system.

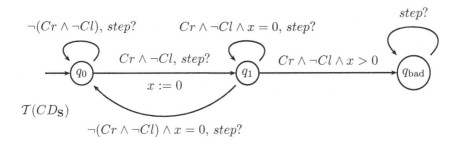

Fig. 6.2. A test automaton for **Safety**

The idea of the test automaton is to observe whether the system reaches a situation in which a train is crossing while the gate is not closed. This observation is done by appropriate edges between the locations q_0 and q_1. If the automaton enters the location q_1 it also resets an auxiliary clock x to 0. If time passes in q_1 the automaton may switch to q_{bad} where it has to reside for ever. Hence, reachability of q_{bad} coincides with the fact that the proposition $Cr \wedge \neg Cl$ holds for a non-point interval in time. Note that the semantics of CDs requires a phase to be observable for longer than a time point. That is why we check the timing condition $x > 0$ at the edge from q_1 to q_{bad}. The following property holds:

$$\mathcal{S} \models_1 CD_\mathbf{S}$$

iff $\qquad\qquad\qquad\qquad\qquad\qquad\qquad\qquad\qquad\qquad\qquad$ (6.6)

$$\mathcal{C}(\mathcal{A}'_1, \dots, \mathcal{A}'_n, \mathcal{T}(CD_\mathbf{S})) \models \forall \Box \, \neg \mathcal{T}(CD_\mathbf{S}).q_{bad}$$

where $\models_1$ is defined as in (6.2) and $\mathcal{A}'_i$ differs from $\mathcal{A}_i$ by an additional communication *step!* without passage of time after each discrete transition.

Utility

Constructing a test automaton for **Utility** by hand is rather difficult. A good recipe is to think in terms of *counterexamples*: what kind of behaviour violates the property? For **Utility** we have to observe the following sequence of phases for a counterexample:

(i) Arbitrary behaviour of the system, i.e. no constraints on duration, track, and gate.

(ii) A phase of duration ξ_2 in which the track satisfies $\neg Cr$.

(iii) After this phase the diagram CD_U requires the gate to be open provided that all assumptions of the CD which lay in the future will be satisfied. In order to observe a counterexample we have to find a phase in which the gate is *not* open. Nevertheless, we may have a phase in which the gate is open as committed by the CD. The track still satisfies $\neg Cr$.

(iv) Then there is a phase in which $\neg Cr \wedge \neg O$ holds. The duration of this phase may be arbitrarily small as long as it is not 0.

(v) After that we only need to observe $\neg Cr$ for ξ_1 time units.

Note that phase (iii) is not mandatory for a counterexample.

In Figure 6.3 a test automaton for **Utility** is given that corresponds to the description of a counterexample above. During the phase (i) the observer is either in location q_0 or q_1 depending on the current status of the track. As soon as ξ_2 time units have elapsed in q_1 the test automaton has seen a behaviour that satisfies the phases (i) and (ii). Hence, it checks the status of the gate to decide whether it can skip phase (iii): If the gate is open it proceeds to state q_2 that corresponds to phase (iii). Otherwise it switches to state q_3 because $\neg Cr \wedge \neg O$ holds. In order to check whether phase (iv) is found it awaits this condition remaining stable for more than just a point in time. If this is true it proceeds to q_4 and otherwise it steps back to q_2 and waits for the next change of the observed system. If the observer reaches state q_4 it is clear that it has found a trace that fulfils the phases (i) to (iv). Hence, it checks the behaviour of the track to observe the last phase in which $\neg Cr$ has to hold for at least ξ_1 time units.

As soon as this is found it proceeds to the location q_{bad} where it remains for ever. Reaching q_{bad} is equivalent to observing a counterexample for **Utility**. Altogether, the following property holds:

$$S \models_1 CD_U$$

iff   (6.7)

$$\mathcal{C}(\mathcal{A}'_1, \ldots, \mathcal{A}'_n, \mathcal{T}(CD_U)) \models \forall \Box \, \neg \mathcal{T}(CD_U).q_{\text{bad}}$$

where $\models_1$ and $\mathcal{A}'_i$ are defined as in (6.6).

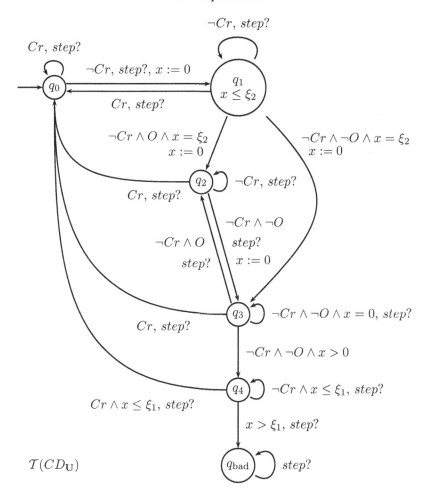

Fig. 6.3. A test automaton for **Utility**

6.2.3 Discussion

The approach presented above has several drawbacks:

(i) The construction of test automata was done *manually*. Hence, this step introduces a risk of errors and thus of misleading verification results, which is unacceptable for safety-critical systems. However, test automata have to be constructed due to the limited expressiveness of UPPAAL's temporal logic.

(ii) To get confidence in the verification result a *proof is necessary* that the test automaton represents exactly the desired property, i.e. the if-and-only-if relation of (6.4) should hold.

(iii) The *size of model* that has to be analysed by the model checker *increases* with the complexity of the test automaton. The best case is a *deterministic* test automaton as for the requirement **Safety**. Then the reachable state space of the model is not increased by the tester, only the memory consumption during model checking is higher because the tester needs additional memory.

(iv) A minor obstacle is the need to *transform the original automata* $\mathcal{A}_i$ into $\mathcal{A}'_i$, but the transformation described in Figure 6.1 can easily be automated.

An approach to solve the first two problems is presented in the following subsection where for subsets of CDs automatic translations into test automata are defined. The fact that the construction is done automatically solves the first problem, whereas the second one is solved by proofs for certain subsets of CDs.

6.2.4 Automatically generated test automata

As explained above, generating test automata from CDs automatically is desirable. However, it is not possible to find a test automaton for every CD. We first give an example of a CD for which an appropriate test automaton does not exist. Afterwards we will consider subsets of CDs:

- which express properties often used to capture requirements, and
- for which test automata are constructible.

Definition 6.1 (Testable CD)
We call a CD P *testable* if a test automaton $\mathcal{T}(P)$ exists such that for all specifications S with timed automaton semantics $\mathcal{C}(\mathcal{A}_1, \ldots, \mathcal{A}_n)$ it holds that:

$$S \models_1 P \qquad \text{iff} \qquad \mathcal{C}(\mathcal{A}'_1, \ldots, \mathcal{A}'_n, \mathcal{T}(P)) \models \forall \Box \neg \mathcal{T}(P).q_{\text{bad}}.$$

Otherwise it is called *untestable*.

Note that this notion of testability requires that the CD can be encoded as a reachability problem. This is sufficient for our purposes in the rest of this chapter.

Example 6.2 (Untestable CD)
Consider the following diagram $CD_{\mathbf{N}}$:

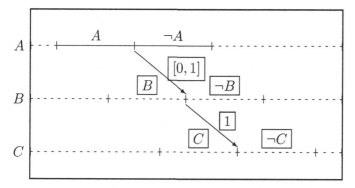

The meaning of $CD_{\mathbf{N}}$ is that whenever we observe a change from A to $\neg A$ at time t_A the system has to produce a change from B to $\neg B$ at some time $t_B \in [t_A, t_A + 1]$ and a change from C to $\neg C$ at time $t_B + 1$. In order to detect a counterexample to this behaviour the test automaton has to verify that all possible instances of t_B do not satisfy the commitment. However, the decision on whether an instance of t_B satisfies the commitment depends on the future. Therefore the test automaton has to remember all possible candidates for t_B, i.e. all time points when the system changes from B to $\neg B$. Intuitively, this is not possible with a finite number of clocks in a test automaton because it is possible that more changes happen than clocks are available. $\blacksquare$

This is made precise in the following proposition:

Proposition 6.3
$CD_{\mathbf{N}}$ is untestable.

Sketch of proof:
Suppose there is a test automaton $\mathcal{T}(CD_{\mathbf{N}})$ for $CD_{\mathbf{N}}$ which has a location q_{bad} and satisfies – as an instance of (6.4) and (6.5) – for all systems $\mathcal{S}$ and corresponding timed automata networks $\mathcal{C}(\mathcal{A}_1, \ldots, \mathcal{A}_n)$ the following equivalence:

$$\mathcal{S} \models_1 CD_{\mathbf{N}} \qquad \text{iff} \qquad \mathcal{C}(\mathcal{A}_1', \ldots, \mathcal{A}_n', \mathcal{T}(CD_{\mathbf{N}})) \models \forall \Box \, \neg \mathcal{T}(CD_{\mathbf{N}}).q_{\text{bad}}.$$

Assume that $\mathcal{T}(CD_{\mathbf{N}})$ has n clocks and consider the following time points:

$$t_A := 1,$$

$$t_B^i := t_A + \frac{2i - 1}{2(n + 1)} \quad \text{for } i = 1, \ldots, n + 1,$$

$$t_C^i \in \left(t_B^i + 1 - \frac{1}{4(n + 1)}, t_B^i + 1 + \frac{1}{4(n + 1)} \right) \quad \text{for } i = 1, \ldots, n + 1$$

where for all $1 \leq i \leq n+1$ we have $t_C^i - t_B^i \neq 1$. Now we assume that the observed system behaves as shown in Figure 6.4, where $n = 3$.

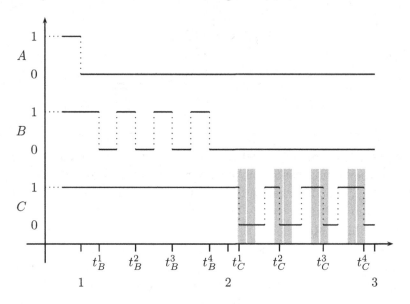

Fig. 6.4. Interpretation for A, B, and C for $n = 3$

Thus the computation path satisfies the assumptions of $CD_{\mathbf{N}}$ and it has $n+1$ candidates of B-changes for which a C-change can be observed 1 time unit later. But due to the choice of the t_C^i the commitment is not satisfied. Since $\mathcal{T}(CD_{\mathbf{N}})$ is a test automaton for $CD_{\mathbf{N}}$, it must have a computation path that reaches q_{bad}. As it has n clocks only, it is not possible for $\mathcal{T}(CD_{\mathbf{N}})$ to save all $n+1$ time points t_B^i by resetting a clock. Hence at time point 2 we can find an i_0 such that all clocks of the test automaton have a value that is not in $2 - t_B^{i_0} + \left(-\frac{1}{4(n+1)}, \frac{1}{4(n+1)}\right)$. Then we construct a new computation path by setting $t_C^{i_0} := t_B^{i_0}+1$. This path satisfies $CD_{\mathbf{N}}$ but the test automaton can reach q_{bad} the same way as before because it cannot observe the changed timing. In other words, $\mathcal{T}(CD_{\mathbf{N}})$ would claim that the property is violated although it is not. This is a *contradiction* to the assumption that there exists a test automaton for $CD_{\mathbf{N}}$. $\qquad\square$

Test automata for DC implementables

Since not all CDs are testable we study subsets of CDs. An important subset are the CDs that represent DC implementables (cf. Theorem 3.22). It turns out that all of these CDs are testable.

Theorem 6.4

The CDs representing DC implementables are testable.

Sketch of proof:
For each Constraint Diagram CD representing a DC implementable we present a test automaton $\mathcal{T}(CD)$. However, we omit the proof that CD and $\mathcal{T}(CD)$ are equivalent in the sense of (6.4) and (6.5) in step (II*):

$$S \models_1 CD \qquad \text{iff} \qquad \mathcal{C}(\mathcal{A}'_1, \ldots, \mathcal{A}'_n, \mathcal{T}(CD)) \models \forall \Box \neg \mathcal{T}(CD).q_{\text{bad}}. \qquad (*)$$

We mention only that this equivalence is decomposed into the following proof obligations:

- Each violation of the requirement expressed by CD is detected by the test automaton $\mathcal{T}(CD)$. To this end, it suffices to show that a violation *can* be detected by $\mathcal{T}(CD)$ because on the right-hand side of (*) *all* possible behaviours of the system together with the test automaton are examined.
- Reaching the location q_{bad} in the test automaton $\mathcal{T}(CD)$ is only possible by violating the requirement expressed by CD. To this end, one has to examine all possible paths of $\mathcal{T}(CD)$ leading into q_{bad}. The construction of the test automaton must then allow us to conclude that a violation of the requirement has occurred.

Now we consider each pattern of a DC implementable, repeat the equivalent CD of Theorem 3.22, and present a corresponding test automaton:

- *Initialisation.* The formula $\lceil\ \rceil \vee \lceil \pi \rceil$; true is represented by the CD

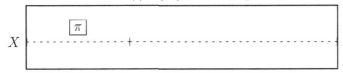

and it can be tested by the following automaton:

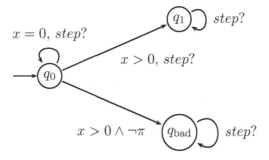

Initially, this test automaton accepts all state changes of the observed system as long as no time has passed ($x = 0$). If time point 0 is left by the system the test automaton can check whether the constraint π is violated in the initial phase $(x > 0 \wedge \neg\pi)$ and in that case switch to q_{bad}. The edge to q_1 is necessary to abort the search when the initial phase is over.

- *Sequencing.* For presentation purposes we assume that the sequencing formula has the form $\lceil\pi\rceil \longrightarrow \lceil\pi \vee \pi_1\rceil$. The corresponding CD is

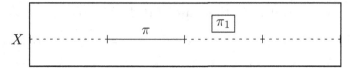

and it can be tested by the following automaton:

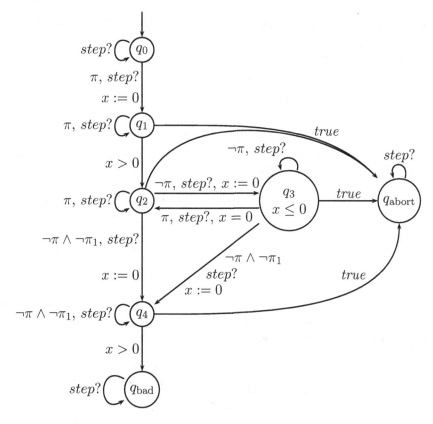

Initially, this test automaton accepts arbitrary behaviour in q_0 until it decides nondeterministically to switch to the location q_1 provided that the observed system satisfies π. Being in state q_1 the observer can verify that π holds for more than a point interval. This is represented by the edge from q_1 to q_2 which is enabled as soon as the clock x is no longer 0. The states q_2 and q_3 represent the knowledge that the observer has found a $\lceil\pi\rceil$ phase and that this phase still holds on. The construction of the states q_2 and q_3 is necessary to deal with the possibility that π is not valid for point intervals within the $\lceil\pi\rceil$-phase. If the observed system invalidates π only for a point in time the observer can switch to q_3 and back to cope with this situation. However, if the observer detects that $\neg\pi$ and $\neg\pi_1$ is satisfied, then it may switch to q_4. Here it remains to be checked that this holds for a non-point interval. If this is the case the observer can switch to q_{bad}.

Note that the basic idea of this test automaton is to find a sequence of phases $\lceil\pi\rceil$; $\lceil\neg\pi\wedge\neg\pi_1\rceil$ in order to disprove the sequencing property. However, the test automaton might fail to do so because it might choose a time point to switch to q_1 when no counterexample can be observed. To avoid a blocking behaviour of the test automaton there are unconstrained edges from all appropriate locations towards q_{abort}.

- *Progress.* The formula $\lceil\pi\rceil \xrightarrow{\;\theta\;} \lceil\neg\pi\rceil$ is represented by the CD

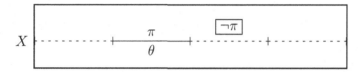

and a test automaton for this property checks for a phase of the form $\lceil\pi\rceil\wedge\ell > \theta$:

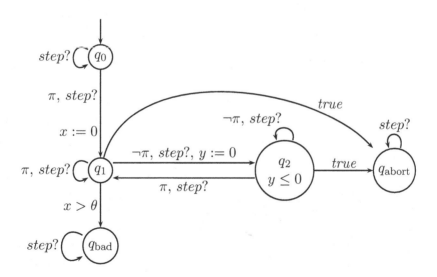

- *Synchronisation.* The formula $\lceil\pi\wedge\varphi\rceil \xrightarrow{\;\theta\;} \lceil\neg\pi\rceil$ is a generalisation of the progress pattern and is represented by the CD

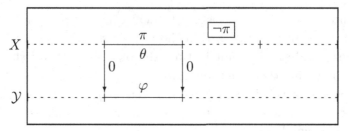

and a test automaton for this property checks for a phase sequence of the form $(\lceil \pi \wedge \varphi \rceil \wedge \ell = \theta) \,;\, \lceil \pi \rceil$:

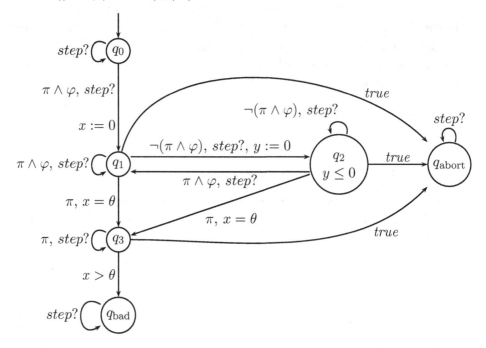

- *Stability.* For presentation purposes we assume that the stability formula has the form

$$\lceil \neg \pi \rceil \,;\, \lceil \pi \wedge \varphi \rceil \xrightarrow{\leq \theta} \lceil \pi \vee \pi_1 \rceil .$$

The corresponding CD is

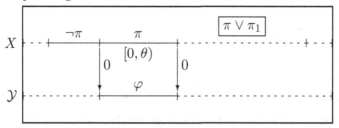

and a test automaton for this property checks for a phase sequence of the form $\lceil \neg \pi \rceil \,;\, (\lceil \pi \wedge \varphi \rceil \wedge \ell < \theta)\,;\, \lceil \neg(\pi \vee \pi_1) \rceil$:

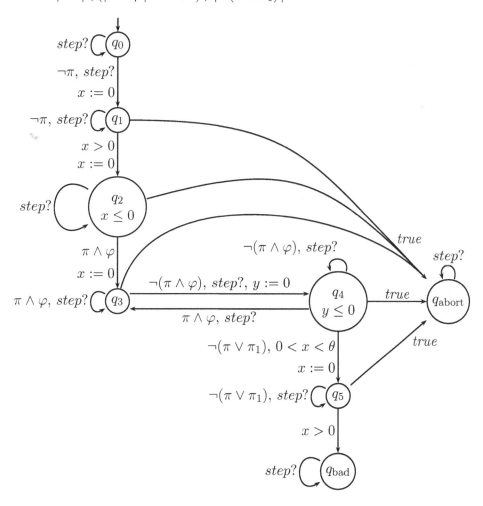

This completes the case analysis of the different CD implementables. □

Test automata for counterexample formulas

So far the test automata were all motivated by concrete CDs or CD patterns. Thus we can generate test automata systematically only when the given CD represents a DC implementable (cf. Theorem 6.4). We now present a construction of test automata for the more general class of so-called counterexample formulas. Thus if we can translate a CD (or a DC formula) into a semantically equivalent counterexample formula (or a finite set thereof) then a test automaton can be constructed systematically.

Definition 6.5 (Counterexample formulas)

- A *counterexample formula* (*CE formula* for short) is a DC formula of the following form:

$$\text{true}\,;\,(\lceil \pi_1 \rceil \wedge \ell \in I_1)\,;\,\ldots\,;\,(\lceil \pi_k \rceil \wedge \ell \in I_k)\,;\,\text{true} \qquad (6.8)$$

  where for $i \in \{1, \ldots, k\}$ the π_i are state assertions and the I_i are non-empty time intervals. They may be open, half-open, or closed of the form (b, e) or $[b, e)$ with $b \in \mathbb{Q}_{\geq 0}$ and $e \in \mathbb{Q}_{\geq 0} \cup \{\infty\}$, and $(b, e]$ or $[b, e]$ with $b, e \in \mathbb{Q}_{\geq 0}$. Intervals (b, ∞) and $[b, \infty)$ denote the unbounded sets $\{t \in \text{Time} \mid b < t\}$ and $\{t \in \text{Time} \mid b \leq t\}$, respectively.†

- Let F be a DC formula. We call a CE formula CEF a *counterexample formula for F* if

$$\models F \iff \neg(CEF)$$

  holds.

- Let $\mathcal{C}$ be a Constraint Diagram. We call a CE formula CEF a *counterexample formula for $\mathcal{C}$* if

$$\models \llbracket \mathcal{C} \rrbracket_{\text{DC}} \iff \neg(CEF).$$

Example 6.6

A counterexample formula for $CD_{\mathbf{S}}$ is

$$\text{true}\,;\,(\lceil Cr \wedge \neg Cl \rceil \wedge \ell \in (0, \infty))\,;\,\text{true}$$

and a counterexample formula for $CD_{\mathbf{U}}$ is

$$\text{true}\,;\,(\lceil \neg Cr \rceil \wedge \ell \in [\xi_2, \xi_2])\,;$$
$$(\lceil \neg Cr \wedge \neg O \rceil \wedge \ell \in (0, \infty))\,;$$
$$(\lceil \neg Cr \rceil \wedge \ell \in [\xi_1, \xi_1])\,;\,\text{true}.$$

We will now show how to construct test automata for such formulas. ∎

Theorem 6.7

Counterexample formulas are testable.

Sketch of proof:

The test automaton in Figure 6.5 checks whether a given real-time system (represented as a network of timed automata and augmented with communications *step*! introduced by the transformation shown in Figure 6.1) is able to perform the counterexample specified by formula (6.8). □

---

† Interval bounds are chosen from $\mathbb{Q}_{\geq 0}$ instead of Time because we wish to construct timed test automata representing counterexample formulas.

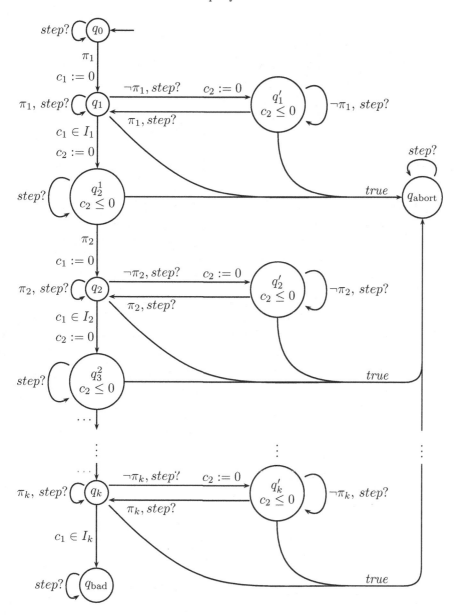

Fig. 6.5. Test automaton for the counterexample formula (6.8)

6.3 Specification

In this section we explain how to express design specifications given by PLC-
Automata in terms of (networks of extended) timed automata. We begin
with the running example and then present a general construction.

6.3.1 *Railroad crossing*

We first specify the controller for the GRC in terms of PLC-Automata and then represent this controller by two timed automata. The control laws of a PLC-Automaton implementing the GRC are simple:

- If the track is not empty the controller should close the gate.
- If the track is empty the controller should open the gate.

The first control law is necessary to satisfy the safety requirement whereas the second one is needed for the utility requirement. In other words, the functionality of the controller is simple and the main concern is the correctness of the timing. The question of correct timing with respect to safety is whether the controller reacts sufficiently fast to close the gate in time (before the train arrives). The utility constraint raises two timing issues. On the one hand, it requires the controller to open the gate sufficiently fast, and on the other hand, it forbids closing the gate too early.

We use these ideas to construct a PLC-Automaton for the GRC, depicted in Figure 6.6. Note that this controller waits a certain amount of time (κ seconds) before it closes the gate. This enables us to implement a delayed closing of the gate which might be necessary to implement the utility property correctly. As usual, ε is the upper time bound for executing a cycle.

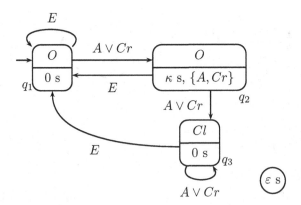

Fig. 6.6. Controller for the GRC

Now we construct a network of extended timed automata that represents the behaviour of the PLC-Automaton in Figure 6.6 *operationally*.

- First we identify the observables and their data types. The input observable of the PLC-Automaton ranges over $\{E, A, Cr\}$ and the output observable over $\{O, Cl\}$. To keep the intuition we will use *Track* and g as names for the data variables in the extended timed automaton. However, recall from Definition 4.39 of extended timed automata that data variables range over finite sets of integers only. Thus the data values have to be encoded, which is straightforward.

Convention. Throughout this chapter a finite data type $\{val_0, \ldots, val_n\}$ of a data variable *var* is encoded as follows:

$$var = val_0 \qquad \text{is encoded by} \qquad var = 0,$$
$$\vdots \qquad\qquad \vdots \qquad\qquad \vdots$$
$$var = val_n \qquad \text{is encoded by} \qquad var = n.$$

If an initial value is given we assume that it is val_0 so that it is encoded by 0, the standard initial value in an extended timed automaton. Assignments are encoded analogously. In the graphic representation of the timed automata we shall use the data values $val_0, \ldots, val_n$.

- The input observable *Track* is unconstrained, i.e. it may change its value arbitrarily. This can be modelled by the simple automaton $\mathcal{A}_{\mathsf{In}}$ shown in Figure 6.7. It resets a clock x with each transition. The purpose of this

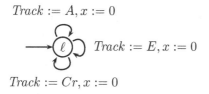

$Track := A, x := 0$

$Track := E, x := 0$

$Track := Cr, x := 0$

Fig. 6.7. The input automaton $\mathcal{A}_{\mathsf{In}}$ for the GRC

construction is to enable the following automaton to check whether the current value was stable for longer than just a point in time.

- The output observable g is under control of the PLC-Automaton. In the corresponding timed automaton we have to represent how g is changed depending on the state of the PLC-Automaton and its input values. To this end, we present two general construction patterns for a given state q in a PLC-Automaton.

Pattern 1. State q without delay: $S_t(q) = 0$.

We introduce the locations q_{p} and q_{cu}, clocks y and z, and the following edges:

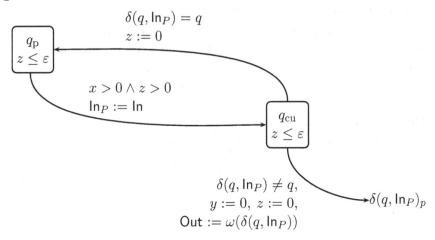

This part of a timed automaton cycles from location q_{p} ("polling") to location q_{cu} ("computing" and "updating") and back. The assignment $\mathsf{In}_P := \mathsf{In}$ models the polling of the input variable In. The current value of In is copied into an auxiliary variable In_P ("polled In"). The clock constraint $x > 0 \wedge z > 0$ ensures that the automaton can only poll a value that holds for a non-point interval during the current cycle.

As long as the transition function satisfies $\delta(q, \mathsf{In}_P) = q$ the cycle continues and the construction of the invariants and transitions ensures that each cycle lasts at most ε seconds. It uses the clock z to measure the duration of the current cycle and both locations have the invariant $z \leq \varepsilon$. Only transitions *towards* q_{p} reset this clock because the execution of these transitions marks the beginning of a new cycle.

If $\delta(q, \mathsf{In}_P) \neq q$ holds, the timed automaton fires a transition towards a location q'_{p} with $q' = \delta(q, \mathsf{In}_P)$ and resets both clocks y and z. The clock y measures the duration for which the system is in the state q. As $S_t(q) = 0$ holds in this case we only have to take care that y is reset when the PLC-Automaton changes the state. If such a state change happens the output variable Out is set to the output value of the target state. Note that the destination $\delta(q, \mathsf{In}_P)$ is not necessarily unique, i.e. it depends on In_P. Hence, the edge may occur in several instances, one instance for each element of $\delta(q, \Sigma) \setminus \{q\}$.

Pattern 2. State q with delay: $S_t(q) > 0$.
We introduce four locations called q_{p}, q_{c} ("computing"), q_{u} ("updating"), and q_{d} ("delayed") in the following edges:

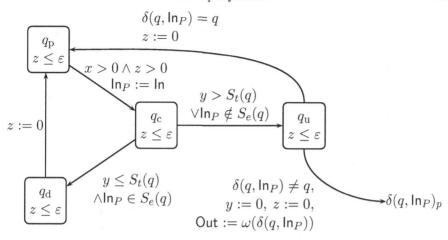

$$\delta(q, \mathsf{In}_P) = q$$
$$z := 0$$

Again, the outgoing edge of q_p models the polling of the PLC-Automaton. Since the system has to consider a delay time the destination location q_c checks whether the PLC-Automaton can ignore the input or not. Depending on the current value of the clock y and the polled input value the timed automaton can switch either to q_d or to q_u. In q_d the timed automaton just finishes the cycle by changing to q_p and resetting the cycle clock z. In q_u it behaves as in the previous pattern, i.e. if the transition function requires a state change of the PLC-Automaton, then the timed automaton switches to a location q'_p with $q' = \delta(q, \mathsf{In}_P)$. Moreover, the output variable is set to $\omega(q')$ and the clocks y and z are reset. Otherwise, the system switches back to q_p and resets the cycle clock z only.

- Finally, the initial location has to be defined. If q_0 is the initial state of the PLC-Automaton, then $q_{0,\mathrm{p}}$ is the initial location of the corresponding timed automaton.

The complete timed automaton $\mathcal{A}_{\mathsf{Out}}$ for the PLC-Automaton of Figure 6.6 is shown in Figure 6.8. It instantiates the pattern for a state without delay twice (q_1 and q_3) and the pattern for a state with delay once (q_2). The latter is shown in the middle and the positions of the locations are rearranged for optical reasons. Note that in the PLC-Automaton $\delta(q_2, E) = q_1$ holds and $\delta(q_2, \{A, Cr\}) = \{q_3\}$. Hence, there are two outgoing edges from $q_{2,\mathrm{u}}$. One towards $q_{1,\mathrm{p}}$ and one towards $q_{3,\mathrm{p}}$ and the guards are appropriately rewritten. Note that there is no self-loop at q_2 in the PLC-Automaton. Therefore, the edge from $q_{2,\mathrm{u}}$ to $q_{2,\mathrm{p}}$, which is drawn dotted in Figure 6.8, would have a guard equivalent to false and thus can be omitted without changing the behaviour. The initial location of the timed automaton is $q_{1,\mathrm{p}}$ because q_1 is the initial state of the PLC-Automaton. Note that the variables

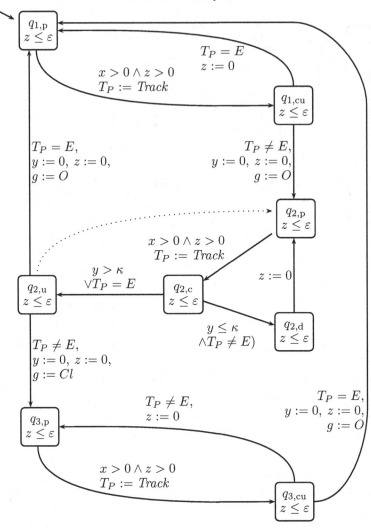

Fig. 6.8. The timed automaton $\mathcal{A}_{\mathsf{Out}}$ describing the semantics of the PLC-Automaton in Figure 6.6

In and Out of the pattern are instantiated with *Track* and g, respectively. The variable In_P of the pattern is instantiated with T_P, which stores the polled value of the input observable *Track*.

6.3.2 Timed automata semantics of PLC-Automata

The previous example prepares the general approach: the formal definition of a timed automata semantics for PLC-Automata. We assign to each PLC-

Automaton a pair of timed automata. The first one is responsible for driving the input variable arbitrarily. The second one represents the operational behaviour of the device executing the PLC-Automaton, i.e. it takes the cycle time and delay times into account. Moreover, it realises the polling behaviour and the reaction of the system.

Definition 6.8 (Timed automata semantics of PLC-Automata)
For a given PLC-Automaton $\mathcal{A} = (Q, \Sigma, \delta, q_0, \varepsilon, S_t, S_e, \Omega, w)$ the following network $T(\mathcal{A})$ of two extended timed automata defines the operational behaviour of $\mathcal{A}$:

$$T(\mathcal{A}) \stackrel{\text{def}}{=} C(\mathcal{A}_{\mathsf{In}}, \mathcal{A}_{\mathsf{Out}}).$$

The timed automaton $\mathcal{A}_{\mathsf{In}} = (L, C, B, U, \mathbb{X}, V, I, E_\Sigma, \ell_{\text{ini}})$ is defined by

$$L = \{\ell\}, \quad C = B = U = \varnothing, \quad \mathbb{X} = \{x\}, \quad V = \{\mathsf{In}\}, \quad I(\ell) = \text{true}, \quad \ell_{\text{ini}} = \ell$$

and has the following set of edges:

$$E_\Sigma = \{(\ell, \tau, \text{true}, \langle\, \mathsf{In} := \sigma, x := 0\,\rangle, \ell) \mid \sigma \in \Sigma\}.$$

The timed automaton $\mathcal{A}_{\mathsf{Out}} = (L, C, B, U, \mathbb{X}, V, I, E, \ell_{\text{ini}})$ has the following components:

- The set L of locations is given by

$$L = \{q_{\mathsf{p}}, q_{\mathsf{cu}} \mid q \in Q \wedge S_t(q) = 0\} \cup \{q_{\mathsf{p}}, q_{\mathsf{c}}, q_{\mathsf{d}}, q_{\mathsf{u}} \mid q \in Q \wedge S_t(q) > 0\}$$

and none of these locations is committed, i.e. $C = \varnothing$

- $B = U = \varnothing$, i.e. no channels are used.
- $\mathbb{X} = \{x, y, z\}$ is the set of clocks.
- $V = \{\mathsf{In}, \mathsf{In}_P, \mathsf{Out}\}$ is the set of data variables.
- $I(\ell) = z \leq \varepsilon$ for all $\ell \in L$.
- $\ell_{\text{ini}} = q_{0,\mathsf{p}}$ is the initial location.
- The set E of edges is given by $E = E_1 \cup E_2$ where E_1 describes the three edges of Pattern 1 for all states q without a delay, i.e. satisfying the condition

$$cond_1(q) \stackrel{\text{def}}{\Longleftrightarrow} q \in Q \wedge S_t(q) = 0$$

and E_2 describes the six edges of Pattern 2 for all states q with a delay, i.e. satisfying the condition

$$cond_2(q) \stackrel{\text{def}}{\Longleftrightarrow} q \in Q \wedge S_t(q) > 0.$$

E_1 and E_2 are defined as follows:

$$E_1 = \left\{ (q_\mathrm{p}, \tau, x > 0 \wedge z > 0, \langle \, \mathsf{In}_P := \mathsf{In} \, \rangle, q_\mathrm{cu}) \, \middle| \, cond_1(q) \right\}$$

$$\cup \ \left\{ (q_\mathrm{cu}, \tau, \mathsf{In}_P = \sigma, \langle \, z := 0 \, \rangle, q_\mathrm{p} \, \middle| \right.$$
$$\left. cond_1(q) \wedge \sigma \in \Sigma \wedge \delta(q, \sigma) = q \right\}$$

$$\cup \ \left\{ (q_\mathrm{cu}, \tau, \mathsf{In}_P = \sigma, \langle \, y := 0, z := 0, \mathsf{Out} := \omega(q') \, \rangle, q'_\mathrm{p}) \, \middle| \right.$$
$$\left. cond_1(q) \wedge q' \in Q \wedge \sigma \in \Sigma \wedge \delta(q, \sigma) = q' \neq q \right\}$$

and

$$E_2 = \left\{ (q_\mathrm{p}, \tau, z > 0, \langle \, \mathsf{In}_P := \mathsf{In} \, \rangle, q_\mathrm{c}) \, \middle| \, cond_2(q) \right\}$$

$$\cup \ \left\{ (q_\mathrm{c}, \tau, y \leq S_t(q) \wedge \mathsf{In}_P = \sigma, \langle \, \rangle, q_\mathrm{d}) \, \middle| \right.$$
$$\left. cond_2(q) \wedge \sigma \in S_e(q) \right\}$$

$$\cup \ \left\{ (q_\mathrm{d}, \tau, \mathsf{true}, \langle \, z := 0 \, \rangle, q_\mathrm{p}) \, \middle| \, cond_2(q) \right\}$$

$$\cup \ \left\{ (q_\mathrm{c}, \tau, y > S_t(q) \vee \mathsf{In}_P = \sigma, \langle \, z := 0 \, \rangle, q_\mathrm{u}) \, \middle| \right.$$
$$\left. cond_2(q) \wedge \sigma \in \Sigma \setminus S_e(q) \right\}$$

$$\cup \ \left\{ (q_\mathrm{u}, \tau, \mathsf{In}_P = \sigma, \langle \, z := 0 \, \rangle, q_\mathrm{p}) \, \middle| \right.$$
$$\left. cond_2(q) \wedge \sigma \in \Sigma \wedge \delta(q, \sigma) = q \right\}$$

$$\cup \ \left\{ (q_\mathrm{u}S, \tau, \mathsf{In}_P = \sigma, \langle \, y := 0, z := 0, \mathsf{Out} := \omega(q') \, \rangle, q'_\mathrm{p}) \, \middle| \right.$$
$$\left. cond_2(q) \wedge q' \in Q \wedge \sigma \in \Sigma \wedge \delta(q, \sigma) = q' \neq q \right\}.$$

Note that neither $\mathcal{A}_{\mathsf{In}}$ nor $\mathcal{A}_{\mathsf{Out}}$ uses channels for communication. However, in conjunction with test automata we need to add appropriate labels *step!* to notify the tester about changes of observables. This can be done by applying the transformation shown in Figure 6.1. In case of the $\mathcal{A}_{\mathsf{In}}$ automaton we obtain the following transformed automaton $\mathcal{A}'_{\mathsf{In}}$:

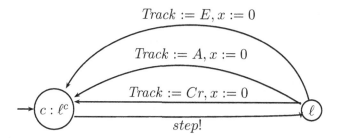

$$Track := E, x := 0$$
$$Track := A, x := 0$$
$$Track := Cr, x := 0$$

$c : \ell^c$ ℓ

step!

For $\mathcal{A}_{\mathsf{Out}}$ we need to apply the modification only to the locations q_{p} for all states q of PLC-Automaton $\mathcal{A}$ because only edges towards locations q_{p} modify the Out observable which is accessible to test automata. For the automaton in Figure 6.8 we get the automaton given in Figure 6.9 where the changes are marked by the shaded areas.

Having a semantics of PLC-Automata in terms of timed automata raises the question of how this semantics is related to its DC semantics given in Definition 5.3. Based on an appropriately defined relation $\approx$ between interpretations (satisfying the DC semantics) and computation paths (of the timed automaton semantics) it is possible to prove the following theorem (cf. [DFMV98]):

Theorem 6.9 (Equivalence of DC and TA semantics)
Let $\mathcal{A}$ be a PLC-Automaton. Then the following holds:

$$\mathcal{T}(\mathcal{A}) \approx [\![\mathcal{A}]\!]_{\mathrm{DC}}^{\mathrm{strong}} \qquad \text{and} \qquad \models [\![\mathcal{A}]\!]_{\mathrm{DC}}^{\mathrm{strong}} \Longrightarrow [\![\mathcal{A}]\!]_{\mathrm{DC}}.$$

The strong DC semantics $[\![\mathcal{A}]\!]_{\mathrm{DC}}^{\mathrm{strong}}$ is a conjunction of $[\![\mathcal{A}]\!]_{\mathrm{DC}}$ and some additional DC formulas.

6.4 Verification

In this section we bring the results of the previous two sections together and discuss the automatic verification of requirements given by Constraint Diagrams for real-time systems given by PLC-Automata on the basis of extended timed automata using the model checker UPPAAL. As we shall illustrate with our running example, an attempt to verify a requirement for a system may fail and yield a counterexample. In that case either the requirement is too strong or the system is too weak.

For the running example we argue that the requirements are too strong and need to be weakened by making explicit hidden *assumptions* about

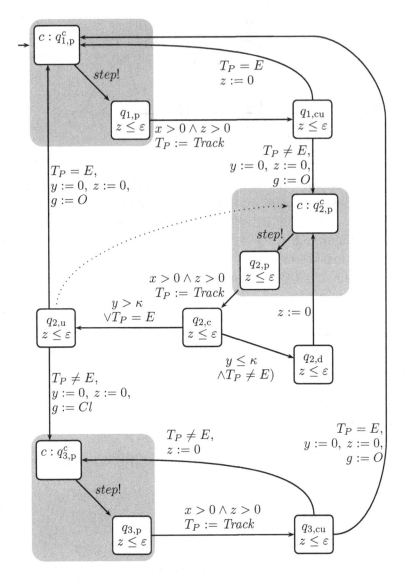

Fig. 6.9. $\mathcal{A}'_{\mathsf{Out}}$, the modified $\mathcal{A}_{\mathsf{Out}}$

the system's environment. With such assumptions the verification succeeds under certain conditions of system parameters like the duration of phases.

We then address two methodological points. First we describe an approach to represent assumptions of the environment as separate timed automata. Then we discuss in more detail sensors and actuators and discuss an approach to represent them by separate timed automata as well.

6.4.1 Railroad crossing

We begin with our running example as a check on whether the PLC-Automaton of Figure 6.6 satisfies the safety and utility requirements.

Verifying safety

For safety, we have to verify

$$\mathcal{C}(\mathcal{A}'_{\mathsf{In}}, \mathcal{A}'_{\mathsf{Out}}, \mathcal{T}(CD_{\mathbf{S}})) \models \forall \square \, \neg \mathcal{T}(CD_{\mathbf{S}}).q_{\mathrm{bad}} \tag{6.9}$$

by applying the model checker UPPAAL. However, the model checker reveals a *counterexample* shown in Figure 6.10. The figure lists a sequence of configurations of the network, called c_0 to c_5, with c_0 being the initial configuration. A configuration of the network consists of the locations of the automata involved, the values of integer variables *Track*, T_P and g, and a clock constraint satisfied by the clock values of the configuration. The downward arrows indicate the automata in which a transition is fired. In case of synchronised transitions we use two downward arrows connected by a horizontal arrow. The direction of this arrow and the annotation with the symbols ! and ? indicate the direction of the communication. The name of the channel is also annotated.

The counterexample given in Figure 6.10 reaches the location q_{bad} as follows. First, the system leaves the initial locations of $\mathcal{A}'_{\mathsf{In}}$ and $\mathcal{A}'_{\mathsf{Out}}$ by firing transitions which synchronise with $\mathcal{T}(CD_{\mathbf{S}})$. With these transitions the system reaches configuration c_2. Since time may pass in this configuration the clocks can change their value uniformly. This is only limited by the invariant $z \leq \varepsilon$ of location $q_{1,\mathrm{p}}$ of $\mathcal{A}'_{\mathsf{Out}}$. In this trace the system now fires the transition of $\mathcal{A}'_{\mathsf{In}}$ that sets the variable *Track* to Cr (configuration c_3). In the next step the test automaton $\mathcal{T}(CD_{\mathbf{S}})$ is informed via the *step* channel. Due to this the test automaton reaches location q_1. In order to reach q_{bad} only time has to pass, which is not forbidden in the current configuration. Hence, in the next configuration c_5 the location of $\mathcal{T}(CD_{\mathbf{S}})$ is q_{bad}, which disproves the safety property.

The explanation of why the current system does *not* implement the safety property is simple. The reason is that the environment is able to change the status of the track without any restriction. In the given counterexample the value of *Track* changes from E to Cr without an approaching phase (representing the value A). In other words, the current system does not reflect assumptions about the physical world.

To cope with that, we have to revise the safety property appropriately such that it incorporates relevant assumptions about the environment. The

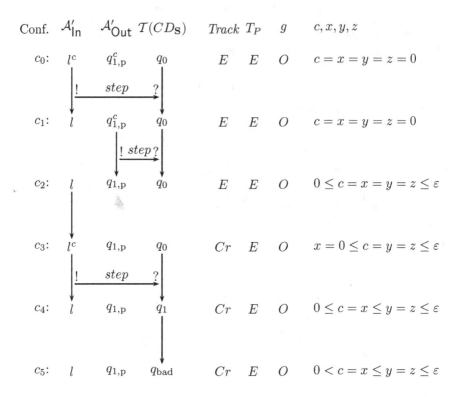

Conf.	A'_{In}	A'_{Out}	$T(CD_S)$	Track T_P	g	c, x, y, z
$c_0:$	l^c	$q^c_{1,p}$	q_0	E E	O	$c = x = y = z = 0$
$c_1:$	l	$q^c_{1,p}$	q_0	E E	O	$c = x = y = z = 0$
$c_2:$	l	$q_{1,p}$	q_0	E E	O	$0 \le c = x = y = z \le \varepsilon$
$c_3:$	l^c	$q_{1,p}$	q_0	Cr E	O	$x = 0 \le c = y = z \le \varepsilon$
$c_4:$	l	$q_{1,p}$	q_1	Cr E	O	$0 \le c = x \le y = z \le \varepsilon$
$c_5:$	l	$q_{1,p}$	q_{bad}	Cr E	O	$0 < c = x \le y = z \le \varepsilon$

Fig. 6.10. The counterexample for the safety property (6.9)

counterexample above clearly demonstrates that we need to consider assumptions about the trains. In Subsection 1.3.2 we specified several assumptions about the train behaviour. For our purposes we need that the track is initially empty and that trains are *not too fast*, i.e. need a given minimal time ρ to approach the crossing. These assumptions allow us to weaken the safety property as formalised by the following Constraint Diagram called CD'_S:

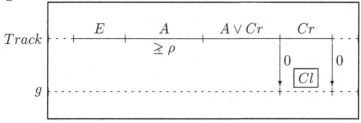

To construct a test automaton for CD'_S we apply the approach described for counterexample formulas. The following CE formula captures all counterexamples of CD_S':

$$
\begin{array}{ll}
\text{true}; \quad ([E] & \wedge \quad \ell \in (0, \infty)); \\
([A] & \wedge \quad \ell \in [\rho, \infty)); \\
([A \vee Cr] & \wedge \quad \ell \in (0, \infty)); \\
([Cr \wedge \neg Cl] & \wedge \quad \ell \in (0, \infty)); \text{true}.
\end{array}
$$

Putting the resulting test automaton in parallel with the Timed Automata semantics of the PLC-Automaton, we can verify that

$$
\rho \geq \kappa + 4\varepsilon \quad \text{implies} \quad \mathcal{C}(\mathcal{A}'_{\text{In}}, \mathcal{A}'_{\text{Out}}, \mathcal{T}(CD_S')) \models \forall \Box \neg \mathcal{T}(CD_S').q_{\text{bad}}. \quad (6.10)
$$

Note that UPPAAL is not able to derive inequalities like $\rho \geq \kappa + 4\varepsilon$ automatically, it needs concrete instances for the parameters $\rho, \kappa, \varepsilon$. If (6.10) must be verified formally, then we can apply Theorem 5.8 on reaction times of PLC-Automata (with $\Pi = \{q_1, q_2, q_3\}$, $A = \neg E$, and $n = 2$) to show that

$$
[\neg E] \xrightarrow{\kappa + 4\varepsilon} [q_3]
$$

holds. With this knowledge and the DC formula (DC-11) of the DC semantics of PLC-Automata we can conclude that

$$
[\neg E] \xrightarrow{\kappa + 4\varepsilon} [Cl]
$$

holds, from which (6.10) obviously follows.

Verifying utility

Now we examine whether the current specification satisfies the utility property, i.e. we check whether

$$
\mathcal{C}(\mathcal{A}'_{\text{In}}, \mathcal{A}'_{\text{Out}}, \mathcal{T}(CD_U)) \models \forall \Box \neg \mathcal{T}(CD_U).q_{\text{bad}} \quad (6.11)
$$

holds. Similar to the safety property, UPPAAL is able to *disprove* this constraint. The details of the counterexample are omitted here because they depend on the concrete instance of the parameters ξ_1, ξ_2, ε, and κ. But the way the counterexample disproves utility is as follows. After initialisation the whole system fires the transition of $\mathcal{A}'_{\text{In}}$ that sets $Track$ to A, i.e. a train is approaching. The rest of the counterexample consists of the appropriate transitions of $\mathcal{A}'_{\text{Out}}$. Eventually, this automaton reaches the states $q_{3,p}^c$, $q_{3,p}$ and $q_{3,\text{cu}}$ in which the variable g is set to Cl. Since $Track$ remains A the value of g cannot change anymore.

This pattern can be extended to an arbitrarily long duration and hence the test automaton $T(CD_U)$ has no problem in finding a sequence of the following form:

$$\text{true;} \quad (\lceil \neg Cr \rceil \qquad \wedge \quad \ell \in [\xi_2, \xi_2]) \,;$$
$$(\lceil \neg Cr \wedge \neg O \rceil \quad \wedge \quad \ell \in (0, \infty)) \,;$$
$$(\lceil \neg Cr \rceil \qquad \wedge \quad \ell \in [\xi_1, \xi_1]) \,; \text{true}$$

because the above pattern satisfies $A \wedge Cl$ arbitrarily long after some time.

As in the previous case the lack of constraints for the trains is the core of the problem. In the introduction we assumed that trains are not *too fast* and this assumption was necessary to prove that the given controller satisfies the safety property. In this case the model checker exploits the fact that our model does allow trains which are *too slow*. In Subsection 1.3.2, this could be avoided by the assumption T-Slow. Here, it is assumed that an approaching train needs at most ρ' time units to reach the crossing. In other words, there is no A-phase with a duration longer than ρ'. We additionally assume that $\rho' < \xi_1 + \xi_2$ holds. This allows us to choose a new parameter $\bar{\rho}$ with

$$0 < \bar{\rho} \leq \min\{\xi_2, \xi_1 + \xi_2 - \rho'\}$$

and revise CD_U to the following Constraint Diagram called CD_U':

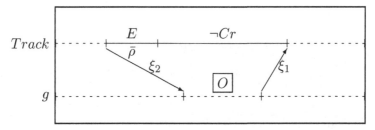

This diagram strengthens the assumptions of utility for the first $\bar{\rho}$ seconds. It requires that the track is empty (E) and not just $\neg Cr$. A test automaton can be constructed from the following CE formula for this CD:

$$\text{true;} \quad (\lceil E \rceil \qquad \wedge \quad \ell \in [\bar{\rho}, \bar{\rho}]) \,;$$
$$(\lceil \neg Cr \rceil \qquad \wedge \quad \ell \in [\xi_2 - \bar{\rho}, \infty)) \,;$$
$$(\lceil \neg Cr \wedge \neg O \rceil \quad \wedge \quad \ell \in (0, \infty)) \,;$$
$$(\lceil \neg Cr \rceil \qquad \wedge \quad \ell \in [\xi_1, \xi_1]) \,; \text{true.}$$

Putting the resulting test automaton in parallel with the timed automaton semantics of the PLC-Automaton we can verify that

$$\left.\begin{array}{r} \rho' < \xi_1 + \xi_2 \\ \wedge \quad \kappa \geq \xi_2 - \bar{\rho} \\ \wedge \quad \varepsilon \leq \frac{1}{2}\bar{\rho} \end{array}\right\} \text{ implies}$$

$$\mathcal{C}(\mathcal{A}'_{\mathsf{In}}, \mathcal{A}'_{\mathsf{Out}}, \mathcal{T}(CD'_{\mathsf{U}})) \models \forall \Box \neg \mathcal{T}(CD'_{\mathsf{U}}).q_{\mathsf{bad}}. \tag{6.12}$$

6.4.2 Discussion

The previous verification results prove correctness of the specification with respect to revised versions of the requirements **Safety** and **Utility**. An overview of the verified behaviour is given in the timing diagram of Figure 6.11.

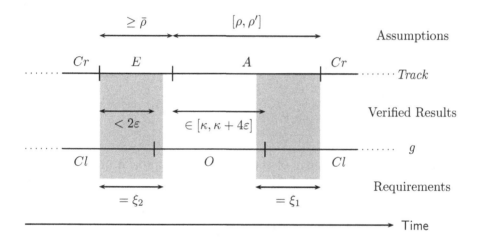

Fig. 6.11. Verified behaviour of the PLC-Automaton for the GRC

For the safety requirement we assumed that the A-phase lasts at least ρ seconds and verified that during this phase the output changes to Cl (and remains there) within at most $\kappa + 4\varepsilon$ seconds.

For the utility requirement we first ruled out situations in which the gate should be opened to satisfy this requirement but the track was not empty, i.e. when a train is approaching while its predecessor is still in the crossing. The problem with this situation is that the controller gets no information when the second train enters the approaching area of the crossing. Hence, it cannot compute when it has to open or close the gate. Therefore, we assumed that the slowest approaching train needs at most ρ' seconds to reach the crossing and that the sum of the time parameters ξ_1 and ξ_2 of utility exceeds this duration. As a consequence, the utility requirement does not restrict anymore the system's behaviour in the above case.

To verify the utility property for the remaining case, in which the track is empty between two crossing trains, we can conclude from the previous assumption that there is a minimal duration $(\bar{\rho})$ of that E-phase. There are two constraints that together are sufficient to verify that utility is satisfied. One constraint is $\varepsilon \leq \frac{1}{2}\bar{\rho}$. It ensures that the gate is open in less than ξ_2 seconds (cf. Figure 6.11) because of $\bar{\rho} \leq \xi_2$. The other constraint is $\kappa \geq \xi_2 - \bar{\rho}$. One would expect that it ensures that the gate does not close too early. Thus it is surprising that ξ_2 appears in this inequality and not ξ_1. Nevertheless, this condition indeed implies that the gate is open sufficiently long. We have to prove that the O-phase ends at most ξ_1 seconds before the Cr-phase begins. We know that the A-phase takes at most ρ' seconds and that the closing reaction of the controller is delayed at least κ seconds. We have to show that $\rho' - \kappa \leq \xi_1$. This is calculated as follows:

$$\rho' - \kappa \leq \rho' - (\xi_2 - \bar{\rho})$$
$$= \rho' - \xi_2 + \bar{\rho}$$
$$\leq \rho' - \xi_2 + (\xi_1 + \xi_2 - \rho')$$
$$= \xi_1.$$

There are two shortcomings of the verification approach presented so far that will be addressed in the following subsections:

- We failed to verify the original requirements, and to overcome this problem we added assumptions *into the requirements*. In general, it is not surprising that initial verification attempts fail; there are three possible reasons for this:

  - The system specification contains an error.
  - An implicit assumption about the environment is not formalised.
  - The requirement is too restrictive.

  In the previous attempts to verify safety and utility we revealed missing assumptions about the train behaviour. However, it is hardly acceptable to revise the requirements such that the missing assumptions become part of the modified requirements. An approach to formally verified correct software should clearly separate the assumptions from the verified requirements.

- The network of Timed Automata considered so far does not take *sensors and actuators* into account. In a more realistic setting the latter represent interface devices between environment and controller. They introduce delays that should be addressed in the verification. In some cases they also introduce specific problems like sporadically occurring wrong sensor results (so-called "glitches") or new requirements that restrict the design space of the controller (for instance, that a motor must not run for more than 5 minutes to avoid overheating).

6.4.3 Separated assumptions

In this subsection we separate the environmental assumptions from the requirements and the system specification. Such a separation improves the structure of the whole verification approach. The idea is to represent the environment as a component in the network of timed automata. The communication structure of the network is shown in Figure 6.12.

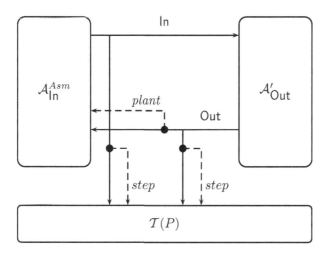

Fig. 6.12. Communication structure of the system model with separated assumptions

The automaton $\mathcal{A}_{In}^{Asm}$ models the environment and the assumptions about its behaviour. It manipulates the input observable In which is read by both the automaton $\mathcal{A}_{Out}'$ representing the controller and the test automaton $\mathcal{T}(P)$ representing the property. The latter is notified by a synchronisation via the channel *step* about input changes immediately after they have happened. This is marked by dashed arrows in the figure. The automaton $\mathcal{A}_{Out}'$ does not need such a notification because it represents a PLC-Automaton, which polls its input variables frequently. Since changes of its output Out have to be observed by the test automaton $\mathcal{T}(P)$, a synchronisation via the channel *step* is needed here as well. In general, the model of the environment needs to be informed about the actions of $\mathcal{A}'_{\mathsf{Out}}$. Hence there is an arrow from $\mathcal{A}'_{\mathsf{Out}}$ to $\mathcal{A}^{Asm}_{\mathsf{In}}$ together with a notification channel called *plant*.

Application to railroad crossing

We instantiate the communication structure in Figure 6.12 for the GRC case study by taking $\mathsf{In} = \mathit{Track}$, $\mathsf{Out} = g$, and as property P the Constraint Diagrams $CD_{\mathbf{S}}$ or $CD_{\mathbf{U}}$, respectively. Recall that the input automaton $\mathcal{A}_{\mathsf{In}}$ modifies the environmental observable In arbitrarily. For the GRC it is shown in Figure 6.7. To represent assumptions about the environment, it has to be changed to an automaton $\mathcal{A}^{Asm}_{\mathsf{In}}$ that produces admissible behaviour only. For the GRC this automaton is called $\mathcal{A}_{\mathit{Track}}$ and shown in Figure 6.13. It captures all assumptions about *Track* stated in Subsection 6.4.1. This model of the environment needs no information about the system's reaction and hence there is no need for synchronisation via a channel *plant*.

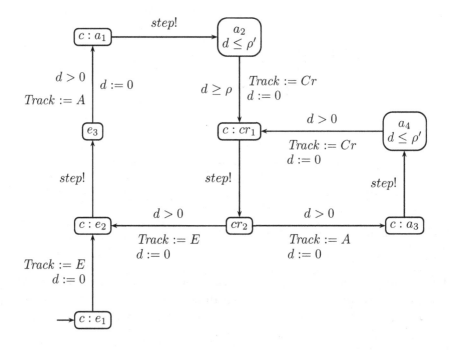

Fig. 6.13. The model $\mathcal{A}_{\mathit{Track}}$ for the assumptions about *Track*

Note that $\mathcal{A}_{\mathit{Track}}$ is equipped with appropriate committed locations and *step* edges to notify the test automaton about the changes of *Track*. The clock d is used to model duration constraints on the phases. This environment automaton starts (from location e_1) with an empty track and can proceed with an approaching phase only. The latter has to obey the assumptions about its duration, i.e. this phase has to last at least ρ seconds (the time the fastest train takes to reach the crossing) and at most ρ' seconds (the time the slowest one takes). This is represented by the invariant $d \le \rho'$ of the location a_2 and the guard $d \ge \rho$ of the outgoing edge modelling the start of the crossing phase. For this crossing phase there are no constraints about its duration except that it should be non-zero as represented by the guards $d > 0$ of the outgoing edges of location cr_2. After the crossing phase the environment can proceed with an empty phase or an approaching phase. In the first case the empty phase has to have a non-zero duration. In the second case the automaton switches back to crossing within the upper bound ρ' for the slowest train. This is represented by the invariant $d \le \rho'$ of the location a_4.

Indeed, we are now able to verify

- For the safety requirement:

$$\rho \ge \kappa + 4\varepsilon \text{ implies}$$

$$\mathcal{C}(\mathcal{A}_{Track}, \mathcal{A}'_{\mathsf{Out}}, \mathcal{T}(CD_{\mathbf{S}})) \models \forall \Box \neg \mathcal{T}(CD_{\mathbf{S}}).q_{\mathrm{bad}}. \tag{6.13}$$

- For the utility requirement:

$$\left.\begin{array}{l} \rho' < \xi_1 + \xi_2 \\ \wedge \quad \rho' - \xi_1 \le \kappa \\ \wedge \quad \varepsilon \le \frac{1}{2}\min(\xi_2,\ \xi_1 + \xi_2 - \rho') \end{array}\right\} \text{ implies}$$

$$\mathcal{C}(\mathcal{A}_{Track}, \mathcal{A}'_{\mathsf{Out}}, \mathcal{T}(CD_{\mathbf{U}})) \models \forall \Box \neg \mathcal{T}(CD_{\mathbf{U}}).q_{\mathrm{bad}}. \tag{6.14}$$

Note that in contrast to (6.10) and (6.12) in Subsection 6.4.1 we check here the original requirements $CD_{\mathbf{S}}$ and $CD_{\mathbf{U}}$ (because the assumptions about the environment are incorporated in the automaton $\mathcal{A}_{Track}$).

Similar to the approach presented there we need some constraints for the parameters to establish the results. We discuss them in the following.

$\rho \ge \kappa + 4\varepsilon$: As in (6.10) this constraint is necessary for the safety requirement; it prevents the PLC-Automaton staying in state q_2 for too long. If $\kappa > \rho - 4\varepsilon$ holds a train with maximum speed could enter the crossing before the gate is closed because in the worst case the PLC-Automaton needs 2ε to reach q_2 and $\kappa + 2\varepsilon$ afterwards to reach q_3 where the gate is closed.

$\rho' < \xi_1 + \xi_2$: This assumption is needed to *exclude* the following scenario: two successive trains are approaching and the time distance between them is large enough that, by the utility requirement, the system has to open the gate. The problem with this scenario is that the system cannot measure this time distance by observing the value of *Track*. Indeed, if the distance is too short the system could violate safety.

Thus the *physical* design of the GRC does not allow us to open the gate in between two approaching trains because we have no means to observe the time distance between these trains and to compute whether the assumptions of the utility requirement are met.

$\rho' - \xi_1 \leq \kappa$: This lower bound for κ is needed to avoid the gate being closed too early. Remember that utility requires the gate to be open at least ξ_1 time units before the approaching train reaches the gate. Hence, whenever the controller detects a new approaching train it must assume that this train runs at minimal speed and thus needs ρ' seconds to reach the crossing. In order to satisfy the utility requirement even in this case the controller must wait at least $\xi_1 - \rho'$ seconds before closing.

$\varepsilon \leq \frac{1}{2}\min(\xi_2, \xi_1 + \xi_2 - \rho')$: This constraint avoids that the gate opens too late for the utility requirement. Remember that the controller keeps the gate closed if it is closed and the track is not empty. As soon as it becomes empty the controller will react to this and open the gate within two cycles, i.e. in less than 2ε seconds. However, this behaviour is only guaranteed if the track is empty during that period. The minimal duration of the empty phase is given by the constant $\xi_1 + \xi_2 - \rho'$, thus 2ε must be less than or equal to this term. However, if $\xi_2 < \xi_1 + \xi_2 - \rho'$ holds the utility requirement is stricter than the minimal duration of the empty phase and the controller must be able to execute two cycles within ξ_2 seconds.

Note that (6.12) and (6.14) have different constraints for the parameters. These difference are due to the fact that CD'_U uses the parameter $\bar{\rho}$ which does not appear in CD_U. However, if the constraint $\varepsilon \leq \frac{1}{2}\bar{\rho}$ of (6.12) is expanded by the definition of $\bar{\rho}$ the last inequality of (6.14) follows immediately. Moreover, in Subsection 6.4.2 we showed that $\kappa \geq \xi_2 - \bar{\rho}$ implies $\rho' - \xi_1 \leq \kappa$, i.e. the second inequality of (6.12) is replaced by its consequence in (6.14).

Discussion

The approach of this subsection has clear advantages in comparison to the previous one. Isolating the environmental assumptions in a dedicated component of the timed automata network makes it simple to find out what the assumptions and what the verified properties are.

The drawback of this approach is that we are forced to construct the automaton model of the environment by hand. Although the assumptions are simple for the GRC, the environmental model is manageable but non-trivial. This model should be the most liberal automaton that satisfies all assumptions. However, there is no obvious way to check whether the constructed environment is the most liberal one. If it allows only for a strict subset of the admissible behaviour – and this can happen easily in such a handmade automaton – then it may lead to a verification result that holds in theory but not in practice. As an extreme case consider an environment automaton that leaves the track empty all the time. In this case even a controller that leaves the gate open for all times would satisfy both the safety and utility requirement.

6.4.4 Plant, sensors, and actuators

In the introduction of this book we described a real-time system as consisting of a plant, a controller, and sensors and actuators (cf. Figure 1.1). However, the previous variants of the GRC did not consider sensors and actuators at all. In reality they can make the design more complicated as they come with delays and in some cases with problems of unreliability. One can conceive sensors and actuators as parts of the environment, but this has two disadvantages:

- As physical devices, sensors and actuators are indeed part of the environment. However, it makes sense to separate the assumptions made about their behaviour from the assumption made about the plant.
- Usually, requirements refer to those variables that are observed by the sensors or manipulated by the actuators. If sensors and actuators are not separated from the plant this can be a source of misunderstandings between the engineers responsible for the requirements and those responsible for the implementation.

In this subsection we integrate sensors and actuators into the system model, leading to a communication structure shown in Figure 6.14. In contrast to Figure 6.12 the changes of In are now read by an additional timed automaton $\mathcal{A}_{Sens}$ modelling the sensor. It will be constructed in such a way

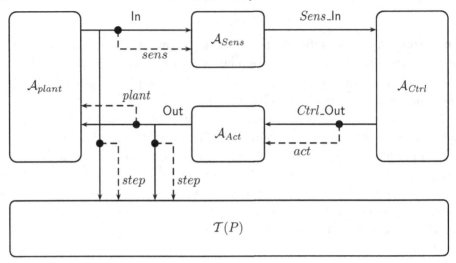

Fig. 6.14. Communication structure of the system model with plant, sensors, and actuators

that it requires a synchronisation on a new channel called *sens*. Therefore, the plant model $\mathcal{A}_{plant}$ has to be extended with additional communications *sens*! in the same way as with communications *step*! before. The sensor automaton computes a value for a new variable *Sens_In* that is polled by $\mathcal{A}_{Ctrl}$ which represents the controller. However, $\mathcal{A}_{Ctrl}$ has now *Sens_In* instead of In as its input variable and *Ctrl_Out* instead of Out as its output variable. The output of $\mathcal{A}_{Ctrl}$ is read by a second additional automaton $\mathcal{A}_{Act}$ modelling the behaviour of the actuator. It reads the output on *Ctrl_Out* if triggered via a channel *act* and computes a new value for Out. Both $\mathcal{T}(P)$ and $\mathcal{A}_{plant}$ are triggered via channel *step* or *plant*, respectively to notify this new value.

Application to railroad crossing

We instantiate the communication structure in Figure 6.14 for the GRC case study by taking

In = *Track*	ranging over	$\{E, A, Cr\},$
Sens_In = *Sens_Track*	ranging over	$\{E, A, Cr\},$
Ctrl_Out = *Ctrl_cmd*	ranging over	$\{open, close\},$ and
Out = *Act_Out*	ranging over	$\{up, dn\}.$

Sensor model $\mathcal{A}_{Sens}$: We specify a simple sensor behaviour by the automaton $\mathcal{A}_{Sens}$ given in Figure 6.16. The idea of this specification is

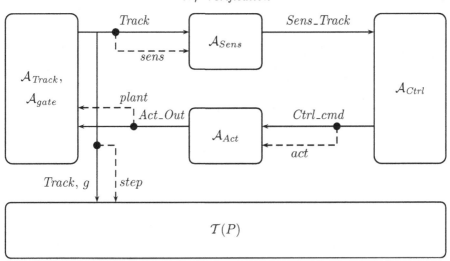

Fig. 6.15. Communication structure of the GRC with sensors and actuators

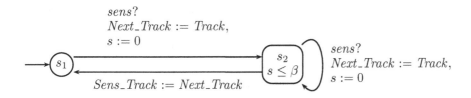

Fig. 6.16. The sensor model $\mathcal{A}_{Sens}$

that the sensor transmits the values from *Track* to *Sens_Track* with a nondeterministic delay that is bounded by a time parameter β. This is modelled by a clock s and the invariant $s \leq \beta$ of the location s_2.

Controller model $\mathcal{A}_{Ctrl}$: The controller is given by the PLC-Automaton *GRC-Ctrl* in Figure 6.17. For verification we employ the extended timed automaton $\mathcal{A}_{Ctrl} = (GRC\text{-}Ctrl)'_{Out}$ of the timed automata semantics where the variables are appropriately renamed.

Actuator model $\mathcal{A}_{Act}$: The simplest way to construct an actuator model is to design an extended timed automaton that is similar to the sensor model and reacts to changes of *Ctrl_cmd* by manipulating the value *up* and *dn* of *Act_Out* appropriately. Here, *up* stands for a mode of the actuator where it opens the gate and *dn* stands for a mode where it closes the gate.

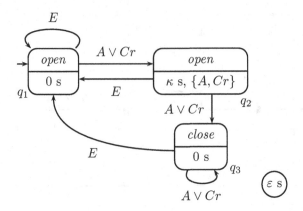

Fig. 6.17. Revised controller *GRC-Ctrl*

Our model of the actuator is given in Figure 6.18. In its initial location a_1 it expects that the controller wants an open gate. Therefore, the initial value of *Act_Out* is *up* and as long as the controller keeps *open* as output the actuator model remains in a_1. As soon as the controller switches its output to *close* and triggers the actuator model via channel *act* the timed automaton fires the transition to a_2 and resets its clock a. In location a_2 it can stay for at most α_1 time unit due to the invariant. It can always leave a_2 by firing the unconstrained transition to a_3 which sets the output *Act_Out* to *dn*, i.e. the actuator now starts to close the gate. In order to notify the gate model about this change, location a_3 is committed and therefore it has to fire the transition to a_4 without delay. This transition triggers via channel *plant* the gate model. In a_4 the actuator model can stay as long as the controller keeps the output *close*. If the controller changes the output to *open* again, then the model can execute the transitions to a_1 via a_5 and a_6 analogously. In case the controller changes its output faster than the actuator can react, the actuator model can fire the transitions between a_2 and a_5.

Plant model $\mathcal{A}_{Track}, \mathcal{A}_{gate}$: In Subsection 6.4.3 we constructed a model of the track behaviour (Figure 6.13). Here we add a second timed automaton $\mathcal{A}_{gate}$ as a specification given in Figure 6.19 of the gate. Similar to the actuator model the gate model reacts to commands of the actuator (triggered via a new channel called *plant*) immediately with a change in the value of g. In contrast to the previous models,

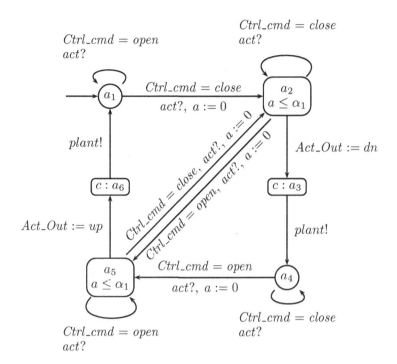

Fig. 6.18. The actuator model $\mathcal{A}_{Act}$

g now has three values. The new value is called X and stands for a gate that is currently moving and thus neither fully open (O) nor fully closed (Cl). Consider that the gate is open and $\mathcal{A}_{gate}$ is in (the initial) location g_1. As long as the actuator outputs the value up on variable Act_Out the gate model remains in g_1 and does not change g. As soon as Act_Out is set to the value dn by the actuator the gate model fires the transition to g_2 and sets the value of g to X. The purpose of g_2 being committed is to trigger the test automaton via channel $step$ by the only outgoing edge to g_3. Here the automaton may stay for a nondeterministic duration limited by the time parameter α_2. This models that the gate needs at most α_2 seconds to close. The event of the gate being closed is modelled by firing the unconstrained transition to g_4. This is again a committed location used to trigger the test automaton by the only edge to location g_5 where the automaton stays as long as the controller does not change the value of Act_Out. If the system is in g_5 and the actuator wants the gate to be open the gate model

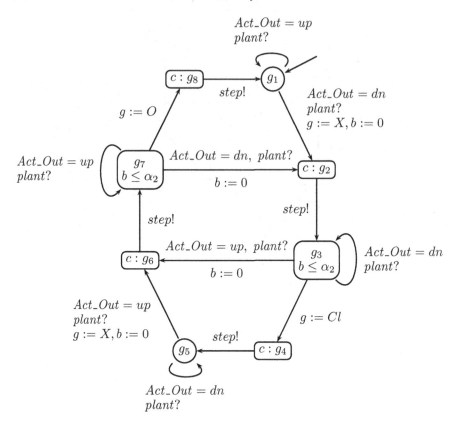

Fig. 6.19. The gate model $\mathcal{A}_{gate}$

moves towards g_1 via g_6, g_7, and g_8 in an analogous manner. Again, the duration to open the gate is limited by α_2.

In the locations g_3 and g_7 the gate model reacts to commands of the actuator although the gate has not reached the desired position. If the actuator has "changed its mind", i.e. the actuator changes *Act_Out* during the movement of the gate, the gate model will react to this appropriately. This is modelled by the transitions from g_3 to g_6 (the gate is closing but the actuator suddenly wants to open it) and from g_7 to g_2 (the gate is opening but the actuator suddenly wants to close it).

Requirement $\mathcal{T}(\mathcal{P})$: As the property P we take the requirements of the GRC given by the Constraint Diagrams $CD_\mathbf{S}$ or $CD_\mathbf{U}$, respectively. Therefore, we have the corresponding test automata as $\mathcal{T}(\mathcal{P})$ at this place.

Introducing a sensor and an actuator into the GRC model changes the behaviour of the overall system, especially timing is affected. Figure 6.20 refines Figure 6.11 and shows where the new timing parameters of both sensor and actuator come into play. Model checking this network of extended Timed Automata yields

- For the safety requirement:

$$\rho \geq \kappa + \beta + \alpha_1 + \alpha_2 + 4\varepsilon \text{ implies}$$

$$\mathcal{C}(\mathcal{A}_{Track}, \mathcal{A}_{gate}, \mathcal{A}_{Sens}, \mathcal{A}_{Ctrl}, \mathcal{A}_{Act}, \mathcal{T}(CD_{\mathbf{S}})) \models \forall \Box \neg \mathcal{T}(CD_{\mathbf{S}}).q_{\text{bad}}.$$
$$(6.15)$$

- For the utility requirement:

$$\left. \begin{array}{l} \rho' < \xi_1 + \xi_2 \\ \wedge \quad \rho' - \xi_1 \leq \kappa \\ \wedge \quad \varepsilon \leq \frac{1}{2}\min(\xi_2 - \beta - \alpha_1 - \alpha_2,\ \xi_1 + \xi_2 - \rho' - \beta) \end{array} \right\} \text{ implies}$$

$$\mathcal{C}(\mathcal{A}_{Track}, \mathcal{A}_{gate}, \mathcal{A}_{Sens}, \mathcal{A}_{Ctrl}, \mathcal{A}_{Act}, \mathcal{T}(CD_{\mathbf{U}})) \models \forall \Box \neg \mathcal{T}(CD_{\mathbf{U}}).q_{\text{bad}}.$$
$$(6.16)$$

Note that these results generalise the results in the previous subsections without the sensor and actuator model. In fact, setting the parameters β, α_1, and α_2 to 0 leads to the same inequalities as in the previous subsection.

When applying UPPAAL to verify (6.15) and (6.16) the user has to instantiate all parameters with concrete integer values because the model checker is not able to derive or prove these inequalities. For a given instantiation of the parameters it is possible to check whether the property holds. By varying a single parameter, the user is able to examine the influence of this parameter on the verification result. This leads to the inequalities as above.

6.5 The tool MOBY/RT

In this section we give an overview of the tool MOBY/RT that implements many results presented in the previous chapters within a single framework. The architecture of MOBY/RT is given in Figure 6.21. It comprises:

- Graphical editors for CDs and PLC-Automata.
- A simulator for networks of PLC-Automata with recording and playback functionality.

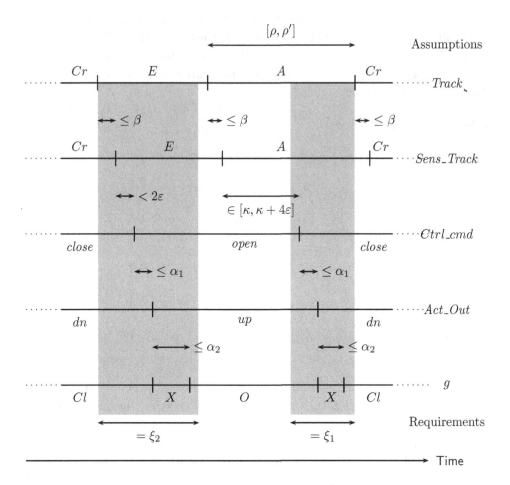

Fig. 6.20. Behaviour of the GRC with sensor and actuator

- Compilers generating code from (networks of) PLC-Automata into the programming language ST for (networks of) PLCs and for (infrared networks of) LEGO Mindstorms (so-called RCX bricks).
- A synthesis algorithm for generating PLC-Automata from DC implementables as described in Section 5.5.
- Algorithms that enable the user to verify specifications (PLC-Automata) against requirements (CDs) even without knowing the theory behind it.

For LEGO Mindstorms, MOBY/RT generates C++ code that can be compiled into executable code for the open source operating system "brickOS" (formerly known as "legOS") for Mindstorms. For verification, the tool offers the translation of an arbitrary set of PLC-Automata together with a CD into the input syntax of UPPAAL. Moreover, the necessary invocation is done automatically and the results of the model checker are presented to the user appropriately: either the requirement is satisfied or the model checker returns a counterexample. In the latter case the counterexample can be *executed* by the simulator of MOBY/RT.

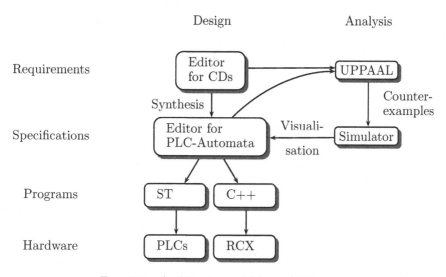

Fig. 6.21. Architecture of MOBY/RT

Figure 6.22 demonstrates the "look and feel" of MOBY/RT. The uppermost box shows a screen-shot of a system that consists of a single PLC-Automaton that corresponds to the automaton in Figure 1.11. The differences are the additional concept of typed variables and assignments to them when transitions are taken. Moreover, self-loop transitions can be omitted in MOBY/RT. The tool can also cope with hierarchical PLC-Automata.

Each of the two boxes in the middle represents a CD. Since both CDs belong to the "testable" patterns for which a timed automata semantics is given, model checking is possible. The results are displayed in the nodes below the CDs, saying that the current model has not changed semantically since the last model-checking attempt ("Export: valid"), that the result of the model checking was positive ("Result: passed"), and that hence no simulation of a counterexample is available ("Simfile: no"). The CD on the left requires the system to hold the output *Test* for less than 9.5 seconds. The CD on the right is the CD for the synchronisation implementable (cf. the proof of Theorem 3.22 in Section 3.3), instantiated for the watchdog.

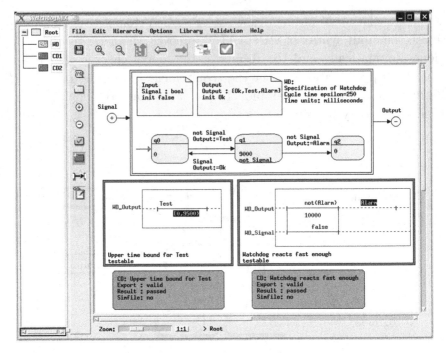

Fig. 6.22. Screen-shot of MOBY/RT

The challenge of model checking is to avoid the state-space explosion. MOBY/RT helps to do this by constructing abstractions of the timed automata models. If a PLC-Automaton $\mathcal{A}$ should satisfy a requirement $\mathcal{R}$ given in terms of a CD, then MOBY/RT feeds UPPAAL with an abstraction $abs(\mathcal{T}(\mathcal{A}))$ instead of $\mathcal{T}(\mathcal{A})$. The abstraction is specified by the user by selecting entities of PLC-Automata like variables or delays before the translation into UPPAAL input takes place.

In Figure 6.23 it is shown how verification with abstraction proceeds. There are three possible outcomes of the model-checking process:

(a) The requirement (here the CD $\mathcal{R}$) is satisfied for the abstract model (here $abs(\mathcal{T}(\mathcal{A}))$. Then $\mathcal{R}$ holds also for the full model $\mathcal{A}$ due to the construction of the abstractions.

(b) Otherwise, the property does not hold for the abstract model and the model checker returns an abstract counterexample. Then MOBY/RT invokes UPPAAL again with the *full* model $\mathcal{T}(\mathcal{A})$ together with a special test automaton which is generated from the abstract counterexample. The outcome of the second model-checking process determines the final result:

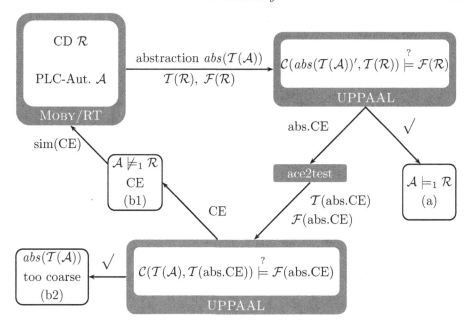

Fig. 6.23. Automatic abstraction refinement loop for PLC-Automata

(b1) If UPPAAL returns another counterexample then it is a counterexample of the full model and the original CD due to the construction of the special test automaton.

(b2) Otherwise the abstraction applied to the model was too coarse and has to be refined.

6.6 Summary

At the end of this chapter let us look back at Figure 1.12 in Chapter 1. It gives an overview of a design process which forms the backbone of the approach to formal specification and automatic verification of real-time systems proposed in this book. The approach covers three levels of abstraction:

- Requirements, specified in Duration Calculus.
- Designs, specified as PLC-Automata.
- Programs, written as C code or PLC code.

Further on:

- Automatic verification is based on timed automata and the model checker UPPAAL.

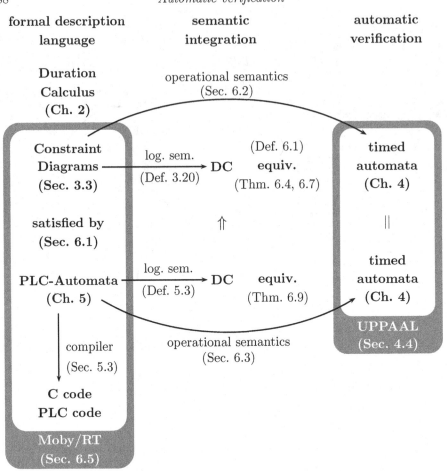

Fig. 6.24. Overview with pointers to the chapters, sections, definitions, and theorems in this book

In Figure 6.24 we refine Figure 1.12 by annotating it with pointers to the chapters, sections, definitions, and theorems in this book that support the approach.

As the most abstract way of specifying real-time requirements we introduced the declarative view of the Duration Calculus (Chapter 2). Since application experts may not be used to reading and writing logical formulas, we introduced Constraint Diagrams as a graphical way of specifying certain subsets of Duration Calculus formulas, among them DC implementables (Section 3.3). To achieve implementability of real-time systems we introduced PLC-Automata and networks thereof (Chapter 5). It was shown how to translate them into code that is executable on PLCs or any other computing device with a simple concept of timers (Section 5.3). Since both Constraint Diagrams and PLC-Automata have a logical semantics in terms of DC formulas (Definitions 3.20 and 5.3), one can employ logical implication to show that a PLC-Automaton satisfies a real-time requirement specified by a Constraint Diagram (or any other DC formula). However, such logical implication could only be established by a manual proof (which is difficult) or by applying general theorems that are proven in advance, like Theorems 5.6 and 5.8 on reaction times.

To achieve a fully automatic verification we resorted to timed automata as an operational model of real-time systems (Chapter 4) because this model comes with a well-developed model checker like UPPAAL (Section 4.4). In this book we therefore presented an automata-based approach to the verification of real-time systems. To this end, we presented in this chapter alternative operational semantics in terms of timed automata for both Constraint Diagrams and PLC-Automata. In separate publications it has been shown that the logical and the operational semantics are indeed equivalent. In this chapter we sketched only the ideas of these equivalence results (Theorems 6.4 and 6.9). The key idea of automatic verification is that a real-time system S (given as a PLC-Automaton) satisfies a requirement P (given as a Constraint Diagram) if and only if the parallel composition of a network of timed automata representing S and a timed test automaton representing P cannot reach a distinguished "bad location" in the test automaton. This reachability problem is decidable (Section 4.3) and can be verified automatically with the model checker UPPAAL. This approach is supported by the tool MOBY/RT (Section 6.5).

A proviso for the success of the automatic verification is that the network of timed automata does not get too large in the number of clocks or the number of parallel components or the size of the data. It is an ongoing research challenge to automatically verify properties of very large real-time systems (see Section 6.8).

6.7 Exercises

Exercise 6.1 (Testing counterexample formulas)
Consider Definition 6.5 and Theorem 6.7 again. Generalise both to cases where a formula or a CD can only be replaced by more than one counterexample formula.

Exercise 6.2 (Constructing test automata)
In Example 6.6 counterexample formulas for CD_S and CD_U are given. Con-

struct the test automaton for both formulas using the pattern given in Figure 6.5 and compare the results with Figures 6.2 and 6.3, respectively.

Exercise 6.3 (Test automata for track assumptions)

In Subsection 6.4.3 we constructed a timed automaton $\mathcal{A}_{Track}$ to model the assumptions about the track. All assumptions are expressed by DC implementables, which are testable. Is it possible to replace $\mathcal{A}_{Track}$ by the set of test automata constructed from the CDs specifying the assumptions about the track?

Exercise 6.4 (Parameters)

The model checker UPPAAL is not able to handle parameters as needed for example in (6.15). However, the tool can handle clock constraints of the form $x \sim v$ in which clocks are compared with data variables. Show that this can be used to verify propositions like (6.15) at least for a limited data range of the variables.

Hint: Instead of concrete integer values the parameters can appear as data variables in the models. Now add an automaton to the network that can guess all instances satisfying the inequalities up to a given limit before time passes the first time.

6.8 Bibliographic remarks

The specification of the safety and utility requirements for the case study "Generalised Railroad Crossing" in terms of Constraint Diagrams is taken from [DD97]. The construction of test automata for certain classes of Constraint Diagrams together with semantic equivalence proofs was first described by M. Lettrari in [Let00]. A conference paper on this topic is [DL02].

Counterexample formulas generalising DC implementables as in Subsection 6.2.4 appeared in [Tap01]. An extended version of these formulas allowing for the specification of events is taken as the set of real-time requirements in [Hoe06].

A timed automata semantics for PLC-Automata together with a proof of equivalence to the Duration Calculus semantics of PLC-Automata was first published in [DFMV98]. For a generalised version of PLC-Automata a corresponding result appeared in [Die00b].

The tool MOBY/RT is the result of a long-standing activity on tool support around PLC-Automata. It has been developed on top of two one-year projects, in which several students at the University of Oldenburg participated, with several Master and Ph.D. theses. An overview of the tool and its underlying theory is presented in the article [OD03], from which Section 6.5 has been adapted. As a comparative benchmark case study, the "Cash-Point Service" has been modelled and verified with MOBY/PLC, a pre-runner of MOBY/RT [DT00]. A variant of MOBY/RT dealing with parametric real-time specifications is MOBY/DC [DT03].

Automatic verification of real-time systems against requirements specified in the Duration Calculus is pushed forward in the context of the research centre AVACS (Automatic Verification and Analysis of Complex Systems, since 2004) [BPD⁺07]. One of its subprojects is called "R1: Beyond Timed Automata"; it is motivated by the observation that model checking with timed automata is limited to real-time systems with finite data only. However, reactive systems often exhibit both real-time and complex, infinite data structures. The goal of R1 is to advance the state of the art in automatic verification of high-level specifications of systems with the three dimensions of process behaviour, data, and real time – beyond the capabilities of timed automata.

In the first phase of R1, the core activities comprised the development of a system specification language, an approach to the automatic verification of real-time properties, and the application to the case study ETCS (European Train Control System). As system specification language, CSP-OZ-DC (combining subsets from Communicating Sequential Processes, Object-Z, and Duration Calculus) was developed [HO02, Hoe06]. A key result in this development was a compositional semantics on the basis of *Phase Event Automata* (PEA), an extension of timed automata to represent data [Hoe06]. It involves a translation of the DC subsets of counterexample formulas (with events) and so-called *test formulas* into equivalent PEA. It was shown that PEA can be translated into *Transition Constraint Systems* (TCS), which serve as input for the *abstraction refinement model checker* ARMC [PR07] and the deductive *slicing abstraction* model checker SLAB [BDFW07]. While ARMC is based on predicate abstraction, SLAB is a combination of deductive model checking (based on Craig interpolation) and slicing. Both tools call *decision procedures* when checking entailment of constraints [GSSW06, SSI07] as well as methods for computing interpolants [SS06, RSS07]. By combining CSP-OZ-DC with ARMC (or SLAB) and decision procedures, properties of systems with both real-time constraints and (certain) infinite data types can be verified automatically, as demonstrated by case studies [HM05]. In particular, real-time properties of *emergency messages* in the ETCS case study were verified [MFR06, FJSS07].

These core activities were complemented by research into reducing the size of the state spaces of specifications with the help of *slicing techniques*. This approach has been applied both at the level of CSP-OZ-DC [BMW06, Brü07] and at the level of TCS [BDFW07].

Another subproject of AVACS that addresses the issues of this chapter is called "R3: Heuristic Search and Abstract Model Checking of Real-Time Systems". It develops *directed model-checking* techniques that accelerate the detection of error states in real-time systems with many clocks and many concurrent components. In R3, the real-time systems are represented as networks of timed automata or of PLC-Automata (with a semantics in terms of timed automata as described in Subsection 6.3.2). Model checking is directed by *heuristics* that estimate the distance to an error state in a given real-time system by computing an *abstraction* of the system. These heuristics are integrated in a version of UPPAAL called UPPAAL/DMC [KDH+07]. Using this tool, error states in the benchmark case study "Single-track Line Segment" for trams (cf. Section 5.2) could be automatically detected. Without the abstraction-based heuristics, this case study had been intractable for automatic verification.

In R3, also a fully automatic approach for *counterexample guided abstraction refinement* [CGJ+03] of real-time systems modelled in a subset of timed automata was developed [DKL07]. This approach is implemented in the MOBY/RT tool environment and thus automates the abstraction refinement loop shown in Figure 6.23. Verification in MOBY/RT is done by constructing variable-based abstractions of the semantics in terms of timed automata which are fed into the model checker UPPAAL. Since the abstractions are over-approximations, the absence of abstract counterexamples implies a valid result for the full model. The new approach deals with the situation in which an abstract counterexample is found by UPPAAL. The generated abstract counterexample is used to construct either a concrete counterexample for the full model or, in case of a counterexample that is caused only by the abstraction, to identify a slightly refined abstraction in which this so-called *spurious* counterexample cannot occur anymore. Hence, the approach allows for a fully automatic abstraction refinement loop starting from the coarsest abstraction towards an abstraction for which a valid verification result is found. Nontrivial case studies demonstrate that this approach computes small abstractions fast without any user interaction [DKL07].

Notations

In this Appendix we collect basic mathematical notations and concepts used throughout this book because they may vary in different sources.

Logic

We assume the reader to be familiar with propositional and predicate logic. In logical formulas we use the connectives

- $\neg$ (*negation*, read as *not*),
- $\wedge$ (*conjunction*, read as *and*),
- $\vee$ (*disjunction*, read as *or*),
- $\implies$ (*implication*, read as *implies*), and
- $\iff$ (*equivalence*, read as *if and only if*)

as well as the quantifiers

- $\forall$ (*universal quantifier*, read as *for all*) and
- $\exists$ (*existential quantifier*, read as *there exists* or *for some*).

We put the symbol $\bullet$ as a separator between the quantified variables and the subsequent formula, for example,

$$\forall x \, \exists z \bullet x < z \quad \text{and} \quad \forall t \in \mathsf{Time} \bullet \neg C(t).$$

In normal text we write "iff" as a shorthand for *if and only if*. Often one wishes to introduce a shorthand for a complex logical formula or a complex expression (not yielding a truth value). In case of a formula we write $F \stackrel{\text{def}}{\iff} formula$ if F is a shorthand for the formula on the right-hand side. In case of an expression we write $e \stackrel{\text{def}}{=} expression$ if e is a shorthand for the expression on the right-hand side.

293

Mathematical proofs are often chains of equivalences between formulas. We present such chains in a special format:

$$formula_1$$
$$\Longleftrightarrow \quad \{\text{explanation why } formula_1 \Longleftrightarrow formula_2\}$$
$$formula_2$$

$$\ldots$$

$$formula_{n-1}$$
$$\Longleftrightarrow \quad \{\text{explanation why formula } formula_{n-1} \Longleftrightarrow formula_n\}$$
$$formula_n.$$

An analogous format is used for $\Longrightarrow$, and relations like $=$ or $\leq$ between expressions. Obvious explanations are omitted.

Sets

Informally, a *set* is a collection of elements. Finite sets may be specified by enumerating their elements between curly brackets. Examples are $\{0, 1\}$ and $\{empty, appr, cross\}$. Of particular interest is the set $\{\mathsf{tt}, \mathsf{ff}\}$ of truth values, standing for "true" and "false", respectively. A special case is the *empty set* $\{\}$, usually denoted by $\varnothing$. For a finite set X let $|X|$ denote its *cardinality*, i.e. the number of elements of X. For example, $|\{empty, appr, cross\}| = 3$ and $|\varnothing| = 0$.

In this book, we shall consider several infinite sets of numbers:

- $\mathbb{N}$ denotes the set of all *natural numbers* $\{0, 1, 2, 3, \ldots\}$,
- $\mathbb{Z}$ the set of all *integers* $\{\ldots, -1, 0, 1, 2, \ldots\}$,
- $\mathbb{Q}$ the set of all *rational numbers*,
- $\mathbb{Q}_{\geq 0}$ the set of all non-negative rational numbers,
- $\mathbb{R}$ the set of all *real numbers*, and
- $\mathbb{R}_{\geq 0}$ the set of all non-negative real numbers.

The notation $x \in X$ expresses that x is an *element* of the set X and $y \notin X$ that y in *not* an element of X. Sets obey the principle of *extensionality* stating that two sets are equal if they have the same elements. For example,

$$\{empty, appr, cross\} = \{cross, empty, appr, empty, cross\}.$$

The notation $X \subseteq Y$ expresses that X is a *subset* of Y, i.e. $x \in Y$ for every $x \in X$. If X is *not* a subset of Y we write $X \nsubseteq Y$. For example, $\mathbb{N} \subseteq \mathbb{R}$ and (trivially) $\mathbb{N} \subseteq \mathbb{N}$, but $\mathbb{Z} \nsubseteq \mathbb{N}$.

From a given set X a new set can be defined by considering only those elements of X that satisfy some property P. This method is called *comprehension*. We denote the new set by $\{x \in X \,|\, P\,\}$; it is a subset of X. For example,

$$M = \{n \in \mathbb{N} \,|\, \exists\, m \in \mathbb{N} \bullet n = 2 \cdot m\}$$

describes the set of all *even* natural numbers. For sets $X, Y \subseteq Z$ the following operations are well known:

$$
\begin{array}{rccl}
\textit{union} & X \cup Y & = & \{z \in Z \mid z \in X \vee z \in Y\}, \\
\textit{intersection} & X \cap Y & = & \{z \in Z \mid z \in X \wedge z \in Y\}, \\
\textit{difference} & X \setminus Y & = & \{z \in Z \mid z \in X \wedge z \notin Y\}, \\
\textit{complement} & \overline{X} & = & Z \setminus X.
\end{array}
$$

Sets X and Y are called *disjoint* if they have no element in common, i.e. if $X \cap Y = \varnothing$. The definitions of intersection and union can be generalised to the case of more than two sets. Let X_i be a set for every element i of an *index set* I. Then

$$\bigcap_{i \in I} X_i = \{a \,|\, a \in X_i \text{ for all } i \in I\},$$
$$\bigcup_{i \in I} X_i = \{a \,|\, a \in X_i \text{ for some } i \in I\}.$$

Let $\mathcal{P}(X)$ denote the *power set* of a set X, i.e. the set of all subsets of X:

$$\mathcal{P}(X) = \{X \,|\, Z \subseteq X\}.$$

Note that in particular $\varnothing \in \mathcal{P}(X)$ and $X \in \mathcal{P}(X)$.

The *Cartesian product* $X \times Y$ of two sets X and Y is the set consisting of all pairs where the first component is an element of X and the second component is an element of Y:

$$X \times Y = \{(x, y) \,|\, x \in X \wedge y \in Y\}.$$

More generally, the *n-fold Cartesian product* $X_1 \times \cdots \times X_n$ of sets $X_1, \ldots, X_n$ is the set consisting of all n-tuples where the ith component is an element of A_i for all $i \in \{1, \ldots, n\}$:

$$X_1 \times \cdots \times X_n = \{(x_1, \ldots, x_n) \,|\, x_1 \in X_1 \wedge \cdots \wedge X_n\}.$$

If all the X_i are the same set X, the n-fold Cartesian product $X \times \cdots \times X$ of X with itself is also written as X^n, the *nth power* of X.

Relations

Relations are special sets. A (*binary*) *relation* R between sets X and Y is a subset of the Cartesian product $X \times Y$; that is, $R \subseteq X \times Y$. If $X = Y$ then

R is called a *relation on* X. For example, the set

$$\{(a, 1), (b, 2), (c, 2)\}$$

is a binary relation between $\{a, b, c\}$ and $\{1, 2\}$. For elements (x, y) of a binary relation R we also write $x \mapsto y$, and membership $(x, y) \in R$ is often written in *infix notation* $x \, R \, y$.

More generally, for any natural number n an *n-ary relation* R between $X_1, \ldots, X_n$ is a subset of the n-fold Cartesian product $X_1 \times \cdots \times X_n$; that is, $R \subseteq X_1 \times \cdots \times X_n$. Note that 2-ary relations are the same as binary relations. Instead of 1-ary and 3-ary relations one talks of *unary* and *ternary* relations, respectively.

The *identity relation* on X is defined by $id_X = \{(x, x) \mid x \in X\}$. The *inverse relation* of $R \subseteq X \times Y$ is $R^{-1} \subseteq Y \times X$, defined as follows:

$$\forall x \in X, y \in Y \bullet (x, y) \in R \iff (y, x) \in R^{-1}.$$

The *composition* $\circ$ of two relations $R \subseteq X \times Y$ and $S \subseteq Y \times Z$ is defined for all $x \in X$ and $z \in Z$ as follows:

$$(x, z) \in R \circ S \iff \exists \, y \in Y \bullet (x, y) \in R \wedge (y, z) \in S.$$

Consider a relation R on a set X. R is called *reflexive* if $(a, a) \in R$ for all $x \in X$, it is called *symmetric* if for all $x, y \in X$ whenever $(x, y) \in R$ then also $(y, x) \in R$, and it is called *transitive* if for all $x, y, z \in X$ whenever $(x, y) \in R$ and $(y, z) \in R$ then also $(x, z) \in R$.

A relation R on X that is reflexive, symmetric and transitive is called an *equivalence relation*. To each element $x \in X$ we can associate the set of elements that are equivalent to x. This set is called the *equivalence class* of x and denoted by

$$[x]_R = \{y \in X \mid (x, y) \in R\}.$$

If R is clear from the context we write $[x]$ instead of $[x]_R$. The element x is called a *representative* of $[x]$ because the whole class can be generated from x by taking equivalent elements. Note that for all elements $x, y \in X$

$$(x, y) \in R \iff [x] = [y] \quad \text{and} \quad (x, y) \notin R \iff [x] \cap [y] = \varnothing.$$

Thus the set X is partitioned into disjoint equivalence classes of R.

The *reflexive, transitive closure* R^* of a relation R on a set X is the *smallest* reflexive and transitive relation on X that contains R as a subset. The *relational composition* $R_1 \circ R_2$ of relations R_1 and R_2 on a set X is defined as follows:

$$R_1 \circ R_2 = \{(a, c) \mid \exists b \in A \bullet (a, b) \in R_1 \wedge (b, c) \in R_2\}.$$

For any natural number n the *n-fold composition* R^n of a relation R on a set X is defined inductively as follows:

$$R^0 = id_X \quad \text{and} \quad R^{n+1} = R \circ R^n.$$

Then the equation

$$R^* = \bigcup_{n \in \mathbb{N}} R^n$$

holds.

Functions

Functions are special relations. A relation $f \subseteq X \times Y$ is called a *partial function* (or *partial mapping*) from X to Y if for each element $x \in X$ there is *at most one* element $y \in Y$ with $x \, f \, y$. In that case we write

$$f : X \xrightarrow{part} Y.$$

The set X is called the *domain* of f and Y the *co-domain* of f. Instead of $(x, y) \in f$ or $x \, f \, y$ we write *function application* in prefix notation: $f(x) = y$.

If for each element $x \in X$ there is *exactly one* element $y \in Y$ with $f(x) = y$ then f is called a *(total) function* (or *mapping* or *operation*) from X to Y. In that case we write

$$f : X \longrightarrow Y.$$

Here $X \longrightarrow Y$ denotes the set of all functions from X to Y. It can itself be the domain or co-domain of a function. For example, for sets X, Y, Z we may consider a function

$$g : X \longrightarrow (Y \longrightarrow Z).$$

Then for all $x \in X$ and $y \in Y$ we have $g(x) : Y \longrightarrow Z$ and $g(x)(y) \in Z$.

We are sometimes interested in functions with special properties. A function $f : X \longrightarrow Y$ is called an *injection* if $f(x_1) \neq f(x_2)$ for any two distinct elements $x_1, x_2 \in X$; it is called a *surjection* if for every element $y \in Y$ there exists an element $x \in X$ with $f(x) = y$; it is called a *bijection* if it is both an injection and a surjection.

Real numbers

In this book (non-negative) real numbers are taken as the time domain. Therefore, we use various notations for real numbers. The binary relations $<, \leq, >, \geq \, \subseteq \mathbb{R} \times \mathbb{R}$ denoting *less than, at most, greater than* and *at least,* respectively, should be clear, as well as the binary functions $+, -, \cdot : \mathbb{R} \longrightarrow \mathbb{R}$ of *addition, subtraction* and *multiplication*, respectively. *Division* x/y or $\frac{x}{y}$ is defined only partially when the divisor satisfies $y \neq 0$.

Real numbers can be approximated by integers. For $x \in \mathbb{R}$ let $\lfloor x \rfloor \in \mathbb{Z}$, the *floor* of x, be the unique integer m with $m \leq x < m + 1$, and $\lceil x \rceil \in \mathbb{Z}$, the *ceiling* of x, be the unique integer n with $n - 1 < x \leq n$. Further on, we define the *fraction* of x by $frac(x) = x - \lfloor x \rfloor$. For example, $\lfloor 1.314 \rfloor = 1$ and $\lceil 1.314 \rceil = 2$ and $frac(x) = 0.314$.

For a non-empty finite set $X \subseteq \mathbb{R}$ let $\min X$ denote the *minimum* of all real numbers in X, and analogously $\max X$ the *maximum*. For two elements, we write $min(x, y)$ instead of $min\{x, y\}$, and analogously for the maximum.

We often consider *intervals*. For $b, e \in \mathbb{R}$ the *closed* interval of real numbers between b and e is

$$[b, e] = \{x \in \mathbb{R} \mid b \leq x \leq e\},$$

and the *open* interval is $(b, e) = \{x \in \mathbb{R} \mid b < x < e\}$. *Half-open* intervals like $(b, e]$ or $[b, e)$ are defined analogously.

From mathematical analysis we use the concept of *Riemann integral*. For an integrable function $f : \mathbb{R} \longrightarrow \mathbb{R}$ and an interval $[b, e] \subseteq \mathbb{R}$ let

$$\int_b^e f(t)dt$$

denote the integral of f on $[b, e]$. In the applications it will be clear that the functions considered are indeed integrable.

Words and languages

An *alphabet* is a finite set of symbols. We use Σ as a typical name for an alphabet and a, b, c for symbols, i.e. elements of Σ. A *word* over Σ is a finite string of symbols from Σ. Special cases are the *empty word* ε (without any symbol) and words consisting of a single symbol only. We use u, v, w as typical names for words. Let Σ^* denote the set of all words over Σ. Then $\varepsilon \in \Sigma^*$ and $\Sigma \subseteq \Sigma^*$. By $|u|$ we denote the *length* of the word u, i.e. the number of symbols from Σ occurring in it. Note that $|\varepsilon| = 0$.

The *concatenation* $u \cdot v$ of words u and v yields the word uv formed by first writing u and then writing v, without intervening space. By $\leq$ we denote the *prefix relation* over words defined as follows:

$$u \leq w \quad \text{iff} \quad \exists u : w = u \cdot v.$$

We then say that u is a *prefix* of w. Special cases are $\varepsilon \leq w$ and $w \leq w$.

Example A.1
Consider the alphabet $\Sigma = \{1, 2, +\}$. Then $1+$ and $2+0$ are words over Σ with $|1+| = 2$ and $|2+0| = 3$. The concatenation of $1+$ and $2+0$ yields $1+2+0$. The prefixes of $1+2+0$ are $\varepsilon, 1, 1+, 1+2, 1+2+,$ and $1+2+0$. ∎

A *(formal) language* over the alphabet Σ is a subset of Σ^*. We use L as a typical name for a language. To languages L, L_1, L_2 we can apply the set operations of

$$
\begin{array}{rl}
\text{union} & L_1 \cup L_2\,, \\
\text{intersection} & L_1 \cap L_2\,, \\
\text{difference} & L_1 \setminus L_2\,, \\
\text{complement} & \overline{L} = \Sigma^* \setminus L\,.
\end{array}
$$

Moreover, there are special operations on languages. The *concatenation* is lifted from words to languages L_1 and L_2 by defining

$$
L_1 \cdot L_2 = \{u \cdot v \mid u \in L_1 \text{ and } v \in L_2\}.
$$

The *nth power* of a language L is defined inductively:

$$
L^0 = \{\varepsilon\} \quad \text{and} \quad L^{n+1} = L \cdot L^n.
$$

The *iteration* or *Kleene star* of L is defined by

$$
L^* = \bigcup_{n \in \mathbb{N}} L^n = \{w_1 \ldots w_n \mid n \in \mathbb{N} \text{ and } w_1, \ldots, w_n \in L\}.
$$

Note that $\varepsilon \in L^*$. To exclude the empty word, one also considers the *non-empty iteration* L^+ defined by $L^+ = L \cdot L^*$.

Finite automata and regular languages

To represent computational processes one uses abstract machines. The simplest model of such a machine is the *finite automaton*. It is a structure $\mathcal{A} = (Q, \Sigma, \delta, q_0, F)$ where

- Q is a finite set of *states*, with typical element q,
- Σ is a finite *input alphabet*, with typical elements a, b, c,
- $\delta : Q \times \Sigma \longrightarrow \mathcal{P}(Q)$ is the *transition function*,
- $q_0 \in Q$ is the *initial* state,
- $F \subseteq Q$ is the set of *final* states.

In classical automata theory, finite automata serve as acceptors of languages. Note that $\mathcal{A}$ is defined as a *nondeterministic* automaton since $\delta(q, a)$ yields a *set* of possible successor states. A *deterministic* finite automaton is one where $\delta(q, a)$ always yields a singleton set. In that case the transition function is defined as $\delta : Q \times \Sigma \longrightarrow Q$. For finite automata, nondeterminism does not extend the class of accepted languages but it can result in substantially smaller state spaces.

It is convenient to represent the transition function as a ternary *transition relation* $\rightarrow \subseteq Q \times \Sigma \times Q$ or as a set of *labelled* binary transition relations

$$\overset{a}{\longrightarrow} \subseteq Q \times Q,$$

one for each symbol $a \in \Sigma$. By definition, these notations are related as follows:

$$q' \in \delta(q, a) \quad \text{iff} \quad (q, a, q') \in \rightarrow \quad \text{iff} \quad q \overset{a}{\longrightarrow} q'$$

for all $q, q' \in Q$ and $a \in \Sigma$. Informally, $q \overset{a}{\longrightarrow} q'$ expresses that the automaton $\mathcal{A}$ can move from state q to state q' by accepting input a. We say that $q \overset{a}{\longrightarrow} q'$ is a *transition labelled with a*. At the level of transitions, *nondeterminism* is visible if at a given state several transitions are possible for the same input label, for example,

$$q \overset{a}{\longrightarrow} q_1 \quad \text{and} \quad q \overset{a}{\longrightarrow} q_2.$$

An advantage of this representation is that binary relations can be composed. For example,

$$\overset{a}{\longrightarrow} \circ \overset{b}{\longrightarrow}$$

denotes the two-step transition of first accepting input a and then input b. This way, the relations $\overset{a}{\longrightarrow}$ for individual symbols a can easily be extended to relations $\overset{w}{\longrightarrow}$ for words $w \in \Sigma^*$. The definition proceeds inductively.

- *Induction basis*: $w = \varepsilon$.
  Then $\overset{\varepsilon}{\longrightarrow} = id_Q$.

  That is, $q \overset{\varepsilon}{\longrightarrow} q'$ iff $q = q'$ holds for all $q, q' \in Q$.
- *Induction step*: $w = av$ for $a \in \Sigma$ and $v \in \Sigma^*$.
  Then $\overset{av}{\longrightarrow} = \overset{a}{\longrightarrow} \circ \overset{v}{\longrightarrow}$.

  That is, $q \overset{av}{\longrightarrow} q'$ iff $\exists\, q'' \in Q \bullet q \overset{a}{\longrightarrow} q''$ and $q'' \overset{v}{\longrightarrow} q'$ holds for all $q, q' \in Q$.

A state q is called *reachable* in $\mathcal{A}$ if $q_0 \xrightarrow{w} q$ holds for some $w \in \Sigma^*$. The automaton $\mathcal{A}$ *accepts* a word w if $q_0 \xrightarrow{w} q$ for some final state q. Thus the *accepted language* of $\mathcal{A}$ is defined as

$$\mathcal{L}(\mathcal{A}) = \{\, w \in \Sigma^* \mid \exists q \in F \bullet q_0 \xrightarrow{w} q \,\}.$$

A language L is called *regular* if $L = \mathcal{L}(\mathcal{A})$ for some finite automaton $\mathcal{A}$. The *set* of regular languages over Σ contains

- the empty set $\varnothing$,
- the set $\{\varepsilon\}$ containing the empty word,
- the singleton set $\{a\}$, for every symbol $a \in \Sigma$,

and is closed under the operations of

- union,
- intersection,
- complement,
- concatenation,
- iteration, and
- non-empty iteration.

It is well known that finite automata can be represented graphically.

Example A.2
The automaton $\mathcal{A} = (Q, \Sigma, \delta, q_0, F)$ with $Q = \{q_0, q_1, q_2\}$, $\Sigma = \{a, b, c\}$, $\delta(q_0, a) = \{q_0, q_1\}$, $\delta(q_0, b) = \{q_0\}$, $\delta(q_0, c) = \{q_0\}$, $\delta(q_1, b) = \{q_2\}$ and $F = \{q_2\}$ is represented as follows:

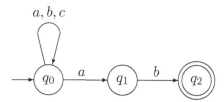

Note that $\mathcal{A}$ is indeed nondeterministic: when accepting a in the initial state q_0 it can either stay in q_0 or move to q_1. The accepted language is

$$\mathcal{L}(\mathcal{A}) = \{wab \mid w \in \Sigma^*\},$$

the set of all words over Σ ending in ab. For example, $abcaacab \in \mathcal{L}(\mathcal{A})$ but $abcaaca \notin \mathcal{L}(\mathcal{A})$. ∎

For finite automata and regular languages various problems are algorithmically decidable. In this book, we refer to three problems.

The *reachability problem* is defined as follows:

Given: A finite automaton $\mathcal{A}$ and a state q.
Question: Is q reachable in $\mathcal{A}$?

The *emptiness problem* is defined as follows:

Given: A regular language L.
Question: Is $L = \varnothing$?

The *infinity problem* is defined as follows:

Given: A regular language L.
Question: Is L an infinite set?

The decidability proofs of the last two problems rest on the *pumping lemma* for regular languages, which in turn exploits the finiteness of the set of states of the accepting automata.

Transition systems

In this book we consider certain kinds of *reactive systems* that continuously interact with their environment by reacting to inputs from the environment with certain outputs. Operationally, such systems can be described by an extension of the finite automaton model called a (*labelled*) *transition system*. This is a structure

$$\mathcal{T} = (C, \Lambda, \{\xrightarrow{\lambda} \mid \lambda \in \Lambda\}, C_0)$$

where:

- C is a (possibly infinite) set of *configurations*, with typical element c.
- Λ is a (possibly infinite) set of *labels*, with typical element λ.
- For each label $\lambda \in \Lambda$ there is a *transition relation* $\xrightarrow{\lambda} \subseteq C \times C$, consisting of all transitions of $\mathcal{T}$ labelled with λ.
- $C_0 \in C$ is the set of *initial* configurations.

Notice the following differences compared with finite automata. The finite sets of states and input symbols are replaced by possibly *infinite* sets of configurations and labels. The unique initial state is replaced by a *set* of initial configurations. There are *no final* states because the purpose of a labelled transition system is not to accept words of labels but to define in which computation paths it can engage. Formally, a *computation path* of a labelled transition system $\mathcal{T}$ is a sequence

$$c_0 \xrightarrow{\lambda_1} c_1 \xrightarrow{\lambda_2} c_2 \xrightarrow{\lambda_3} \cdots$$

of labelled transitions starting in an initial configuration $c_0 \in C_0$ with $c_i \in C$ and $\lambda_i \in \Lambda$ for $i \geq 1$ that is either infinite or maximally finite, i.e. the sequence cannot be extended any further by some transition.

Bibliographic remarks

For an introduction to logic the reader may consult the books by D. Gabbay [Gab98], or by H.-D. Ebbinghaus, J. Flum and W. Thomas [EFT96]. The symbol • as a separator in quantified formulas is taken from the specification language Z (see e.g. [WD96]). Mathematical proofs are often chains of equalities between expressions. The proof format for chains of equivalences or equalities was suggested by E.W. Dijkstra and C.S. Scholten [DS90].

The concepts and notations for sets, relations, and functions are introduced in most undergraduate mathematical textbooks (see e.g. [Hal98]). An introduction to mathematical analysis can be found, for example, in the book by W. Rudin [Rud76]. For an introduction to automata theory, formal languages and decidability we refer to the classic book by J.E. Hopcroft and J.D. Ullman [HU79] or its extended version [HMU01].

The notion of a transition system is due to R.M. Keller [Kel76]. The systematic and structured use of transition systems for the definition of the semantics of programming and specification languages was advocated by G.D. Plotkin [Plo81].

Bibliography

[ABL96]   J.R. Abrial, E. Börger, and H. Langmaack, editors. *Formal Methods for Industrial Applications: Specifying and Programming the Steam Boiler Control*, volume 1165 of *Lecture Notes in Computer Science*. Springer, 1996.

[ACD93]   R. Alur, C. Courcoubetis, and D. Dill. Model-checking in dense real-time. *Information and Computation*, 104(1):2–34, 1993.

[AD94]   R. Alur and D.L. Dill. A theory of timed automata. *Theoretical Computer Science*, 126:183–235, 1994.

[AILS07]   L. Aceto, A. Ingólfsdóttir, K.G. Larsen, and J. Srba. *Reactive Systems – Modelling, Specification and Verification*. Cambridge University Press, 2007.

[AL92]   M. Abadi and L. Lamport. An old-fashioned recipe for real time. In J.W. de Bakker, C. Huizing, W.-P. de Roever, and G. Rozenberg, editors. *Real-Time: Theory in Practice*, volume 600 of *Lecture Notes in Computer Science*, pages 1–27. Springer, June 1992.

[Alu98]   R. Alur. Timed automata. In *Verification of Digital and Hybrid Systems*, NATO ASI Series. Springer, 1998. Marktoberdorf Summer School.

[AS85]   B. Alpern and F.B. Schneider. Defining liveness. *Information Processing Letters*, 21(4):181–185, October 1985.

[AS87]   B. Alpern and F.B. Schneider. Recognizing safety and liveness. *Distributed Computing*, 2:117–126, 1987.

[Bac90]   R.J.R. Back. Refinement calculus, part II: Parallel and reactive programs. In J.W. de Bakker, W.-P. de Roever, and G. Rozenberg, editors. *Stepwise Refinement of Distributed Systems: Models, Formalisms, Correctness*, volume 430 of *Lecture Notes in Computer Science*, pages 67–93. Springer, 1990.

[BB91]   J. Baeten and J. Bergstra. Real time process algebra. *Formal Aspects of Computing*, 3:142–188, 1991.

[BBD+02]   G. Behrmann, J. Bengtsson, A. David, K.G. Larsen, P. Pettersson, and W. Yi. UPPAAL implementation secrets. In Damm and Olderog [DO02], pages 2–22.

[BDFW07]   I. Brückner, K. Dräger, B. Finkbeiner, and H. Wehrheim. Slicing abstractions. In F. Arbab and M. Sirjani, editors. *International Symposium on Fundamentals of Software Engineering*, volume 4767 of *Lecture Notes in Computer Science*, pages 17–32. Springer, 2007.

[BdS91]   F. Boussinot and R. de Simone. The ESTEREL language. *Proceedings of the IEEE*, 79(9):1293–1304, September 1991.

[BE02]   N. Bauer and S. Engell. A comparison of sequential function charts and statecharts and an approach towards integration. In *Workshop: Integration of Software Specification Techniques*, ETAPS, pages 58–69, 2002.

[Bel57] R. Bellman. *Dynamic Programming*. Princeton University Press, 1957.

[BHL+96] J. Bowen, C.A.R. Hoare, H. Langmaack, E.-R. Olderog, and A.P. Ravn. *ProCoS II: A ProCoS II Project Final Report*, chapter 7, pages 76–99. Number 59 in Bulletin of the EATCS. European Association for Theoretical Computer Science, June 1996.

[Bir35] G. Birkhoff. On the structure of abstract algebras. *Proceedings of the Cambridge Philosophical Society*, 31:433–454, 1935.

[BlGJ91] A. Benveniste, P. le Guernic, and C. Jacquemot. Synchronous programming with events and relations: the SIGNAL language and its semantics. *Science of Computer Programming*, 16(2):103–149, September 1991.

[BM02] J.C.M. Baeten and C.A. Middelburg. *Process Algebra with Timing*. Monographs in Theoretical Computer Science. An EATCS Series. Springer, 2002.

[BMW06] I. Brückner, B. Metzler, and H. Wehrheim. Optimizing slicing of formal specifications by deductive verification. *Nordic Journal of Computing*, 13(1–2):22–45, August 2006.

[BPD+07] B. Becker, A. Podelski, W. Damm, M. Fränzle, E.-R. Olderog, and R. Wilhelm. SFB/TR 14 AVACS – automatic verification and analysis of complex systems. *it – Information Technology*, 49(2):118–126, 2007. See also `http://www.avacs.org`.

[Brü07] I. Brückner. Slicing concurrent real-time system specifications for verification. In J. Davies and J. Gibbons, editors. *IFM 2007: Sixth International Conference on Integrated Formal Methods*, volume 4591 of *Lecture Notes in Computer Science*, pages 54–74. Springer, July 2007.

[But02] G. Buttazzo. Real-time operating systems: Problems and novel solutions. In Damm and Olderog [DO02], pages 37–51.

[BW90] J.C.M. Baeten and W.P. Weijland. *Process Algebra*. Cambridge University Press, 1990.

[BW01] A. Burns and A. Wellings. *Real-Time Systems and Programming Languages*. Addison-Wesley, 3rd edition, 2001.

[BY03] J. Bengtsson and W. Yi. Timed automata: Semantics, algorithms and tools. In J. Desel, W. Reisig, and G. Rozenberg, editors. *Lectures on Concurrency and Petri Nets*, volume 3098 of *Lecture Notes in Computer Science*, pages 87–124. Springer, 2003.

[CE81] E.M. Clarke and E.A. Emerson. Synthesis of synchronization skeletons for branching time temporal logic. In D. Kozen, editor. *Logic of Programs*, volume 131 of *Lecture Notes in Computer Science*, pages 52–71. Springer, May 1981.

[CES86] E.M. Clarke, E.A. Emerson, and A.P. Sistla. Automatic verification of finite-state concurrent systems using temporal logic specifications. *ACM Transactions on Programming Languages and Systems*, 8:244–263, 1986.

[CGJ+03] E.M. Clarke, O. Grumberg, Somesh Jha, Yuan Lu, and H. Veith. Counterexample-guided abstraction refinement for symbolic model checking. *Journal of the ACM*, 50(5):752–794, 2003.

[CGP00] E.M. Clarke, O. Grumberg, and D. Peled. *Model Checking*. MIT Press, 2000.

[CPHP87] P. Caspi, D. Pilaud, N. Halbwachs, and J. Plaice. LUSTRE: A declarative language for programming synchronous systems. In *14th ACM Symposium on Principles of Programming Languages*, January 1987.

[Dal04] D. van Dalen. *Logic and Structure*. Springer, 4th edition, 2004.

[Dav93] J.W. Davies. *Specification and Proof in Real-Time CSP*. Cambridge University Press, 1993.

[DD97] H. Dierks and C. Dietz. Graphical specification and reasoning: Case study "Generalized Railroad Crossing". In J. Fitzgerald, C.B. Jones, and P. Lucas, editors. *FME'97*, volume 1313 of *Lecture Notes in Computer Science*, pages 20–39, Graz, Austria, September 1997. Springer.

[DFMV98] H. Dierks, A. Fehnker, A. Mader, and F.W. Vaandrager. Operational and logical semantics for polling real-time systems. In A.P. Ravn and H. Rischel, editors. *FTRTFT'98*, volume 1486 of *Lecture Notes in Computer Science*, pages 29–40, Lyngby, Denmark, September 1998. Springer.

[DH01] W. Damm and D. Harel. LSCs: Breathing life into message sequence charts. *Formal Methods in System Design*, 19(1):45–80, 2001.

[Die96] C. Dietz. Graphical formalization of real-time requirements. In Jonsson and Parrow [JP96], pages 366–385.

[Die97] H. Dierks. Synthesising controllers from real-time specifications. In *Tenth International Symposium on System Synthesis*, pages 126–133. IEEE Computer Society Press, September 1997. Short version of [Die99].

[Die99] H. Dierks. Synthesizing controllers from real-time specifications. *IEEE Transactions on Computer-Aided Design of Integrated Circuits and Systems*, 18:33–43, 1999.

[Die00a] H. Dierks. PLC-Automata: A new class of implementable real-time automata. *Theoretical Computer Science*, 253(1):61–93, 2000.

[Die00b] H. Dierks. *Specification and Verification of Polling Real-Time Systems*. PhD thesis, Report Nr. 1/2000, University of Oldenburg, January 2000.

[Die06] H. Dierks. Time, abstraction and heuristics – automatic verification and planning of timed systems using abstraction and heuristics. Technical report, Nr. 1/06, University of Oldenburg, January 2006. Habilitationsschrift.

[DKL07] H. Dierks, S. Kupferschmid, and K.G. Larsen. Automatic abstraction refinement for timed automata. In J.-F. Raskin and P.S. Thiagarajan, editors. *Formal Modelling and Analysis of Timed Systems (FORMATS 2007)*, volume 4763 of *Lecture Notes in Computer Science*, pages 114–129. Springer, 2007.

[DL02] H. Dierks and M. Lettrari. Constructing test automata from graphical real-time requirements. In Damm and Olderog [DO02], pages 433–453.

[DO02] W. Damm and E.-R. Olderog, editors. *Formal Techniques in Real-Time and Fault-Tolerant Systems*, volume 2469 of *Lecture Notes in Computer Science*. Springer, 2002.

[Dri88] L. van den Dries. Alfred Tarski's elimination theory for real closed fields. *Journal of Symbolic Logic*, 53(1):7–19, 1988.

[DS90] E.W. Dijkstra and C.S. Scholten. *Predicate Calculus and Program Semantics*. Springer, 1990.

[DS95] J.W. Davies and S.A. Schneider. A brief history of timed csp. *Theoretical Computer Science*, 138(2):243–271, 1995.

[DT00] H. Dierks and J. Tapken. Modelling and verifying of 'cash-point service' using moby/plc. *Formal Aspects of Computing*, 12:221–222, 2000.

[DT03] H. Dierks and J. Tapken. Moby/DC – a tool for model-checking parametric real-time specifications. In *Tools and Algorithms for the Construction and Analysis of Systems (TACAS)*, volume 2619 of *Lecture Notes in Computer Science*, pages 271–277. Springer, 2003.

[Dut95] B. Dutertre. Complete proof systems for first order interval temporal logic. In *Tenth IEEE Annual Symposium on Logic in Computer Science*, pages 36–43.

IEEE Press, 1995.

[EFT96] H.-D. Ebbinghaus, J. Flum, and W. Thomas. *Mathematical Logic.* Springer, 2nd edition, 1996.

[FH07] M. Fränzle and M.R. Hansen. Deciding an interval logic with accumulated durations. In Orna Grumberg and Michael Huth, editors. *Tools and Algorithms for the Construction and Analysis of Systems (TACAS)*, volume 4424 of *Lecture Notes in Computer Science*, pages 201–215. Springer, 2007.

[FJSS07] J. Faber, S. Jacobs, and V. Sofronie-Stokkermans. Verifying CSP-OZ-DC specifications with complex data types and timing parameters. In J. Davies and J. Gibbons, editors. *Integrated Formal Methods*, volume 4591 of *Lecture Notes in Computer Science*, pages 233–252. Springer, July 2007.

[Frä04] M. Fränzle. Model-checking dense-time duration calculus. *Formal Aspects of Computing*, 16(2):121–139, 2004.

[FVH02] K. Fischer and B. Vogel-Heuser. UML for real-time applications in automation. *Automatisierungstechnische Praxis*, 44, 2002. In German.

[FW96] S. Fowler and A. Wellings. Formal analysis of a real-time kernel specification. In Jonsson and Parrow [JP96], pages 440–458.

[Gab98] D. Gabbay. *Elementary Logics: A Procedural Perspective.* Prentice-Hall International, 1998.

[GNRR93] R. Grossmann, A. Nerode, A. Ravn, and H. Rischel, editors. *Hybrid Systems*, volume 736 of *Lecture Notes in Computer Science.* Springer, 1993.

[GSSW06] H. Ganzinger, V. Sofronie-Stokkermans, and U. Waldmann. Modular proof systems for partial functions with Evans equality. *Information and Computation*, 204(10):1453–1492, 2006.

[Hal98] P.R. Halmos. *Naive Set Theory.* Undergraduate Text in Mathematics. Springer, 1998.

[Har87] D. Harel. Statecharts: A visual formalism for complex systems. *Science of Computer Programming*, 8(3):231–274, June 1987.

[HC68] G.E. Hughes and M.J. Cresswell. *An Introduction to Modal Logic.* Methuen, 1968.

[Hei99] S.T. Heilmann. *Proof Support for Duration Calculus.* PhD thesis, Department of Computer Science, Technical University of Denmark, January 1999.

[HHF+94] He Jifeng, C.A.R. Hoare, M. Fränzle, M. Müller-Olm, E.-R. Olderog, M. Schenke, M.R. Hansen, A.P. Ravn, and H. Rischel. Provably correct systems. In H. Langmaack, W.-P. de Roever, and J. Vytopil, editors. *Formal Techniques in Real-Time and Fault-Tolerant Systems*, volume 863 of *Lecture Notes in Computer Science*, pages 288–335, Lübeck, Germany, September 1994. Springer.

[HHW97] T.A. Henzinger, P.-H. Ho, and H. Wong-Toi. HyTech: a model checker for hybrid systems. *STTT – International Journal on Software Tools for Technology Transfer*, 1(1+2):110–122, December 1997.

[HL94] C. Heitmeyer and N. Lynch. The generalized railroad crossing. In *IEEE Real-Time Systems Symposium*, pages 120–131. IEEE Computer Society Press, 1994.

[HM96] C. Heitmeyer and D. Mandrioli, editors. *Formal Methods for Real-Time Computing*, volume 5 of *Trends in Software.* Wiley, 1996.

[HM05] J. Hoenicke and P. Maier. Model-checking of specifications integrating processes, data and time. In J.S. Fitzgerald, I.J. Hayes, and A. Tarlecki, editors. *FM 2005*, volume 3582 of *Lecture Notes in Computer Science*, pages 465–480. Springer, 2005.

[HMU01] J.E. Hopcroft, R. Motwani, and J.D. Ullman. *Introduction to Automata Theory, Langages, and Computation.* Addison-Wesley, 2nd edition, 2001.

[HNSY94] T. Henzinger, X. Nicollin, J. Sifakis, and S. Yovine. Symbolic model checking for real-time systems. *Information and Computation,* 111:193–244, 1994.

[HO02] J. Hoenicke and E.-R. Olderog. CSP-OZ-DC: A combination of specification techniques for processes, data and time. *Nordic Journal of Computing,* 9(4):301–334, 2002.

[Hoa85] C.A.R. Hoare. *Communicating Sequential Processes.* Prentice-Hall International, 1985.

[Hoe06] J. Hoenicke. *Combination of Processes, Data, and Time.* PhD thesis, Report Nr. 9/2006, University of Oldenburg, July 2006.

[HU79] J.E. Hopcroft and J.D. Ullman. *Introduction to Automata Theory, Langages, and Computation.* Addison-Wesley, 1979.

[HZ97] M.R. Hansen and Zhou Chaochen. Duration calculus: Logical foundations. *Formal Aspects of Computing,* 9:283–330, 1997.

[IEC93] IEC international standard 1131-3, programmable controllers, part 3, programming languages, 1993.

[ITU94] ITU-T recommendation Z.120: Message sequence chart (MSC), 1994. ITU General Secretariat, Geneva.

[Jos96] M. Joseph, editor. *Real-time Systems – Specification, Verification and Analysis.* Prentice-Hall International, 1996. Available under http://www.tcs.com/techbytes/htdocs/book_mj.htm.

[JP96] B. Jonsson and J. Parrow, editors. *Formal Techniques in Real-Time and Fault-Tolerant Systems,* volume 1135 of *Lecture Notes in Computer Science,* Uppsala, Sweden, 1996. Springer.

[KDH⁺07] S. Kupferschmid, K. Dräger, J. Hoffmann, B. Finkbeiner, H. Dierks, A. Podelski, and G. Behrmann. Uppaal/DMC – abstraction-based heuristics for directed model checking. In O. Grumberg and M. Huth, editors. *Tools and Algorithms for the Construction and Analysis of Systems,* volume 4424 of *Lecture Notes in Computer Science,* pages 679–682. Springer, 2007.

[Kel76] R.M. Keller. Formal verification of parallel programs. *Communications of the ACM,* 19(7):371–384, 1976.

[Kle00] C. Kleuker. *Constraint Diagrams.* PhD thesis, Report Nr. 3/00, University of Oldenburg, December 2000.

[KM01] N. Klarlund and A. Møller. MONA version 1.4 user manual. Technical report, Department of Computer Science, Aarhus University, January 2001.

[Kop97] H. Kopetz. *Real-Time Systems – Design Principles for Distributed Embedded Applications,* volume 395 of *The Springer International Series in Engineering and Computer Science.* Springer, 1997.

[Koy90] R. Koymans. Specifying real-time properties with metric temporal logic. *Real-Time Systems,* 2(4):255–299, 1990.

[KPOB99] B. Krieg-Brückner, J. Peleska, E.-R. Olderog, and A. Baer. The UniForM workbench, a universal development environment for formal methods. In J. Wing, J. Woodcock, and J. Davies, editors. *FM'99 – Formal Methods,* volume 1709 of *Lecture Notes in Computer Science,* pages 1186–1205. Springer, 1999.

[Lar02] K.G. Larsen. Advances in real-time model checking, 2002. Tutorial presented at the FTRTFT 2002.

[LEG01] LEGO. PLC-Automata and LEGO Mindstorms, 2001. See http://csd.

`Informatik.Uni-Oldenburg.DE/teaching/fp_realzeitsys_ws0001/`
`result/eindex.html`.

[Let00] M. Lettrari. Eine Testautomatensemantik für Constraint Diagrams und ihre Anwendung. Master's thesis, University of Oldenburg, Department of Computer Science, April 2000.

[Lew95] R.W. Lewis. *Programming industrial control systems using IEC 1131-3*. The Institution of Electrical Engineers, 1995.

[Liu00] J.W.S. Liu. *Real-Time Systems*. Prentice-Hall International, 2000.

[LL73] C.L. Liu and J.W. Layland. Scheduling algorithms for multiprogramming in a hard-real-time environment. *Journal of the ACM*, 20(1):40–61, 1973.

[LPW97] K.G. Larsen, P. Petterson, and Wang Yi. Uppaal in a nutshell. *STTT – International Journal on Software Tools for Technology Transfer*, 1(1+2):134–152, December 1997.

[Lue79] D.G. Luenberger. *Introduction to Dynamic Systems. Theory, Models & Applications*. Wiley, 1979.

[MFR06] R. Meyer, J. Faber, and A. Rybalchenko. Model checking duration calculus: A practical approach. In K. Barkaoui, A. Cavalcanti, and A. Cerone, editors. *3rd International Colloquium on Theoretical Aspects of Computing, ICTAC*, volume 4281 of *Lecture Notes in Computer Science*, pages 332–346. Springer, 2006.

[Mil89] R. Milner. *Communication and Concurrency*. Prentice-Hall International, 1989.

[Mil99] R. Milner. *Communicating and Mobile Systems*. Cambridge University Press, 1999.

[Min67] M.L. Minsky. *Computation: Finite and Infinite Machines*. Prentice-Hall International, 1967.

[Mos85] B. Moszkowski. A temporal logic for multilevel reasoning about hardware. *Computer*, 18(2):10–19, 1985.

[Mos86] B. Moszkowski. *Executing Temporal Logic Programs*. Cambridge University Press, 1986.

[MP90] Z. Manna and A. Pnueli. A hierarchy of temporal properties. In *Proceedings of the 9th ACM Symposium on Principles of Distributed Computing (PODC)*, pages 377–410. ACM, 1990.

[MP91] Z. Manna and A. Pnueli. *The Temporal Logic of Reactive and Concurrent Systems – Specification*. Springer, 1991.

[MP95] Z. Manna and A. Pnueli. *Temporal Verfication of Reactive Systems – Safety*. Springer, 1995.

[MR94] S. Mauw and M.A. Reniers. An algebraic semantics of basic message sequence charts. *Computer Journal*, 37(4):269–277, 1994.

[OD03] E.-R. Olderog and H. Dierks. Moby/RT: A tool for specification and verification of real-time systems. *Journal of Universal Computer Science*, 9:88–105, 2003.

[OL82] S. Owicki and L. Lamport. Proving liveness properties of concurrent programs. *ACM Transactions on Programming Languages and Systems*, 4(3):455–495, 1982.

[Old99] E.-R. Olderog. Correct real-time software for programmable logic controllers. In E.-R. Olderog and B. Steffen, editors. *Correct System Design*, volume 1710 of *Lecture Notes in Computer Science*, pages 342–362. Springer, 1999.

[ORS92] S. Owre, J. Rushby, and N. Shankar. PVS: a prototype verification system.

In D. Kapur, editor. *Automatic Deduction – CADE-11*, volume 607 of *Lecture Notes in Computer Science*, pages 748–752. Springer, 1992.

[ORS96] E.-R. Olderog, A.P. Ravn, and J.U. Skakkebæk. Refining system requirements to program specification. In Heitmeyer and Mandrioli [HM96], pages 107–134.

[Pan01] P.K. Pandya. Specifying and deciding quantified discrete-time duration calculus formulae using DCVALID: An automata theoretical approach. In *Workshop on Real-Time Tools (RTTOOLS'2001)*, Aalborg, 2001.

[Plo81] G.D. Plotkin. A structural approach to operational semantics. Technical Report DAIMI-FN 19, Department of Computer Science, Aarhus University, 1981.

[Plo04] G.D. Plotkin. A structural approach to operational semantics. *Journal of Logic and Algebraic Programming*, 60–61:17–139, 2004. This is a revised version of the original report [Plo81].

[Pnu77] A. Pnueli. The temporal logic of programs. In *Foundations of Computer Science*, pages 46–57. IEEE Computer Society Press, October 1977.

[PR07] A. Podelski and A. Rybalchenko. ARMC: the logical choice for software model checking with abstraction refinement. In M. Hanus, editor. *PADL'2007: Practical Aspects of Declarative Languages*, volume 4354 of *Lecture Notes in Computer Science*, pages 245–259. Springer, 2007.

[QS82] J.-P. Queille and J. Sifakis. Specification and verification of concurrent systems in CESAR. In M. Dezani-Ciancaglini and U. Montanari, editors. *Proceedings of the 5th International Symposium on Programming*, volume 137 of *Lecture Notes in Computer Science*, pages 337–371. Springer, 1982.

[QS06] J.-D. Quesel and A. Schäfer. Spatio-temporal model checking for mobile real-time systems. In K. Barkaoui, A. Cavalcanti, and A. Cerone, editors. *Theoretical Aspects of Computing – ICTAC 2006*, volume 4281 of *Lecture Notes in Computer Science*, pages 347–361. Springer, 2006.

[Ras02] T.M. Rasmussen. *Interval Logic – Proof Theory and Theorem Proving*. PhD thesis, Technical University of Denmark, July 2002.

[Rav95] A.P. Ravn. Design of embedded real-time computing systems. Technical Report ID-TR 1995-170, Technical University of Denmark, October 1995.

[Rei85] W. Reisig, editor. *Petri Nets – An Introduction*. Springer, 1985.

[Ros98] A.W. Roscoe. *The Theory and Practice of Concurrency*. Prentice-Hall International, 1998.

[RRH93] A.P. Ravn, H. Rischel, and K.M. Hansen. Specifying and verifying requirements of real-time systems. *IEEE Transactions on Software Engineering*, 19:41–55, January 1993.

[RSS07] A. Rybalchenko and V. Sofronie-Stokkermans. Constraint solving for interpolation. In B. Cook and A. Podelski, editors. *8th International Conference on Verification, Model Checking and Abstract Interpretation (VMCAI 2007)*, volume 4349 of *Lecture Notes in Computer Science*, pages 346–362. Springer, 2007.

[Rud76] W. Rudin. *Principles of Mathematical Analysis*. McGraw-Hill, 3rd edition, 1976.

[Sch95] S.A. Schneider. An operational semantics for Timed CSP. *Information and Computation*, 116:193–213, 1995.

[Sch99] M. Schenke. Transformational design of real-time systems – Part 2: from program specifications to programs. *Acta Informatica*, 36:67–99, 1999.

[Sch05] A. Schäfer. A calculus for shapes in time and space. In Z. Liu and K. Araki, editors. *Theoretical Aspects of Computing – ICTAC 2004*, volume 3407 of *Lecture Notes in Computer Science*, pages 463–478. Springer, 2005.

[Sch06] A. Schäfer. *Specification and Verification of Mobile Real-Time Systems*. PhD thesis, Report Nr. 1/07, University of Oldenburg, December 2006.

[Sch07] A. Schäfer. Axiomatisation and decidability of multi-dimensional duration calculus. *Information and Computation*, 205:25–64, 2007.

[SD93] R. Schlör and W. Damm. Specification and verification of system level hardware designs using timing diagrams. In *European Conference on Design Automation*, pages 518–524. IEEE Computer Society Press, 1993.

[Ska94] J.U. Skakkebæk. *A Verification Assistant for a Real-Time Logic*. PhD thesis, Department of Computer Science, Technical University of Denmark, November 1994.

[SO99] M. Schenke and E.-R. Olderog. Transformational design of real-time systems – Part 1: from requirements to program specifications. *Acta Informatica*, 36:1–65, 1999.

[SS06] V. Sofronie-Stokkermans. Interpolation in local theory extensions. In U. Furbach and N. Shankar, editors. *Automated Reasoning: Third International Joint Conference, IJCAR 2006*, volume 4130 of *Lecture Notes in Computer Science*, pages 235–250. Springer, 2006.

[SSI07] V. Sofronie-Stokkermans and C. Ihlemann. Automated reasoning in some local extensions of ordered structures. In *Proceedings of the 37th International Symposium on Multiple-Valued Logics (ISMVL 2007)*. IEEE Press, 2007.

[Tap01] J. Tapken. *Model-Checking of Duration Calculus Specifications*. PhD thesis, Report Nr. 3/01, University of Oldenburg, June 2001.

[Tho90] W. Thomas. Automata on infinite objects. In J. van Leuwen, editor. *Handbook of Theoretical Computer Science, Volume B: Formal Models and Semantics*. Elsevier, 1990.

[WD96] J. Woodcock and J. Davies. *Using Z – Specification, Refinement, and Proof*. Prentice-Hall International, 1996.

[Yi91] W. Yi. CCS + time = an interleaving model for real-time systems. In J. Leach Albert, B. Monien, and M. Rodríguez, editors. *Automata, Languages and Programming*, volume 510 of *Lecture Notes in Computer Science*, pages 217–228. Springer, 1991.

[Yov97] S. Yovine. Kronos: a verification tool for real-time systems. *STTT – International Journal on Software Tools for Technology Transfer*, 1(1+2):123–133, December 1997.

[ZH04] Zhou Chaochen and M.R. Hansen. *Duration Calculus: A Formal Approach to Real-Time Systems*. Monographs in Theoretical Computer Science. An EATCS Series. Springer, 2004.

[ZHR91] Zhou Chaochen, C.A.R. Hoare, and A.P. Ravn. A calculus of durations. *Information Processing Letters*, 40/5:269–276, 1991.

[ZHS93] Zhou Chaochen, M.R. Hansen, and P. Sestoft. Decidability and undecidability results for duration calculus. In P. Enjalbert, A. Finkel, and K.W. Wagner, editors. *Symposium on Theoretical Aspects of Computer Science (STACS 93)*, volume 665 of *Lecture Notes in Computer Science*, pages 58–68. Springer, 1993.

Index